Animal Models
of Human Behavior

Animal Models
of Human Behavior
Conceptual, Evolutionary, and
Neurobiological Perspectives

Edited by

Graham C. L. Davey
The City University
London

JOHN WILEY AND SONS
Chichester · New York · Brisbane · Toronto · Singapore

Library of Congress Cataloging in Publication Data:
Main entry under title:

Animal models of human behavior.

  Includes indexes.
  1. Psychology, Comparative. 2. Human behavior—
Animal models. I. Davey, Graham.
BF671.A54 1983 156 82–13714

ISBN 0 471 90038 9

British Library Cataloging in Publication Data:

Animal models of human behavior.
  1. Psychology, Physiological
  2. Psychology, Comparative
  I. Davey, Graham C. L.
  156'.2   QP356

ISBN 0 471 90038 9

Phototypeset by Input Typesetting Limited, London SW19 8DR
and printed at the Pitman Press Limited, Bath, Avon.

Contents

v

Section III   Neurobiological Aspects

List of Contributors

JEROME H. BARKOW, *Department of Sociology and Social Anthropology, Dalhousie University, Halifax, Nova Scotia, B3H 1T2, Canada.*

DAVID BENTON, *Psychology Department, North Arts Building, University College of Swansea, Singleton Park, Swansea, SA2 8PP, UK.*

D. E. BLACKMAN, *Department of Psychology, University College, Cardiff, PO Box 78, Cardiff, CF1 1XL, UK.*

N. G. BLURTON JONES, *Graduate School of Education, and Departments of Psychiatry and Anthropology, University of California, Los Angeles, Ca. 90024, USA.*

ROBERT A. BOAKES, *Laboratory of Experimental Psychology, Sussex University, Brighton, BN1 9QG, UK.*

DOUGLAS CARROLL, *Department of Psychology, University of Birmingham, Elms Road, PO Box 363, Birmingham, B15 2TT, UK.*

A. CHARLES CATANIA, *Department of Psychology, University of Maryland, Baltimore County, Catonsville, Maryland 21228, USA.*

GRAHAM C. L. DAVEY, *Department of Social Science and Humanities, The City University, Northampton Square, London EC1V 0HB, UK.*

SIMON GREEN, *Department of Psychology, Birkbeck College, Malet Street, London, WC1E 7HX, UK.*

C. R. LEGG, *Department of Social Science and Humanities, The City University, Northampton Square, London EC1V 0HB, UK.*

C. FERGUS LOWE, *Department of Psychology, University College of North Wales, Bangor, Gwynedd, LL57 2DG, UK.*

T. R. MILES, *Department of Psychology, University College of North Wales, Bangor, Gwynedd, LL57 2DG, UK.*

DAVID A. OAKLEY, *Department of Psychology, University College, London, Gower Street, London, WC1E 6BT, UK.*

MARK A. J. O'CALLAGHAN, *Department of Psychology, University of Birmingham, B15 2TT, UK.*

F. J. ODLING-SMEE, *Department of Psychology, Brunel University, Uxbridge, Middlesex, UB8 3PH, UK.*

H. C. PLOTKIN, *Department of Psychology, University College, London, Gower Street, London WC1E 6BT, UK.*

J. T. RICK, *Department of Psychology, University of Sheffield, Sheffield, S10 2TN, UK.*

PETER K. SMITH, *Department of Psychology, University of Sheffield, Sheffield, S10 2TN, UK.*

DAVID M. WARBURTON, *Department of Psychology, Building 3, Earley Gate, Whiteknights, Reading, RG6 2AL, UK.*

Editor's Preface

In effect, comparative studies of humans and non-human animals commenced only following the Darwinian revolution of the nineteenth century. Prior to this, both academic and religious dogma had strictly enforced the human–animal dichotomy on the basis of intellectual capacity, social achievement, and divine pronunciation. Nevertheless, even today 100 years after Darwin's death, anthropologists, biologists, and psychologists are still unsure about the significance and even the morality of making human–animal comparisons. To the uninformed reader this might imply that little progress has been achieved in our understanding of the biological and psychological relations between animals and humans, but this is to ignore the tortuous history that this topic possesses. Immediately after the publication of Darwin's thesis on the origin of species, and more specifically after the publication of *The Descent of Man* the search began for human traits in non-human animals: even to the extent of attempting to detect such characteristics as inductive reasoning, imagination, aesthetic appreciation, and even religious belief. This endeavor failed, and not only because its adherents were enthusiastic amateurs such as farmers, zoo-keepers, and animal breeders who relied for most of their evidence on anecdotes and casual observations. Their place was taken by the positivists and the experimentalists of the early twentieth century, and the question of human–animal comparisons was turned on its head. Animal experimentalists and later behavioristic psychologists, such as Lloyd Morgan, J. B. Watson, and B. F. Skinner advocated a psychological understanding of the non-human animal as the yardstick for judging and understanding human characteristics. They based their approach on the common important influence of evolutionary factors in determining behavioral and psychological processes in all living organisms, and the need to confine behavioral studies to concepts in keeping with the strictures of scientific experimentation. Both the Darwinian and behaviorist/reductionist approaches have been seen as attempts either to elevate non-human animals to the psychological level of man or to reduce humans to the apparently more mechanistic level of animals, and unfortunately for psychology in general this polarization has tended to create more heat than light. Arguably, the question is not 'Can we equate the behavioral and psychological processes of humans and animals?' but 'What, if any, is the heuristic value of doing so?'. At the very least the question of *how* animals and humans can be compared has traditionally been a secondary one, and one which has only recently been broached with any commitment.

The present volume is an attempt to illustrate some of the contemporary approaches to the 'How' and 'Why' questions raised by human–animal comparisons in psychology and behavioral biology. Many of the contributors to this book attended a symposium on 'Extrapolation from Animals to Man in Psychology' held at the City University, London, in March 1980. The symposium was convened in the first instance to try and survey some of the many diverse ways in which psychologists were attempting to extrapolate animal findings to human behavior. There were clearly many areas in which psychologists were willing to use extrapolation: learning theory, brain–behavior relationships, sociobiology, psychopathology, to name but a few. What became clearer as the symposium progressed, however, was that there was no clear consensus on *how* we should extrapolate from animals to humans, even though a majority of contributors agreed that extrapolation was a useful exercise from both a practical and heuristic point of view. It is from these considerations that this volume stems. It is not only an attempt to look at the practical benefits of elaborating animal models of human behavior (as in the use of animal models of human psychopathy—Section III), nor just of comparing various psychological processes or mechanisms across animals and man, but—perhaps most importantly—it is an attempt to come to terms with a few of the conceptual problems inherent in extrapolation and to try and piece together the bare bones of a conceptual framework which will provide some answers to the 'How?' question posed by animal–human comparisons.

Whilst compiling the contributions to this book it became clearer to me that there was a framework within which all interspecific comparisons could be made—that of evolutionary biology. Even as specific research workers concerned with process biology, cognitive psychology, or functional analyses of behavior, our findings—and our extrapolations—must conform with the principles of biological evolution, and biological evolution is a process afflicting the whole gamut of living organisms. This is not to say that one must directly attack animal to human extrapolation from a purely evolutionary angle: given that the researcher has comparable analytic techniques for the study of animals and humans (and an evolutionary analysis can help to clarify what might and might not be comparable techniques—see Chapter 12), then we can begin to experimentally compare the various behavioral and psychological mechanisms possessed by animals and humans. A variety of the contributions to this volume express this line of approach (Chapters 4, 5, 6, 12, and 13). However, making interspecific comparisons is not strictly the same as extrapolation from one species to another. Extrapolation implies that our findings with one species tell us something about a second, different, species, without us necessarily conducting similar rigorous investigations on that second species. Here extrapolation itself is useful in at least two important ways. First, it allows us to understand human psychological processes in circumstances where constructing animal models of those processes is potentially the most rewarding and practical line of approach in the short term. This is particularly true in the case of psychopathology (see Chapters 13, 14, 15, 16, and 17). Secondly, extrapolation allows us to test very general theories of behavior; for instance, sociobiology (see Chapters 9, 10, and 11). The rules for extrapolation, it seems, must in the last analysis be extracted from principles of evolutionary biology. But even here it is not yet obvious how these principles should be interpreted to provide the rules for extrapolation. Some possibilities are outlined in Chapters 7 and 8.

Finally, this volume has trodden a long and tortuous path to reach its present form, but I hope it provides a cross-section of contemporary views on interspecific comparisons in general and animal models of human behavior in particular. The book would not have come to fruition if it had not been for some early conversations with Chris Cullen on the topic of extrapolating from animal to man in psychology, nor if the Nuffield Foundation had not kindly funded the original symposium in 1980; I am grateful to both. I must also acknowledge a long-standing debt to B. F. Skinner. Whilst hesitating to label myself as a 'Skinnerian', it was Skinner's writings that originally aroused my interest in extrapolation from animals to humans and largely contributed to maintaining that interest over the past ten years or so. Last, but not least, my wife Sian deserves an acknowledgment; although she is not aware of the fact yet, she will probably contribute generously to the reading of proofs and compiling of the index. To her I am very greatful in advance.

GRAHAM C. L. DAVEY

London, May 1982

Section I

Conceptual and Historical Issues

It is clearly important to understand how conceptual and historical factors influence the way we use animal models as aids to explanation of human behavior. The way in which we talk about human behavior in an everyday sense is often quite different from the way in which we talk about animal behavior. As a start we are more willing to use mentalistic and uniquely cognitive concepts to describe the causes of human behavior—if only because we can all individually testify to the existence of our thoughts, feelings, and memories. But as psychologists we are much less willing to use these concepts with animals. For instance, it is only recently that we have acknowledged that animals may have complexly organized memories of the world, and, for instance, possess such attributes as elaborate cognitive maps. Only in the last decade have we really begun to shake off the legacy inherited from the early behaviorists which implored us to interpret the actions of animals in relatively mechanistic terms. Even when animal behaviorists were willing to admit the existence of such things as memories in animals these were the crudest of neural traces. Clearly, one factor that has enabled animal models to become more relevant to human behavior is the willingness of researchers to construct cognitive rather than purely behavioral models of animal behavior. In the 1950s and 1960s extrapolation from animals to man was almost entirely the domain of the Skinnerians, and they conducted extrapolation on the basis of an understanding of behavior at the level of controlling variables (the empirical law of operant reinforcement is an instance of this). However, throughout the 1970s, the Skinnerian analysis was in decline—for a number of reasons. First, an analysis at the level of controlling variables is useful only if the empirical laws evolved from a study of controlling variables exhibit some kind of general consistency. Two branches of evidence began to suggest that many of the Skinnerian laws did not exhibit this consistency: humans did not appear to learn in the same way as rats or pigeons (see Chapters 5 and 6), and more ethologically orientated behavioral tasks suggested that there were clearly limits to which general behavioral laws could be applied even to animals. The second contribution to the gradual demise of the Skinnerian approach was, I believe, the burgeoning of research in human cognition in the 1970s. This appears to have spurred animal psychologists to develop techniques for investigating uniquely cognitive aspects of non-human behavior. And they have subsequently discovered that, in many cases, a cognitive analysis helps to ameliorate some of the apparent anomalies arising from purely behavioral analyses. Of course, there are those who do not see cognitive analyses as being any improvement over traditional behavior analyses, and some of these arguments are expressed in the first section of this book. However, at the very least, recently evolved cognitive analyses of animal behavior do have the advantage of opening up new avenues of psychological research in animals and, as a consequence, developing models of animal behavior which could have more than just superficial relevance to human behavior.

Animal Models of Human Behavior
Edited by G. C. L. Davey
© 1983 John Wiley & Sons Ltd

Chapter 1

Responsibility in the Cockroach: An Exercise in Linguistic Phenomenology

T. R. MILES

1. INTRODUCTION

Lest there should be any misunderstanding I should like to make clear that this is not a chapter describing research into the behavior of cockroaches. I know very little about the cockroach—almost certainly less than most of my audience. I do know, however, that it sounds odd, or uncomfortable, to speak of *responsibility* in the cockroach. In general, there are many expressions which we use without qualms in speaking of human beings but which become progressively more uncomfortable as we attempt to apply them to species of lesser degrees of complexity. The theme of this chapter is that similarities and differences between humans and other organisms are reflected in the ways in which we talk. Careful examination of such talk, therefore, can highlight features in a particular situation which we might otherwise have overlooked. The exercise is one which Austin (1961, p. 130), perhaps with his tongue in his cheek, has called 'linguistic phenomenology'.

In this kind of enquiry it is of course important to distinguish conceptual analysis from conceptual revision (compare Harzem and Miles, 1978). In the case of conceptual analysis one is examining the classifications implicit in language systems as they exist at present; in the case of conceptual revision one is explicitly or implicitly making proposals for change. I shall be concerned in this chapter mostly with the former. Just because we talk as we do about humans and animals it does not of course follow that there are no better ways of talking; but it is arguable that one should try to be clearheaded about existing classifications before one sets out to advocate change.

Before I embark on my main argument three preliminary points require mention. In the first place, despite the pressures to classify *homo sapiens* as a member of the animal kingdom, in this chapter I shall follow popular practice in using the word 'animal' to mean 'non-human animal'. Secondly, if it makes no sense to speak of 'responsibility' in the case of cockroaches, then it is as inappropriate to say of a cockroach that it was *not* responsible for a particular state of affairs as to say that it *was* responsible; similarly, if it is inappropriate to say of a worm that it recognized me, then it is also inappropriate to say that it failed to recognize me. During much of this chapter I shall be calling attention to expressions where the negative form is as inappropriate as the positive. Thirdly, I shall not be talking about situations where animals are portrayed in fiction. Some of you may remember that Christoper Robin had a beetle called Alexander who

> . . . . had a sort of look as if he thought he ought to say
> I'm very, very sorry that I tried to run away.

Clearly in fiction, or in a child's imagination, any animal can be endowed with human qualities, and indeed in some stories, for example the Dr Dolittle books, the animals retain in a delightful way their animal characters despite talking and acting like humans. Interesting, however, though such characterization is, I shall not refer to it here.

Many different words are interesting from the point of view of linguistic phenomenology. Those which I shall be considering can conveniently be classified under three main heads, namely (1) words which imply planning and cognitive skills, in particular *want, choose, intelligent, recognize, mistake, guess*, and *say*, (2) words which are descriptive of *personality*, such as *placid, nervous, obstinate*, and *wilful*, and (3) words which are closely connected with social institutions, in particular *punishment* and *responsibility*. I shall thus be asking three questions, namely (1) to what extent do we describe the cognitive skills of humans and those of animals in the same terms?, (2) to what extent do we describe their personalities in the same terms?, and (3) to what extent do we describe their social institutions in the same terms? In attempting to answer these three questions I hope to highlight both similarities and differences. I shall end with some brief comments on behaviorism and on Lloyd Morgan's canon.

2. MEN, DOGS, RATS, AND COCKROACHES

2.1. Planning and cognitive skills

I begin with the concept of *wanting*; and for this purpose I shall consider the following four sentences: (a) The man wanted to go into the field, (b) The dog wanted to go into the field, (c) The rat wanted to go into the field, (d) The cockroach wanted to go into the field. It seems to me plain that (a) and (b) are comfortable and that (c) and (d) are uncomfortable. Why should this be so? It cannot simply be that the man is in a position to put into words what he wants, else how could one say that the dog wanted . . .? I suggest that we would be willing to say of a dog that he wanted to go into a field if we had evidence that he was in some way aware of what was going on in the field (for example if his master were there or even a rabbit), and if his movements, perhaps towards a gate, had the character of being purposeful. Michotte (1963) has made us aware of all kinds of nuances which can be studied experimentally in connection with 'movement towards' and 'movement away from', and in particular he has shown that living movement has certain distinctive features. It seems to me that the presence of the right kind of living movement in the right kind of context could justify the claim that a dog wanted to go into a field; and it is an obvious fact that the same sorts of purposive movement are not made by rats or cockroaches. One cannot envisage them jumping the height of a hedge, seeing their owner and then making for the nearest gate. Similarly one can say that a dog wants a drink, for example if he is panting and looking hopefully in one's direction; in contrast, though a rat or a cockroach—or even a plant—may *need* water they do not pant and look hopefully at people, and I suggest that it is the absence of these kinds of behavior which makes it uncomfortable to use the word 'want'.

It is worth noting that in the above discussion I have referred to the dog as 'he' rather than 'it'. This decision was not made without hesitation since there are pressures in both directions. In contrast the pressures to refer to a rat as 'he' are appreciably smaller and the pressures to refer to a cockroach as 'he' are virtually non-existent. I suspect that we use the personal pronoun in the case of organisms to whom we have given names, for example a pet rabbit as opposed to a wild one.

If we now pass to the concept of *choosing*, the position appears somewhat different. One is almost happy to say of any organism, even the cockroach, that it chose to go down one of two routes, for example the darker of two alleys. Possibly, however, in this context the word 'choose' is doing very little work. Certainly there are situations where we say of a human that 'he had no choice'; but if we exclude situations where previous pressure is brought to bear and consider only those situations where the 'correct' response is rewarded, it is not entirely clear that 'the cockroach chose the darker alley' means any more than that it *went down* the darker alley. Possibly in the case of a very young baby one might feel hesitant in saying that he *chose* the red smartie (in a context where—so it might be said—it is true only that he put out his hand and grabbed the red smartie and not the blue one). There is a possible case for saying that the word 'choose' is applicable only when there is a conscious consideration of consequences or even actual verbalization. However, there is nothing self-contradictory in the expression, 'I chose it without thinking'; and if the existence of alternative possibilities is the key notion then one need have no hesitation in saying that a cockroach makes choices and certainly none in the case of the young baby. There is in fact a sizeable literature on choice in the pigeon (see, for example, Catania and Sagvolden, 1980), and I see no reason in this context for putting the word 'choice' in inverted commas.

Let us now consider the following four expressions: (a) an intelligent man, (b) an intelligent dog, (c) an intelligent rat, (d) an intelligent cockroach.

It is certainly uncomfortable to speak of an intelligent cockroach; and it must surely be significant that when he studied skill in maze running Tryon (1940) did not speak of 'intelligent' rats but characterized them as 'maze-bright' and 'maze-dull'. Many investigators do indeed speak of 'naive' rats—and mischievously I envisage the rats as making rather simple-minded remarks!—but clearly in this case one is expected to discount many of the ideas which normally accompany the word 'naive'. Dogs can certainly be—or fail to be—intelligent. On the other hand, one does not expect an intelligent dog to do the same kinds of thing as an intelligent human and it would be decidely uncomfortable to say that one dog had a higher IQ than another dog. The manifestations of intelligence are likely to vary from one species to another. An important point here is that humans, more than animals, perform courses of actions which are interconnected; thus, to adapt an example from Professor Ryle, whistling from *joie de vivre* may be physically indistinguishable from whistling in order to train a puppy but one describes the behavior differently because of the difference in context. If human actions are to be termed meaningful, purposeful, or intelligent they need to be interconnected; and we do in fact speak of an intelligent sheep-dog if he performs certain actions in the right order; and in saying this we are stressing the similarities with correctly ordered behavior in humans.

One may, of course, be tempted to say of the sheep-dog, 'It was not intelligence but instinct which made him do it'. Now part of what is meant by attributing behavior to instinct is that certain relatively simple mechanisms are involved; and, consequently, if behavior is to be termed intelligent as opposed to instinctive, certain predictions follow as to what *other* behavior can and cannot be expected. For example, if nest-building in birds were a manifestation of intelligence, this entails an ability to adapt to new situations which birds do not in fact possess. It is interesting that 'instinctive' is sometimes loosely used to imply behavior that is carried out without conscious thought, as in expressions such as 'his fingers instinctively grasped the trigger'. It is no doubt the degree of adaptability which a trained sheep-dog can show that leads us to describe his behavior as 'intelligent'; he adjusts to new circumstances in ways in which birds, spiders, and sticklebacks do not.

With regard to recognition, one can say of a dog that he recognized or failed to recognize someone, but there are at least twinges of discomfort in using the word 'recognize' of the behavior of a rat or a cockroach. It is not obvious why this should be so, but the following consideration is perhaps relevant: to recognize a person, animal, or object is not merely to be able to respond differentially when that person, animal, or object is present but to be able to emit a *series* of correct responses, as when a dog wags his tail when his master appears and then fetches his master's walking stick! We are hesitant, I think, to say of a rat which had jumped correctly from a Lashley jumping-stand that it *recognized* the difference between triangles and circles, since no appreciable *series* of behaviors was involved; and if a rat or a cockroach were to respond differentially to its mate we would still hestitate to use the word 'recognize' unless there was a series of behaviors which occurred involving adaptability to fresh circumstances. This is an area where familiar expressions such as 'recognize' and 'possess the concept of' are best avoided, since they do not specify what happened with sufficient accuracy.

The making of *mistakes* is, I believe, largely though not exclusively a characteristic of humans. An obvious example of a mistake is the situation where one intends to do or say X but ends up by doing or saying Y, and it is very doubtful if one could say even of a dog—let alone of a rat or cockroach—that he made that kind of mistake. There may, however, be situations where without conscious intent an organism adopts a sequence of behaviors, and in these situations any performance involving the wrong sequence could without too much discomfort be termed a mistake. A chimpanzee might well make a mistake in his efforts to earn tokens.

Guessing is a term which seems to me applicable only to humans. The contrast, I take it, is between those situations where a person acts out of knowledge or at any rate out of fairly well assured belief and those situations where he acts with minimal or no grounds for foreseeing the outcome. Thus I may guess—rightly or wrongly—that my opponent at bridge holds the king of spades, but it is no longer a guess if I deduce this on the basis of evidence and still less if I am unscrupuluous enough to peep into his hand! In contrast it is difficult to think of situations where animals succeed or fail in comparable deductions, and one therefore has no occasion to use the word 'guess', since this implies *absence* of such deduction, which in its turn implies the possibility of its *presence*. Only an organism which possesses the capacity to act from knowledge can guess or fail to guess.

I now pass to the concept of *saying*. Uttering words or writing them is the usual way of saying things, but it is possible to say things without using words and it is possible to use words without saying anything. Thus a look in a person's eye may, as we say, 'speak volumes', and some of you may remember the florists' advertisement of many years ago, 'Say it with flowers!' Equally, one may ask of an obscure lecturer, 'But what did he really *say*?' Talking does not imply saying, and the expression in Greek, *ouden legein* (literally 'to say nothing') often means 'talk nonsense' rather than 'remain silent'. The implication is that there was no *logos*—no rationality—in what was uttered.

There is a complication in that we sometimes use the word 'said' of a parrot when it produces an intelligible phrase, but this is perhaps a witticism. It is a similar witticism to say of a phonograph, tape-recorder, or telephone that it 'said' something, since we know in such a context that it was a person who said it. There would be a further conceptual complication if a speech synthesizer were coupled with a sufficiently adaptive computing device. If appropriate words were emitted in a suitably varied range of situations, there would be pressures to assert that the device was *saying* something. On the other hand, if careful examination showed a greater number of stereotyped responses than one had at first supposed, there would be counter-pressures to assert that a clever device had been made which *appeared* to be able to say things. The fact that humans are made of flesh, blood, etc. and such devices are made mostly of metal is not necessarily important for all purposes; but since over many millennia *de facto* conjunctions have been observed between flesh and blood objects and the ability to 'say' things, one can at least see the case for not using the word 'say' of devices which are made mostly of metal. If human tissue were grafted on to the metal the conflicting pressures of different conceptualizations would be even more complex!

There is an interesting passage in Plato's *Sophist* (262 B) which runs as follows:

> STRANGER: A statement never consists solely of nouns spoken in succession, nor yet of verbs apart from nouns . . . For example, 'walks runs sleeps' . . . does not make a statement . . . and again if you say 'lion stag horse' . . . such a string never makes up a statement

One might adapt this view by saying that if a person is to say something a necessary condition is that, at least in a rudimentary way, the words should obey syntactical rules. If this is correct it follows that, on existing evidence, one should be hesitant in claiming that animals ever say anything. Possibly one reason why this area has been controversial is that the presence or absence of syntax is not always obvious. For example it is recorded (Terrace *et al.*, 1979) that Nim Chimpsky signaled the words 'Give orange me give eat orange me eat orange give me eat orange give me you'. My impression, when reading reports of this kind, is that one is like a spectator at an auction sale who sees someone's raised hand but has insufficient evidence on which to decide whether that person was bidding. In some cases one is unsure how to describe a situation because one does not know what other behaviors to expect. It may eventually transpire that the boundary between those verbal responses which obey syntactical rules and those which do not is itself imprecise. Whether animal language has ever been unambiguously syntactical, however, seems to me questionable.

There has been a curious twist to this controversy as a result of a paper by Epstein *et al.* (1980), who, after citing an earlier paper by Savage-Rumbaugh *et al.* (1978) purporting to demonstrate symbolic communication between chimpanzees, claim that what is in all relevant respects the same phenomenon could be made to occur in two pigeons, Jack and Jill. They report that, after appropriate training, Jack initiated a conversation 'by asking Jill for information about the hidden color. In response Jill looked at the color behind the curtain and then depressed the key with the symbolic name for that color, illuminating the symbol. Having seen Jill accomplish this, Jack depressed the THANK YOU key, rewarding Jill with food . . .' Later in the paper, however, the authors argue that 'an alternative account of this exchange may be given in terms of the prevailing contingencies of reinforcement' and in their concluding sentence they claim that such an account is also applicable to symbolic communication between humans (compare Skinner, 1957).

Now it is not clear to me whether, or to what extent, Epstein *et al.* are writing with their tongues in their cheeks. I suspect, however, that the authors' intention could be expressed somewhat as follows: 'You claim to have demonstrated symbolic communication in primates. . . . Very well, we can demonstrate it in pigeons. In both cases, however, it is possible to avoid talk of symbolic communication if one talks instead of the conditions in which particular behaviors are reinforced; and a similar redescription is also possible in the case of humans'.

If this is the argument, however, it is by no means clear what has happened to the relatively simple-minded view that humans can communicate symbolically while other species cannot. Savage-Rumbaugh *et al.* appear to be saying that chimpanzees *can* so communicate, which implies that the alleged differences between humans and other species are not as great as one might have supposed. Similarly Skinner's (1957) conceptual scheme appears at first glance to exclude any basic difference between species, since a description in terms of contingencies of reinforcement is applicable whatever type of organism is being studied. It seems to me, however, that it is still open to us to say that what both Savage-Rumbaugh *et al.* and Epstein *et al.* reproduced was a *clever imitation* of symbolic behavior, and that one is entitled to speak of genuine symbolic communication only if certain behaviors occur in a context where the organism could also have displayed other behaviors, namely those demonstrating the ability to use syntax correctly. The advantages of re-describing symbolic communication in terms of behavior-being-reinforced are not in dispute; but, as Skinner himself has pointed out (1972, p. 215), 'No theory changes what it is a theory about', and the fact that infra-human species can be taught to reproduce certain *other* characteristics of symbolic communication does not refute the view that only humans produce language which obeys syntactical rules. It seems to me that this view has not so far been shown to be wrong.

2.2. Personality

Words descriptive of personality can be used with minimum 'stretch' in the case of many animal species. Domestic animals, including cats and dogs in particular, have their own characters and can be described, e.g. as *placid* or *nervous*. A horse can be *obstinate* or even *wilful*. Animals which display such characteristics behave in much the same ways as humans who display them. The extent to which a rat has its own character, however, is more dubious, and I doubt if anyone would wish to use the words 'placid' or 'nervous', let alone 'obstinate' or 'wilful', of a cockroach. It is important in this kind of context to distinguish genuine attribution from what may be called 'tongue-in-cheek' attribution. Thus in an experimental situation one might say of a rat which failed to respond in a particular way, 'It is being very obstinate this morning', but this is not a genuine attribution of obstinacy any more than it is if one describes one's car as obstinate when it fails to start.

2.3. Social situations

Words whose applicability arises from particular social contexts can seldom be used comfortably of animals unless the social context is very similar. One can speak of punishing a dog as part of his training; and psychologists do indeed speak of punishing rats, for example if electric shock is administered contingent upon the emission of the 'wrong' response. By analogy one might even, in this sense, punish cockroaches, for example if they went down the 'wrong' alley. However, it is arguable that the uses of the word 'punishment' have been extended in ways which are less than comfortable (compare Harzem and Miles, 1978, Chapter 11); and certainly it does not make sense to speak of *responsibility* in a cockroach, or even in a rat or dog. The notion of 'responsibility' is applicable only within a particular social system and only in the case of organisms which are capable of considering the consequences of what they do. A schoolmaster may be responsible for the children in his care or a policeman for the maintaining of law and order, but a sheep-dog, however skilled, is not responsible for managing the sheep nor is he acting irresponsibly if he fails to do so.

3. BEHAVIORISM

It is sometimes supposed that if one takes behaviorism seriously one is thereby committed to minimizing the differences between humans and animals: according to the familiar caricature a behaviorist believes that man is nothing more than a rather complicated kind of rat.

This is a stupid caricature. Quite apart from the difficulties over the correct analysis of sentences of the form 'A is "nothing more" than B' (or 'A can be "reduced" to B'), its target is clearly a man of straw, while, in contrast, it ignores some of the most compelling arguments within the behaviorist tradition. As I have argued elsewhere (Harzem and Miles, 1978, Chapter 6), the important feature of any worthwhile version of behaviorism is the recognition that for many research purposes we need a 'language without extra-episodic words'. That is to say, we need a record of what movements the organism made in a particular situation in language which is as free as possible from any prediction as to what the organism might do in other situations. The fact that a lever was depressed by more than a specified amount provides such a record, whereas statements about the subject's wishes, intentions, etc. carry implications as to what he can be expected to do in a range of conditions outside the episode in question. On this showing it ceases to be mere dogma that teleological explanations (that is, explanations in terms of the subject's purposes) are 'unscientific' or that mentalistic concepts can play no part in a 'scientific' psychology; it is rather than it is often convenient for research purposes to use expressions which refer to here-and-now events rather than expressions which theorize about such events by relating them to other events, actual or possible.

The fact, of course, that the cumulative record is a suitable device whether one is studying human or animal behavior does not of itself guarantee either that human patterns of responding are the same as those of animals or that they are different. As was pointed out above, ordering one's concepts in a particular way, for example by making use of the concept of 'response rate', does not make the similarities and differences between humans and animals any different from what they would otherwise have been; to that extent behaviorism is neutral with regard to the central topic of this book.

4. LLOYD MORGAN'S CANON

How exactly Morgan intended his canon to be interpreted is not by any means a straightforward issue (cf. Boakes, in press), and for present purposes I shall limit myself to two quotations.

Morgan (1903, p. 296) writes:

A dog, heading to cut off a rabbit scuttling in a circular path does not necessarily understand the chord of a circle to be shorter than the arc.

In a later work (Morgan, 1926, pp. 60–61) he writes:

Some 30 years ago I accepted as part of my policy in comparative psychology a rule which I may here re-state. In no instance should we interpret an act as the outcome of a higher mental process if it can adequately be interpreted as the outcome of a process that stands lower in the psychological scale.

In the light of emergent evolution this policy and the canon which it implies may be extended in range. In no instance should we interpret events in terms of concepts appropriate to a higher level of emergence if they can adequately be interpreted in terms of concepts appropriate to a lower level of emergence.

In these two passages it is perhaps helpful to think of Morgan as being concerned with conceptual proposals. In the case of the dog which takes a short cut to head off the rabbit one need not dispute that there are things about the situation which the dog *understands*; but the extent of his understanding is determined by considerations of what he would do on other occasions, and there is no suggestion that he would ever draw a diagram or verbalize, even in a rudimentary way, about the geometrical properties of the circle. Similarly a human being—or indeed a cat or dog—who has learned, say, to catch a ball could not necessarily formulate the laws of Newtonian mechanics even though he may be implicitly using them. For the same reasons one is correct in saying that Clever Hans did not really know the answers to the mathematical questions that he was asked even though he emitted the correct number of taps. Had he genuinely understood the situation he would have responded correctly even when the members of his audience did not know what was being asked (compare Katz, 1937, pp. 2–7). Morgan is in effect reminding us that in the case of animals we should not use words whose extra-episodic commitment goes further than is justified. To be 'anthropomorphic' is to make precisely this mistake: it is to overestimate the extent of an animal's repertoire.

Now because humans can plan ahead we are often more interested in their intentions and achievements than in the physical movements by which these intentions and achievements are expressed. To adapt the example given earlier, if I am bidding at an auction sale I may raise my arm, but I might achieve the same end-product by a nod. Conversely, I might carry out what is physically the same movement of my arm without this being a bid. Moreover if a dog carried out a physically similar movement of his paw the issue of whether he was bidding would not arise, nor if he dropped from his mouth a playing card which was the three of spades would anyone ask whether this was a revoke. The fact that certain words are used distinctively of humans is closely associated with the fact that humans are more able than animals to plan ahead.

5. CONCLUSION

Some words, then, are uncomfortable when used of certain types of organism ('responsibility in the cockroach' being simply one example); other words, however, can be used of other types of organism without discomfort (as when we use 'obstinate' of a horse). Such considerations reflect not just curiosities about English or any other language; they arise because humans and animals are alike and different in all kinds of subtle and complex ways.

Linguistic phenomenology does not change these similarities and differences, but it offers us a technique by which we can make ourselves more aware of them.

ACKNOWLEDGMENTS

I am grateful to Professor G. B. B. Hunter for many of the ideas contained in the section on 'saying' and for calling my attention to the interesting passage in the *Sophisl*. I am grateful to Dr C. F. Lowe for his discussion of the paper by Epstein, Lanza, and Skinner, and to Dr R. A. Boakes for letting me see a preview of his book, *Psychologists and Animals. From Darwin to Behaviourism*. Finally I am grateful to Dr A. W. Heim who first pointed out to me the incongruity of speaking of 'naive rats' and to Professor H. H. Price who called my attention to that delightful expression, 'Say it with flowers'.

REFERENCES

Austin, J. L. (1961) A plea for excuses. *Philosophical Papers*. Oxford: Clarendon Press.
Boakes, R. A. (in press) *Psychologists and Animals. From Darwin to Behaviourism*. Cambridge: Cambridge University Press.
Catania, A. C. and Sagvolden, T. (1980) Preference for free choice over forced choice in pigeons. *J. Exp. Anal. Behav.*, **34**, 77–86.
Epstein, R., Lanza, R. P., and Skinner, B. F. (1980) Symbolic communication between two pigeons. *Science*, **207**, 543–545.
Harzem, P., and Miles, T. R. (1978) *Conceptual Issues in Operant Psychology*. Chichester: John Wiley.
Katz, D. (1937) *Animals and Men: Studies in Comparative Psychology*. London: Longman's Green.
Michotte, A. (1963) *The Perception of Causality*. London: Methuen.
Morgan, C. L. (1903) *An Introduction to Comparative Psychology*. 2nd edition. London and Newcastle-on-Tyne: Walter Scott Publishing.
Morgan, C. L. (1926) *Life, Mind, and Spirit*. London: Williams & Norgate.
Savage-Rumbaugh, E. S., Rumbaugh, D. M., and Boysen, S. (1978) Symbolic communication between two chimpanzees. *Science*, **201**, 641–644.
Skinner, B. F. (1957) *Verbal Behavior*. New York: Appleton-Century-Crofts.
Skinner, B. F. (1972) *Beyond Freedom and Dignity*. London: Jonathan Cape.
Terrace, H. S., Petitto, L. A., Saunders, R. J., and Bever, T. G. (1979) Can an ape create a sentence? *Science*, **206**, 891–902.
Tryon, R. C. (1940) Genetic differences in maze learning ability in rats. *39th Yearbook, National Society for the Study of Education (Part 1)*. Bloomington: Public School Publishing Co.

Animal Models of Human Behavior
Edited by G. C. L. Davey
© 1983 John Wiley & Sons Ltd

Chapter 2

Behaviorism and the Nature–Nurture Controversy

Robert A. BOAKES

In the autumn of 1971 Leon Kamin was chairman of the psychology department of Princeton University and consequently became involved in heated arguments over the imminent visit of a psychologist from another university who had been invited to talk about his research. The problem did not arise from the research itself, but from a popular article on intelligence tests which the prospective visitor had published some weeks earlier. Although the article avoided the subject of race, it was none the less sympathetic in general to the opinions expressed by Jensen (1969) whose claims about the inherent intellectual inferiority of some races had aroused bitter attacks over the preceding few years. As controversy over the visit grew within the university, Kamin decided to examine the primary sources of data on the heritability of intelligence, something that few recent disputants had done very carefully.

He concentrated on the research reported by Burt, since this was the most important set of results on the IQs of identical twins. Kamin was the first to notice that the consistency of the reported correlations between the scores of separated twins appeared too good to be true and came to suspect that Burt's claims were fraudulent (Kamin, 1974). Subsequent investigations have shown that these suspicions were well grounded (Hearnshaw, 1979).

Few who followed the development of Kamin's case are likely to have found it inappropriate or startling that an American psychologist whose major research contributions had been to the study of conditioning (e.g. Kamin, 1969) and who had not previously been involved in intelligence testing should have mounted this challenge to the hereditarian claims of a British psychologist who had been a leading pioneer of mental testing. If challenged to say why this seemed quite natural, then the obvious answer would be that American behaviorism, the tradition within which Kamin's work on conditioning was set, has always been fiercely environmentalist and hostile towards the Galtonian tradition of mental testing.

The next question, how did American behaviorism acquire such attitudes, is not so easy to answer. After all, as European ethology has shown, the study of animal behavior, from which behaviorism developed, can just as well be combined with an hereditarian attitude towards human differences. Also, it is worth emphasizing that theories of learning only became a central aspect of behaviorism after it had acquired an environmentalist stance; both Pavlov and Thorndike, the father figures of modern conditioning research, believed there to be a strong hereditary component in human personality. The identification of behaviorism as the major movement within modern psychology at the nurture end of the continuum has been taken for granted so much that there has been little discussion of how it occurred. The main aim of this chapter is to make up for this neglect (for some previous discussion, see Logue, in press; Cravens, 1978).

GENERAL TRENDS

In very general terms the question is easily answered. There were a number of major changes occurring within American psychology during the first thirty years of this century; these changes coincided with a general reaction towards entrenched hereditarian attitudes within American science; behaviorism was the movement in psychology that best represented these trends and, by association based on temporal contiguity, it acquired a strong anti-hereditarian stance. The main concern of this paper is with the details of this last claim and the extent to which it was a matter of association rather than intellectual connectedness. But before looking at the implications of particular events in the development of behaviorism it may be helpful to consider briefly the more general changes.

From around 1870 until the First World War the biological and social sciences in the English-speaking world and, to a lesser extent, in Germany were dominated by what might be called 'speculative Darwinism'. Some of the elements of this ideology were current before the *Origin of Species* (Darwin, 1859) was published or conflicted with Darwin's own specific views, but 'Darwinism' has become the accepted term, even if 'evolutionism' might be more accurate. Those elements that bore on the concept of man were: Lamarckism, the idea that well-practiced skills could become partly hereditary; recapitulation, the idea that the development of an individual directly reflects the evolutionary history of the species; instinct theory, the idea that behavior reflects the operation of integrated motivational systems with which characteristic emotions and goal-directed action patterns are innately associated; racism, the belief that there are several pure 'types' of human being which possess well-defined physical characteristics; and, 'neo-phrenology', the belief that there are organic factors that give rise directly to psychological differences between individuals (Boakes, in press; Cravens and Burnham, 1971; Young, 1973). The underlying hereditarian outlook of Darwinism was most closely related to this last idea; it was widely believed that criminality or dementia on the one hand and intelligence or moral fibre on the other were a direct result of 'breeding' operating on some physical aspect of the nervous system, which might range from something as simple as brain size or number of convolutions to some hypothetical lesion which neuroanatomical techniques could not yet detect. The political and social implications of these beliefs were initially blunted by Lamarckian theory; thus, Darwin himself characteristically believed that within a few generations of appropriate training in the habits and customs of Europe even the wretched natives of Terra del Fuego would develop an innately civilized outlook.

It is of course something of a simplification to cluster these beliefs together under a single label; many who held some of them were less sure about the remainder. Nevertheless there were enough leading nineteenth century theorists who held strongly to all of these ideas to justify such labeling. One example was the leading German evolutionist, Ernst Haeckel, (e.g. Haeckel, 1900); another was the pioneer of American psychology, G. Stanley Hall (Ross, 1972).

Beginning with Lamarckism the central tenets of speculative Darwinism were subjected to sustained examination by those who may be called the 'skeptical empiricists', scientists whose roots were mainly in German physiology and who asked in positivistic fashion for good evidence, preferably experimental, that such-and-such was true. Behaviorism can be seen as the main product of leveling such criticism at those elements of Darwinism still strong within American psychology in the early part of the century, as part of the general ascendancy of laboratory-based science that was also seen, for example, in embryology and genetics (Allen, 1978).

The attack on Darwinism was pressed by scientists in Europe and America. There were other changes of more limited scope which were taking place as behaviorism was launched and with which behaviorism became identified. One was the institutional separation between psychology and philosophy in American universities that arose as laboratories of psychology sought to become independent of the philosophy departments in which they had grown. A second was the search for practical applications to justify psychology's already well-established position in American academia. In Watson's first paper on behaviorism (Watson, 1913) the need for independence from philosophy and for enabling 'the educator, the physician, the jurist, and the businessman to utilize our data in a practical way' were both major themes. But these were trends that were already well under way. Independent psychology departments had existed in several universities for some years and journals like *Psychological Review* contained a steadily decreasing proportion of papers on philosophical issues. In America the belief, widely held in Germany, that psychology should first get on its feet as a pure science, before it became diverted by attempts to solve specific practical problems, was principally expounded by Titchener and he had become increasingly isolated in this respect by 1913 (O'Donnell, 1979).

The final general change to note here was the growing self-confidence of American science. The most important event in this respect was the First World War. Before the war most leading American scientists had spent at least one post-graduate year in Europe, usually at one of the German universities, and a fluent knowledge of German was regarded as an essential skill for any reputable scientist. The horrors and mindlessness of the war itself, and in particular the nationalistic diatribes published by many a hitherto respected European scientist, helped considerably to end the deference many sciences in America felt towards the transatlantic traditions from which they had sprung.

In view of these general trends it is not surprising that the leading movement in American psychology, as behaviorism had become by the 1940s, was highly antagonistic towards philosophy and speculative theory in general, much concerned with practical issues and very definitely an all-American product. However, none of this directly suggests why it should also have been so environmentalist. To pursue this question further requires looking at the successive stages by which Watson's behaviorism acquired its various characteristics (for more detailed treatment, see Boakes (in press)).

STAGES IN THE DEVELOPMENT OF WATSON'S BEHAVIORISM

A psychologist of today, if asked what he or she associated with behaviorism, would probably list the following elements: relevance of animal research; study of behavior for its own sake and antagonism towards 'mentalistic' psychology; emphasis on conditioning; applications in clinical psychology; and belief that all the important aspects of human behavior are acquired. The above ordering is deliberate, for this is the sequence in which these elements became part of Watson's views on psychology.

Watson entered the University of Chicago as a graduate student in 1900 and a year or so later, when his research career began, his experiments were designed to find out about the learning abilities at various ages of a new laboratory animal, the rat (Watson, 1903). This study was a very early one in the history of experimental studies of learning; the methods used by Watson were mainly derived from the first systematic experiments using mammals which Thorndike had described in 1898. In view of this piece of graduate research and of the later development of behaviorism it is tempting to assume that the nature of learning processes was the major issue for behaviorists from the very beginning; indeed contemporary textbooks on learning that provide a historical framework tend to list Watson as one of the early giants of animal learning theory.

For a dozen years Watson was indeed busily involved in research and all of his experiments involved animals as subjects. However, the questions addressed by this work were largely ones that would nowadays be grouped under 'animal psychophysics' or 'stimulus control'. What sensory inputs control a rat's progress through a maze (Watson, 1907)? Do rats or monkeys possess color vision (Watson, 1909)? What is the visual acuity of a tern and is it sufficient to allow it to locate its nesting site from a distance (Watson, 1908a)? The work with noddy and sooty terns on the Dry Tortugas that Watson began in the summer of 1906 was as much on instinct, in the style of classical ethology, as on learning.

In the few years prior to the First World War there were two central issues which occupied every member of the small group of comparative psychologists working in the United States. One was whether Thorndike (1898; 1901) was correct in concluding that the intelligence of non-human animals, including monkeys, is limited to trial-and-error learning with accidental success and that this is best understood in terms of the establishment of stimulus-response connections, 'S–R bonds', that are strengthened by satisfying events that follow the response. Most of the empirical work inspired by this claim was directed towards obtaining evidence for learning by imitation, which common sense, aided by every authority on animal intelligence since Romanes (1882) except Thorndike, suggested should be easy to find. Watson's failure to find any good sign of imitation learning in his own limited work with monkeys (Watson, 1908b) and his very critical attitude towards the positive evidence offered by others (e.g. Watson, 1914) led him to decide that Thorndike was probably right. His skepticism was also directed towards claims made on behalf of various wonder animals, of which Clever Hans (Pfungst, 1908) has remained the most famous. Over the years Watson's outlook changed from one of tentative skepticism to the strong position that the only way an animal's behavior can change is by the acquisition of habits based on S–R bonds and that not even monkeys or apes possess high-level cognitive processes (Watson, 1908c; Watson, 1914).

The other general issue provoking heated controversy among American comparative psychologists was that of consciousness. On one wing there were the traditionalists like Washburn (1908) who followed Morgan (1894) in believing that for psychology the point of understanding an animal's behavior was to gain an understanding of its mental life which could then be compared to that of man. From the observation of a monkey's differential reactions to lights of different wavelength one might infer that monkeys experience color. The validity of such inferences was disputed by Watson on the grounds that no empirical evidence could either confirm or disconfirm them. More important than the arguments themselves was the gradual realization that comparative psychology was proceeding with the business of generating interesting experimental research and appeared able to do so despite continued failure to resolve the issues of how to decide whether or not an animal possesses consciousness and what its characteristics are. Comparative psychologists could simply study behavior without concerning themselves with subjective experience or with philosophical arguments on the subject.

The extension of this argument to human psychology was the main theme of Watson's 1913 paper. Because Watson had already adopted an S–R outlook, the message that psychologists should restrict themselves to behavior was from early on intertwined with arguments that man is just a bundle of habits (see Watson, 1914, Ch. 1). Thus, there has always been the ambiguity surrounding behaviorists' attacks on 'mentalism', which present-day critics have noted in Skinner's work (e.g. Dennet, 1978), as to whether the arguments are directed at dualistic appeals to non-physical causes of psychological phenomena or, much more broadly, at any kind of theory that proposes the existence of processes which may be labeled 'thinking'. As has often been noted, Tolman's (1932) self-description as a behaviorist was valid in the broad sense of the term, but not in the narrower, Watsonian one that became the major tradition for later versions of behaviorism.

The first time that Watson wrote anything that was noticeably more environmentalist than his peers was in 1916. In this year he began to study the behavior of new-born babies, looking at their emotional reactions and their reflexes. On the one hand he found that only a limited number of stimuli elicited fear, rage or love responses, which he regarded as the three fundamental emotions, and it occurred to him that a process of rapid conditioning could produce the wide range of emotionally-laden stimuli found later in life. Up to this point his interest in Russian research on conditioning had arisen because of its potential as a method for studying perception that did not involve the reporting of subjective experience (Watson, 1916). Now he recognized its appeal as a general process of learning for explaining the psychological development of an individual.

The second aim of Watson's research on babies was to discover what reflexes they possessed at birth. In this work the outcome was in the opposite direction to that on emotional reactions, in that Watson and the student working with him were surprised by the range of well-developed reflexive reactions that they found (Blanton, 1917).

For Watson the study of reflexes was a necessary preliminary for analyzing instincts, which he regarded as integrated sequences of reflexes. As described below, a critical onslaught on the concept of instinct began in 1919 and it is interesting that in the book Watson published that year, *Psychology from the Standpoint of Behaviorist* (Watson, 1919), the section on instincts is modest and tentative compared to its many predecessors, but not highly critical. Presumably reflecting the ambivalence of the initial results from the baby research, whereby the mind of a new-born child seemed to be more of a *tabula rasa* than anticipated with respect to emotion, but less with respect to reflexive action, Watson's book contains no real hint of the extreme environmentalism that was advanced by some protagonists in the instinct debate only two years later (Kuo, 1921).

For Watson to have put forward such views would have been to fly in the face of what was still his cardinal principle: don't go beyond the evidence. He had hopes of being able to carry out a full-scale study, in which the environments of a group of children would be controlled and the results monitored over several years. One would then have something substantial at last to say on the subject of nature versus nurture. But in 1920 his affair with a graduate student and his subsequent divorce ended his academic career and his prospects for further full-time involvement in research (Boakes, in press; Cohen, 1979).

At this point there was not a great deal to mark off Watson's ideas on human development from those of other psychologists of his generation, except for his conclusion that handedness is learned and his views on emotional development. In his final year he had carried out the famous experiment with little Albert, but this is more appropriately regarded as a demonstration of an idea he had already been propounding than as the source of a new discovery (Harris, 1979; Samelson, 1980; Watson and Rayner, 1920). A noticeable aspect of his outlook on such matters is his lack of commitment to the strong hereditarian beliefs held by many of his close associates. Unlike Thorndike, for example, Watson had no enthusiasm for mental testing and, unlike both Thorndike and his friend and fellow comparative psychologist, Robert Yerkes, Watson stayed clear of the eugenics movement. On the question of racial differences he seems to have been more skeptical than many, but his only published reference to this question was the suggestion that a baby somehow transferred from Ancient Egypt to a modern Bostonian family would grow to acquire just the same habits and abilities as the typical freshman entering Harvard (Watson, 1917).

With hindsight one can detect a gradual shift in Watson's outlook (cf. Logue, 1978), but all in all there was not a lot of warning when, after five years of combining a very successful career in advertising and residual links with psychology, a combative environmentalism appeared as the central theme of Watson's third book, *Behaviorism* (Watson, 1924). The substantive content was not much changed from his previous book five years earlier. What had changed was the style—short, punchy statements designed to hold the interest of a wide public—and the emphasis on the conditional reflex as the basic process underlying habit formation, which in turn was the key to understanding any aspect of human behavior.

What caused this change? Since leaving academic life Watson had eventually managed to obtain some funding for a research project on child development in which he served as a consultant to Mary Cover Jones (Jones, 1924; 1974). This research extended his earlier work on babies and included the first attempt at behavior therapy. But no major discovery emerged from this work that might account for Watson's new emphasis on environmentalism and no one else was carrying out comparable studies on human development. It seems that one must look outside Watson's own career for signs of why this might have come about. The obvious place to start is the general state of American psychology that provided the immediate context in which Watson's behaviorism developed.

AMERICAN PSYCHOLOGY FOR THE FIRST TWO DECADES OF THE CENTURY

The most important features of early American psychology were its rapid expansion at the turn of the century and the influence of William James. For reasons that had mainly to do with the growth and reform of the American university system psychological laboratories were founded at a rapid rate in the 1890s and 1900s, so that by the First World War there were already more people calling themselves psychologists and publishing more professional papers in America than anywhere in Europe (O'Donnell, 1979). The greatest personal contribution to this development was James' *Principles of Psychology* (1890). This book inspired a whole generation of young Americans looking to science for guidance both on personal issues and on the social changes of their time. At the same time James' considerable reputation helped to put psychologists in good standing among their university colleagues from more traditional disciplines.

Although James imparted enthusiasm, he was not a clear guide to the direction psychology should take. The ideology sustaining the expansion of psychology was that the scientific, experimental approach would provide solid factual information on crucial issues which for centuries speculative philosophy had left in an unresolved muddle. But this was all promise and there were no really substantial achievements to back such claims and no ready home-based models to follow of the psychological researcher beavering steadily away at a connected series of important problems. James himself was ambivalent in this respect, just as he was on many other crucial issues. By 1890 he had long given up his previous light involvement in laboratory research and the *Principles* contains many barbed comments about experimental work that have been quoted with glee ever since.

James' opinions on two crucial points were relatively straightforward. One was that psychology should not remain a purely academic exercise, but should involve itself in the real world; by 1900 James believed that mental illness was the field in which psychology might make its most useful contribution in the immediate future (see Hale, 1971). The other issue was heredity and here James, in discussing instincts (James, 1890, Ch. 24), proposed an innate basis for various aspects of human behavior to a degree that now seems ludicrous; for example, he suggested that there was 'a native impulse in everyone to conceal love affairs', a 'genuine instinct of cleanliness', an 'instinctive impulse to hide certain parts of the body' and an 'instinct of personal isolation (which) in women is called coyness.'

One consequence of this aspect of James' thought was that, while other social sciences were beginning to move away from the strong hereditarian outlook associated with Darwinism, James helped to ensure that psychology did not. The other was that he prepared the scene for the subsequent popularity of 'instinct' theories of human behavior that blossomed after William McDougall wrote persuasively about this approach in his *Introduction to Social Psychology* (McDougall, 1908).

In the early 1900s widespread interest in the potential contribution psychology might make to the treatment of mental illness culminated in the invitation extended to Freud and Jung to attend a major psychology conference held in 1909 (Ross, 1972; Clark, 1980). At this time psychoanalysis had been almost totally ignored by psychologists in Europe. For reasons that are not completely clear this visit did not after all lead to the inclusion of psychoanalysts within university departments of psychology, nor did it mark the beginning of a rapid growth of clinical psychology in America. If anything, the conference initiated a renewed search for a path that would be both scientific and practical. Subsequent debates over the question of whether thinking always involves imagery added to dissatisfaction with what had become the conservative position, that the aim of psychology should be the analysis of subjective experience without regard to the need for practical applications (Titchener, 1914).

It was in this context that Watson's announcement of his behaviorist approach to human psychology was made in 1913. Others were beginning to produce similar suggestions, but for the first few years such ideas had little impact (Samelson, 1981). The other new development that attracted much more attention was mental testing. The earlier Galtonian approach, based on simple psychological measures such as reaction times and sensory thresholds, had lost conviction by 1900 (see Cairns and Ornstein, 1979), but a few years later Binet's different approach attracted attention and the first English-language version of his test was published in 1916 (Terman, 1916).

The development of mental testing was well under way when America entered the war. On that same day in April, 1917 Yerkes, as President of the American Psychological Association, wrote to members of the association's council with the suggestion that psychologists immediately put their expertise at the service of their country. Within a remarkably short time a massive program was under way whereby all entrants to the United States army were given a psychological test designed to assess their suitability for

various kinds of training. It is doubtful whether this exercise contributed
very much to the army's efficiency, but it certainly had an enormous effect
on the prestige and self-confidence of psychology (Gould, 1981; Samelson,
1977; 1979).

After the war mental testing was in the ascendant, which meant that the
hereditarian stream in American psychology was now more pronounced than
ever. Testing enthusiasts like Yerkes and Thorndike may not all have shared
the more extreme views expressed by fellow members of the eugenics society
to which they belonged. However, they certainly believed that 'bad breeding'
was a source of many of society's ills and that changes in human reproductive
practices were at least as important as changes in social conditions to alleviate
problems of crime, prostitution or feeblemindedness (Haller, 1963; Samelson, 1975).

Within psychology the attack on hereditarianism started in an indirect
manner, not with a challenge to the assumptions of the mental testers, but
with a lively debate over the subject of instinct. This started as an argument
over conceptual issues with a paper that questioned the facile way in which
numerous instincts had been identified over the previous decade or so without
any agreement over the criteria for deciding what an instinct is (Dunlap,
1919). It then moved to the general issue of whether appeals to an instinct
have any explanatory power whatsoever; to explain someone's suicide as a
result of his or her suicidal instinct is clearly unsatisfactory, but perhaps no
more so than examples that had been generally accepted up to the time of
this debate (Herrnstein, 1972).

Starting with a paper by Kuo (1921) the debate over instincts shifted from
such conceptual issues to the more substantial one of how heredity determines behavior (see Cravens, 1978; Herrnstein, 1972; Krantz and Allen,
1967). Kuo argued that since any behavior develops as a result of a complex
interaction between the genes and the environment that starts from the
moment the egg is fertilized, neither 'instinct' nor 'habit' are useful concepts
in the study of behavior, and they obstruct detailed analysis of developmental
processes. Watson was much more cautious and, although he later rejected
the use of instinct with regard to human behavior, he found it perfectly
serviceable as a label to use for some kinds of animal behavior (Watson,
1924). But this was when the debate had already begun to die down; at its
height Watson had presumably been too occupied with personal matters to
become involved and, in any case, his position while still in academic life
had always been that factual information was needed in advance of conceptual argument.

One aspect of the instinct debate that is of interest here is that, as in
Watson's own research career, there was no particular experimental study,
or empirical finding of any kind, that featured strongly in the exchanges.
Some of the papers (e.g. Kuo, 1921) referred to the recent discovery of

sexual imprinting in pigeons (Whitman, 1919) as an illustration of the long lasting effect that early experience can have on behavior, but that was about all. This again suggests that the roots of the attack on hereditarianism within psychology are to be found outside. The most likely candidates are the important shifts in outlook which occurred in genetics and in anthropology; these have been discussed extensively elsewhere (e.g. Stocking, 1968; Cravens, 1978), but are rarely mentioned in histories of psychology.

GENETICS AND ANTHROPOLOGY: 1900–1920

Early in this chapter various components of speculative Darwinism were described as being successively challenged in the first part of this century. In fact the critical attack on Lamarckism was already well under way (Weismann, 1889) and by the turn of the century many influential psychologists (e.g. Baldwin, 1894; Morgan, 1896) no longer believed in any inheritance of acquired characteristics, not even of engrained habits acquired by generation after generation. The failure of ducklings to recognize the visual signs of water was a crucial piece of evidence for Morgan (1896). The lack of any satisfactory theory of heredity had been very generally recognized as a central weakness of Darwin's theories from the time of the debates that surrounded publication of the *Origin of Species*. In retrospect it is surprising that for forty years so little progress was made on this problem. The turning point was the rediscovery in 1900 of Mendel's results. Two aspects of early twentieth century genetics were important for psychology: one was that for the next twenty or more years Mendelian genetics were viewed as incompatible with Darwinian theory, and the other was the delay of up to fifteen years before the modern concept of the gene was widely accepted by geneticists. During this time various theories involving what would now be termed macro-mutations were put forward to explain speciation (Cravens, 1978). It was only after years of intensive experimental work on the fruit-fly that certain crucial features of modern genetics became clear; one was that there is rarely a simple one-to-one correspondence between a unit of heredity, the gene, and some specific characteristic of an individual organism and, second, that any developmental process involves complex interactions between the genes and the environment (Morgan *et al.*, 1915).

What did these issues have to do with psychology? In the 1900s mutation theory was taken up by many psychologists involved in the eugenics movement who adopted what is called 'unit character theory' for their own purposes. This involved the assumption of a very direct link between some unit of the 'germ' and a psychological trait. The retreat of Lamarckism and the emergence of Mendelian genetics initially led to a reinforcement of hereditarian attitudes. Galton had been preaching eugenics for over thirty years (since Galton, 1869) and it was only with this change of outlook on the mechanisms of heredity that scientists in any number took his social ideas very seriously (Haller, 1963).

The theory of the gene developed by Morgan and his associates was slower to affect psychology than mutation theory had been a decade or so earlier. Watson, for example, was well placed to appreciate such ideas, since a close colleague, H. S. Jennings, was one of the leading workers in genetics research. The two of them took part in a symposium on the implications of modern science for education, in which Watson spoke of his new research on babies, while Jennings outlined the way in which current genetics undermined the assumption that psychological traits could be inherited in some simple, direct fashion (Jennings *et al.*, 1917). Yet there is little discussion of this point in Watson's own writings over the next few years; it was emphasized by a psychologist for the first time in Kuo's attack on instinct theory (Kuo, 1921).

The other outside influence on psychology came from anthropology. It is in this field alone that one can find indication of changes in opinions on human nature occurring as the direct result of new discoveries.

One kind of discovery was of the immense diversity of human customs. Many of the Darwinians, but emphatically not Darwin himself, had believed both in a simple ordering, the *scala naturae*, of organisms from 'lower' to 'higher' and a similar single scale for human societies, usually with Australian aborigines at one end and always with Europeans at the other. By the turn of the century anthropologists who had started to look at the habits, customs and social relationships of various non-European peoples were beginning to reject simple biological models (Cravens, 1978). One widely read account of the results from such field studies was *Folkways* (Sumner, 1906) which detailed the huge variety of customs related to child care, courtship, and marriage in different societies. Waston (1936) later cited this as the most influential book he ever read. It seemed now that writers like James were dignifying as 'natural' what were completely arbitrary mores of their own particular social group.

The other kind of discovery emerged from the study of racial differences and here a major part was played by the anthropologist, Franz Boas (Stocking, 1968). The most important of his findings were obtained from a study of the physical changes occurring among the members of immigrant groups. To his considerable surprise he discovered that such changes were very marked, even in measures of head-shape which had been widely regarded as the most stable indicator of racial type. What aspects of the environment produced such changes, whether it was the climate, diet or more subtle modifications of ways of life after reaching America, was unclear; but it was quite plain that physical characteristics hitherto taken as expressions of racial inheritance were more likely to reflect the particular circumstances in which some group of people had been living for generations in the Old World.

Such results were summarized by Boas in the *Mind of Primitive Man* (1911) which served to undermine the assumptions about race held in anthropology and which strongly reinforced the idea that the really important problem in the study of man is that of understanding how one generation passes on to the next its *culture*, a problem to which biology can contribute very little. Other studies of immigrant groups, including those that looked at the way national customs were affected by arrival in America, as in a celebrated study of Polish immigrants (Thomas and Znanecki, 1918; see Deegan and Burger, 1981), encouraged this environmentalist trend within the American social sciences.

As with the new theories of genetics, these developments do not appear to have made an immediate impact on psychology (Samelson, 1978). One reason may have been simply one of timing: they occurred just before the war and American psychology became almost totally involved in its contributions to the war effort so that it is hard to find any psychologist under the age of forty-five who was not caught up in testing and training soldiers. Furthermore, while the success of the army program added to the importance of the mental testers within psychology, in the other social sciences American involvement in the war temporarily isolated the Boasians, many of whom were suspected of insufficient patriotism (Cravens, 1978).

An attack on the hereditarian assumptions of the mental testing movement began by concentrating on its social and political implications. This had been heralded by an address to the American Psychological Association given just before the war by Dewey (1917), who discussed in very general terms the connection between structural approaches in psychology and conservative attitudes towards social problems. 'The ultimate refuge of every standpatter in every field, education, religion, politics, industrial, and domestic life, has been the notion of an alleged fixed structure of mind. As long as mind is conceived as an antecedent and ready-made thing, institutions and customs may be regarded as its offspring. By its own nature the ready-made mind works to produce them as they have existed and now exist. There is no use in kicking against necessity' (Dewey, 1917; p. 273). He went on to welcome 'the advent of a type of psychology which builds frankly on the original activities of man and asks how these are altered, qualified and reorganized in consequence of their exercise in specifically different environments'.

A more detailed version of Dewey's arguments came later from outside the profession when the journalist, Walter Lippman, wrote a series of articles in the *New Republic* which castigated Terman's claims concerning the 'mental age' of Americans and expressed alarm that the promise of Binet's work was 'in danger of gross perversion by muddleheaded and prejudiced men.' Lippmann was primarily concerned with education: 'the danger of intelligence tests is that in a wholesale system of education, the less sophisticated or the more prejudiced will stop when they have classified and forget that their duty is to educate. They will grade the retarded child instead of fighting the causes of his backwardness' (Lippmann, 1922; p. 297). He argued that Terman's correlations between social status and intelligence were 'hardly an argument for hereditary differences in the endowment of social classes. They are a rather strong argument for the traditional American theory that the public school is an agency for equalizing the opportunities of the privileged and the unprivileged' (Lippmann, 1922; p. 329). Lippmann's articles were well-informed, closely argued and—in contrast to Dewey's elaborate and difficult style—very forceful. They ended with the plea that 'psychologists will save themselves from the reproach of having opened up a new chance for quackery in a field where quacks breed like rabbits, and they will save themselves from the humiliation of having furnished doped evidence to the exponents of the New Snobbery' (Lippmann, 1923; p. 10).

At the same time intelligence testing was attracting great interest in another context, the public debate over immigration that came to the fore in 1922 when a congressional committee began hearings in preparation for new legislation. Some recent accounts of these events have stressed the role played by the eugenicists and mental testers in the moves towards more restrictive quotas drawn up on racist grounds (e.g. Gould, 1981; Kamin, 1974). However there are good reasons for regarding the psychologists as Johnies-come-lately to a movement which had campaigned against further immigration from southern and eastern Europe long before anyone thought to cite eugenics arguments or intelligence test data in its support (Samelson, 1978; 1979). There were a variety of banners to wave other than what one supporter of restricted immigration dismissed as 'highbrow Nordic superiority stuff' (Samelson, 1979; p. 136).

Independent of its actual effectiveness was the publicity given to psychology's support for a movement that within a short time began to arouse deep revulsion among other American intellectuals. The geneticists were horrified by the distortions of genetics theory employed to justify racist arguments, as were the anthropologists by the way in which the importance of environmental factors and cultural differences was ignored as expert witnesses paraded their prejudices on racial stereotypes. In 1924 the new and highly restrictive immigration law was passed, but by then the kind of belief that had helped its passage was seen as disreputable among American scientists. In the early stages of the congressional hearings Yerkes, for example, had helped publicize those aspects of the Army test results which he saw as reflecting inherited differences in intelligence between various groups, but by 1923 he had been impressed by Lippmann's arguments and anyhow had decided that such ideas had become too controversial to discuss publicly any more (Cravens, 1978; Samelson, 1979).

What is the connection between these events and behaviorism? There is little evidence of direct links between the immigration debates and the strong environmentalism of Watson's *Behaviorism* that was published in the year that the immigration act was passed. The book was based on a series of evening lectures he had been giving and he wrote that during these lectures the question that came up again and again was: what is innate and what is learned?[1] One can only surmise that the central environmentalist theme of *Behaviorism* reflects the interests of the students who attended Watson's lectures and the pressure he felt to abandon his position of suspended judgment and come down on one side or the other.

With Watson's past interest in learning, his enthusiasm for the conditioned reflex and his skeptical attitude towards claims about human instincts, it was perhaps inevitable that he should have chosen the nurture side. There were also his close contacts with Jennings and with sociologists like Thomas to nudge him in this direction. Perhaps not least, although most speculative, was Watson's sense of where the action was going to be; American psychology would surely have become much less hereditarian even if Watson had broken all contact with psychology after 1920, but by making this the major issue in his book he ensured that his brand of behaviorism was already well-established in a strong environmentalist position before any other movement in psychology arrived there.

IMPLICATIONS FOR PSYCHOLOGY TODAY

After covering so much ground it might be helpful at this point to summarize some of the main points. Starting with Watson's own career, the various features that later came to characterize behaviorism were adopted by him at different times, with commitment to the primacy of habit and to an objective definition for the subject matter of psychology coming early on and environmentalism coming very late. There was a gap of eight years between Watson's adoption of the conditioned reflex and the announcement of a full-blooded environmentalist view of human nature. Whereas there is a certain logic in terms of his own research career and intellectual development to account for other elements of Watsonian behaviorism, it is difficult to find events or discoveries to explain where the sudden fierce emphasis on nurture came from. However, there was one important change in his life that may be quite crucial and deserves some comment here. His four years in advertising taught Watson to express his ideas in a more direct and challenging way than ever.

As Kamin (1974) noted, Watson's oft-quoted claim that he could take a healthy infant at random and train him to become any type of specialist he might select, was followed by the infrequently cited disclaimer, admitting that he was going beyond his facts, but so equally had advocates for the contrary position and this for thousands of years. Looked at carefully the main theme of *Behaviorism* is not that the hereditarian view of man is mistaken, but that there is no evidence in its support and that the environmentalist alternative has never been seriously explored. The presentation is such that these qualifications, which would stand out if phrased in standard scholarly style, are as easy to miss now as presumably they were when the book first appeared.

If we ask whether the appearance of environmentalism as an important element of behaviorism followed some general trend in American psychology, the answer is no. There was a strong hereditarian tradition dating back at least to James' discussion of human instincts and, if anything, this was accentuated by the growth of the mental testing movement. The Army program encouraged the belief that intelligence and aptitude testing was the way that psychology could make the major contribution to society that so many had been looking for.

Although initially used in an attempt to distinguish the 'feeble-minded' from the rest of the population, in the early 1920s the data from the Army tests was used to draw conclusions about inherent racial differences in intellect (Brigham, 1923). This further extension of the belief in the 'biological' determinants of individual differences came at an unpropitious time, in that it flew in the face of new ideas in genetics and the critique of traditional ideas on race that was mounted in anthropology. Watson seems to have associated behaviorism with a strong environmentalist approach just as the tide was about to turn in psychology as it had already in other American social sciences.

An interesting contrast is provided by British psychology where in the early 1920s the mental testing tradition was if anything more strongly entrenched than in America (Hearnshaw, 1979). However, the general expansion of psychology within British universities occurred much later. When eventually a challenge to the mental testing approach was mounted within psychology, it did not occur at a time of general reaction to hereditarian ideas as it had over twenty years earlier in the United States. The professional critique of mental testing in Britain based its case mainly on the lack of any analysis of cognitive processing and of an experimental methodology. There does not seem to have been as intense suspicion of the hereditarian assumptions made by someone like Burt as in the United States. And this seems to be the reason why the flaws in Burt's data were not spotted until an American conditioning theorist, Kamin, looked closely at this work (Hearnshaw, 1979; but see Clarke and Clarke, 1974).

The events described in this chapter happened over fifty years ago and readers might well ask whether they are of any interest apart from satisfying curiosity about the origins of behaviorism. In suggesting that there is something more than this and that one can go beyond the glib expression of sentiments on 'the advisability of viewing current work in its historical context', I would like to discuss briefly the relationship between animal research on conditioning and human development.

We have seen that Watson adopted the conditioned reflex as a model of learning well before behaviorism became committed to an environmentalist view of man and that this occurred in the absence of any new discoveries or insights about human learning. Since then, of course, various theories of conditioning have continued to remain a central part of the behaviorist tradition. As sociology and anthropology developed the concept of cultural transmission, it was hoped that the process by which this transmission occurred at a molecular level would be illuminated by psychology's new emphasis on learning (e.g., Bernard, 1924).

This hope has still not been fulfilled. Mainstream psychology, as represented by the standard textbooks, has had very little to say about why one child develops in one direction and a second in another. When a new student of psychology turns to a text on the psychology of learning he or she is usually disappointed to find that it is mainly about conditioning experiments using animals. Is this disappointment naive or unjustified? The standard behaviorist reply is that the principles of conditioning when fully elucidated will provide the essential basis for an understanding of human development (see Blackman, Chapter 3). But such assertions are almost as much dogma and as little supported by empirical evidence now as they were when first made by Pavlov and then by Bechterev and Watson. At least Bechterev and Watson proposed to study children directly, whereas most of their successors have simply asserted, slightly less fiercely in recent years, that those problems that provide the focus of most research on conditioning hold the key to understanding human development; there has been remarkably little effort expended on empirical attempts to demonstrate the validity of this claim (but see Lowe, Chapter 5).

Disappointment over what experimental psychology has to say about learning is not confined to the beginning student. Educational psychologists feel that they need more than the basics of classical conditioning, details of different reinforcement schedules and two-factor theories of avoidance to help them in their work. Perhaps they are wrong, but, if so, the argument needs to be made more convincingly.

In a letter to *The Times* (15 November 1976) in response to an editorial on the Burt affair, the following request was made: 'Would the experts debating the question of whether intelligence is inherited please say why the intelligence of children of the same parents can differ so much when their intellectual environment is usually so similar.' In answering such a plea the behaviorist today can suggest, as Watson did in 1924, why certain events in infancy might produce marked differences between individuals whose environments in gross terms seem so alike. But none, including Kamin, can go much beyond plausible appeals to possible factors.

To her request *The Times* correspondent added: 'Surely the explanation is genetic?' It is because the psychology of learning has maintained its emphasis on the study of conditioning in animals and allowed the environmentalist position on human development to go largely unexplored that a simple hereditarian interpretation of human differences has been able to maintain its long appeal.

In discussing these consequences of the early days of behaviorism I am not maintaining that the study of conditioning in animals is unrelated to important issues in human development or in the everyday behavior of adults. The suggestion is simply that prior commitment to the study of 'habits' has deflected effort away from the study of other important aspects of human learning. For some of these it may be as appropriate to use animal models as in the study of conditioning. Clearly one major reason for the continued interest in conditioning is that it can be studied experimentally in animals, whereas Watson's successors have felt more keenly than he did the ethical and practical considerations that limit experiments on human learning. But there are other kinds of learning, those involving language or imitation—to take examples from behaviorism's origins—where animal models are likely to be of limited help. In obtaining some understanding of these the psychology of learning will have to be more willing than in the past to accept evidence of a less conclusive kind than can be obtained by experiment. If it does this and puts more effort into exploring the relationship between phenomena found in the animal laboratory and apparently similar effects found in everyday life then it will have some expert knowledge to use in answering *The Times'* correspondent's request.

NOTE

1. J. B. Watson to H. S. Jennings, January 24th, 1924. Unpublished letter in the Jennings Collection, Library of the American Philosophical Society, Philadelphia, Penn.

ACKNOWLEDGMENTS

I am very grateful for the suggestions and comments on a draft of this chapter made by Leon Kamin, Lexa Logue, Tim Roper, and Franz Samelson, although they might disagree with some of the views expressed in this final version. Its preparation was helped by a grant from the Royal Society and the assistance of the Library of the American Philosophical Society, Philadelphia.

REFERENCES

Allen, G. E. (1978) *Life Science in the Twentieth Century*. Cambridge: Cambridge University.
Baldwin, J. M. (1894) *Mental development in the Child and the Race*. New York: Macmillan.
Bernard, L. L. (1924) *Instinct*. London: George Allen & Unwin.

Blanton, M. G. (1917) The behavior of the human infant during the first thirty days of life. *Psychological Review*, **24**, 456–483.

Boakes, R. A. *From Darwin to Behaviourism*. Cambridge: Cambridge University, in press.

Boas, F. (1911) *The Mind of Primitive Man*. New York: Macmillan.

Brigham, C. C. (1923) *A Study of American Intelligence*. Princeton, N.J: Princeton University.

Cairns, R. B., and Ornstein, P. A. (1979) Developmental psychology. In E. Hearst (ed.) *The First Century of Experimental Psychology* Hillsdale, N.J: Erlbaum, pp. 459–512.

Clark, R. W. (1980) *Freud*. London: Jonathan Cape and Weidenfeld & Nicolson.

Clarke, A. D. B., and Clarke Ann M. (1974) *Mental Deficiency*. 3rd Edition. London: Methuen.

Cohen, D. (1979) *J. B. Watson: The Founder of Behaviourism*. London, Routledge & Kegan Paul

Cravens, H. (1978) *The Triumph of Evolution*. Philadelphia: University of Pennsylvania.

Cravens, H., and Burnham, J. C. (1971) Psychology and evolutionary naturalism in American thought, 1890–1914. *American Quarterly*, **23**, 635–657.

Darwin, C. (1859) *The Origin of Species*. London: Murray.

Deegan, M. J., and Burger, J. S. (1981) W. I. Thomas and social reform. *Journal for the History of the Behavioral Sciences*, **17**, 114–125.

Dennet, D. C. (1978) *Brainstorms*. Montgomery, Vt: Bradford.

Dewey, J. (1917) The need for social psychology. *Psychological Review*, **24**, 266–277.

Dunlap, K. (1919) Are there any instincts? *Journal of Abnormal Psychology*, **14**, 307–311.

Galton, F. (1869) *Hereditary Genius*. London: Macmillan.

Gould, S. J. (1981) *The Mismeasure of Man*. New York: Norton.

Haeckel, E. (1900) *The Riddle of the Universe*. (Transl. by J. McCabe). London: Watts.

Hale, N. G. (1971) *Freud and the Americans*. New York: Oxford University.

Haller, M. H. (1963) *Eugenics*. New Brunswick: Rutgers University.

Harris, B. (1979) Whatever happened to little Albert? *American Psychologist*, **34**, 151–160.

Hearnshaw, L. S. (1979) *Cyril Burt*. London: Hodder & Stoughton.

Herrnstein, R. J. (1972) Nature as nurture: behaviorism and the instinct doctrine. *Behaviorism*, **1**, 233–252.

James, W. (1890) *Principles of Psychology*. New York: Henry Holt.

Jennings, H. S., Watson, J. B., Meyer, A., and Thomas, W. (1917) *Suggestions of Modern Science Concerning Education*. New York: Macmillan.

Jensen, A. R. (1969) How much can we boost IQ and scholastic achievement. *Harvard Educational Review*, **39**, 1–123.

Jones, M. C. (1924) A laboratory study of fear: the case of Peter. *Pedagogical Seminary*, **31**, 308–315.

Jones, M. C. (1974) Albert, Peter and John B. Watson. *American Psychologist*, **29**, 581–583.

Kamin, L. J. (1969) Predictability, surprise, attention and conditioning. In B. A. Campbell and R. M. Church (eds) *Punishment and Aversive Behavior*. New York: Appleton-Century-Crofts.

Kamin, L. J. (1974) *The Science and Politics of IQ*. Hillsdale, N. J: Erlbaum.

Krantz, D. L., and Allen, D. (1967) The rise and fall of McDougall's instinct doctrine. *Journal of the History of the Behavioral Sciences*, **3**, 326–338.

Kuo, Z–Y. (1921) Giving up instincts in psychology. *Journal of Philosophy*, **18**, 645–664.

Lippmann, W. (1922) The mental age of Americans. *New Republic*, **32**, 213–215 (Also 246–248; 257–278; 297–298; 328–330.)

Lippmann, W. (1923) A future for the tests *New Republic*, **33**, 9–10. (See also 116–120; 145–146.)

Logue, A. (1978) Behaviorist John B. Watson and the continuity of the species. *Behaviorism*, **6**, 71–79.

Logue, A. The growth of behaviorism. In C. Buxton (ed.) *Points of View in the Modern History of Psychology*. New York: Academic, in press.

McDougall, W. (1908) *An Introduction to Social Psychology*. London: Methuen.

Morgan, C. L. (1894) *An Introduction to Comparative Psychology*. London: Walter Scott.

Morgan, C. L. (1896) *Habit and Instinct*. London: Edward Arnold.

Morgan, T. H., Sturtevant, A. H., Muller, H. J., and Bridges, C. B. (1915) *The Mechanisms of Mendelian Heredity*. New York:

O'Donnell, J. M. (1979) *The Origins of Behaviorism: American Psychology, 1870–1920*. Unpublished Ph.D. thesis, University of Pennsylvania. (University Microfilms International.)

Pfungst, O. (1965) *Clever Hans: the Horse of Mr. von Osten*. (Original German edition, 1908.) English edition, New York: Holt.

Romanes, G. J. (1882) *Animal Intelligence*. London: Kegan, Paul, Trench & Co.

Ross, D. G. (1972) *Stanley Hall: the Psychologist as Prophet*. Chicago: University of Chicago.

Samelson, F. (1975) On the science and politics of the IQ. *Social Research*, **42**, 467–488.

Samelson, F. (1977) World War I intelligence testing and the development of psychology. *Journal of the History of the Behavioral Sciences*, **13**, 274–282.

Samelson, F. (1978) From 'race psychology' to 'studies in prejudice'; some observations on the thematic reversal in social psychology. *Journal of History of the Behavioral Sciences*, **14**, 265–278.

Samelson, F. (1979) Putting psychology on the map: ideology and intelligence testing, In A. R. Buss (ed.) *Psychology in Social Context*. New York: Irvington. pp. 103–168.

Samelson, F. (1980) J. B. Watson's Little Albert, Cyril Burt's Twins, and the need for a critical science. *American Psychologist*, **35**, 619–625.

Samelson, F. (1981) Struggle for scientific authority: the reception of Watson's behaviorism, 1913–1920. *Journal for the History of the Behavioral Sciences*, **17**, 399–425.

Stocking, G. W. (1968) *Race, Culture and Evolution: Essays in the History of Anthropology* New York: Free Press.

Sumner, G. (1906) *Folkways* Boston: Ginn.

Terman, L. M. (1916) *The Measurement of Intelligence*. Boston: Houghton Mifflin.

Thomas, W. I., and Znanecki, F. (1918) *The Polish Peasant in Europe and America*. Boston: Badger. (Reprinted New York: Dover, 1951.)

Thorndike, E. L. (1898) Animal intelligence Monograph supplement, No. 8 *Psychological Review*, 1898. (Reprinted in Thorndike, E. L., *Animal Intelligence*. New York: Macmillan, 1911.)

Thorndike, E. L. (1901) The mental life of monkeys. Monograph supplement, No.

15 *Psychological Review*. (Reprinted in Thorndike, E. L., *Animal Intelligence*. New York: Macmillan, 1911.)

Titchener, E. B. (1914) On 'Psychology as the Behaviorist views it'. *Proceedings of the American Philosophical Society*, 53, 1–17.

Tolman, E. C. (1932) *Purposive Behavior in Animals and Men*. New York: Appleton-Century-Crofts.

Washburn, M. F. (1908) *The Animal Mind*. New York: Macmillan.

Watson J. B. (1903) *Animal Education*. Chicago: University of Chicago.

Watson, J. B. (1907) Kinaesthetic and organic sensations: their role in the reactions of the white rat to the maze. *Psychological Monographs*, 8, No. 33.

Watson, J. B. (1908a) Behavior of noddy and sooty terms. *Carnegie Publications*, 103, 187–255.

Watson, J. B. (1908b) Imitation in monkeys. *Psychological Bulletin*, 5, 169–179.

Watson, J. B. (1908c) Review of Pfungst's *Clever Hans*. *Journal of Comparative Neurology & Psychology*, 18, 329–331.

Watson, J. B. (1909) Experiments bearing on color vision in monkeys. *Journal of Comparative Neurology and Psychology*, 19, 1–28.

Watson, J. B. (1913) Psychology as the Behaviorist views it. *Psychological Review*, 20, 158–178.

Watson, J. B. (1914) *Behavior: An Introduction to Comparative Psychology*. New York: Holt.

Watson, J. B. (1916) The conditional reflex in psychology. *Psychology Review*, 23, 89–117.

Watson, J. B. (1917) An attempted formulation of the scope of behavior psychology. *Psychological Review*, 24, 329–352.

Watson, J. B. (1919) *Psychology from the Standpoint of a Behaviorist*. Philadelphia: Lippincott.

Watson, J. B. (1924) *Behaviorism*. New York: Norton.

Watson, J. B. (1936) Autobiography. In C. Murchison (ed.) *A History of Psychology in Autobiography*. Worcester, Mass: Clark University.

Watson, J. B., and Rayner, R. (1920) Conditioned emotional reactions. *Journal of Experimental Psychology*, 3, 1–14.

Weismann, A. (1889) Professor Weismann's theory of heredity. *Nature*, 41, 317–323.

Whitman, C. O. (1919) The behavior of pigeons. *Carnegie Institute Publications*, No. 257.

Young, R. M. (1973) The role of psychology in the nineteenth-century evolutionary debate. In M. Henle, J. Jaynes, and J. Sullivan (eds) *Historical Conceptions of Psychology*. New York: Springer.

Animal Models of Human Behavior
Edited by G. C. L. Davey
© 1983 John Wiley & Sons Ltd

Chapter 3

On Cognitive Theories of Animal Learning: Extrapolation from Humans to Animals?

D. E. BLACKMAN

A major part of 'comparative psychology' has by tradition focused on experimental studies of learning in animals. In turn, 'learning theory' has traditionally played an influential role in the development of general models in psychology. As psychologists have struggled to come to grips with the complexities of human behavior, learning theorists such as Watson, Guthrie, Tolman, Hull and Skinner have all in their time been seen as offering distinctive ways of interpreting behavior, including the behavior of humans. Almost without exception, the impact of learning theory in this sense rests on the extrapolation to human psychology of principles which emerged from rigorously controlled experimental studies of learning in laboratory animals.

There is no need here to comment on what some see as the distorting impact of studies of learning in rats on 'comparative psychology', nor on what others see as the distorting impact of 'learning theory' on general psychology. But it is worth noting that these influences, whether or not they are seen as distorting, arrive from a conventional chain of reasoning. It is difficult to carry out rigorously controlled experiments on human behavior, for human subjects bring to any laboratory investigation a host of expectations, prejudices and aspirations based on their past experiences. By transferring our experimental interests to the animal laboratory, we may gain in our ability to control individual differences which stem from past experience or indeed from genetic inheritance. We may also gain in our ability to control the experimental conditions and even to broaden the range of variables which can be ethically investigated.

There are also costs to be considered, of course, in focusing experimental

attention on the behavior of animals. Extrapolations of some kind are necessary if animal studies are to be perceived as having any relevance to human
psychology. In addition, it must be recognized that the behavioral repertoires
of animals (or, at least of laboratory rats) are extremely limited in comparison
with the complexities of human behavior. Recognition of this limitation may
in part be the reason why experimental psychologists have favored studies of
learning, since the learning process can at least be said to reflect some degree
of behavioral plasticity, which may in turn be seen as a key to an understanding of the richness of differences in human behavior, both within and between
individuals. With respect to extrapolations from experiments on learning in
animals to the behavior of humans, it is normal to extrapolate not the
quantitative data or 'facts', but general principles. Such principles are represented in Skinnerian theory, for example, by the *concepts* of reinforcement,
punishment, or discriminative control or by *generalizations* concerning the
broad effects on behavior of intermittent schedules of reinforcement, response shaping, or stimulus fading.

Extrapolation of principles of this kind fits readily within the strictures of
a principle of parsimony. Lloyd Morgan's dictum has become conventional
wisdom in requiring interpretations of animal behavior to be couched in
terms of the 'lowest' 'psychical' faculty necessary to explain any particular
pattern of behavior. This principle has been used generally in comparative
psychology and in ethology, though its hegemony may sometimes now appear
to be challenged in some of the more engagingly daring aspects of sociobiology. Concepts such as reinforcement, and generalizations such as those
concerning intermittent schedules, are neutral with respect to levels of psychical functioning, or at least can be expressed in such a way as to appear
neutral. Furthermore, their extrapolation may in turn encourage attempts to
explain and understand even human behavior without appealing to higher
psychical faculties as *explanatory* devices.

The increasing complexity of more recent experimental analyses of animal
behavior has sometimes identified the necessary and sufficient environmental
conditions for behavior to occur which could be seen to reflect 'preference'
'choice', 'self-control', 'awareness' and other higher psychical processes (see
Rachlin, 1976). The thrust of such experimentation, taken in conjunction
with the principle of parsimony, has been to produce explanations of increasingly complex animal behavior in environmentalistic terms. This in turn has
led to extrapolations which reinterpret increasingly complex patterns of human behavior in essentially non-cognitive environmentalistic terms.

Dickinson (1980) has described this general approach well, characterizing
it as that of the 'behavior analyst'. Such analysts are said to focus directly on
behavior, hoping to formulate behavioral laws and principles which transcend
the confines of the laboratory and the species of animal whose behavior is
investigated. Behavior analysts see their task, according to Dickinson, as

'specifying the relationship between some physical event in the environment, the stimulus, and . . . some acquired behavioral pattern, the response, without reference to mental processes' (1980, p. xi).

The behavior analysts' wish to eschew mental processes in the interpretation of animal learning may reflect their general orientation with respect to theory in psychology or it may arise in a more limited way from the conventional use of Lloyd Morgan's principle of parsimony in interpreting the animal behavior studied in the analysts' laboratories. However, Dickinson considers that the analysts' program is doomed to failure, for he believes that 'it turns out that most interesting behavioural capacities are just not susceptible to this type of explanation' (1980, p. 4). Thus he argues that learning theorists, even those studying the behavior of non-human animals, should formulate their interests in terms of 'the way in which animals acquire knowledge through experience' (1980, p. xi). He believes that 'the conditioning experiment is primarily an analytically tractable tool for studying the cognitive changes that take place during learning' (1980, p. xi).

Dickinson is not alone in advocating such a seemingly fundamental reorientation. Mackintosh has argued that '. . . simple associative learning is simple in name only. Animals do not automatically associate all events that happen to occur together. If they did, they would surely be at the mercy of every chance conjunction of events. In fact, they behave in an altogether more rational manner' (1978a, p. 54). 'It is time', Mackintosh has asserted, 'that psychologists abandoned their outmoded view of conditioning and recognised it as a complex and useful process whereby organisms build an accurate representation of their world' (1978a, p. 54).

Contemporary learning theory therefore now includes some who seem to assert that the complexities of conditioning experiments are such that even animals should be seen as active information processors, and that changes in behavior must be reflections of events at some other level, such as 'expectations' (Wagner, 1978), 'selective attention' (Riley and Roitblat, 1978), 'surprise' (Mackintosh, 1978b), and others described by similar essentially cognitive terms. Learning theorists should seek 'the associative processes underlying learned modifications of behaviour' (Mackintosh, 1974, p. 1), and they should recognize that 'learning may occur in the absence of any current changes in behaviour' (Mackintosh, 1974, p. 4).

Such views appear to attribute to animals psychological (or 'psychical' in Lloyd Morgan's terminology) functions in a way that is somewhat different from what has become conventional in comparative psychology. It is important to note, however, that this is not in itself to imply that a principle of parsimony has necessarily been infringed, for cognitive learning theorists presumably would assert that such forms of psychological functioning *are* required in order to explain some (or even all) changes in behavior in conditioning experiments in the most parsimonious way.

Such a claim can be resisted, however. The argument here is exactly that addressed by Skinner (1950) in his seminal paper 'Are theories of learning necessary?' Skinner argued in that paper (and elsewhere, of course), that explanations of behavior couched in terms of events taking place at other levels are not of necessity and inherently better than explanations which seek to relate behavior to environmental conditions. The 'cognitive' concepts advocated by Mackintosh, Dickinson and others clearly rest at some other level. Their status with respect to level can sometimes seem a little unclear. Are the 'associative mechanisms' which are said to 'underlie' behavior merely to be envisaged in a scientifically conservative manner as having some physiological entity, thereby allowing an essentially mechanistic analysis (albeit with increased complexity)? Dickinson suggests that 'whether or not we shall be able at some time to identify the neurophysiological *substrate* of these cognitive structures is an open question' (1980, p. 5, italics added). (He continues: 'It is clear, however, that we cannot do so at present'.) From this, at least, the 'cognitive structures' could seem to be something other than 'merely' physiological structures. Is, then, the vocabulary of human cognition now used to explain animal learning well chosen in order to imply that animals can be said to enjoy the psychological functions that humans can talk about with respect to their own *experience*? Is the rat even perhaps aware of his own psychological processes, expecting, selectively attending, or being surprised? If this is *not* the case, it might seem that the cognitive terminology may be no more than an attractively daring (and potentially grossly misleading) choice of words to identify hypothetical constructs—or even perhaps merely intervening variables (MacCorquodale and Meehl, 1948) which are not presumed to have any existence at all. The attraction of this approach may come, it seems, from some degree of conceptual vagueness coupled with a willingness to appear to extrapolate *from* humans *to* animals.

Honig (1978) has considered the conceptual status of cognitive concepts with respect to animal learning, and would doubtless not accept the above suggestion that their status can be ambiguous. However, with respect to the direction of extrapolation, he has argued 'If psychologists were consistent in applying the principle of biological continuity amongst species, they would find it easier to adopt concepts based on human experience to characterize behavior in other species and to suggest theoretical formulations. The principle of continuity implies the possibility of moving in both directions along the phylogenetic continuum. Traditionally psychologists have started with a S–R analysis founded on animal behavior and have moved "up" the scale for the analysis of human behavior. The study of cognitive processes in animals may open the way to movement in the other direction. Once the behavioral analysis has been soundly established, subjective or mentalistic concepts arising from human experience can perhaps be used for explanation or theory' (Honig, 1978, p. 13). But, we may ask, is it *necessary* to do this?

If 'the behavioral analysis is soundly achieved', will mentalistic concepts attributed to non-verbal animals *add* any explanatory power? Or instead will premature transitions to the level of mentalism deflect psychologists *away* from sound behavioral analyses and the recognition of their explanatory power, as Skinner has suggested (1950)?

In any case, current environmentalistic analyses of both simple and complex behavioral adjustments in animals should be scrutinized carefully before being discarded as unsatisfactory. It seems that much of the cognitive theorists' dissatisfaction arises from their belief that environmentalistic analyses can be characterized by 'stimulus-response' analyses (see quotations above from Dickinson, 1980, Honig, 1978, and Mackintosh, 1974). Such S–R relationships are clearly thought to be the basis of 'associationism' (e.g., Mackintosh, 1978b) and to be seen as automatic and inevitable. However, it has been argued elsewhere (Blackman, 1980) that the terms stimulus and response may be misleading, at least for operant conditioning experiments. Such studies investigate the reliable correlations that develop over time between environmental conditions and emitted behavior. Discriminative control may be exerted by a light if the light sets the occasion for a pattern of behavior to be followed by a reinforcer. The frequency of that pattern of behavior may then be interpreted as a function of the schedule by which reinforcers are related to behavior. Thus functional analyses of behavior attempt to identify how the frequency with which behavior is emitted can be understood in relation to the setting conditions in the environment and the (possibly occasional) consequences of that behavior in those conditions. To call the light a *stimulus* and the operant behavior a *response* may be seriously misleading if it is taken to imply an easy similarity to the 1 : 1 relationship of an unconditional stimulus and an unconditioned response in conventional Pavlovian conditioning experiments. To this extent, the terms discriminative stimulus and operant response are unfortunate jargon. *Any* 'voluntary' pattern of behavior is potentially amenable to a functional analysis, which seeks simply to explain and understand the occurrence of such behavior in its environmental context, and which does not thereby commit the behavior analyst to the 'associationism' which appears to be seen as the antithesis to contemporary cognitive learning theory (Mackintosh, 1978b).

This point can perhaps be developed by considering the relationships between behavior and consequence in the so-called shock-frequency reduction phenomenon. Herrnstein and Hineline (1966) reported that the lever-pressing of rats occurred at higher frequencies if it led to an *overall* (but not necessarily immediate) reduction in the frequency with which shocks are delivered. Thus a functional relationship between the frequency of environmental events and the frequency of emitted behavior was demonstrated experimentally (in this case an *inverse* correlation). Herrnstein and Hineline went to some length in their paper to argue that their experiment began to identify effectively a functional relationship between behavior and environmental conditions, and thus the necessary and sufficient conditions for operant behavior to be sustained by negative reinforcement. Mackintosh (1974) reviews data which makes it clear that the experiment by Herrnstein and Hineline identifies only one part of the necessary and sufficient conditions for behavior to be maintained, since the *momentary* probability of shock can also be important. Nevertheless, in a real sense the explanation of lever-pressing behavior in the shock-frequency reduction procedure could be seen by behavior analysts as lying *within* the exposition of the functional relationship between behavior and the environment.

Although the original investigators explicitly did not interpret their data in any other way, Mackintosh, when reviewing the experiment by Herrnstein and Hineline, suggested '. . . it must be assumed that animals are calculating variations in the overall rate of shock per session, and correlating these with variations in their own patterns of responding' (1974, p. 328). It could be argued that Mackintosh's assumption adds nothing to the explanatory power of the empirically identified functional relationship between behavior and environment, and that it serves merely to deflect theoretical attention to a spuriously explanatory and unidentifiable inner mechanism whose cognitive characteristics are perhaps once more somewhat ambiguous.

Exactly this dispute between functional and cognitive analyses can be (and has been) extended to *all* aspects of operant behavior: for example, the functional relationship between the frequency of operant behavior and the frequency of positive reinforcement in interval schedules could be 'explained' by recourse to the computing of frequencies by rats, though this was not thought by the behavior analysts to be necessary or helpful for twenty years. Even the basic unit of analysis, the single lever press, can serve as an example here. Functional analyses rest their explanatory power on the observation that this unit of behavior is increased in frequency when followed by reinforcer. If we insist on asking *why* this is so, we may be drawn, along with Estes, to note approvingly that Konorski was '. . . the first to see clearly that we do not need to look beyond or above conditioning experiments for evidence of higher processes, such as those of perception and memory' (Estes, 1979, p. 421). The behavior analyst would surely query the nature of this 'evidence', and indeed what the nature of the 'higher processes' might be. But Konorski was certainly correct in one sense: we *can* certainly use such cognitive 'explanations' to deflect us from recognizing the adequacy of explaining behavior by identifying functional relationships between it and environmental events, even in the simplest of behavioral situations. But what do we gain if we assert that our rat presses its lever because it perceives its presence and remembers its purpose, or that the rat wants food and knows how to get it? The further questions remain as to *why* the rat perceives the lever or wants food, and *how* he has come to know how to get food.

Furthermore, the behavior analyst would argue that these further questions are amenable to investigation *only* by identifying the environmental circumstances in which the functional relationship between behavior and reinforcement obtains.

Although cognitive learning theory has been applied to the interpretation of operant conditioning experiments, its main thrust has undoubtedly been in the domain of classical conditioning. Here experimental associations arranged between two external stimuli by an investigator lead perhaps all the more easily to explanations of changes in behavior based on the assumption of 'associations' being formed *within* the experimental animal which are then expressed through behavior.

Even in experiments in which there is no dependency between behavior and the environment and which can therefore be seen as classical conditioning, it has become clear in recent years that the traditional concepts of stimulus and response can be misleading. For example, Rescorla (1968) has shown that the differential probability of conditioned behavior during a conditional stimulus is a function of the differential probability of occurrence of an unconditional stimulus during the conditional stimulus. Again this statement captures the necessary and sufficient conditions for an acquired reflex to develop. It broadens our previous analyses based on the Pavlovian pairing of stimuli. Behavior analysts might rest content with this expression of a relationship between behavior and environment as an explanation of behavior. Again it is possible, however, for cognitive theorists to offer the further explanation that the functional relationship between behavior and environment results from the experimental animal computing the differential probabilities of the unconditional stimulus in the presence and absence of the conditional stimulus. And again behavior analysts might ask what has been gained by this device. They would argue that the increasing complexity of the experimental arrangements which give rise to conditioning may need to be summarized by increasingly sophisticated mathematical or algebraic functions, but such functions clearly summarize the relationships between events rather than possibly represent hypothetical structures within an animal.

Certainly the impressive empirical advances in the study of classical conditioning provide challenges for any explanatory system. Cognitive learning theorists appear to be much concerned by studies which show that the behavioral effects of experimentally associating two stimuli may be changed by the past history of the experimental animals. One example is provided by sensory preconditioning. This phenomenon can be demonstrated by pairing S_1 and S_2, then by pairing S_2 and an unconditional stimulus. Subsequent presentation of S_1 alone reveals a conditioned response appropriate to the unconditional stimulus, although S_1 has never been paired with it. According to Dickinson, 'For the cognitive psychologist, sensory preconditioning, at least in principle, provides no difficulty; obviously, during the first stage the (S_1-S_2) pairings set up some internal representation of this relationship which remained behaviourally silent because neither of these stimuli were of any significance to the rat at that time. When (S_2) subsequently acquired significance by being paired with (the unconditional stimulus), the internal structure representing S_1 as a predictor of S_2 resulted in S_1 becoming (a conditional stimulus)' (1981, p. 5).

Dickinson claims that there is no difficulty in principle in the cognitive psychologist finding such an explanation, but perhaps this is because he is doing no more than translating the observed relationships between events and between events and behavior into another language, referring to unobservable constructs, and being too easily impressed by the 'explanatory' power of these constructs. In fact, it seems that sensory preconditioning can be explained in a similar but more objective way by the behavior analyst: given that S_1 and S_2 have occurred in a specified temporal relationship, and that S_2 then occurred in a specified relationship with an unconditional stimulus, S_1 will elicit a conditioned response when presented alone. Of course this is 'just' a restatement of the procedure and its findings. But it begins to identify the necessary and sufficient conditions for the behavioral phenomenon of sensory preconditioning, and thereby explains it without recourse to putative events at other, unobservable, levels which may add nothing to the power of the explanation and again might be said to shelter behind some degree of conceptual ambiguity.

As with operant conditioning, this dispute between behavior analysts and cognitive learning theorists can be extended through the whole field of classical conditioning. It is clear that the effects of environmental events in classical conditioning experiments can be understood only in a broader context and not by means of an outmoded form of 'associationism'. For example, one element of a compound conditional stimulus will acquire less control over behavior if the other element has previously been presented alone with the unconditional stimulus than if both elements are presented together *ab initio* in relation to the unconditional stimulus. This description identifies a behavioral phenomenon, and explains it by providing its context. Alternatively one might say that the behavioral effect of one element of the compound stimulus can be 'blocked' by prior pairing of the other element with the unconditional stimulus (Mackintosh, 1978b). This describes the behavioral effects again, but in a way that may be easier for us to remember. One could go on to suggest that this blocking results from animals failing to notice or attend to a second element of a compound stimulus after having perceived the causal relationship between the first element and the unconditional stimulus. But is this to do more than describe the behavioral effect yet again in an attempt to explain it? If this explanation adds anything, it is done at the cost of directing us to other levels of analysis where variables are not observable and can no longer be measured directly. The introduction of the concept of 'surprise' (e.g. Dickinson, 1980, p. 49) may add little but conceptual confusion to a description of the conditions in which the blocking effect can be reduced or enhanced (as for example when one element of a compound conditional stimulus has previously been explicitly correlated with the *absence* of the unconditional stimulus: Rescorla, 1971).

A particularly interesting paper in the field of cognitive learning theory is that of Church (1978). The paper reports the results of an extensive series of experiments which reveal how rats' lever-pressing behavior can become functionally related to the passage of time, that is how temporal patternings develop in operant behavior as a result of certain schedules of reinforcement. Behavior analysts would seek ways of capturing and describing (a) the temporal pattern of behavior, (b) the temporal patterning of environmental events, and (c) the functional relationships between these two measures. Church himself (p. 282) recognizes that his experiments 'provide ample evidence that there is a relationship between time and behavior'. However the evolution of Church's attempts to *explain* this relationship is illuminating, and deserves to be presented at some length in his own words:

> When a significant event occurs at a predictable time, an animal can learn to adjust its behavior in an appropriate manner. An observer can then use the animal's behavior as a clock to guess quite accurately the time of occurrence of the significant event. What clock did the animal use to predict the event? No external clock was available, so the fact of temporal discrimination suggests that the animal has some sort of internal clock which it can read. Our general question is, what are the properties of this internal clock? (p. 277).

> Although the concept of an internal clock is not required to explain the results of any of the experiments described in this chapter, there are three types of arguments in favor of the concept. First, it is possible that there is a physiological reality to the internal clock, and that we are more likely to find it if we know its properties. Second, there is the argument of theoretical elegance. An intervening variable may simplify the input–output relationships. (. . .) Finally, there is the pragmatic argument. It is possible that the concept of the internal clock will lead to the discovery of capacities of animals that otherwise could not have been identified . . . (p. 284).

> . . . the clock can run in at least two modes: run or stop (p. 307).

> If a rat cannot be trained to behave as if its clock had a particular property (e.g. running backward), this is evidence that the internal clock does not have the property in question (p. 308).

> In addition to maintaining an accurate internal representation of time that they can read, there is some evidence that animals are able to control the operation of the internal clock—to vary the relationship between real time and its internal representation (p. 309).

> When we began research on timing . . ., the concept of internal clock was, for us, simply a metaphor. As our research progressed, however, we found ourselves searching for the properties of the internal clock. After we discovered some char-

acteristics of the internal clock, our attitude toward it gradually began to change. The concept was no longer a metaphor; we began to believe that the clock actually exists (p. 284).

. . . the rat reads the value of the clock and makes a decision to respond . . . (p. 284).

By the end of this progression, Church's data describing functional relationships between behavior and environmental events take second place to a clock that runs, stops, or runs at different speeds, but which cannot be seen by the experimenter. The clock apparently has to be consulted by a positive decision on the part of the rat, who then decides how to behave as a result of his reading. The behavior analysts' reaction to this account is to suggest that it offers a spurious explanation by means of an imaginative exercise of translation. The behavior analysts' position can be succinctly conveyed by the suggestion that it would be more profitable to conceptualize the rat *as* the clock.[1] Rather than reflecting the operation *of* a clock, the rat's behavior would now be said to *have* the properties of a clock in certain environmental conditions. The functioning of this clock (i.e. this behavior) may differ in different environmental conditions, and it is the task of experimental analysis to identify these conditions and their effects on the clock (behavior).

It can be seen that the different emphases of behavior analysts and cognitive learning theorists rest essentially on disagreements about the most appropriate *level* of 'explanations' for behavior. For the former, the identification of the necessary and sufficient environmental conditions for a behavioral phenomenon to occur identifies also an appropriate explanation. Skinner's rat presses the lever because the tone is present and lever-pressing in the presence of the tone is occasionally followed by food (i.e. because the tone is a discriminative stimulus and the food is a reinforcer). The rats in the experiment by Herrnstein and Hineline pressed the lever because their behavior was inversely correlated with the overall frequency of shock. The behavior of rats in a blocking experiment does not come under the control of one element of a compound conditional stimulus because the other element has previously been paired with the unconditional stimulus. In all these cases, the explanation is open to public inspection, offers a direct means of experimental test (by changing environmental conditions), and nests a particular behavioral phenomenon in a broader body of empirical knowledge or potential knowledge. Such environmental explanations of behavior are not condemned to a simplistic stimulus–response model which implies a 1 : 1 and automatic association between environmental 'input' and behavioral 'output'. The relationships which have been established between behavior and environmental events, both in operant and in classical conditioning experiments, require more subtle descriptions of behavior, of the environmental contingencies, and of the relationships between these.

Of course, this is not to argue that environmental explanations are the only 'scientific' explanation of behavior. Rats are certainly physiological systems as well as behavioral systems. Investigations of their physiological structure and functioning have revealed relationships with behavior, and there is no doubt that such relationships are open to investigation by appropriate methods in the study of learning. However, behavior analysts assume that physiological explanations of behavior will expand adequate environmental explanations, and not replace them. Perhaps the cognitive learning theorists believe that the cognitive structures in animals which they infer from their studies of behavior will ultimately yield to physiological analysis. It is not clear whether their cognitive structures are necessarily or invariably thought to be of this nature, and certainly cognitive theorists have not been particularly active as yet in seeking the physical existence of their structures at a physiological level.

The cognitive structures now favored by some in contemporary learning theory may be of a different kind, however, operating at the level not of the *central* but of the *conceptual* nervous system (Skinner, 1950). They may gain their apparent attractiveness by offering no more than translations of observable behavioral phenomena, but in this case drawing additional strength for moving to a different level of analysis from their preparedness to extrapolate cognitive concepts from humans to animals.

Skinner (1977) has considered this form of theorizing at some length in his paper 'Why I am not a cognitive psychologist'. He suggests:

'Cognitive association is an invention. Even if it were real, it would go no further toward an explanation than the external contingencies upon which it is modelled' (p. 1).

Skinner continues:

Having moved the environment inside the head in the form of conscious experience and behavior in the form of intention, will, and choice, and having stored the effects of contingencies of reinforcement as knowledge and rules, cognitive psychologists put them all together to compose an internal simulacrum of the organism, a kind of Doppelgänger, not unlike the classical homunculus . . . The mental apparatus studied by cognitive psychology is simply a rather crude version of contingencies of reinforcement and their effects (p. 9).

Before concluding the present review, it will be useful briefly to consider two additional points. First, it should not be thought that an emphasis on environmental analyses of behavior denies existence of cognitive events and awareness in *humans*. Skinner (e.g., 1973) has attempted to find appropriate ways of incorporating conscious experience in humans within his theoretical analysis. He has emphasized his view that we develop our awareness as a result of interacting with others in our verbal community. In his system, consciousness is therefore seen as the result of a social process. Explanations of human behavior couched in terms of the cognitive processes perceived by (and perhaps described by) the behaving person are not accorded special status, however, and explanations expressed in terms of observable functional relationships between behavior and the environment are still favored. Skinner's account of cognitions in humans therefore acknowledges their experiential reality (their existence as 'higher psychical functions'), but attacks their conventional pre-eminence as special causes of behavior.

The question of whether this view of consciousness can be extended to animals is a difficult one which would require extensive argument (but see, for example, Schoenfeld, 1981, for a discussion of the concept of pain in animals). With humans, Skinner considers consciousness to result from reinforcement of verbal behavior. It should be remembered that Skinner's definition of verbal behavior is eccentric, emphasizing as it does not the use of words but the functional significance of reinforcement mediated by other people (Skinner, 1957). The behavior of inarticulate animals can clearly also be reinforced by the behavior of other animals. A Skinnerian analysis might therefore not simply rule out of court *some* concept of awareness in animals. Here too though, it must be emphasized, any cognitive concepts of this kind would be given no logical priority by behavior analysts in their attempts to explain animal behavior.

An interesting and somewhat ironic point can be made with respect to recent *empirical* work in the field of animal learning. It can be argued that the contributions of the cognitive learning theorists have been particularly impressive in recent years. Their theories have given rise to predictions about behavior which have then been put to experimental test. As a result, they have increased significantly the complexity of the relationships between environmental conditions and behavior which have been studied. This empirical contribution made by cognitive learning theorists to behavioral analysis has been more striking perhaps than that of the behavior analysts themselves, working within their environmentalistic tradition. The essentially cognitive theories developed by Rescorla and Wagner (1972) and by Pearce and Hall (1980), for example, have given rise to much research within a traditional hypothetico-deductive model. Perhaps it should be recognized that cognitive concepts applied in the field of animal learning may provide a heuristic device with respect to empirical investigations of the environmental conditions in which behavior changes. The conceptual status of these cognitive concepts may therefore be that of intervening variables for researchers rather than of hypothetical constructs in animals (MacCorquodale and Meehl, 1948). The idea of extrapolating cognitive capacities from humans to animals (Honig, 1978) then becomes less forceful and daring.

To conclude, contemporary cognitive theories of animal learning appear to provide an unusual example of a 'backward' extrapolation from humans to animals. They may also seem daring in sometimes appearing to attribute conscious processes to animals, though in fact the precise logical status of these processes can be unclear. The conventional principle of parsimony requires us to ask if it is *necessary* to attribute cognitive processes to animals, and to seek explanations of behavior couched in terms of the 'lowest' possible 'psychical' processes. It is argued in this chapter that the attribution of cognitive processes to animals is *not* necessary in this sense. The functional analyses of behavior advocated by behavior analysts of the Skinnerian school are not limited to an outmoded and automatic 'associationism'. They attempt instead to explain behavior by relating it to the necessary and sufficient environmental conditions for its occurrence at varying frequencies. Recent developments in our knowledge of the complexities of these functional relationships between behavior and environment may be difficult for us to summarize in words or mathematical formulae, but this should not necessarily drive us to explain animal behavior in terms of cognitive processes.

NOTE

1. I am grateful to A. C. Catania for making this point to me.

REFERENCES

Blackman, D. E. (1980) Images of man in contemporary behaviourism. In A. J. Chapman and D. M. Jones (eds), *Models of Man*. Leicester: British Psychological Society.

Church, R. M. (1978) The internal clock. In S. H. Hulse, H. Fowler, and W. K. Honig (eds), *Cognitive Processes in Animal Behavior*, pp. 277–310, Erlbaum Associates, Hillsdale, N.J.

Dickinson, A. (1980) *Contemporary Animal Learning Theory*. Cambridge University Press, Cambridge.

Estes, W. K. (1979) Cognitive processes in conditioning. In A. Dickinson and R. A. Boakes (eds), *Mechanisms of Learning and Motivation*, pp. 417–442, Erlbaum Associates, Hillsdale, N.J.

Herrnstein, R. J., and Hineline, P. N. (1966) Negative reinforcement as shock-frequency reduction. *J. exp. Anal. Behav.*, **9**, 421–430.

Honig, W. K. (1978) On the conceptual nature of cognitive terms: an initial essay. In S. H. Hulse, H. Fowler, and W. K. Honig (eds), *Cognitive Processes in Animal Behavior*, pp. 1–14, Erlbaum Associates, Hillsdale, N.J.

MacCorquodale, K., and Meehl, P. E. (1948) On a distinction between hypothetical constructs and intervening variables. *Psychol. Rev.*, **55**, 95–107.

Mackintosh, N. J. (1974) *The Psychology of Animal Learning*. Academic Press, London.

Mackintosh, N. J. (1978a) Conditioning. In B. M. Foss (ed.), *Psychology Survey No. 1*, pp. 43–57, George Allen and Unwin, London.

Mackintosh, N. J. (1978b) Cognitive or association theories of conditioning: implications of an analysis of blocking. In S. H. Hulse, H. Fowler, and W. K. Honig (eds), *Cognitive Processes in Animal Behavior*, pp. 155–176, Erlbaum Associates, Hillside, N.J.

Pearce, J. M., and Hall, G. (1980) A model for Pavlovian learning: variations in the effectiveness of conditioned but not of unconditioned stimuli. *Psychol. Rev.*, **87**, 532–553.

Rachlin, H. (1976) *Behavior and Learning*. W. H. Freeman, San Francisco.

Rescorla, R. A. (1968) Probability of shock in the presence and absence of CS in fear conditioning. *J. comp. physiol. Psychol.*, **66**, 1–5.

Rescorla, R. A. (1971) Variations in the effectiveness of reinforcement and nonreinforcement following prior inhibitory conditioning. *Learning and Motivation*, **2**, 113–123.

Rescorla, R. A., and Wagner, A. R. (1972) A theory of Pavlovian conditioning: variations in the effectiveness of reinforcement and nonreinforcement. In A. H. Black and W. K. Prokasy (eds), *Classical Conditioning II: Current Research and Theory*, pp. 64–99. Appleton-Century-Crofts, New York.

Riley, D. A., and Roitblat, H. C. (1978) Selective attention and related cognitive processes in pigeons. In S. H. Hulse, H. Fowler, and W. K. Honig (eds), *Cognitive Processes in Animal Behavior*, pp. 249–276, Erlbaum Associates, Hillsdale N.J.

Schoenfeld, W. N. (1981) Pain: a verbal response. *Neurosci. and Biobeh. Rev.*, **5**, 385–389.

Skinner, B. F. (1950) Are theories of learning necessary?. *Psychol. Rev.*, **57**, 193–216.

Skinner, B. F. (1957) *Verbal Behavior*. Appleton-Century-Crofts, New York.

Skinner, B. F. (1973) *About Behaviorism*. Knopf, New York.

Skinner, B. F. (1977) Why I am not a cognitive psychologist. *Behaviorism*, **5**, (2) 1–10.

Wagner, A. R. (1978) Expectancies and the priming of STM. In S. H. Hulse, H. Fowler, and W. K. Honig (eds), *Cognitive Processes in Animal Behavior*, pp. 177–210, Erlbaum Associates, Hillsdale, N.J.

Animal Models of Human Behavior
Edited by G. C. L. Davey
© 1983 John Wiley & Sons Ltd

Chapter 4

Behavior Analysis and Behavior Synthesis in the Extrapolation from Animal to Human Behavior

A. Charles CATANIA

To extrapolate is to extend a function beyond the range of values over which its form is known. It is implicit in this operation that the extended function must be smooth; *extrapolate* is related etymologically to *polish*. Thus, to discover a discontinuity is to disconfirm an extrapolation. In extrapolating from animal to human behavior, the crucial questions are usually about the presence or absence of discontinuities rather than about the form of functions, but the quantitative properties of the relevant variables are elusive. Do we measure fitness or activity or some index of behavioral abilities? Do we plot our measure against evolutionary time or genetic overlap or some scale of higher and lower organisms? The enterprise hardly seems feasible. Clearly the arguments are not to be taken so literally, and the language of extrapolation must be regarded as metaphorical. How then should a science of behavior proceed in dealing with these issues?

1. EXPLANATION AND BEHAVIORAL TAXONOMY

Some accounts are couched in terms of explanation. For example, a learning theory might be said to explain some complex performance in terms of a conditioning process. If the complex performance is a human one and the conditioning process is one derived from animal research, it might be argued that the explanation of one by the other justifies the extrapolation of the conditioning process to humans. But the weight of tradition notwithstanding, this is an indirect way to assess the scope of a behavioral process. One

51

difficulty is that phenomena often allow several internally consistent but mutually incompatible explanations.

Earlier in the development of psychological theory, there was less concern with explanation *per se*. Research was conducted not so much to explain phenomena as to decide whether they occurred and what properties they had. Thus, the most important components of the psychology of learning that have come down to us from Thorndike (1911) and Pavlov (1927) and Skinner (1938) are categories of learning phenomena rather than explanations of behavior. It is essential to say whether a particular change in behavior is an instance of instrumental learning or respondent conditioning or stimulus control, but saying which is not to explain the behavior (cf. Catania, 1973; 1978; 1979; 1980b; in press). What follows explores some research examples, to illustrate experimental strategies available as alternatives to those primarily concerned with explanation (cf. Sidman, 1960). An effective science of behavior must be able to discover elementary behavioral phenomena, to analyse complex performances in terms of these elementary components, and to demonstrate the adequacy of the analysis by appropriate synthesis.

One way to organize the elementary phenomena of behavior is to ask where particular responses or classes of responses come from. Some responses are simply produced by the presentation of stimuli, and are said to be elicited or are called respondents. Others are produced because responses like them have in the past had consequences, and are said to be emitted or are called operants. Some responses occur in the presence of stimuli that often precede other, eliciting stimuli, and are said to be conditioned or conditional responses. Others occur in the presence of stimuli that typically set the occasion for particular consequences of responding, and are said to be discriminated. Further distinctions can be made within these classes, as when consequences that produce increases or decreases in responding are respectively called reinforcers or punishers. Barring a 'none-of-the-above' category, there are no guarantees that such a taxonomy of behavioral phenomena will be exhaustive (cf. Gallistel, 1980), and there are a few if any criteria independent of the behavior itself for distinguishing classes within the taxonomy or for adding new ones to it. Investigators observe behavior in various settings, and the taxonomy summarizes some of the useful discriminations they make.

2. ELEMENTARY VERSUS COMPLEX PHENOMENA: REINFORCEMENT, AUTOSHAPING, AND CONTRAST

Consider reinforcement as an example. A class of responses is said to be reinforced if responses in the class have some consequence and by virtue of doing so become more frequent. Each component of the definition is critical. If a child's schoolwork is praised but the child does schoolwork less often, we cannot call the praise a reinforcer, no matter how well received by the child it seemed to be. Even though it was a consequence of schoolwork, it did not make schoolwork increase. If a child's crying leads to a spanking and the child then cries more, we would not ordinarily call the spanking a reinforcer, but we might do so if we could show that the crying increases only after spankings produced by crying and not after just any spankings. The language of masochism would be of little help here. We must know whether the spanking alone was sufficient to produce crying, or whether the contingent relation between crying and spanking was necessary.

Reinforcement is the name of a behavioral phenomenon; it is not an explanation. Identifying the phenomenon says nothing about its ubiquity. Reinforcement is no more to be disproved in behavior analysis than is osmosis in biology. The problems arise only in particular cases, when the question sometimes is whether the name is appropriate. Thus, if a monkey presses a lever faster when the presses produce electric shocks at the end of a fixed interval than when they do not (e.g., Kelleher and Morse, 1968; Morse and Kelleher, 1977), the eliciting effects of shock on lever pressing in this context must be ruled out before the shock can be called a reinforcer. Like the investigator, a student must learn to discriminate those cases that may be spoken of in terms of reinforcement from those that may not.

The point is illustrated by the phenomenon of autoshaping (Brown and Jenkins, 1968; Jenkins and Moore, 1973). If, in a standard pigeon chamber, a light on the key is reliably followed by the delivery of food, the pigeon comes to peck the lighted key even though the food delivery does not depend on key pecks. Early accounts sought to explain the pecks in terms of adventitious reinforcement of orienting toward the lit key or of other responses. These accounts became untenable with additional data, such as the finding that autoshaped pecks often continued even when they prevented the food deliveries that were presumed to maintain them (Williams and Williams, 1969). But the autoshaped pecking was not explained; instead, it was assimilated into the class of phenomena dealt with in terms of respondent conditioning and not into the class dealt with in terms of reinforcement. (Its theoretical interest was that the response was skeletal rather than autonomic; its significance was therefore comparable to the demonstration of the operant conditioning of autonomic responses: e.g., Miller and Banuazizi, 1968; Miller and Carmona, 1967.)

The language of explanation becomes more appropriate when a complex performance is reduced to simpler components. For example, when reinforcement schedules maintaining a pigeon's key pecks operate in the presence of alternating stimuli (multiple schedules: Ferster and Skinner, 1957), an increase in responding in the presence of one stimulus typically accompanies the decrease in responding produced by terminating reinforcement in the presence of the other stimulus; this phenomenon is called behavioral contrast (Reynolds, 1961). One explanation is that after food deliveries cease in the presence of one stimulus, pecks are elicited as in autoshaping by the differential relation that exists between the other stimulus and food. The increase thus comes about because these elicited pecks summate with those engendered by the continuing reinforcement contingency (Keller, 1974; Schwartz and Williams, 1972). Leaving aside the controversial features of this account (e.g., Hamilton and Silberberg, 1978; Williams and Heyneman, 1981), it works as explanation because one phenomenon is found to be implicit in the known properties of other, simpler behavioral processes. Explanations typically involve reductions to simpler terms; those that are not parsimonious are not particularly effective.

But the success of an explanation depends on the adequacy of the classification of the basic processes to which it must appeal. The analysis of a complex phenomenon may sometimes lead to the discovery of new elements, but analytic procedures become efficient and synthesis becomes feasible only when the elements are known (the obvious analogy here is with chemistry). Part of the present argument is that the science of behavior is still at the stage of discovering its elements, and therefore that much of what is offered as explanation (e.g., the reduction of all modifications of behavior to one kind of learning) is at best premature. It is therefore ironic that Skinner, in suggesting an extended behavioral classification that included phylogenic behavior as a new category, was taken to task on the grounds that he should instead have explained the distinctions with which he was concerned in terms of a self-reinforcement theory (Herrnstein, 1977a; 1977b; Skinner, 1977).

3. BEHAVIOR ANALYSIS AND LEARNING: PARAMECIUM EXAMPLES

One historical difficulty is the tendency to equate behavior analysis and the psychology of learning, at least with respect to the problems with which each is concerned. A peculiar feature of the psychology of learning is that the scope of its subject matter often diminishes with the success of its analyses. Once a particular change in behavior is attributed to the class of variables called artifacts, it is excluded from systematic treatment. For example, throughout the history of the psychology of learning, studies of the behavior of lower organisms (Jennings, 1906) have often duplicated in microcosm learning procedures also developed with mammals (e.g., Thorpe and Davenport, 1964; Warden, *et al.*, 1940). The literature for paramecium alone includes studies of maze learning (Lepley and Rice, 1952), escape from enclosed spaces (Day and Bentley, 1911; French, 1940), respondent conditioning (Smith, 1908), discrimination learning (Metalnikow, in Thorpe, 1956), and operant responding (Gelber, 1952, 1957). In each case, however, performances could be attributed to (or explained in terms of) variables other than learning. Reactive inhibition in a maze, in which the likelihood of a turn in one direction decreased given a prior turn in the same direction, depended on the interaction between segment lengths in the maze and the consistent helical swimming pattern of the paramecium (Bullington, 1930); the first choice-point selected paramecia oriented so that they would be likely to turn in a particular direction when they came to the next choice-point. Observations of decreasing latencies of escape from a capillary tube did not control adequately for the effects on movement of mechanical stimulation and the accumulation in the medium of the paramecium's metabolic products (e.g., Gunn, 1942; Wichterman, 1953). The avoidance by the paramecium of light after light had been paired with heat occurred because heated paramecia become photosensitive and not because they learn the light-heat contingency (Best, 1954). Experiments on food selection did not adequately distinguish between the discriminative experience of the paramecium and such variables as its reaction to a particle it had previously ingested (Thorpe, 1956). Increases in the likelihood of approach to the presentation of a food-baited needle depended on the gradient of food particles dispersed in the medium by the presentations, and not on a reinforcing effect of food (Jensen, 1957; Katz and Deterline, 1958). The point is that each case, as it was resolved, dropped out of the subject matter of the psychology of learning. Even disregarding the argument for the relevance of unicellular studies that could be made by those who claim that learning involves changes in the local environments of individual neurons, a serious objection to limiting the subject matter in this way is that the phenomena of learning are to be understood in the context of behavior in general. The analysis of behavior includes within it the topic of learning; the psychology of learning must not be insulated from non-learning phenomena in behavior.

Let us now turn to some more contemporary experimental issues, for the purpose of exploring some alternatives to explanation as an objective of research. First we will examine the development of distinctions that may allow a more finely grained analysis of behavioral processes. In this connection we will consider treatments of chaining and the serial integration of behavior and of stimulus control and the nature of the three-term contingency. Then we will move on to behavior synthesis and some of its implications, with examples from experiments on self-control and on preference for free choice. Finally, we will return to the issue of extrapolation, with some comments on the nature of experimental analyses of behavior, in the context of research on instructional control and the functions of language and on productivity and the structural properties of verbal behavior.

4. SEQUENTIAL BEHAVIOR

The serial integration of behavior is a problem of long standing (e.g., Lashley, 1951). Some accounts have appealed to chaining (e.g., Skinner, 1934): each response in a sequence produces stimuli that reinforce that response and that set the occasion for the next one. The insufficiency of such an analysis to deal with many instances of rapid response sequences has been argued in various ways. In one series of experiments (Bever *et al.*, 1980; Straub *et al.*, 1979), four keys in a pigeon chamber were lit green, white, red, and blue in different permutations of position on each trial. If the pigeon pecked the keys in the order of colors listed, the final peck on blue produced food; pecks out of order, excluding repetitions of pecks on a single color, cancelled the trial. Thus, the pigeon learned to peck white after pecking green and red after pecking white and blue after pecking red even though the positions of the colors on the keys changed from trial to trial. Furthermore, the pigeon's pecks were likely to adhere to the reinforced sequence even if one of the colors was deleted (e.g., with red missing, pecking blue more often than green after pecking white). To accommodate such data, a chaining account must define the discriminative and reinforcing stimuli of the sequence independent of changing locations and of differential feedback other than the pigeon's own behavior. The alternative to chaining proposed by these investigators was that the pigeon was responding on the basis of a representation of the color sequence.

We need not judge the adequacy of chains or representations as explanations to observe that the concern in either case is to explain the sequential behavior: the question posed is whether sequential behavior is reducible to a succession of discriminative stimuli and responses or to the matching of overt responses to an internal representation. A behavioral analysis, however, need not be limited to such choices, nor to the assumption that there is only one kind of sequential behavior the explanation for which is to be derived from some crucial experiment. Instead, we can recognize the possibility of behavior sequences of different sorts.

Some behavior sequences, called chains, are successions of responses in which each is defined by the reinforcing consequence of producing an opportunity to engage in the next. The sequence is reducible to smaller units, and this analysis can be confirmed experimentally by seeing how independent the components are from each other. For example, consider the rat's lever press, involving movement to the lever, pressing the lever, movement to the food pellet, and eating. If lever pressing no longer produces pellets, pressing decreases, but the delivery of a pellet independent of pressing will still occasion movement to the food cup. The integrity of one part of the sequence is not altered by changing the reinforcement contingencies for another. In other words, partitioning the chain is one technique for diagnosing its characteristics.

The problem is that not all sequences can be analyzed in this way. Some sequences occur too rapidly for their components to have discriminative effects (e.g., the musician's arpeggio), and some, especially in verbal behavior, have such variable potential continuations that they cannot be regarded as effective discriminative stimuli (e.g., for what subsequent words are *thus* or *but* or *in other words* unique discriminative stimuli?). Some sequences can be put together so that each response produces stimulus conditions that occasion the next, and others must be integrated so that responses occur in the proper order without depending on the consequences of earlier responses. For any sequence, the task of an experimental analysis is the experimental one of deciding which kind it is.

The distinction is implicit in Skinner's account of verbal behavior (Skinner, 1957). The chaining of verbal behavior was included in a response class called the intraverbal, but other classes involving temporally extended behavior were also recognized as coherent units. The very fact that intraverbals were discussed as a specific and non-exhaustive class of verbal responses implies that other sequential processes were assumed in other instances. In any case, once it is recognized that some sequences can be fractioned in ways that others cannot, behavioral analyses can include both chaining and extended temporal structure as alternative classes of sequential behavior. The problem is not one of explaining the sequences. It is one of developing a taxonomy of sequential behavior. We can see how little progress we have made by noting how few are the alternative classes available to us for constructing such a taxonomy.

5. STIMULUS CONTROL, MATCHING, AND EQUIVALENCE RELATIONS

The three-term contingency is a cornerstone of contemporary behavior analysis: in the presence of a stimulus a response has a consequence (Skinner, 1938). The first of the three terms in this relation is a discriminative stimulus; its presence sets the occasion for the contingent relation between the two remaining terms, the response and its reinforcer. The discriminative function that it specifies has been invoked not only in relatively simple instances of stimulus control, such as discriminations of wavelength, intensity, and other readily quantifiable properties of environmental events, but also in cases that involve complex relations among stimuli, such as in matching and oddity tasks (e.g., Cumming and Berryman, 1965; Skinner, 1950). For example, given two different side-key or comparison colors, a pigeon's peck may be reinforced only if it is on the key the color of which matches a center-key or sample color. The pigeon may master this task either by learning responses to particular color configurations on the three keys, or, as may be tested by presenting novel color combinations, by learning the general relation called matching. Either performance may be explained by invoking mediating behavior, coding responses, representations, or other inferred processes (e.g., Carter and Werner, 1978).

Matching to sample and related performances have been referred to as conditional discriminations. The response reinforced in the presence of one stimulus is conditional upon other stimuli that accompany it. Now consider the case of symbolic matching, in which the sample and comparison stimuli are arbitrarily related. For example, in symbolic matching of color to form, a pigeon's peck on a red or a green comparison key may be reinforced given respectively a circle or a triangle as the sample stimulus. Once a pigeon has mastered this task, it is tempting to describe the performance in terms of a symbolic equivalence of red and circles and of green and triangles. But such an equivalence is not implicit in the discriminative functions of circles and triangles. The crucial test is in the reversal of the sample and comparison stimuli: does the pigeon now peck circles given a red sample and triangles given a green sample?

Findings to date suggest that non-verbal as well as verbal humans master these and related tasks in terms of symbolic equivalences, whereas non-human organisms learn them only as conditional discriminations (Lazar, 1977; Sidman et al., 1974; Sidman et al., 1982; Sidman and Tailby, 1982). In other words, humans continue to perform consistently after the reversals, whereas other organisms have to learn the reversals as new conditional discriminations. One research strategy might be to attempt to show how the equivalence relations in humans are reducible to conditional discriminations; such a reduction might constitute an explanation. But more progress is likely to follow from recognizing equivalence relations as demonstrations of a stimulus function different from that of a discriminative stimulus. This function may be the criterion for distinguishing symbolic behavior from other kinds of behavior with respect to stimuli (see also Gillan, 1981; Gillan et al., 1981). Just as it is important to distinguish chained response sequences from sequences that are temporally integrated in other ways, it may be important to distinguish stimulus control based on equivalence relations from that based on the discriminative functions of stimuli. A taxonomy of stimulus-control functions will not explain symbolic behavior, but it will be essential to any effective analysis.

6. THE BEHAVIOR SYNTHESIS OF SELF-CONTROL

Behavior analysis begins with complex behavioral relations and breaks them down into their components. One test of the adequacy of such an analysis is an experimental synthesis (e.g., Catania, 1972b; Catania and Keller, 1981). But not all syntheses are of this sort. Sometimes we begin with concepts from human affairs as the basis for producing novel behavioral relations. The synthesis consists of creating within the laboratory a performance in some respects analogous to human behavior outside the laboratory. If producing an analog were the only function of the synthesis, however, a thought experiment would do as well. Instead, once a phenomenon has been demonstrated by a behavior synthesis, its defining properties and its range of applicability can be refined by subsequent research. The success of the synthesis is then judged not only on the basis of the empirical results but also on the extent to which the refined understanding of the phenomenon has implications for the human non-laboratory situations from which the analog emerged.

Self-control provides an example. Human situations discussed in terms of self-control typically involve two different consequences of responding that are pitted against each other (Skinner, 1953). The immediate effects of smoking increase its future likelihood, but its delayed effects may be aversive. Spending an allowance makes inexpensive commodities immediately available, but may rule out the later purchase of a more expensive item that might have been affordable if the money had been saved. The delayed aversive consequences of failing to visit a dentist may be greater than the immediate aversive consequences of the visit itself. To bring such behavioral relations into the laboratory, the investigator must create reinforcement schedules with analogous temporal properties, preferably using comparable and quantifiable reinforcers as the immediate and delayed consequences.

Here is one experimental analog. When a pigeon's pecks on one key produce an immediate 2-second access to food and those on a second key produce a 4-second access to food after a delay of 4 seconds, the pigeon reliably produces the immediate small reinforcer rather than the delayed larger one (Rachlin and Green, 1972; see also Grosch and Neuringer, 1981, for a related procedure). But if an additional 10-second delay is imposed before this choice during which, by pecking, the pigeon may commit itself to the larger though later reinforcer, the pigeon will do so. This commitment response, it is argued, may be analogous to human self-control commitments, as in public pledges to stop smoking or drinking. Such commitments are most easily made when the moment of temptation is distant.

In the pigeon analog, the difference in delays does not outweigh the difference in reinforcer magnitudes when the smaller reinforcer is 10 seconds away and the larger is 14 seconds away, but it does when the smaller is immediate and the larger is 4 seconds away. For this reason, some accounts of the development and maintenance of the pigeon's commitment response appeal mainly to the forms of the delay-of-reinforcement gradients for the two reinforcers (e.g., Green and Snyderman, 1980; Navarick and Fantino, 1976). They therefore aim for an explanation of the complex performance in terms of simpler behavioral processes. The gradients have a common form but they start at different times and approach different maxima, so that they cross as time passes. The pigeon's behavior depends on the proximity of the reinforcers because the pigeon responds on the basis of which gradient is higher at the moment. A difficulty is that the form of delay-of-reinforcement gradients has not been determined directly (e.g., Catania and Keller, 1981), so that the phenomenon to be explained provides some of the support for the assumed properties of the processes that are explanatory.

An explanation of a performance, however, does not necessarily bear on its adequacy as an analog. It may be more important instead to examine the ways in which the performance is modifiable and to determine whether the essential components of the prototype performance have all been included in the experimental analog. In the present context, for example, it may be useful to consider procedures that might reduce the likelihood of the pigeon's choice of the small reinforcer even when that reinforcer is immediate (e.g., Mazur and Logue, 1978), and it may be critical to know whether verbal behavior is an effective component in human instances of self-control (e.g., Bem, 1967). Either direction might have implications for human performance, but neither would be explanatory.

Experimental syntheses can contribute to behavior analysis even when they fail as analogs. In the case of those self-control procedures called self-reinforcement, individuals are supposed to be able to modify their own behavior by delivering reinforcers to themselves contingent on some criterion performance (e.g., Bandura, 1971). An attempt to synthesize an analog with pigeons (Mahoney and Bandura, 1972) showed that the variables controlling the self-delivery of the reinforcers were confounded with those controlling the criterion performance, and that the important feature of the behavior engendered by thse procedures was not that behavior was reinforced but rather that individuals learned to discriminate among those aspects of their own behavior that distinguished criterion from non-criterion performance (Catania, 1975; 1976).

A similar extension to the distinction between intrinsic and extrinsic reinforcers (e.g., Lefcourt, 1976) may be instructive. Intrinsic reinforcers characteristically are inevitable consequences of behavior, whereas extrinsic reinforcers are artificial consequences. For example, a child might master a musical instrument either on the basis of the quality of the sounds produced or on the basis of tokens or grades or other consequences arranged by a teacher. It has been argued that performances maintained by intrinsic reinforcers are sometimes weakened when extrinsic reinforcers are superimposed (Lepper and Greene, 1978). One point is that this argument should not discourage the use of extrinsic reinforcers when intrinsic reinforcers have not been effective. But more important for the present purposes is that the feasibility of a behavior synthesis may clarify the characteristics of the distinction between intrinsic and extrinsic reinforcers. The distinction is not simply one between conditioned and unconditioned reinforcers, because many important intrinsic reinforcers (e.g., those that maintain reading) develop in relation to other consequences. How then would a laboratory analog be synthesized from the behavior of a pigeon? The answer is not obvious, but if the distinction cannot be extrapolated to non-human behavior, we must look elsewhere than to reinforcement processes for an account of the empirical findings. It may be significant that the effectiveness of tokens and other artificial consequences is often established through instructions rather than through the direct operation of reinforcement contingencies, and thus human verbal behavior may be implicated. In this instance, the difficulty even of formulating what would be the effective synthesis of a non-human analog reveals some assumptions upon which the distinction is based.

7. PREFERENCE FOR FREE CHOICE OVER FORCED CHOICE

Some questions about the value of freedom can be regarded as questions about whether we prefer the availability of alternatives. Are free choices preferred to forced choices? The problem of synthesis then becomes one of defining choices. For example, if two keys are available to a pigeon in a standard chamber and pecks on either key produce food, the pigeon's pecking on one key or the other might be called a choice. On the other hand, it might not be appropriate to speak of choice between two keys if pecks on only one produce food, or to speak of choice between pecking and not pecking if only a single key is available.

In research on free-choice preference (Catania, 1980a; Catania and Sagvolden, 1980), a pigeon could enter one condition with two or more keys available on which pecks produced food or a second with only a single key available. These conditions, the terminal links of concurrent-chain schedules, were respectively treated as instances of free choice and of forced choice. During the initial links of the schedules, preference for free choice or forced choice was determined on the basis of the responding that produced entries into one or the other terminal link.

In these procedures, pigeons prefer free choice to forced choice, even with the two conditions equated in terms of responses per reinforcer and relative frequency of exposure. The preference has not been reducible to simpler variables, such as number of stimuli, properties of terminal-link performances, and the pigeon's previous history with choices. Had such variables been shown to be determinants of the preference, they would have served as its explanation.

As in previous cases, however, explanation may be secondary to other research objectives. For example, once a free-choice preference is demonstrated, the definition of choice can be refined on the basis of explorations of the boundary conditions of the preference. Experiments comparing preferences for keys of different sizes with preferences for different numbers of keys indicate that the free-choice preference is based on the availability of more than one response class (operant) rather than simply on the availability of a larger area for pecking. Thus, the preference is determined by the functional rather than by the topographical properties of the response classes that constitute the alternatives. The free-choice preference therefore becomes relevant to the definition of behavioral units.

The synthesis may also lead to distinctions among different types of choices. Consider the pigeon in the self-control procedure of the preceding section. Confronted with a choice between an immediate 2-second food reinforcer and a 4-second reinforcer after a 4-second delay, it chooses the smaller but immediate one. This cannot be called a free choice if it is then discovered that the pigeon does not prefer it to a condition of forced choice, with only a single key available (Hayes *et al.*, 1981). An alternative to seeking an explanation for the difference between this choice and free choice is that of recognizing the difference and determining which features of choice are critical to it. Perhaps it may become appropriate to differentiate the choices in free-choice procedures from those in self-control procedures by calling some of the latter coerced choices, with coercion defined on the basis of whether the situation maintains commitment responses. A taxonomy of choice may then supplement those of sequential behavior and stimulus control. Parallel arguments for analysis and synthesis rather than explanation can also be made for such other areas as foraging behavior (Kamil and Sargent, 1981) and economics (Rachlin *et al.*, 1976).

8. THE ANALYSIS AND SYNTHESIS OF VERBAL BEHAVIOR

What of extrapolation in all of this? The processes and taxonomies and phenomena of the preceding sections are not extrapolations. Rather, they suggest how inquiries into behavioral continuities might be conducted. When the issues are concerned with concepts derived from human behavior, the assumption of evolutionary continuity is implicit. In the case of free-choice preference, for example, the human concept of freedom becomes more fundamental with the demonstration that such preferences are not limited to human behavior. If the preference exists even in the behavior of pigeons, it cannot be based simply on the practices of human cultures. It may be a product of ontogeny, in that organisms may learn that momentarily preferred alternatives are more often available in free than in forced choice, or of phylogeny, in that evolutionary contingencies may favour the survival of organisms that prefer free to forced choice. In either case, free choice provides opportunities for more varied behavior than does forced choice, and is therefore consistent with the important biological role of variability.

In some instances, however, human and animal behavior can persuasively be argued to be separated by discontinuities. Language in particular, or at least some of its components, appears unique to humans. Thus, it provides one of the most controversial areas of extrapolation. The topic has motivated analyses of the properties of animal communication (e.g., Beer, 1976; Peters, 1980; Sebeok, 1977; Smith, 1977) and syntheses of animal verbal behavior (e.g., Gardner and Gardner, 1969; Premack, 1970; Rumbaugh and Gill, 1976; Terrace *et al.*, 1979). It has also received its share of attempts at explanation, in such constructs as deep structure and transformational grammar (Chomsky, 1959), innate language-acquisition devices (McNeill, 1970), and dual-coding processes (Paivio and Begg, 1981). What follows recapitulates what has gone before in a brief treatment of the analysis of instructional control and the synthesis of syntactically structured behavior.

One advantageous feature of human verbal behavior is that new behavior can be established by instruction rather than by shaping or other indirect procedures. An instruction is a verbal discriminative stimulus for the listener, and the following of the instruction may reinforce the behavior of the speaker. The effectiveness of instructions presumably derives from a history of contingencies arranged by the verbal community. Instructions may direct verbal as well as non-verbal behavior, as when a student is taught the appropriate use of a technical term. The significance of instructions in the taxonomy of verbal behaviour (Skinner, 1957), however, depends on whether the functional properties of instructions differ from those of other discriminative stimuli.

One feature of behavior controlled by instructions, or rule-governed behavior (Skinner, 1966; 1969), is its insensitivity to the current consequences of behavior. In fact, instructions are not ordinarily given if current contingencies will produce the relevant behavior anyway. Children are not told to do things that they are already doing. Although instructions may override current contingencies, their effectiveness may depend on more remote contingencies arranged by the verbal community on rule-following and on the correspondence between verbal and non-verbal behavior (Risley and Hart, 1968). Such an account may explain why rule-governed behavior differs from contingency-governed behavior, but it would not diminish the importance of recognizing their different properties.

When human button-pressing is instructed, responding does not change with the schedule of consequences for pressing as it does when the button-pressing is shaped (Harzem *et al.*, 1978; Kaufman *et al.*, 1966; Matthews *et al.*, 1977; Shimoff *et al.*, 1981). If a skilled performance is defined as one in which behavior is sensitive to its consequences from moment to moment, as when a woodcarver adjusts to the changing patterns of grain in a woodblock or as when a ballet dancer accommodates to slight deviations in the steps of a partner, then skilled performance is contingency-governed and not rule-governed. The distinction therefore may have important educational implications.

Furthermore, if a speaker's instructions control the behavior of a listener, what happens when the speaker and the listener are the same individual? The question is whether what one says about what one does affects what one does (e.g., Burron and Bucher, 1978; Israel and O'Leary, 1973; Lovaas, 1964), and whether one has come to say it through instructions or through non-verbal contingencies. In any case, for the present purposes the point is that the distinction between rule-governed and contingency-governed behavior is part of the taxonomy of verbal behavior, and that the behavior controlled by either rules or by contingencies can itself be either verbal or non-verbal. There is nothing to be explained until the properties of these several classes have been explored. The classes then may serve in the analysis of more complex performances (cf. Baer et al., 1967, on imitative classes).

The issues involved in the analysis of rule-governed behavior concern the functions of language, but language also has structure, and concern with structure engenders different and often complementary problems (Catania, 1972a). One research strategy is to synthesize non-verbal behavior the structural properties of which are analogous to those of verbal behavior (e.g., Catania, 1980c). For example, a pigeon in a three-key chamber may be presented with one or two circles or triangles, first on the top key and then on each of the two bottom keys. On the top key the pigeon learns to peck rapidly in the presence of triangles and slowly in the presence of circles, and on the bottom keys it learns to peck left when the stimuli are singular (one circle or one triangle) and right when they are plural (two circles or two triangles). The fast triangle pecking and slow circle pecking, established only for the top key, emerge during left and right bottom-key pecking, even though they are not required in this part of the discrimination task. The analogy is to phonological structure in human speech (Berko, 1958): the plural -s is voiced after voiced consonants, as in *dogs*, but is unvoiced after unvoiced consonants, as in *cats*. The rate of pecking, required only early in the sequence, continues like voicing to the end of the sequence. The novel combination of two response properties (right–left and fast–slow) is also a simple instance of productivity in non-verbal performance (cf. Esper, 1918, 1933; Guess et al., 1968).

The above performance does not demonstrate language in the pigeon. Instead, the synthesis shows that some structural features of behavior often cited as crucial to the definition of language are rather properties of behavior in general. If so, we must look elsewhere for the defining properties of language than in its structure. Although syntheses of primate language have been criticized on the grounds of syntactic inadequacy (Terrace et al., 1979), semantics might provide more appropriate criteria than syntax for assessing such non-human behavior. The interaction of verbal units in the processes called autoclitic (Skinner, 1957) provides a basis for syntax, and implies that the capacity to discriminate properties of one's own behavior is a necessary condition for propositional language.

We need not worry whether our extrapolations lead us to continuities or discontinuities in the behavior of humans and other organisms. It is more important that we recognize the role of behavioral taxonomies in our analyses and syntheses. The essential taxonomies will be those of behavioral function and not those of topography. They will not be explained, but will provide the prerequisites for explanation. Explanation will then be tied less closely to rule-governed systems of psychological theory. It will correspond more to its everyday sense of showing how something works. We may then be able to advance from relatively simple response systems to such complexities as imagery and thought (Paivio, 1971; Skinner, 1945, 1953), the organizing functions of metaphor and of simulation (Dawkins, 1976; Lakoff and Johnson, 1980), and perhaps even the development of cultures (Harris, 1977). We will get there only if our scientific behavior is contingency-governed rather than rule-governed. In other words, as Wittgenstein (1921) might have predicted, if we get there we will have taken our discriminative capacities with us but we will have left our explanatory theories at the bottom of the ladder.

REFERENCES

Baer, D. M., Peterson, R. F., and Sherman, J. A. (1967) The development of imitation by reinforcing behavioral similarity to a model, *J. Exp. Anal. Behav.*, **10**, 405–416.

Bandura, A. (1971) Vicarious and self-reinforcement processes, in *The Nature of Reinforcement* (ed. R. Glaser), pp. 228–278, Academic Press, New York.

Beer, C. (1976) Some complexities in the communication behavior of gulls, *Annals N.Y. Acad. Sci.*, **280**, 413–432.

Bem, S. L. (1967) Verbal self-control: the establishment of effective self-instruction, *J. Exp. Psychol.*, **64**, 485–491.

Berko, J. (1958) The child's learning of English morphology, *Word* **14**, 150–177.

Best, J. B. (1954) The photosensitization of paramecia aurelia by temperature shock, *J. Exp. Zool.*, **126**, 87–99.

Bever, T. G., Straub, R. O., Terrace, H. S., and Townsend, D. J. (1980) The comparative study of serially integrated behavior in humans and animals. in *The Nature of Thought* (eds P. W. Jusczyk and R. M. Klein), pp. 51–93, Erlbaum, Hillsdale, N.J.

Brown, P. L., and Jenkins, H. M. (1968) Auto-shaping of the pigeon's key-peck, *J. Exp. Anal. Behav.*, **11**, 1–8.

Bullington, W. E. (1930) A further study of spiralling in the ciliate *paramecium*, with a note on morphology and taxonomy, *J. Exp. Zool.*, **56**, 423–449.

Burron, D., and Bucher, B. (1978) Self-instructions as discriminative cues for rule-breaking and rule-following. *J. Exp. Child Psychol.*, **26**, 46–57.

Carter, D. E., and Werner, T. J. (1978) Complex learning and information processing by pigeons: a critical analysis, *J. Exp. Anal. Behav.*, **29**, 565–601.

Catania, A. C. (1972a) Chomsky's formal analysis of natural languages: a behavioral translation, *Behaviorism*, **1**, 1–15.

Catania, A. C. (1972b) Concurrent performances: synthesizing rate constancies by manipulating contingencies for a single response, *J. Exp. Anal. Behav.*, **17**, 139–145.

Catania, A. C. (1973) The psychologies of structure, function, and development, *Amer. Psychol.*, **28**, 434–443.

Catania, A. C. (1975) The myth of self-reinforcement, *Behaviorism*, **3**, 192–199.

Catania, A. C. (1976) Self-reinforcement revisited, *Behaviorism*, **4**, 157–162.

Catania, A. C. (1978) The psychology of learning: some lessons from the Darwinian revolution, *Annals N.Y. Acad. Sci.*, **309**, 18–28.

Catania, A. C. (1979) *Learning*, Prentice-Hall, Englewood Cliffs, N.J.

Catania, A. C. (1980a) Freedom of choice: a behavioral analysis, in *The Psychology of Learning and Motivation. Volume 14* (ed. G. H. Bower), pp. 97–145, Academic Press, New York.

Catania, A. C. (1980b) Operant theory: Skinner, in *Theories of Learning* (eds G. M. Gazda and R. J. Corsini), pp. 135–177, Peacock, Itasca, Ill.

Catania, A. C. (1980c) Autoclitic processes and the structure of behavior, *Behaviorism*, **8**, 175–186.

Catania, A. C. (in press) The two psychologies of learning: blind alleys and nonsense syllables, in *A Century of Psychology as Science* (eds S. Koch and D. E. Leary), McGraw-Hill, New York.

Catania, A. C., and Keller, K. J. (1981) Contingency, contiguity, correlation, and the concept of causation, in *Predictability, Correlation, and Contiguity* (eds P. Harzem and M. D. Zeiler), pp. 125–167, Wiley, Chichester.

Catania, A. C., and Sagvolden, T. (1980) Preference for free choice over forced choice in pigeons, *J. Exp. Anal. Behav.*, **34**, 77–86.

Chomsky, N. (1959) Review of B. F. Skinner's *Verbal behavior*, *Language*, **35**, 26–58.

Cumming, W. W., and Berryman, R. (1965) The complex discriminated operant: Studies of matching-to-sample and related problems, in *Stimulus Generalization* (ed. D. I. Mostofsky), pp. 284–330, Stanford Univ. Press, Stanford, Calif.

Dawkins, R. (1976) *The Selfish Gene*, Oxford, New York.

Day, L. M., and Bentley, M. (1911) Note on learning in paramecia, *J. Animal Behav.*, **1**, 67–73.

Esper, E. A. (1918) A contribution to the experimental study of analogy, *Psychol. Rev.*, **25**, 468–487.

Esper, E. A. (1933) Studies in linguistic behavior organization, *J. Gen. Psychol.*, **8**, 346–381.

Ferster, C. B., and Skinner, B. F. (1957) *Schedules of Reinforcement*, Appleton-Century-Crofts, New York.

French, J. W. V. (1940) Trial and error learning in paramecia, *J. Exp. Psychol.*, **26**, 609–613.

Gallistel, C. R. (1980) *The Organization of Action: A New Synthesis*, Erlbaum, Hillsdale, N.J.

Gardner, R. A., and Gardner, B. T. (1969) Teaching sign language to a chimpanzee, *Science*, **165**, 664–672.

Gelber, B. (1952) Investigations of the behavior of paramecium aurelia: I. Modification of behavior after training with reinforcement, *J. Comp. Physiol. Psychol.*, **45**, 58–65.

Gelber, B. (1957) Food or training in paramecium, *Science*, **126**, 1340.

Gillan, D. J. (1981) Reasoning in the chimpanzee: II. Transitive inference, *J. Exp. Psychol.: Animal Behav. Processes*, **7**, 150–164.

Gillan, D. J., Premack, D., and Woodruff, G. (1981) Reasoning in the chimpanzee: I. Analogical reasoning, *J. Exp. Psychol.: Animal Behav. Processes*, **7**, 1–17.

Green, L., and Snyderman, M. (1980) Choice between rewards differing in amount and delay: toward a choice model of self control, *J. Exp. Anal. Behav.*, **34**, 135–147.

Grosch, J., and Neuringer, A. (1981) Self-control in pigeons under the Mischel paradigm, *J. Exp. Anal. Behav.*, **35**, 3–21.

Guess, D., Sailor, W., Ruthorford, G., and Baer, D. M. (1968) An experimental analysis of linguistic development: the productive use of the plural morpheme, *J. Appl. Behav. Anal.*, **1**, 297–306.

Gunn, D. L. (1942) Klinokinesis in paramecia, *Nature*, **149**, 78–79.

Hamilton, B. E., and Silberberg, A. (1978) Contrast and autoshaping in multiple schedules varying reinforcer rate and duration, *J. Exp. Anal. Behav.*, **30**, 107–122.

Harris, M. (1977) *Cannibals and Kings*, Random House, New York.

Harzem, P., Lowe, C. F., and Bagshaw, M. (1978) Verbal control in human operant behavior, *Psychol. Rec.*, **28**, 405–423.

Hayes, S. C., Kapust, J., Leonard, S. R., and Rosenfarb, I. (1981) Escape from freedom: choosing not to choose in pigeons, *J. Exp. Anal. Behav.*, **36**, 1–7.

Herrnstein, R. J. (1977a) The evolution of behaviorism, *Amer. Psychol.*, **32**, 593–603.

Herrnstein, R. J. (1977b) Doing what comes naturally: a reply to Professor Skinner, *Amer. Psychol.*, **32**, 1013–1016.

Israel, A. C., and O'Leary, K. D. (1973) Developing correspondence between children's words and deeds, *Child Dev.*, **44**, 575–581.

Jenkins, H. M., and Moore, B. R. (1973) The form of the auto-shaped response with food or water reinforcers, *J. Exp. Anal. Behav.*, **20**, 163–181.

Jennings, H. S. (1906) *Behavior of the Lower Organisms*, Macmillan, New York.

Jensen, D. D. (1957) Experiments on learning in paramecia, *Science*, **125**, 191–192.

Kamil, A. C., and Sargent, T. D. (1981) *Foraging Behavior*, Garland, New York.

Katz, M. S., and Deterline, W. A. (1958) Apparent learning in paramecia, *J. Comp. Physiol. Psychol.*, **51**, 243–247.

Kaufman, A., Baron, A., and Kopp, R. E. (1966) Some effects of instructions on human operant behavior, *Psychonomic Monogr. Suppl.*, **1**, 243–250.

Kelleher, R. T., and Morse, W. H. (1968) Schedules using noxious stimuli. III. Responding maintained with response-produced electric shocks, *J. Exp. Anal. Behav.*, **11**, 819–838.

Keller, K. (1974) The role of elicited responding in behavioral contrast, *J. Exp. Anal. Behav.*, **21**, 249–257.

Lakoff, G., and Johnson, M. (1980) *Metaphors We Live By*, Univ. of Chicago Press, Chicago.

Lashley, K. S. (1951) The problem of serial order in behavior. in *Cerebral Mechanisms in Behavior* (ed. L. A. Jeffress), pp. 112–136, Wiley, New York.

Lazar, R. (1977) Extending sequence-class membership with matching to sample, *J. Exp. Anal. Behav.*, **27**, 381–392.

Lefcourt, H. M. (1976) *Locus of Control*, Erlbaum, Hillsdale, N.J.

Lepley, W. M., and Rice, G. E., Jr. (1952) Behavior variability in paramecium as a function of guided act sequences, *J. Comp. Physiol. Psychol.*, **45**, 283–286.

Lepper, M. R., and Greene, D. (1978) *The Hidden Costs of Reward: New Perspectives on the Psychology of Human Motivation*, Erlbaum, Hillsdale, N.J.

Lovaas, O. I. (1964) Cue properties of words: the control of operant responding by rate and content of verbal operants, *Child Dev.*, **35**, 245–246.

Mahoney, M. J., and Bandura, A. (1972) Self-reinforcement in pigeons, *Learning and Motiv.*, **3**, 293–303.

Matthews, B. A., Shimoff, E., Catania, A. C., and Sagvolden, T. (1977) Uninstructed human responding: sensitivity to ratio and interval contingencies, *J. Exp. Anal. Behav.*, **27**, 453–467.

Mazur, J. E., and Logue, A. W. (1978) Choice in a 'self-control' paradigm: effects of a fading procedure, *J. Exp. Anal. Behav.*, **30**, 11–17.

McNeill, D. (1970) *The Acquisition of Language*, Harper and Row, New York.

Miller, N. E., and Banuazizi, A. (1968) Instrumental learning by curarized rats of a specific visceral response, intestinal or cardiac, *J. Comp. Physiol. Psychol.*, **65**, 1–7.

Miller, N. E., and Carmona, A. (1967) Modification of a visceral response, salivation in thirsty dogs, by instrumental training with water reward, *J. Comp. Physiol. Psychol.*, **63**, 1–6.

Morse, W. H., and Kelleher, R. T. (1977) Determinants of reinforcement and punishment, in *Handbook of Operant Behavior* (eds W. K. Honig and J. E. R. Staddon), pp. 174–200, Prentice-Hall, Englewood Cliffs, N.J.

Navarick, D. J., and Fantino, E. (1976) Self-control and general models of choice, *J. Exp. Psychol.: Animal Behav. Processes*, **2**, 75–87.

Paivio, A. (1971) *Imagery and Verbal Processes*, Holt, Rinehart and Winston, New York.

Paivio, A., and Begg, I. (1981) *Psychology of Language*, Prentice-Hall, Englewood Cliffs, N.J.

Pavlov, I. P. (1927) *Conditioned Reflexes* (Tr. G. V. Anrep), Oxford University Press, London.

Peters, R. (1980) *Mammalian Communication*, Brooks/Cole, Monterey, Calif.

Premack, D. (1970) A functional analysis of language, *J. Exp. Anal. Behav.*, **14**, 107–125.

Rachlin, H., and Green, L. (1972) Commitment, choice and self-control, *J. Exp. Anal. Behav.*, **17**, 15–22.

Rachlin, H., Green, L., Kagel, J. H., and Battalio, R. C. (1976) Economic demand theory and psychological studies of choice, in *The Psychology of Learning and Motivation. Volume 10* (ed. G. H. Bower), pp. 129–154, Academic Press, New York.

Reynolds, G. S. (1961) Behavioral contrast, *J. Exp. Anal. Behav.*, **4**, 57–71.

Risley, T. R., and Hart, B. (1968) Developing correspondence between the nonverbal and verbal behavior of preschool children, *J. Appl. Behav. Anal.*, **1**, 267–281.

Rumbaugh, D. M., and Gill, T. V. (1976) The mastery of language-type skills by the chimpanzee (*Pan*), *Annals N.Y. Acad. Sci.*, **280**, 562–578.

Schwartz, B., and Williams, D. R. (1972) Two different kinds of key peck in the pigeon: some properties of responses maintained by negative and positive response-reinforcer contingencies, *J. Exp. Anal. Behav.*, **18**, 201–216.

Sebeok, T. A. (1977) *How Animals Communicate*, Indiana University Press, Bloomington, Ind.

Shimoff, E., Catania, A. C., and Matthews, B. A. (1981) Uninstructed human responding: sensitivity of low-rate performance to schedule contingencies, *J. Exp. Anal. Behav.*, **36**, 207–220.

Sidman, M. (1960) *Tactics of Scientific Research*, Basic Books, New York.

Sidman, M., Cresson, O., Jr., and Willson-Morris, M. (1974) Acquisition of matching to sample via mediated transfer, *J. Exp. Anal. Behav.*, **22**, 261–273.

Sidman, M., Rauzin, R., Lazar, R., and Cunningham, S. (1982) A search for symmetry in Rhesus monkeys, baboons, and children, *J. Exp. Anal. Behav.*, **37**, 23–44.

Sidman, M., and Tailby, W. (1982) Conditional discrimination *vs* matching to sample: an expansion of the testing paradigm, *J. Exp. Anal. Behav.*, **37**, 5–22.

Skinner, B. F. (1934) The extinction of chained reflexes, *Proc. Nat. Acad. Sci.*, **20**, 234–237.

Skinner, B. F. (1938) *The Behavior of Organisms*, Appleton-Century-Crofts, New York.

Skinner, B. F. (1945) The operational analysis of psychological terms, *Psychol. Rev.*, **52**, 270–277.

Skinner, B. F. (1950) Are theories of learning necessary?, *Psychol. Rev.*, **57**, 193–216.

Skinner, B. F. (1953) *Science and Human Behavior*, Macmillan, New York.

Skinner, B. F. (1957) *Verbal Behavior*, Appleton-Century-Crofts, New York.

Skinner, B. F. (1966) An operant analysis of problem-solving, in *Problem Solving* (ed. B. Kleinmuntz), pp. 225–257, Wiley, New York.

Skinner, B. F. (1969) 'Notes', in *Contingencies of Reinforcement. A Theoretical Analysis*, pp. 157–171, Appleton-Century-Crofts, New York.

Skinner, B. F. (1977) Herrnstein and the evolution of behaviorism, *Amer. Psychol.*, **32**, 1006–1012.

Smith, S. (1908) The limits of educability of paramecia, *J. Comp. Neurol.*, **18**, 499–510.

Smith, W. J. (1977) *The Behavior of Communicating*, Harvard University Press, Cambridge, Mass.

Straub, R. O., Seidenberg, M. S., Bever, T. G., and Terrace, H. S. (1979) Serial learning in the pigeon, *J. Exp. Anal. Behav.*, **32**, 137–148.

Terrace, H. S., Petitto, L. A., Sanders, R. J., and Bever, T. G. (1979) Can an ape create a sentence?, *Science*, **206**, 891–902.

Thorndike, E. L. (1911) *Animal Intelligence*, Macmillan, New York.

Thorpe, W. H. (1956) *Learning and Instinct in Animals*, Methuen, London.

Thorpe, W. H., and Davenport, D. (1964) *Learning and Associated Phenomena in Invertebrates. Animal Behaviour Supplement 1*. Bailliere, Tindall and Cassell, London.

Warden, C. J., Jenkins, T. N., and Warner, L. H. (1940) *Comparative Psychology. Volume 2. Plants and Invertebrates*, Ronald, New York.

Wichterman, R. (1953) *The Biology of Paramecia*, Blakiston, New York.

Williams, B. A., and Heyneman, N. (1981) Determinants of contrast in the signal-key procedure: evidence against additivity theory, *J. Exp. Anal. Behav.*, **35**, 161–173.

Williams, D. R., and Williams, H. (1969) Auto-maintenance in the pigeon: sustained pecking despite contingent non-reinforcement, *J. Exp. Anal. Behav.*, **12**, 511–520.

Wittgenstein, L. (1961) *Tractatus Logico-Philosophicus* (tr. by D. F. Pears and B. F. McGuinness from the 1921 German edition), Routledge and Kegan Paul, London.

Animal Models of Human Behavior
Edited by G. C. L. Davey
© 1983 John Wiley & Sons Ltd

Chapter 5

Radical Behaviorism and Human Psychology[1]

C. Fergus LOWE

> *Other species (than humans) are . . . conscious in the sense of*
> *being under stimulus control. They feel pain in the sense of*
> *responding to painful stimuli, as they see a light or hear a sound*
> *in the sense of responding appropriately. . . . A person becomes*
> *conscious in a different sense when a verbal community arranges*
> *contingencies under which he not only sees an object but sees*
> *that he is seeing it. In this special sense consciousness or aware-*
> *ness is a social product.* (Skinner, 1974)

INTRODUCTION

In the history of psychology, the most effective advocate of an animal model of human behavior has been J. B. Watson. Reviewing the progress of behaviorism in 1930, Watson characterized it explicitly as being the extension of an animal orientated perspective to humans: 'Behaviorism . . . was an attempt to do one thing—to apply to the experimental study of man the same kind of procedure and the same language of description that many research men had found useful for so many years in the study of animals lower than man' (p. ix). Earlier, in 1913, he had argued that the behavior of man and the behavior of animals must be considered on the same plane; human behavior should be studied, as was animal behavior without reference to consciousness: 'Psychology, as the behaviorist views it, . . . needs introspection as little as do the sciences of chemistry and physics'. This rejection of introspection, together with Watson's recommendation that psychologists should study and formulate laws concerning only observable events, greatly affected the subsequent development of the behaviorist movement, and psychology in general.

71

The positivist features of Watson's approach were extended and formalized by those behaviorists who were influenced by the development of logical positivism and operationism in the 1920s.[2] According to their account, which became known as *methodological behaviorism*, there could be no public agreement about mental events or what happens in consciousness; as far as the scientific community was concerned, such events were 'private' and, hence, could not be included in a scientific analysis. With human consciousness and introspection out of the reckoning overt behavior alone remained as the rightful subject matter of scientific psychology. The way lay open for the methodology and findings of animal research, which had advanced so remarkably well without the notion of consciousness (cf. Boakes, in press), to be applied directly to human behavior.

Skinner's *radical behaviorism* arose largely in opposition to the positivist excesses of methodological behaviorism and it explicitly disavowed the taboo on private events and introspection. However, with respect to the issue of extrapolating from animals to humans, the position of most radical behaviorists has hardly differed from that of methodological behaviorism. The prevailing view has been, and remains, that the best and certainly the most convenient, way of finding out about the principles which govern human behavior is by conducting research with animals (see Boakes, Chapter 2). This is clearly reflected in the research literature on operant behavior. For example, the principal publisher of basic operant research is *The Journal of the Experimental Analysis of Behavior*, in which, over the past decade, the number of papers published on animal research has exceeded those on human operant behavior by a factor of almost twenty to one (Buskist and Miller, 1982). And yet, although comparatively few studies have been conducted with human subjects, extensive claims have been made for the direct applicability of animal research to human behavior (e.g. Baer, 1978; Deluty, 1981; Morse, 1966; Rachlin, 1980; Skinner, 1969; Whaley and Malott, 1971).

Schedules of reinforcement have been the context in which animal behavior has been most intensively studied. This research is of central importance because it has provided the data base upon which has been erected an analysis of behavior which is extended to all areas of human activity. The effects of scheduled reinforcement are orderly and generally replicable within and across animal species, and the characteristic patterns of behavior generated by the basic schedules have become widely known (Ferster and Skinner, 1957; Morse, 1966; but see also Lowe and Harzem, 1977). These findings are used to explain human behavior under conditions which appear to resemble the reinforcement schedules of animal studies. For example, the performance of the gambler working at a slot machine is cited as an example of variable-ratio[3] schedule performance in humans, and factory employees on a piecework payment system are said to behave as animals do on fixed-ratio[3] schedules (Baer, 1978; Karoly, 1980; Reynolds, 1975; Skinner, 1953).

Many psychologists working in the clinical and educational areas eagerly seized upon the animal model since it provided, not only an explanatory system, but, more importantly for them, the means to change behavior. Moreover, with its focus upon overt behavior and environmental stimuli, and the apparent exclusion of troublesome 'cognitive' factors, behavior modification seemed an attractively simple business. And, since, in these early years, the various behavior modification procedures appeared successful, there seemed little need to question the assumption of generality, despite objections that most therapeutic interventions did not permit an adequate assessment to be made of controlling variables (cf. Beech, 1974; Bloomfield, 1976; Wolf, 1973).

The intellectual ferment created by behaviorism and, particularly, by the writings of Skinner, was the result not just of innovations in therapy and educational practice but of an all-encompassing view of human behavior which attempted to recast age-old epistemological, ethical, social, and political issues in behavioral terms. Skinner, moreover, offered solutions for impending social crises and suggested ways in which, for the commonweal, entire societies might be redesigned in line with behaviorist conceptions of human nature (Skinner, 1953; 1972). In all of this endeavor the animal model was paramount and the principles of animal learning were constantly invoked to illuminate and, hopefully, to transform the human condition.

But the power to predict and control complex human behavior, which behaviorism promised, proved to be decidedly elusive. Recently, behaviorists themselves have soul-searched (cf. Brigham, 1980; Cullen, 1981; Michael, 1980; Branch and Malagodi, 1980; Repucci and Saunders, 1974), outsiders have been eager to announce behaviorism's demise (Mackenzie, 1977), and out of the disillusionment the hydra-headed monster of mentalism, once thought to have been subdued by Watson and finally despatched by Skinner and Ryle, has resurfaced in the form of contemporary cognitivism. Within clinical psychology, for example, an alternative movement to behavior modification, known as *cognitive behavior modification* (Mahoney, 1974; Meichenbaum, 1977), has burgeoned in recent years.

Apart from the fact that the 'powerful technology of behavior change' has not materialized, an even more serious threat to the traditional account, and to the assumption of generality, has come from recent research on human operant behavior which has shown that the behavior of humans with respect to scheduled reinforcement differs in fundamental respects from that of other animal species. The differences appear so extensive, applying as they do to all the basic schedules of reinforcement, that they throw into doubt much of the theorizing about human learning which is based upon animal experimentation. And if the animal model does not hold good for human operant behavior under controlled experimental conditions why should it do so in the hospital, school, or stock exchange? What, if any, is the relevance of the vast body of research on conditioning in animals to human psychology? The present chapter addresses these and related questions. It will try to show how, as far as the study of human behavior is concerned, much of contemporary behaviorism has lost its way and will attempt to indicate new directions for theory and research. I shall argue that exclusive reliance upon the animal model was a mistake for behaviorism, that it has led to the neglect of human behavior as an object of study in its own right and that it has provided those who wish to use behaviorist principles in research and therapy with an inadequate model in so far as it ignores important determinants of human behavior.

HOW HUMAN OPERANT BEHAVIOR DIFFERS FROM THAT OF ANIMALS

One of the most striking and impressive features of the early work of Skinner and others was their demonstration that behavior could be related in an orderly way to contingencies of reinforcement. As Morse (1966) observed: 'Even people with a minimum of training can follow simple specified procedures for producing stable, standard behavior patterns of various types in any individual of a variety of different species. . . . Furthermore, any member of most species will give a similar performance on the same schedules' (pp. 58–59). In recent years, however, it has become clear that there is at least one species which does not conform to this general prescription, namely man.

Consider, for example, performance on the fixed-interval (FI) schedule, where the first response is reinforced after a stated interval has elapsed since the previous reinforcement. When humans aged four and upwards perform on conventional FI schedules the resulting patterns of behavior are, not the classic FI 'scallop' which is characteristic of animal performance, but variations on one of two forms, shown in Figure 5.1: (a) a continuous and high rate of responding between reinforcers, or (b) a very low response rate consisting of just one or two responses at the end of the inter-reinforcement interval. Both forms of behavior have frequently been observed in different subjects in the same study and, occasionally, in the same subject at different stages of an experiment. The rate of responding of the high-rate subjects is unaffected by changes in the FI schedule, over a wide range of schedule values and many experimental sessions (cf. De Casper and Zeiler, 1972; Leander et al. 1968; Lippman and Meyer, 1967; Long et al., 1958; Lowe, 1979; Weiner, 1969). This is in marked contrast to animal performance which shows great sensitivity to variations in schedule parameter in terms of response rate, post-reinforcement pause and other measures (Hanson and Killeen, 1981; Lowe et al., 1979; Lowe and Wearden, 1981; Zeiler, 1977).

The picture which thus emerges of human performance on conventional FI schedules is one of an unpredictable and uncontrolled subject matter and certainly one which differs greatly from other animal species.

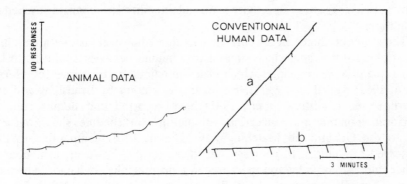

Figure 5.1 Cumulative records of typical animal and human performance on fixed-interval schedules showing the stable performance of a rat and of two human subjects on an FI 60-sec. schedule. The record labeled 'a' exemplifies the high-rate pattern while that labeled 'b' shows low-rate performance. The two human subjects pressed a panel for points which were later exchanged for money. (After Lowe, 1979)

A great deal of research has also been conducted with animals on the effects of reinforcement delivered under fixed-ratio[3] (FR) schedules. The standard pattern of FR behavior is a pause following reinforcement followed by a constant and relatively high rate of responding until the occurrence of the next reinforcer. The duration of the pause is an increasing function, and response rate a decreasing function, of FR value (Felton and Lyon, 1966; Gott and Weiss, 1972; Powell, 1968). The pattern of responding shown in most human studies, on the other hand, is very different and resembles the high-rate pattern, shown in Figure 5.1; there are no post-reinforcement pauses and the rate of responding is unaffected by changes in the schedule parameter (Holland, 1958; Weiner, 1964a; 1965; 1970).

Behavioral 'rigidity', of a kind not found in animal experiments, has been observed consistently in human operant research (cf. Leander et al., 1968; Long et al., 1958; Lowe, 1979; Weiner, 1965, 1969). For example, if human subjects first perform on FR schedules constant high rates of responding are generated which persist unaltered for many sessions when the schedule is changed to FI. Alternatively if the initial schedule generates a low rate of responding, e.g., a differential-reinforcement-of-low-rate[4] (DRL) schedule, then subsequent performance on FI will be of the low-rate type (Weiner,

1964b; 1969). Similar findings have been reported in studies of human performance on variable-interval[5] (Weiner, 1965) and concurrent (Poppen, 1982) schedules. Such marked and persistent effects of reinforcement history on these and other schedules are not evident in animal performance which shows much greater sensitivity and adaptability to changing schedule conditions.

The study of choice in concurrent schedules, however, is one area which has yielded some data which suggest that human behavior conforms to the same quantitative principles which describe animal performance (cf. Herrnstein, 1961; de Villiers, 1977). For example, studies by Bradshaw and colleagues (see Bradshaw et al., 1981) have reported that human subjects performing on multiple concurrent variable-interval schedules show conformity to the Generalized Matching Law (Baum, 1974) comparable to that observed in animals. In contrast with these results, however, a number of other studies have failed to report animal-type 'matching' behavior in humans (e.g., Oscar-Berman et al., 1980; Pierce et al., 1981; Schmitt, 1974). In view of these contradictory findings, a series of experiments (Horne and Lowe, 1982) has recently been conducted in the writer's laboratory to investigate the determinants of human choice. Under various conditions, the majority of subjects performing on multiple concurrent variable-interval schedules showed gross departure from the matching relationship with forms of responding not previously encountered in animal studies of concurrent performance. As has been observed in previous studies of human performance on single schedules, there was considerable variability in responding, both within and between subjects (see also Poppen, 1982; Wearden et al., 1982).

These are but a few of many possible examples which show the difficulty of obtaining with humans any of the well-known functional relationships of animal operant behavior (for a review of the literature, see Lowe, 1979).

WHY HUMAN BEHAVIOR IS DIFFERENT

There have been two recent attempts to account for differences in the operant behavior of animals and humans and both have appealed to verbal behavior as a critical variable. One analysis (Catania, 1981; Matthews et al., 1977; Shimoff et al., 1981) stresses the importance of instructions provided by the experimenter in human studies and draws a distinction between instruction-controlled and contingency-controlled responding along the lines of Skinner's (1966) distinction between rule-governed and contingency-governed behavior. According to this account, human operant behavior in some situations may not be sensitive to scheduled reinforcement because it is already controlled by instructions provided by the experimenter at the beginning of the experiment. On the other hand, it is argued, if instructions are minimized and responding is shaped by the technique of successive approximations, in a manner similar to that employed with animals, then human performance will come under contingency control and will show sensitivity, i.e., performance will change appropriately when contingencies change (Shimoff *et al.*, 1981).

Although this account has many virtues, particularly in drawing attention to the role of instructions, it also presents some problems. First, explicit experimental instructions do not invariably produce performance which is insensitive to changes in the schedule contingencies. On the contrary, studies have shown accurate instructions to be sometimes *necessary*, though not always sufficient, to produce behavior which is sensitive to schedule parameters; when minimal instructions were given behavior was generally insensitive to reinforcement (Baron *et al.*, 1969; Ayllon and Azrin, 1964). The available evidence suggests that whether performance changes when the schedule changes may depend upon the nature of the instructions. Accurate instructions which help to specify the initial set of contingencies and further variations may lead to very sensitive performance (Baron *et al.*, 1969; Weiner, 1969). On the other hand, instructions which accurately describe the initial contingency but are misleading about subsequent changes may produce insensitivity (Shimoff *et al.*, 1981). What is more important as far as the central issues of the present chapter are concerned, however, is that the account under consideration does not explain why it is that, even when human operant performance is shaped and minimal instructions are given, performance does not show the kinds of patterning and sensitivity displayed by animals on schedules of reinforcement (cf. Matthews *et al.*, 1977; Lowe, 1979).

To account for these and related problems, the present author (Lowe, 1979) has proposed that in studies of human operant behavior the experimenter does not have a monopoly over rule-making; the human subject can, and frequently does, make his own rules, particularly when none are provided by the experimenter. Thus 'uninstructed' behavior may be just as much rule-governed as instructed behavior, but the rules are different, being produced by the subjects themselves. (Hence, uninstructed behavior may be more adaptive than instructed behavior if experimental instructions are misleading—see, for example, Kendler and Kendler, 1962.) It is human subjects' capacity to formulate their own descriptions of reinforcement contingencies, to 'self-tact' (Skinner, 1957, p. 138), and to use these descriptions to formulate rules to govern their behavior which results in human operant behavior being so different from that of lower animals. What individual subjects say to themselves may be an accurate or an inaccurate description of the contingencies but it may, nevertheless, be an important influence on the rest of their behavior.

The evidence in support of this latter account is now considerable and comes from a variety of sources. One important, and often primary, source of evidence is introspective or, perhaps more accurately, retrospective, since it comes from subjects' verbal reports about their behavior and its determinants after the behavior has occurred, and usually at the end of an experiment. For example, subjects who produce the low-rate pattern on conventional FI schedules will generally report that they had a time-based formulation of the contingencies and that they counted out the interval before responding; on the other hand, subjects who produce the high-rate pattern usually report that they considered that more responses would produce more reinforcement and so responded as fast as possible (Leander *et al.*, 1968; Lippman and Meyer, 1967). Subjects who initially respond on an FR schedule almost invariably report, correctly, that the more they responded the more reinforcement was produced. However, when the FR schedule is changed to FI this formulation, and the accompanying high-rate behavior, may persist and, hence, behavior will not be sensitive to changes in the schedule parameter (Lowe, 1979; Weiner, 1969). It has frequently been pointed out, from Watson onwards, that introspective evidence may be problematic (Nisbett and Wilson, 1977). Because it is difficult to deal with subjects' verbal reports, however, does not mean that such evidence has no place in a scientific analysis. Whether or not introspective evidence is of value should not be a matter of dogma; if subjects are able to tell experimenters about some of the factors which influence their behavior then this can provide fruitful information about controlling variables which may be experimentally verifiable (cf. Laties and Weiss, 1963).

The program of experimental research conducted by the present author and colleagues may serve as a case in point. In a number of early experiments conducted in our laboratory, subjects reported idiosyncratic formulations of contingencies and covert behavior, such as counting, which seemed greatly to affect their overt operant behavior. One way of experimentally testing whether this was the case was to introduce another task, designed to interfere with covert counting, and observe whether schedule performance was disrupted. Lowe and Hughes (Lowe, 1979) carried out an experiment along these lines which showed that human FI behavior, under conditions which generate time-based formulations, was disrupted when subjects were given a concurrent verbal shadowing task; in most cases the effects lasted only a short time until, according to the subjects, new strategies for counting the interval were devised (see also Laties and Weiss, 1963; Sokolov, 1972).

Two further studies of human FI behavior (Lowe, Harzem, and Bagshaw, 1978; Lowe, Harzem, and Hughes, 1978) attempted to achieve more permanent attenuation of covert counting by providing a response-produced clock which displayed time into the fixed interval. Subjects under these conditions reported that they did not count but responded for the clock 'automatically'. All subjects showed the scalloped pattern of responding characteristic of animal FI performance (Figure 5.1) and different measures of responding were sensitive to changes in the schedule parameter in a manner closely resembling that reported in the animal literature. These are the only two studies of FI performance in adult humans which have shown close agreement between human and animal behavior with respect to both patterning and schedule sensitivity (but see also Harris and Wilkins, 1982).

Another, perhaps critical, test of hypotheses concerning verbal control lies in an experimental investigation of: (i) the schedule performance of humans who have not developed language sufficiently well to be able to describe their own behavior and its consequences; according to Lowe's (1979) account, infants should behave like animals, but not like adult humans, on schedules of reinforcement, (ii) changes in the operant behavior of children who are in the process of acquiring self-descriptive verbal skills, and (iii) the effects of instructional interventions, including self-instructional training, on operant performance at different stages of childhood. Such an investigation is in progress and has begun to yield results which throw some light on the interactions between verbal behavior and other operant performance.

Lowe et al. (in press) have investigated the operant performance of infants less than one year old. When the infants touched a cylinder either music or food was presented according to FI schedules ranging in value from 10 to 50 seconds. Figure 5.2 shows cumulative records, from two subjects, Ann and Jon, after performance had been stabilized on each FI schedule, with the exception of Jon's record on FI 50 seconds which was obtained after only three sessions on this schedule. These records, and other analyses, show that the predominant response pattern consisted of a pause after reinforcement followed by an accelerated rate of responding which terminated when the next reinforcement was delivered. This is the 'scalloped' pattern which is characteristic of animal but not adult human performance (Figure 5.1). Analyses of other measures, i.e., response rate, duration of post-reinforcement pause and successive inter-response times, all showed a sensitivity to the schedule parameter closely resembling that shown by animals on FI schedules. Indeed, in all respects considered, the behavior of these infants was indistinguishable from that of animals (for further details see Lowe et al., in press). Similar procedures have been employed to investigate the performance of infants on FR, VI and DRL schedules;[6] preliminary findings suggest that on these schedules also there is a close resemblance, in terms of patterning and sensitivity, to animal behaviour.

A study by Bentall and Lowe (1981) compared performance of young infants on FI schedules with that of older children of different ages and language ability. With respect to both pattern of responding and schedule

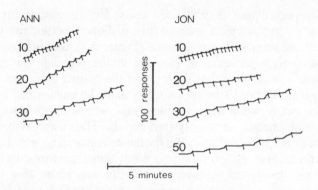

Figure 5.2 Cumulative records of responding for each
infant on FI 10, 20, and 30 sec. and, in the case of Jon,
FI 50 sec. The order of exposure to schedule values was
different for the two subjects. The records are from the
final session on each schedule value. (After Lowe et al.,
in press)

sensitivity, the performance of children in age ranges 5–6½ years and 7½–
9 years resembled that of adults, with individual subjects exhibiting either
the high or low-rate pattern. (Figure 5.1). The performance of children aged
2½–4 years differed both from that of infants and the older children, though
containing some patterning elements similar to those produced by the older
and younger subjects. Observation of both verbal and non-verbal behavior
in the 2½–4 year-old group suggested that, while verbal control over operant
performance was present, it was not as consistent or as effective as in the
older children.

However, when children in this very young group (2½–4 years) are given
verbal instructions and taught appropriate self-instructions they can regulate
their own behavior and perform like older children and adults on reinforcement schedules. In a recent study (Bentall and Lowe, 1982), children from
three age groups (2½–4, 5–6½, and 7½–9 years) responded on an FI 40-
second schedule: (i) some were instructed to respond at a high rate, others
at a low rate, and (ii) they were subsequently taught either high or low-rate
self-instructions, respectively. All subjects who received high-rate instructions (i.e., they were told that it was necessary to respond often in order to
produce the reward) responded at a steady high rate (pattern 'a' in Figure
5.1), which was maintained following self-instructional training. The effects
of the low-rate instructions (i.e. the children were told that they should not
respond between reward deliveries) were directly related to the age of the
children. The two older groups produced low-rate patterns (pattern 'b' in

Figure 5.1), with the oldest group responding so slowly that some reinforcements were missed; the effects of instructions were least noticeable in the youngest group. After self-instructional training in low-rate responding (i.e. the children were told to count out the interval or, in the case of the youngest subjects, to sing a song before responding), children in all three groups showed adult-like low-rate behavior; children in the older groups showed an improved ability to estimate the interval length and fewer reinforcements were missed. Thus, whether or not performance was like that of adults was dependent upon the kinds of verbal behavior which the children, particularly those in the youngest group, could produce to control their own performance.

The evidence from the studies described here suggest that, without language, humans behave like animals; when language is well-established, operant performance is markedly different (see also Horne and Lowe, 1982; Poppen, 1982; Sidman et al., 1982). In the early stages of language acquisition, young children whose behavior is initially different from that of adults will come to behave like adults when provided with training in appropriate verbal skills. It would appear then that it may be language which spans the hiatus between animal and human operant performance. Clearly a great deal of research is now needed to extend these findings and to determine more precisely the ways in which verbal behavior, both overt and covert, interacts with other behavior. Indeed, it is remarkable that, prior to the studies described here, there has been no systematic investigation of the ways in which the development of language alters the operant performance of humans. When children's behavior has been studied (e.g. Long et al., 1958), subjects of different ages and verbal skills have been treated as a homogeneous grouping without considering whether there might be qualitative differences in performance related to age or verbal ability (cf. Lowe et al., in press; Bentall and Lowe, 1981; 1982). Similarly, at the level of adult human operant behavior, there has been no systematic attempt to show under what conditions and to what extent there can be 'pure' contingency control which is unaffected by rule-following and other verbal factors.

IMPLICATIONS FOR THEORY AND RESEARCH:
WHO'S AFRAID OF 'PRIVATE' EVENTS?

The foregoing account raises the question of why so little behavioral research has been concerned with an investigation of the determinants of human operant behavior. It also raises the question of whether radical behaviorism is capable of providing the theoretical basis for such an investigation. In answering these questions the role of covert or 'private' events in behavioral science will be a critical consideration. The evidence suggests, for example, that it is not normally possible to explain the vagaries of adult human schedule performance without recourse to inferences about subjects' covert behavior, such as the way they describe the contingencies to themselves or formulate rules for responding. But these inferred events are not publicly observable (hence the label 'private') and as such would not be considered a valid subject matter for science by some behaviorists. Assertions to the effect that radical behaviorism can only deal with publicly observable events and that it eschews inference, are widespread and categoric (see, for example, Chomsky, 1975; Harré and Secord, 1972; Kendall and Hollon, 1979; Koestler, 1967; Ledwidge, 1978; Locke, 1979; Strupp, 1979; Wilson, 1978). However, as a cursory glance at any of several of Skinner's writings since 1945 would reveal, this characterization is almost entirely false and represents a point of view which Skinner has consistently opposed, claiming that it misguidedly adheres to the tenets of logical positivism and operationism (Skinner, 1945; 1953; 1957; 1963; 1974). Indeed the principal distinguishing feature of his radical behaviorism is that it considers that a science of behavior, like other sciences, *must* deal with events which are not publicly observable; inference, therefore, is held to be essential in the study of behavior, regardless of parsimony. Recognition of the importance of private events in human psychology thus poses no problems, in principle, for radical behaviorism. On the contrary, Skinner has repeatedly argued that an analysis of the role of private events is essential for an understanding of human behavior and of how human 'consciousness' differs from that of animals. This is well expressed in the passage from *About Behaviorism* cited at the beginning of this chapter and in the statement that: 'A science of behavior must consider the place of private stimuli. . . . The question then is this: What is inside the skin, and how do we know about it? The answer is, I believe, the heart of radical behaviorism' (Skinner, 1974, pp. 211–12).

But even when covert behavior is accepted as a legitimate subject matter for study there remains the question of its role, if any, in the determination of other behavior. There are, for example, many avowed radical behaviorists who would deny that private events can determine any other behavior (cf. Branch and Malagodi, 1980; Brigham, 1980; Rachlin, 1977) and some have gone so far as to suggest that 'It makes little sense that verbal behavior should cause other behavior' (Rachlin, 1977, p. 662). But this 'epiphenomenalist' position has little in common with the radical behaviorism of Skinner which explicitly recognizes that verbal behavior, both overt and covert, functions as a determinant of other behavior. This is clearly stated in many of his theoretical writings (see also Lowe and Higson, 1981), as the following passage from *Verbal Behavior* exemplifies:

> Behavior generally stimulates the behaver. Only because it does so can coordinated behavior, in which one response is in part controlled by another, be executed.

Verbal behavior exemplifies the co-ordination which requires self-stimulation. The speaker may be his own listener—for example, when intraverbal responses generate 'free association'—and automatic self-stimulation from verbal behavior is crucial in the analysis of syntactical and other processes involved in composition and thinking. We are concerned here with self-tacts—with verbal behavior controlled by other behavior of the speaker, past, present, or future. The stimuli may or may not be private. Self-descriptive verbal behavior is of interest for many reasons. Only through the acquisition of such behavior does the speaker become 'aware' of what he is doing or saying, and why. . . . So long as covert behavior continues to stimulate the individual . . . it may control other behavior. (pp. 138–142)

But it is at this point that we encounter an extraordinary paradox in contemporary behaviorism. Skinner's radical behaviorism, in contra-distinction to the methodological variety, has established its theoretical identity largely on the basis of its recognition of the importance of covert events in human behavior and Skinner, moreover, has argued that being able, through language, to describe our own behavior to ourselves has resulted in a form of 'consciousness' which is unique in the animal world (Skinner, 1957, p. 140; 1978, p. 220). It is remarkable, therefore, that the role of covert events and the transformation in human behavior brought about by language, have been almost completely ignored in radical behaviorist research. Instead, the major journals in this area publish experimental work almost exclusively concerned with animal behavior or with human behavior which is treated as if it did not differ significantly, in terms of controlling variables, from the key-peck of the pigeon or the lever-press of the rat.[7]

Why then, in ignoring covert behavior, have radical behaviorists lost their 'heart' (Skinner, 1974) and given the animal model almost undisputed hegemony over the affairs of man? This is not an easy question to deal with and one can only speculate about the factors which have brought about the apparent *volte face*. First, it appears to be the case that for many there never was a *volte face*; what was attractive about the Skinnerian system was the new methodology and techniques which it introduced for the prediction and control of behavior, together with the basic conceptual apparatus within which the effects of the environment on behavior could be expressed. Skinner's writings on philosophy of science and on the development of human, as opposed to animal, 'consciousness' (e.g. his seminal paper 'The operational analysis of psychological terms', 1945) were perhaps not known, and certainly were not appreciated, by many who were enthusiastic about these other aspects of his system. Instead, earlier notions, dating from Watson, of what behaviorism was about, and the prevailing *zeitgeist* within psychology of positivism, overshadowed radical behaviorism's principal theoretical innovation. Thus, for many aspiring behavior analysts, it became almost a matter of ideological purity to deny the existence or efficacy of any event which could not be publicly and directly observed and measured. Watson's ban on introspection, although no longer justified by Skinnerian theory, continued to hold sway and had particularly bad effects. If, as Skinner had argued, what is unique about humans is their capacity to reflect upon their own actions then not allowing subjects to report such behavior effectively removed it from analysis.

The study of human behavior in its own right has also been impeded by extravagant claims made for animal research and by premature extensions of animal findings to complex clinical, social, and political issues. A number of authors, for example, have argued that the results of animal experimentation are just as true of humans as they are of animals (cf. Morse, 1966; Whaley and Malott, 1971) and when Skinner (1953, 1969, 1972) writes that the concepts and principles first developed from the study of lower organisms have been successfully applied to human behavior in basic analysis, and that we are now in possession of a powerful technology for changing human behavior then it would seem to follow that there is no longer any need for basic research with humans—the work has already been conducted and the basic principles established with animals. Nothing remains, it would seem, save the engineering tasks involved in using these principles to change society. In spite of the ringing confidence of the claims they are almost wholly unsupported by evidence.

While critical issues in human operant behavior have gone uninvestigated, animal performance, on the other hand, has been studied in remarkable detail under a myriad different schedule conditions. This is not to suggest that animal experimentation is not valuable. Indeed, the case for differences between human and animal behavior, which is outlined here, could not have been made without findings from animal studies. But, whereas Skinner (1972) has rightly argued that 'we cannot discover what is "essentially" human until we have investigated nonhuman subjects' (pp. 201–202), I wish to stress the corollary: we cannot discover what is essentially human until we have also investigated humans.

IMPLICATIONS FOR APPLIED BEHAVIOR ANALYSIS

If the principles of behavior derived from animal experiments cannot adequately describe the behavior of humans in relatively controlled experimental settings it must follow that they are also, in themselves, an inadequate basis upon which to construct a technology of human behavior. The central problem in the applied analysis of behavior is the same as that which besets basic research, namely, there has been a failure to understand the importance of verbal behavior and private events. In a recent paper on behavioral approaches to therapy, Zettle and Hayes (1981) have voiced similar misgivings:

A radical behavioral view of common clinical issues has been poorly developed or has been developed in a way that has not lead to the needed research (e.g., Skinner's 1957 book on verbal behavior). Presently, it is sadly true that radical behaviorists have 'consistently eschewed the analysis and modification of private events'.

That this problem is fundamental is now becoming increasingly evident. There has been a growing disillusionment with the practical achievements of applied behavior analysis and a recognition that most of the basic experimental research presently being conducted no longer informs the practice of behavior modification (cf. Branch and Malagodi, 1980; Brigham, 1980; Cullen, 1981; Michael, 1980; Pierce and Epling, 1980; Repucci and Saunders, 1974). Cullen (1981) sums up the situation as follows '. . . the promise of the early sixties does not appear to have been met. While applied behavior analysis has undoubtedly had some impact, many of the applications have been trivial or transitory in effect. There has been a drift away from the kind of "science" which was once the hallmark of behavior modification' (p. 81). Various solutions have been proposed. Pierce and Epling (1980) have suggested that applied analysts should make greater efforts to use the findings of operant research, such as the matching law (Herrnstein, 1961; Baum, 1974) which very effectively describes behavioral 'choice' in animals (cf. Bradshaw et al., 1981). On the other hand, Cullen (1981) has argued that most current research is irrelevant to the needs of psychologists dealing with human problems; he claims that applied analysts know enough about general principles to move away from the laboratory and deal directly with problems of social importance.

On the basis of the present evidence, however, a 'flight from the laboratory' would be unwise, precisely because so little is known about the general principles governing human behavior. It is the nature of the laboratory which is critical. If much of contemporary operant research does not inform clinical and educational practice it is because it is primarily concerned with animal performance and with accounts of behavior which rely exclusively upon an animal model. There may not be a great deal to gain from a direct application of, for example, the matching law, if, as is suggested by recent research, the variables governing 'choice' in animals and humans differ (Horne and Lowe, 1982; Oscar-Berman et al., 1980; Schmitt, 1974; Wearden et al., 1982). Clearly, an experimental analysis of *human* behavior can be the only proper scientific foundation for applied behavior analysis.

The failure of radical behaviorists to deal adequately with human language and private events is shown most clearly in the rapid growth of cognitive behavior modification as a major influence within clinical psychology. The defining characteristic of the various therapeutic activities which go under this label, is that they seek to change, not just overt performance, but also clients' covert behavior. This is very often achieved through 'talking-therapies' of different kinds, which provide clients with problem-solving strategies, different ways of describing their problems and specific self-instructional techniques to enhance adaptive behavior. The effectiveness of many of these procedures in changing behavior cannot any longer be doubted (cf. Kendall and Hollon, 1979; Lowe and Higson, 1981). What is noteworthy here, however, is that those involved in this movement have found it necessary to reject radical behaviorism in favor of the 'new', and in many respects problematic, conceptual apparatus of cognitivism.

The term 'cognitive' appears to have been grafted on to that of behavior modification for the following reasons: (i) taking evidence from a variety of sources, it was shown that private events were important determinants of behavior (Mahoney, 1974; Meichenbaum, 1977), (ii) it was assumed that radical behaviorism was concerned only with controlling relationships between environmental stimuli and overt behavior and that it rejected the study of private events (Bandura, 1978; Kendall and Hollon, 1979; Locke, 1979; Mahoney, 1977; Strupp, 1979; Wilson, 1978), and (iii) given that private events were not behavioral, it was concluded, drawing upon earlier mentalistic traditions, that they must be 'cognitive'. But the flight from behaviorism was not confined to the simple relabeling of covert behavior as 'cognitions'. The new approach also sought a different conceptual base and found it, principally, in neo-Kantian philosophy. The 'new' perspective is clearly expressed in Castenada's (1972) much quoted dictum 'The world is such-and-such or so-and-so only because I tell myself that is the way it is' (cf. Mahoney, 1974; Meichenbaum, 1977) and in the following passage from Mahoney (1974):

> An individual responds—not to some real environment—but to a perceived environment. The frightened airline passenger reacts not to a purely external stimulus (loud noises after take-off) but to his perception (i.e. labeling) of those stimuli ('My God, we've lost an engine!'). The compulsive hand-washer reacts not to any real environmental contingencies, but to a perceived (but equally powerful) set (e.g., 'If I don't wash my hands, God will punish me'). Data from several different lines of research offer converging evidence on the critical role of cognitive factors in human behavior. (p. 5)

Thus the response to those behaviorists who argued that psychology should be concerned only with environmental effects on overt behavior, was the assertion that individuals never respond to a 'real environment' but to one which is, at least partly, created by their own cognitions.

We have attempted elsewhere (Lowe and Higson, 1981; in press) to show how a bifurcation of human activity into 'cognition' and 'behavior', needlessly introduces insoluble epistemological problems and dualistic confusion, and we have argued that a behavioral analysis of what takes place in cognitive behavior modification should provide not only a coherent conceptual basis for these techniques but also the means of enhancing their effectiveness. The cornerstone of any such analysis must surely be the recognition of the role of verbal behavior and private events in determining human behavior (see also Zettle and Hayes, 1981). My writing of this chapter and your, the reader's, consideration of it, indicate that we already share the tacit assumption that verbal events do indeed count for something—that they can influence and perhaps change the practice of others. There is, moreover, no reason to believe that the individuals whose behavior applied analysts attempt to modify inhabit a different behavioral plane and that most are not affected by description, explanation, instruction, self-instruction, and 'rational' argument. In spite of this, contemporary behaviorism, constrained by the animal model, has failed to grapple with the effects of what therapists say to their clients and, perhaps more importantly, what clients say to themselves.

CONCLUSION—TOWARDS A DIALECTICAL BEHAVIORISM

To psychologists, animal research becomes valuable when it tells us, not just about the performance of animals, but also, however indirectly, about the variables controlling human behavior. In this respect, the contribution of animal experimentation has been and will, undoubtedly, continue to be great. The challenge appears to be whether, in studying human behavior, we can integrate and build upon the animal findings. Assertions to the effect either that human behavior is not in any fundamental respects different from that of animals, or, on the other hand, that it is governed by entirely different principles, are equally unhelpful in this endeavor.

A dialectical view suggests that whilst there is a great deal in common between animal and human behavior there are also qualitative differences. To take a classic analogy from Hegelian dialectics, water and steam are the same in that they are both composed of two parts hydrogen and one part oxygen; but, in many respects, they 'behave' differently and obey different scientific laws. The related question of whether human behavior is determined by the environment or by our 'cognitions' (Mahoney, 1974) should also be regarded dialectically. Such an account might run, in brief, as follows:

1. In the lifetime of the normal individual, the world exists prior to his being able to talk, i.e., there is an environment which exists independently of us.

2. The behavior of the human infant is, *pace* Mahoney (1974), directly affected by the environment in the same way as is animal behavior; neither infants nor animals are capable of verbally describing their environment.

Hence, for example, both are affected in similar ways by schedules of reinforcement (Lowe et al., in press).

3. His particular social environment, a verbal community, establishes in the child the skill of being able to talk about the world and his relationship to it.

4. Being able to speak about his interactions with the environment has a profound effect on the way he behaves. In terms of psychological functioning, he has now altered qualitatively with respect both to his earlier infant self and to animals. Only at this stage may it be true to say that he reacts not simply to external stimuli alone, such as the noises heard after take-off by Mahoney's (1974) frightened airline passenger, but also to his own labeling of these events (e.g. 'My God, we've lost an engine!'), which can greatly alter his reactions.

5. But labeling or describing events to oneself, whether overtly or covertly, is itself behavior and subject to a behavioral analysis. It has been established by a particular social environment and is maintained and altered by the consequences it produces for the individual.

This account is similar in terms of its central focus to that put forward by Soviet psychologists such as Vygotsky (1962), Luria (1961) and Sokolov (1972) and to the social behaviorism of G. H. Mead (1934). It is entirely consistent with Skinner's radical behaviorism. Unlike the simpler animal paradigm, it rules out none of the phenomena of human psychology and offers an analysis of human consciousness which makes no concessions to mentalism (cf. Ryle, 1949). The environment remains the *primary* determinant of all behavior, both animal and human, verbal and non-verbal, but the qualitatively new effects produced by language are recognized. It is the study of these effects which may provide the most fruitful area of investigation for behavioral psychology in the coming years.

NOTES

1. I wish to thank R. P. Bentall, R. A. Boakes, P. Horne, and T. R. Miles for their comments on an earlier draft of this chapter and Jennifer Sloan and Llio Ellis Williams for their help in the preparation of the manuscript.

2. The influence was not entirely one way. Early American behaviorism also served as inspiration for members of the Vienna Circle in the 1920s (cf. Bergmann, 1954, p. 5).

3. In a variable-ratio schedule reinforcement occurs after a specified number of responses, the number varying from reinforcement to reinforcement. A fixed-ratio schedule consistently requires the same number of responses for each reinforcement.

4. In a differential-reinforcement-of-low-rate schedule a response is reinforced only if a specified minimum interval has elapsed since the preceding response.

5. The variable-interval schedule resembles fixed-interval but the intervals between reinforcements vary from one reinforcement to the next in a random or nearly random fashion.

6. This study is being conducted in collaboration with Richard Bentall, Julie Hird, and Alan Beasty.

7. Recently, there have been indications that the editors of *The Journal of the Experimental Analysis of Behavior* are very much aware of the problems discussed here (see Nevin, 1982).

REFERENCES

Ayllon, T., and Azrin, N. T. (1964) Reinforcement and instructions with mental patients. *Journal of the Experimental Analysis of Behavior*, **7**, 327–331.

Baer, D. M. (1978) The behavioral analysis of trouble. In K. E. Allen, V. A. Holm, and R. M. Schiefelbusch (eds), *Early Intervention—A Team Approach*. Baltimore: University Park Press, 57–93.

Bandura, A. (1978) The self system in reciprocal determinism. *American Psychologist*, **33**.

Baron, A., Kaufman, A., and Stauber, K. A. (1969) Effects of instructions and reinforcement feedback on human operant behavior maintained by fixed-interval reinforcement. *Journal of the Experimental Analysis of Behavior*, **12**, 701–712.

Baum, W. M. (1974) On two types of deviation from the matching law; bias and undermatching. *Journal of the Experimental Analysis of Behavior*, **22**, 321–342.

Beech, H. R. (1974) Behaviour therapy. In P. Morris (ed.), *Behaviourism*. Milton Keynes, UK: The Open University Press.

Bentall, R. P., and Lowe, C. F. (1981) Developmental aspects of human operant behavior. Paper presented to the annual conference of the Experimental Analysis of Behaviour Group, University of Oxford.

Bentall, R. P., and Lowe, C. F. (1982) Developmental aspects of human operant behavior: the role of instructions and self-instructions. *Behaviour Analysis Letters*, **2**, 186 (abstract)

Bergmann, G. (1954) *The Metaphysics of Logical Positivism*. New York: Longmans.

Bloomfield, T. M. (1976) About Skinner: notes on the theory and practice of 'Radical Behaviourism'. *Philosophy of the Social Sciences*, **6**, 75–82.

Boakes, R. A. *From Darwin to Behaviourism*. Cambridge: Cambridge University Press. (in press)

Bradshaw, C. M., Ruddle, H. V., and Szabadi, E. (1981) Studies of concurrent performances in humans. In C. M. Bradshaw, E. Szabadi, and C. F. Lowe (eds), *Quantification of Steady-State Operant Behaviour*. Amsterdam: Elsevier/North Holland Biomedical Press. 49–64.

Bradshaw, C. M., Szabadi, E., and Lowe, C. F. (1981) *Quantification of Steady-State Operant Behaviour*. Amsterdam: Elsevier/North Holland Biomedical Press.

Branch, M. N., and Malagodi, E. F. (1980) Where have all the behaviorists gone? *The Behavior Analyst*, **3**, 31–38.

Brigham, T. A. (1980) Self-control revisited: or why doesn't anyone actually read Skinner anymore? *The Behavior Analyst*, **3**, 25–33.

Buskist, W. F., and Miller, H. L. (1982) *The analysis of human operant behavior: recapitulations and reflections*. Unpublished manuscript. Adams State College, Colorado.

Castaneda, C. (1972) *A Separate Reality: Further Conversations with Don Juan*. New York: Pocket Books.

Catania, A. C. (1981) The flight from experimental analysis. In C. M. Bradshaw, E. Szabadi, and C. F. Lowe (eds) *Quantification of Steady-State Operant Behaviour*. Amsterdam: Elsevier/North Holland Biomedical Press. 49–64.

Chomsky, N. (1975) *Reflections on Language*. Glasgow, UK: William Collins.

Cullen, C. (1981) The flight to the laboratory. *The Behavior Analyst*, 4, 81–83.

De Casper, A. J., and Zeiler, M. D. (1972) Steady-state behavior in children: A method and some data. *Journal of Experimental Child Psychology*, 13, 231–239.

Deluty, M. Z. (1981) Self-control and impulsiveness involving short-term and long-term punishing events. In C. M. Bradshaw, E. Szabadi, and C. F. Lowe (eds), *Quantification of Steady-State Operant Behaviour*. Amsterdam: Elsevier/North Holland Biomedical Press, 127–138.

de Villiers, P. (1977) Choice in concurrent schedules and a quantitative formulation of the law of effect. In W. K. Honig and J. E. R. Staddon: *Handbook of Operant Behavior*. Englewood Cliffs, N.J.: Prentice-Hall.

Felton, M., and Lyon, D. O. (1966) The post-reinforcement pause. *Journal of the Experimental Analysis of Behavior*, 9, 131–134.

Ferster, G. B., and Skinner, B. F. (1957) *Schedules of Reinforcement*. New York: Appleton-Century-Crofts.

Gott, C. F., and Weiss, B. (1972) The development of fixed-ratio performance under the influence of ribonucleic acid. *Journal of the Experimental Analysis of Behavior*, 18, 481–497.

Harré, R., and Secord, P. F. (1972) *The Explanation of Social Behaviour*. Oxford: Blackwell.

Harris, J. E. and Wilkins, A. J. (1982) Remembering to do things: A theoretical framework and an illustrative experiment. *Human Learning*, 1, 123–136.

Hanson, S. J., and Killeen, P. R. (1981) Measurement and modeling of behavior under fixed-interval schedules of reinforcement. *Journal of Experimental Psychology: Animal Behavior Processes*, 7, 129–139.

Herrnstein, R. J. (1961) Relative and absolute strength of response as a function of frequency of reinforcement. *Journal of the Experimental Analysis of Behavior*, 4, 167–272.

Holland, J. G. (1958) Human vigilance. *Science*, 128, 61–67.

Horne, P. J., and Lowe, C. F. (1982) Determinants of human performance on multiple concurrent variable-interval schedules. *Behaviour Analysis Letters*, 2, 186–187 (abstract).

Karoly, P. (1980) Operant methods. In F. H. Kanfer and A. P. Goldstein (eds), *Helping People Change*. New York: Pergamon, 210–247.

Kendall, P. C., and Hollon, S. D. (1979) *Cognitive-Behavioral Interventions: Theory, Research and Procedures*. New York: Academic Press.

Kendler, H. H., and Kendler, T. S. (1962) Vertical and horizontal processes in problem-solving. *Psychological Review*, 69, 1–16.

Koestler, A. (1967) *The Ghost in the Machine*. London: Hutchinson.

Laties, V. G., and Weiss, B. (1963) Effects of a concurrent task on fixed-interval responding in humans. *Journal of the Experimental Analysis of Behavior*, 6, 431–436.

Leander, J. D., Lippman, L. G., and Meyer, M. E. (1968) Fixed-interval performance as related to subjects' verbalizations of the reinforcement contingency. *Psychological Record*, 18, 469–474.

Ledgwidge, B. (1978) Cognitive-behavior modification: a step in the wrong direction? *Psychological Bulletin*, 85, 353–375.

Lippman, L. G., and Meyer, M. E. (1967) Fixed-interval performance as related to instructions and to subjects' verbalizations of the contingency. *Psychonomic Science*, 8, 135–136.

Locke, E. A. (1979) Behavior modification is not cognitive and other myths: a reply to Ledgwidge. *Cognitive Therapy and Research*, **3**, 119–125.

Long, E. R., Hammack, J. T., May, F., and Campbell, B. J. (1958) Intermittent reinforcement of operant behavior in children. *Journal of the Experimental Analysis of Behavior*, **1**, 315–339.

Lowe, C. F. (1979) Determinants of human operant behavior. In M. D. Zeiler and P. Harzem (eds), *Advances in Analysis of Behaviour (Vol. 1): Reinforcement and the Organisation of Behaviour*. Chichester, U.K.: Wiley. 159–192.

Lowe, C. F., Beasty, A., and Bentall, R. P. The role of verbal behavior in human learning: infant performance on fixed-interval schedules. *Journal of the Experimental Analysis of Behavior*. (in press)

Lowe, C. F., and Harzem, P. (1977) Species differences in temporal control of behavior. *Journal of the Experimental Analysis of Behavior*, **28**, 189–201.

Lowe, C. F., Harzem, P., and Bagshaw, M. (1978) Species differences in temporal control of behavior II: Human performance. *Journal of the Experimental Analysis of Behavior*, **29**, 351–361.

Lowe, C. F., Harzem, P., and Hughes, S. (1978) Determinants of operant behavior in humans: Some differences from animals. *Quarterly Journal of Experimental Psychology*, **30**, 373–386.

Lowe, C. F., Harzem, P., and Spencer, P. T. (1979) Temporal control of behavior and the power law. *Journal of the Experimental Analysis of Behavior*, **31**, 333–343.

Lowe, C. F., and Higson, P. J. (1981) Self-instructional training and cognitive behaviour modification: A behavioural analysis. In G. C. L. Davey (ed.), *Applications of Conditioning Theory*. London: Methuen. 162–188.

Lowe, C. F., and Higson, P. J. Is all behaviour modification 'cognitive'? In E. Karans (ed.), *Current Issues in Clinical Psychology*. London: Plenum.

Lowe, C. F., and Wearden, J. H. (1981) A quantitative model of temporal control on fixed-interval schedules: Dynamic properties of behaviour. In C. M. Bradshaw, E. Szabadi, and C. F. Lowe (eds), *Quantification of Steady-State Operant Behaviour*. Amsterdam: Elsevier/North Holland Biomedical Press, 177–188.

Luria, A. (1961) *The Role of Speech in the Regulation of Normal and Abnormal Behaviors*. New York: Liveright.

Mackenzie, B. D. (1977) *Behaviourism and the Limits of Scientific Method*. London: Routledge.

Mahoney, M. J. (1977) Reflections on the cognitive-learning trend in psychotherapy. *American Psychologist*, **32**, 5–13.

Matthews, B. A., Shimoff, E., Catania, C., and Sagvolden, T. (1977) Uninstructed human responding to ratio and interval contingencies. *Journal of the Experimental Analysis of Behavior*, **27**, 453–467.

Mead, G. H. (1934) *Mind, Self and Society: from the Standpoint of a Social Behaviorist*. Chicago: University of Chicago Press.

Meichenbaum, D. (1977) *Cognitive-Behavior Modification: An Integrative Approach*. New York: Plenum Press.

Michael, J. (1980) Flight from behavior analysis. *The Behavior Analyst*, **3**, 1–21.

Morse, W. H. (1966) Intermittent reinforcement. In W. K. Honig (ed.), *Operant Behavior: Areas of Research and Application*. New York: Appleton-Century-Crofts, 52–108.

Nevin, J. A. (1982) Editorial. *Journal of the Experimental Analysis of Behavior*, **37**, 1–2.

Nisbett, R. E., and Wilson, T. D. (1977) Telling more than we can know: Verbal reports on mental processes. *Psychological Review*, **84**, 231–259.

Oscar-Berman, M., Heyman, G. M., Bonner, R. T., and Ryder, J. (1980) Human neuropsychology: some differences between Korsakoff and normal operant performance. *Psychological Research*, **41**, 235–247.

Pierce, W. D., and Epling, W. F. (1980) What happened to analysis in applied behavior analysis? *The Behavior Analyst*, **3**, 1–9.

Pierce, W. D., Epling, W. F., and Greer, S. M. (1981) Human communication and the matching law. In C. M. Bradshaw, K. Szabadi, and C. F. Lowe (eds), *Quantification of Steady-State Operant Behaviour*. Amsterdam: Elsevier/North Holland Biomedical Press. 345–348.

Poppen, R. (1982) Human fixed-interval performance with concurrently programmed schedules: a parametric analysis. *Journal of the Experimental Analysis of Behavior*, **37**, 251–266.

Powell, R. W. (1968) The effect of small sequential changes in fixed-ratio size upon the post-reinforcement pause. *Journal of the Experimental Analysis of Behavior*, **11**, 589–593.

Rachlin, H. (1977) A review of M. Mahoney's *Cognition and Behavior Modification*. *Journal of Applied Behavior Analysis*, **10**, 369–374.

Rachlin, H. (1980) *Behaviorism in Everyday Life*. Englewood Cliffs, N.J.: Prentice-Hall.

Repucci, N., and Saunders, J. (1974) Social psychology of behavior modification: problems of implementation in natural settings. *American Psychologist*, **29**, 649–660.

Reynolds, G. S. (1975) *A Primer of Operant Conditioning*. Glenview, Illinois: Scott Foresman.

Ryle, G. (1949) *The Concept of Mind*. Middlesex, England: Penguin.

Schmitt, D. R. (1974) Effects of reinforcement rate and reinforcer magnitude on choice behavior of humans. *Journal of the Experimental Analysis of Behavior*, **21**, 409–419.

Shimoff, E., Catania, A. C., and Matthews, B. A. (1981) Uninstructed human responding: sensitivity of low-rate performance to schedule contingencies. *Journal of the Experimental Analysis of Behavior*, **36**, 207–220.

Sidman, M., Rauzin, R., Lazar, R., Cunningham, S., Tailby, W., and Carrigan, P. (1982) A search for symmetry in the conditional discrimination of rhesus monkeys, baboons, and children. *Journal of the Experimental Analysis of Behavior*, **37**, 23–45.

Skinner, B. F. (1945) The operational analysis of psychological terms. *Psychological Review*, **52**, 270–277.

Skinner, B. F. (1953) *Science and Human Behavior*. New York: Macmillan.

Skinner, B. F. (1957) *Verbal Behavior*. New York: Appleton-Century-Crofts.

Skinner, B. F. (1963) Behaviorism at fifty. *Science*, **134**, 566–602.

Skinner, B. F. (1966) An operant analysis of problem solving. In B. Kleinmuntz (ed.), *Problem Solving: Research, Method and Teaching*. New York: John Wiley.

Skinner, B. F. (1969) *Contingencies of Reinforcement: A Theoretical Analysis*. New York: Appleton-Century-Crofts.

Skinner, B. F. (1972) *Beyond Freedom and Dignity*. London: Jonathan Cape.

Skinner, B. F. (1974) *About Behaviourism*. London: Jonathan Cape.

Sokolov, A. N. (1972) *Inner Speech and Thought*. New York: Plenum.

Strupp, H. H. (1979) Psychotherapy research and practice: an overview. In S. L. Garfield, and A. E. Bergin (eds), *Handbook of Psychotherapy and Behavior Change: An Empirical Analysis* (2nd edn) New York: Wiley.

Vygotsky, L. (1962) *Thought and Language*. New York: Wiley.

Watson, J. B. (1913) Psychology as the behaviorist views it. *Psychological Review*, **20**, 158–177.

Watson, J. B. (1930) *Behaviorism*. New York: Norton.

Wearden, J. H., Lochery, M., and Oliphant, S. (1982) Human variable-interval performance. *Behaviour Analysis Letters*, **2**, 187 (abstract).

Weiner, H. (1964a) Response cost and fixed-ratio performance. *Journal of the Experimental Analysis of Behavior*, **7**, 79–81.

Weiner, H. (1964b) Conditioning history and human fixed-interval performance. *Journal of the Experimental Analysis of Behavior*, **7**, 383–385.

Weiner, H. (1965) Conditioning history and maladaptive human operant behavior. *Psychological Reports*, **17**, 935–942.

Weiner, H. (1969) Controlling human fixed-interval performance. *Journal of the Experimental Analysis of Behavior*, **12**, 349–373.

Weiner, H. (1970) Human behavioral persistence. *The Psychological Record*, **20**, 445–456.

Whaley, D. L., and Malott, R. W. (1971) *Elementary Principles of Behavior*. New York: Appleton-Century-Crofts.

Wilson, T. (1978) Cognitive behavior therapy: Paradigm shift or passing phase? In J. Foreyt and D. Rathjen (eds), *Cognitive Behavior Therapy: Research and Application*. New York: Plenum Press. 7–32.

Wolf, M. M. (1973) Quoted in K. Goodall. 'This little girl won't interact with other little girls and she crawls around a lot'. *Psychology Today*, **7**, 64–72.

Zeiler, M. D. (1977) Schedules of reinforcement: the controlling variables. In W. K. Honig and J. E. R. Staddon (eds), *Handbook of Operant Behavior*. Englewood Cliffs: Prentice Hall. 201–232.

Zettle, R. D., and Hayes, S. C. (1981) Rule-governed behavior: a potential theoretical framework for cognitive behavior therapy. In P. C. Kendall (ed.), *Advances in Cognitive-Behavioral Research and Therapy* (Vol. 1). New York: Academic Press.

Animal Models of Human Behavior
Edited by G. C. L. Davey
© 1983 John Wiley & Sons Ltd

Chapter 6

An Associative View of Human Classical Conditioning[1]

Graham C. L. DAVEY

In the past ten years or so theoretical accounts of conditioning in both animals[2] and humans have diverted from the strict path of behaviorism to encompass concepts which are distincly 'cognitive' in nature. This development seems to have come about for at least two important reasons. First, theorists had become more inquisitive about the mechanisms which subserve learning. Explanations of behavior change in terms of controlling variables seemed a reasonable intermediate goal, but if techniques could be developed which would unlock the dynamics of the mechanisms which mediate environment–behavior relationships, why not use them? The second reason for the burgeoning of cognitive accounts of conditioning can be located in what is known as the 'constraints on learning' literature. Throughout the 1970s it became apparent that many laws of conditioning which had previously been considered as both universal and sacrosanct, were being violated by species other than the rat and pigeon. Basic principles such as operant conditioning, the equipotentiality of stimuli, and temporal contiguity appeared to operate only when both the species and the conditioning context were taken into consideration (cf. Shettleworth, 1972; Breland and Breland, 1966; Davey, 1981, pp. 154–214). This literature fostered the belief that species differences in learning abilities must be reflective of species differences in learning mechanisms, and thus the only means of solving the enigma created by the constraints on learning literature was to develop means of studying associative and performance mechanisms directly.

Meanwhile, it was also being discovered that humans too violated traditional laws of learning. They often emitted inappropriate rates of responding on simple schedules of reinforcement (Lowe, 1979; Davey, 1981, pp. 345–63), frequently failed to extinguish responding with non-reinforcement

95

(Buchwald, 1959; Bijou and Baer, 1966), and would not always develop a conditioned response (CR) following the pairing of a conditioned stimulus (CS) with an unconditioned stimulus (UCS) (Dawson and Biferno, 1973; Erwin, 1978; Dawson and Furedy, 1976; Brewer, 1974). These apparent discrepancies also led to the theoretical implication of cognitive variables postulated to mediate the relationship between conditioning contingencies and learning.

However, these theoretical re-orientations were not part of a single unitary development in the field of learning. The drift towards cognitive explanations of animal and human conditioning occurred in parallel, and, what is more, involved different types of 'cognition'. In animal learning, 'cognitive' refers to the learning of new cognitive structures that are inferred from behavior. More specifically, the cognitive psychologist would here claim that the animal learns to mentally represent events in the learning situation and subsequently to associate these events. For instance, it might be the case that the bell CS in Pavlov's prototypical salivary conditioning experiment comes, through its association with food, to evoke a cognitive representation of the food UCS; this representation in turn evokes salivation. The association between bell and food is a learned cognitive structure which, although unobservable, might be detected using any one of a variety of inferential techniques (these techniques will be discussed in a later section of this chapter). However, theorists of human learning have tended to avoid the question of 'what is learned?' in favor of putative cognitive variables that modulate learning. Such variables as have already been postulated include 'awareness of contingencies', 'self-efficacy', 'compliance', 'expectancy', and so on. Thus, rather than elaborating the cognitive structure of what is learned—which is the 'animal' theorist's approach—the 'human' theorist is still in the throes of cataloging the cognitive functions that contribute to learning.

The view that I wish to argue in this chapter is that an understanding of conditioning in humans might be served better by adopting the approach to learning advocated by cognitive animal psychologists. That is, it might be more beneficial to understand exactly *what* is learnt in a conditioning situation—in terms of associations and representations of events. Once we know what is learnt we can then begin to understand the effects of variables such as 'awareness', 'expectancy', etc. by observing their effect on the cognitive structures that have been learnt. I will elaborate this possibility later, but first a brief summary of cognitive accounts of human and animal conditioning is necessary.

COGNITIVE ACCOUNTS OF CLASSICAL CONDITIONING IN HUMANS

Studies of human classical conditioning carried out in the 1960s and 1970s tended to suggest that factors other than the simple contingent pairing of CS and UCS significantly influenced conditioning. The most obvious effect was that of instructions. Simply informing Ss of the CS–UCS relationship, with no actual pairings, can produce immediate conditioning (e.g. Dawson and Grings, 1968; Katz et al., 1971; McComb, 1969; Wilson, 1968); whilst informing the S of extinction can also produce a dramatic and rapid drop in responding (e.g. Colgan, 1970; Koenig and Castillo, 1969). Similarly, Ss who are told to try and withhold the CR whilst being given continued pairings of CS and UCS, are frequently able to reduce the magnitude of the CR (e.g. Swenson and Hill, 1970; Dawson and Reardon, 1969; Fishbein, 1967; Norris and Grant, 1948; Prokasy and Allen, 1969; cf. Brewer, 1974, for a review of these studies).

One of the apparently crucial factors in mediating some of these instructional effects is 'awareness of contingencies'. First, only Ss who can verbalize the correct CS–UCS relations in post-experimental questionnaires appear to exhibit conditioning (Baer and Fuhrer, 1968, 1970). Secondly, when level of awareness of CS–UCS relations is measured on a trial-to-trial basis throughout conditioning, differential CRs occur only after the time that contingency awareness has developed (e.g. Dawson and Biferno, 1973; Biferno and Dawson, 1977; Fuhrer and Baer, 1980). Thirdly, studies which have deliberately attempted to 'mask' the CS–UCS relationship and prevent Ss from becoming aware of the CS–UCS contingency have largely failed to find evidence for conditioning (Dawson, 1973; Grings and Dawson, 1973; Ross et al., 1974; Dawson et al., 1979).

These and other results on the relation between contingency awareness and conditioning have given rise to what has come to be known as the dual-level view of human classical conditioning[3] (Baer and Fuhrer, 1973; Grings, 1965; Mandel and Bridger, 1967; Razran, 1971). This view asserts that a CS–UCS contingency can lead to either of two distinct levels of learning: (i) 'true' primitive conditioning (Razran, 1955) in which learning occurs at an autonomic, non-cognitive level, and (ii) 'cognitive relational learning' (Grings, 1973; Dawson and Furedy, 1976) which involves the S's cognitive and conscious processes and 'can be usefully conceptualized as a complex and active information processing task with the autonomic indices of conditioning reflecting in large part the sequence of central cognitive processes' (Dawson et al., 1979, p. 38). The majority of the demonstrations of human autonomic conditioning in the laboratory are considered to be examples of the latter process, and the more primitive non-cognitive process is retained in order to explain a smattering of findings which appear to be anomalous with the cognitive view (e.g. Fuhrer and Baer, 1969; Wilson et al., 1973; Bridger and Mandel, 1965; Mandel and Bridger, 1967).

So, the currently popular model of human classical conditioning is basically an information processing one (cf. Öhman, 1979), and Dawson *et al.* (1979) have suggested some of the conscious cognitive processes that might be necessary for successful conditioning. These include (i) detection and recognition of the CS, (ii) retrieval of information about the significance of the CS, (iii) anticipation of the signaled reinforcer, and (iv) post-trial rehearsal and encoding of the trial events. Some preliminary studies do indicate the importance of these kinds of conscious processes in some situations (e.g. Ross *et al.*, 1974; Dawson *et al.*, 1978), but as yet no real attempt has been made to specify whether such processes are unique to 'cognitive relational learning' or are shared by the putative lower level 'true' conditioning. Indeed, if a separate mechanism exists for primitive unconscious conditioning in humans, theorists have to date been singularly unsuccessful in specifying with any certainty the empirical conditions which are necessary for engaging this learning mechanism rather than the higher-level cognitive mechanism.

COGNITIVE ACCOUNTS OF CLASSICAL CONDITIONING IN ANIMALS

The brief preceding review of cognitive accounts of human classical conditioning emphasizes the theorist's desire to describe the cognitive processes through which learning proceeds. The translation of environmental contingencies into learned response requires mediation through a series of information processing mechanisms. Whilst cognitive theorists of animal conditioning have also recently viewed conditioning in information processing terms (e.g. Pearce and Hall, 1980; Wagner, 1978)—and indeed there is much room for integration between the human and animal spheres here—I wish to devote this section to reviewing those studies of animal conditioning which have attempted to define the cognitive content of learning rather than describe the cognitive processing mechanism itself. My reasons for doing this are two-fold: (i) it will allow me to elaborate the techniques available for determining what is learned during a conditioning episode—a task which is necessary if the reader is to appreciate the reasoning behind the experiments which are subsequently to be described; and (ii) as I indicated earlier, a knowledge of the content of learning can provide valuable clues to an understanding of the mechanisms by which learning takes place. For instance, it may be the case that CRs learned through the primitive mechanism in the dual-level view are mediated by reflexive S–R associations, while CRs learned through the cognitive mechanism are mediated by associations representing relationships between external events (i.e. stimulus–stimulus associations). The fact that these different types of associations are not immediately distinguishable in observed behavior could clearly deceive the theorist, and thus a knowledge of them might help to elucidate a dual-level account.

In order to investigate the kinds of associations formed during learning, techniques have been devised which involve the post-conditioning modification of stimulus values. For instance, Holland and Rescorla (1975), investigating conditioned activity in hungry rats, first paired a CS with a food UCS. Then they reduced the palatability of that food by pairing it with illness (taste aversion learning). Following this 'devaluation' of the UCS for the rat, subsequent testing indicated reduced activity to the CS. Rescorla (1973; 1977; 1980) has claimed that these results supported a view that first-order Pavlovian conditioning involves the establishment of internal representations of the CS and UCS and the formation of an association between them. Thus, presentation of the CS comes to activate the UCS representation which in turn generates conditioned responding. Within this view, then, the strength of conditioning would depend on the integrity or 'value' of the UCS representation. Other studies which have manipulated UCS value in both appetitive and aversive first-order Pavlovian conditioning have found results consistent with the view that CS–UCS associations mediate conditioning (Rescorla, 1973; Colby and Smith, 1977; Holland and Straub, 1979).

This rationale can be extended to study the types of associations formed in higher-order Pavlovian conditioning, and it is these studies which have arguably produced the most interesting results. In second-order conditioning a CS_1 is initially paired with a UCS, subsequently the S is given pairings of a new CS_2 with the original CS_1. Under these conditions, conditioned responding usually develops to CR_2 (cf. Rescorla, 1980, pp. 1–10). For this kind of learning to take place, what has been learnt during the CS_1–UCS episode has to be integrated in some way with what is subsequently learnt during CS_2–CS_1 episodes. Oddly enough, initial studies found that CR_2 was quite resistant to revaluation of both CS_1 and UCS: that is, responding to CS_2 persisted even if (i) S underwent post-conditioning habituation to the original shock UCS in aversive conditioning (Rescorla, 1973), (ii) S underwent post-conditioning taste aversion learning to the food UCS in appetitive conditioning (Holland and Rescorla, 1975), or (iii) responding to CS_1 was extinguished independently of CS_2 (Rizley and Rescorla, 1972). These results intimated that the contents of second-order learning were quite different from the contents of first-order learning. More specifically, since CR_2 persisted in spite of revaluations of UCS and CS_1 it seemed likely that CR_2 was *not* mediated by the integration of independently learnt CS_1–UCS and CS_2–CS_1 associations. The most obvious alternative here was that the S had learnt an association between CS_2 and the response to CS_1—i.e. an S–R association (Rescorla, 1977).

However, not all second-order studies supported the findings of these earlier studies. The content of second-order learning seems in some part to depend on the conditioning paradigm. For instance, studies of appetitive (rather than aversive) conditioning which have used the post-conditioning re-valuation technique with autoshaped key-pecking in the pigeon, have found that CR_2 does not survive revaluation of CS_1 (Rashotte *et al.*, 1977; Leyland, 1977) implying that CS_2–CS_1 associations and their integration with CS_1–UCS associations are supporting CR_2.

Of course, there is no caveat which states that only one kind of association can be formed during a particular conditioning procedure, nor indeed do those results just reviewed imply different associative mechanisms for first- and second-order conditioning. It seems reasonable to assume that what associations are formed will depend to a great extent on the salience and attentional properties of the various elements in the learning situation. For instance, during second-order conditioning CS_2 is followed more or less simultaneously by a number of internal and external events such as (i) the sensory properties of the CS_1 itself, (ii) the $S's$ reaction to CS_1, and probably (iii) evocation of the UCS representation. If we assume that formation of associations is an information processing task taking place in a limited ca-pacity processor, then these elements would be vying for associative strength and presumably only the most salient events will be processed. In second-order conditioning it is arguably the animal's own reaction to CS_1 which is the most important event to it: for example, in second-order aversive con-ditioning it is likely that the $S's$ fear reaction to CS_1 will overshadow pro-cessing of the biologically neutral sensory characteristics of CS_1 and result in learnt associations between CS_2 and CR_1 rather than CS_2 and CS_1 itself. However, in first-order conditioning the sensory characteristics of the UCS *are* important for the animal (since it would be biologically or experientially primed to approach or avoid these characteristics) and we might be more inclined to expect CS_1–UCS associations. However, there are at present few studies in the literature addressed to the problem of association formation and the relative salience of the elements in the learning situation, but the relative importance of the attention-provoking properties of the various ele-ments vying for association will be discussed again later in this chapter.

SOME EXPERIMENTS ON HUMAN CLASSICAL CONDITIONING USING THE POST-CONDITIONING REVALUATION TECHNIQUE

The preceding reviews emphasize that accounts of human classical condi-tioning have tended to ignore the role played by the associative substructure underlying learning in favor of mediating variables which stress the import-ance of conscious cognitive processes during learning. It is the view to be expressed here that a study of human classical conditioning in terms of associative factors has been sorely neglected—especially since animal studies have refined experimental techniques which allow a greater understanding of the associations underlying conditioning.

The experiments to be described here are a preliminary attempt to apply post-conditioning revaluation techniques to human classical conditioning in the hope of casting some light on the associations underlying human learning. They are all concerned with the associations formed during second-order conditioning—not because I feel that these are any more important theoretically than the associations formed during first-order conditioning, but because second-order conditioning potentially provides greater scope for manipulation of the characteristics of the referents of the association (CS_1 and CS_2) than does first-order conditioning (see also, Rescorla, 1980).

Experiment I. Post-conditioning extinction of CR_1 following second-order electrodermal conditioning.[4]

Many of the studies of second-order conditioning in animals that have been reviewed here have discovered that CR_2 survives extinction of CR_1, suggesting that CR_2 is frequently not mediated via CS_2–CS_1 associations. This first experiment looks at this possibility in human second–order electrodermal conditioning.

Subjects. The *Ss* were 27 undergraduate volunteers of both sexes, all naive as to the purpose of the experiment. These *Ss* were then divided into three groups of nine. These groups were labeled Group E (experimental), Group A (avoidance), and Group C (control).

Procedure. On introduction to the experimental room *Ss* were given written instructions which told them that the experiment was designed to measure sweat gland activity. They were seated in a comfortable chair facing a screen on which slides of various outline figures were to be projected. They were then fitted with anodized thimble finger electrodes on the distal phalanx of the middle and ring finger of the left hand. (Details of recording apparatus, response measurement, and response measurement controls are given in Davey and Arulampalam, 1982.) *Ss* were also fitted with headphones which continually emitted white noise (65 ± 2 dB) but which could also present a brief (0.5 sec) 1000 H_z tone of 115 dB which was used as the reinforcer (UCS). Following a brief adaptation period, the experiment, which consisted of four phases, commenced.

Phase 1 consisted of first-order electrodermal conditioning in which, for Groups E and A, the 115 dB tone always followed the 6-sec presentation of a slide showing a triangle (CS_1). These *Ss* were prewarned of this correlation and they received 10 pairings of CS_1 and UCS, each trial being separated by a 30 sec inter-trial interval. Group C also received 10 presentations of CS_1 and tone but these were unpaired (a random control procedure).

Phase 2 consisted of second-order conditioning in which for all groups CS_1 always immediately followed the 6-sec presentation of a slide of an outline drawing of a telephone (CS_2^+). Interspersed amongst these pairings was the individual presentation of an outlined drawing of a kitchen tap (CS_2^0). CS_2^0 was a second-order control stimulus which was never paired with CS_1 (telephone and tap were counter-balanced as CS_2^+ and CS_2^0 across Ss). This phase consisted of five pairings of CS_2^+ and CS_1, and five independent presentations of CS_2^0. All Ss were informed of the relationship between the two new stimuli and CS_1 prior to the start of this phase. However, Group A was also told that the UCS could be avoided if they pressed a small lever (situated near to their right hand) during the presentation of CS_1. Group C were simply told to press the lever whenever they saw CS_1. The UCS was never presented during this phase, so in effect Group A had pairings of CS_2^+ and CS_1 whilst believing they were avoiding the UCS by pressing the lever. Groups E and C simply had pairings of CS_2^+ and CS_1.

In phase 3 all groups were given 10 trials in which CS_1 was presented alone (designed to extinguish CR_1). In phase 4, all groups were given eight individual slide presentations, two of these presentations were of CS_2^+ and two were of CS_2^0. The remaining four were interspersed randomly amongst these and were slides which were novel to the Ss (outline drawings of an aeroplane, square, star, and circle). Slides were separated by an ITI of 30 sec.

Results. Figure 6.1 shows range-corrected skin conductance responses (SCRs) for all groups for phases 1, 2, and 4 of the experiment. First-order conditioning is indicated for Groups A and E, but not Group C, when SCR measures during CS_1 and randomly selected ITI periods are compared (see Davey and Arulampalam, 1982, for full statistical analyses).[5] Both Groups A and E exhibit second-order conditioning to CS_2^+ and responding to CS_2^0 was no higher than that recorded during ITI. Since the original UCS was never presented during this phase, the SCR acquired by CS_2^+ must have been due to the reinforcing properties of its pairing with CS_1. At the end of phase 3 all groups had shown extinction of the SCR to CS_1, and phase 4 was used to test for a retention of the conditioned responding to CS_2^+ even though CR_1 had been extinguished.

During phase 4, for Group A, SCR to CS_2^+ was not significantly different (at the 5% level) to that emitted to CS_2^0 or to the novel stimuli, nor during randomly selected ITI periods. However, in Group E, responding to CS_2^+ did appear to survive extinction of CR_1. SCR to CS_2^+ was greater than that to CS_2^0 ($t=3.164$, $p<0.05$), greater than that to the novel stimuli ($t=2.69$, $p<0.05$), and greater than spontaneous responses measured during selected ITI periods ($t=2.873$, $p<0.05$).

Discussion. The results of this first experiment demonstrate: (i) that second-order electrodermal conditioning can readily be acquired by human Ss, and (ii) under some conditions, this second-order response can survive extinction of responding to the original first-order CS. However, this latter

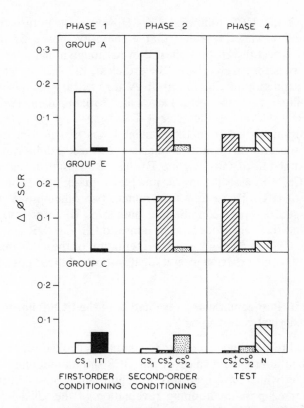

Figure 6.1 Mean ϕ SCR values for all three groups for phases 1, 2, and 4 of Experiment I. CS response values during phases 1 and 2 are calculated from the last three trials in each phase. In phase 4, means are calculated from the two presentations of CS_2^+ and CS_2^0 and the four presentations of novel stimuli (N). ITI values are a mean of two samples taken during individual 6-sec. periods of each phase ($\triangle$ ϕ SCR = change in SCR (range-corrected micromho)). (From Davey and Arulampalam, 1982, copyright 1982 by Pergamon Press Ltd. Reprinted by permission)

finding was only true with Ss who were not given a supposed avoidance response to perform during CS_1 in phase 2. Prior to the experiment we felt that Ss in Group E might not exhibit second-order conditioning since CS_2 might rapidly become a stimulus predicting non-delivery of the UCS following CS_1 (i.e. CS_2 could become a conditioned inhibitor). In order to attenuate this possibility we included Group A in the experiment: a group of Ss who, whilst still not receiving UCS in phase 2, would still presumably have an expectancy of the UCS following CS_1. However, as it turned out, post-experimental interviews revealed that a majority of the Ss in Group E continued to expect the UCS in phase 2 even though it had not followed CS_1 on the five trials they were given. Nevertheless, the reasons why CR_2 does not survive extinction of CR_1 in Group A are unclear. We have expounded some possibilities elsewhere (e.g. Davey and Arulampalam, 1982), but they are not directly relevant to the present discussion.

The important finding from Experiment I was that in a procedure quite similar to that used with animals, human subjects also exhibit survival of CR_2 following extinction of CR_1 (Group E). The conclusion to be drawn from this is that CS_2–CS_1 associations do not play a major role in mediating the appearance of CR_2. There therefore remain two other prime possibilities: that during second-order conditioning human Ss (i) form associations between CS_2 and their electrodermal response to CS_1 (an S–R association), or (ii) associate CS_2 directly with the representation of the UCS that is evoked by CS_1. The second experiment investigates some of these possibilities.

Experiment II. Post-conditioning revaluation of the UCS following second-order electrodermal conditioning

If conditioned responding is mediated by stimulus-evoked representations of the UCS, then altering the value of the UCS should modulate responding. Animal studies which have used this procedure have suggested that in aversive conditioning post-conditioning revaluation of the UCS influences responding to a first-order CS_1, but does not affect responding to a second-order CS_2 (Rescorla, 1973; 1977; Holland and Rescorla, 1975).

One method of achieving UCS-revaluation in aversive conditioning paradigms is to habituate the S to the UCS after conditioning has taken place. If conditioned responding is mediated by the S's response to an internal representation of the UCS, then a reduced reaction to the UCS should also attenuate CRs. Although with animals these revaluations have to be incurred through actual experience with the UCS, this need not be so with human Ss—revaluation of events can take place through many media. In the experimental setting one method is by instructions. In Experiment I we used instructions to facilitate association formation (each S was informed of the experimental contingencies prior to phases 1, 2, and 3), in the next experiment to be described an attempt was made to compare experimental and instructional methods of producing UCS revaluation following first- and second-order electrodermal conditioning.

Subjects. The Ss were 28 undergraduate volunteers of both sexes, all of whom were naive as to the purpose of the experiment. These Ss were divided into four groups of 7. These groups were called Group E (extinction), Group H (habituation), Group $\bar{T}$ (no-tone expectancy), and Group R (random control).

Procedure. The apparatus was identical to that used in Experiment I, except that the response lever was no longer required and was removed from the room. This experiment also consisted of four phases following an initial adaptation period.

Phase 1 was identical to phase 1 in Experiment I except that the slide of the triangle (CS_1) and tone (UCS) were paired for only six trials for Groups E, H, and $\bar{T}$. Group R received six unpaired presentations of both CS_1 and UCS.

Phase 2 consisted of second-order conditioning. This was identical to phase 2 in Experiment I except there were only three pairings of CS_2^+ and CS_1, and only three independent presentations of CS_2^0.

In phase 3, Groups E, $\bar{T}$, and R received independent periodic presentations of CS_1 alone. This continued until each S had received three successive CS_1 presentations without emitting a CR. As in Experiment I this was designed to extinguish responding to CS_1. However, instead of extinction of CR_1 in phase 3, Group H received a 'pseudo-habituation' treatment designed to develop a more favorable revaluation of the tone UCS. At the end of phase 2, *Ss* in Group H were asked to mark on a 9 point scale how they felt about the tone 'at this point in the experiment' (on the scale 1=pleasant, 3=neutral, 5=loud, 7=aversive, 9=unbearable). They were then given the following instructions: 'In the following part of the experiment you will receive a number of presentations of the tone. When a series of relatively loud noises are presented to you, your hearing system usually compensates for the intensity by making them seem less intense. This process is known as "habituation". As a consequence you may perceive the tone as getting quieter as the number of presentations increases'. This was followed by 15 presentations of the tone UCS, with each presentation separated by a 20-sec ITI. Unbeknown to the *Ss*, however, over these 15 presentations the experimenter was progressively reducing the volume of the tone from 115 dB to 90 dB. In a post-experimental interview only one *S* admitted being suspicious that anything other than the prewarned habituation process was occurring. At the end of phase 3 all *Ss* in Group H were asked to re-evaluate the tone on the 9 point scale.

At the beginning of phase 4 all groups were informed that in 'the following part of the experiment you will be presented with a number of slides'. Group $\bar{T}$, however, were further informed that 'there will be *no more* presentations of the tone.' All groups then received eight individual slide presentations, two of these presentations were of CS_2^+ and two were of CS_2^0. Interspersed amongst these presentations were four blank slides which projected white light on to the screen for 6 sec and acted as controls for reactions to stimulus change.

Results. At the end of phase 1 (last three trials) Group E (Wilcoxon $t=0$, $p<0.05$, Group H ($t=0$, $p<0.05$), and Group $\bar{T}$ ($t=0$, $p<0.05$) were all exhibiting first-order conditioning when SCRs to CS_1 and during randomly selected ITI periods were compared. Group R did not exhibit conditioning ($t=15$, $p>0.05$). Figure 6.2 shows the results obtained from the second-order conditioning in phase 2. Groups E, H, and $\bar{T}$ all show significantly greater responding to CS_2^+ than to CS_2^0 (Group E, $t=1$, $p<0.05$; Group H, $t=0$, $p<0.05$; Group $\bar{T}$, $t=2$, $p<0.05$); and significantly greater responding during CS_2^+ than during ITI periods (Group E, $t=0$, $p<0.05$; Group H, $t=0$, $p<0.05$; Group $\bar{T}$, $t=2$, $p<0.05$). There was no significant difference between CRs to CS_2^+ and CS_2^0 for Group R ($t=5\frac{1}{2}$, $p>0.05$).

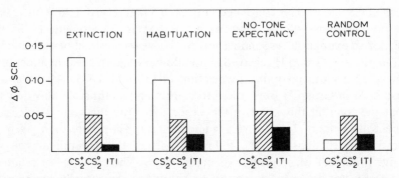

Figure 6.2 Mean ϕ SCR values for all groups during phase 2 of Experiment II. CS response values are taken as a mean from the three trials in phase 2 for CS_2^+ and CS_2^0. ITI values are a mean of two 6-sec. samples taken during this phase ($\triangle\varnothing$ SCR = change in SCR (range-corrected micromho))

Figure 6.3 presents mean ϕ SCR to CS_2^+, CS_2^0, the blank control slides, and selected ITI periods during phase 4. For Group E, responding to CS_2^+ was significantly greater than that to CS_2^0 ($t=0$, $p<0.05$), the blank slides ($t=0$, $p<0.05$), and ITI periods ($t=1$, $p<0.05$). This confirms the result obtained in Experiment I that post-conditioning extinction of responding to CS_1 fails to suppress CR_2. For Group H, however, although mean ϕ SCR to CS_2^+ was greater than that to the other stimuli, these differences were not statistically significant (CS_2^+ − ITI, $t=5$, $p>0.05$). All *Ss* in Group H showed a more favorable re-evaluation of the UCS following the habituation phase with the mean scale point for the group dropping from 5.62 (5=loud) to 4.05 (3=neutral). The section of Figure 6.3 referring to Group $\bar{T}$, however, clearly shows that in phase 4 CS_2^+ responding was no greater than that to CS_2^0 ($t=5$, $p>0.05$). All *Ss* in Group $\bar{T}$ claimed in a post-experimental interview that

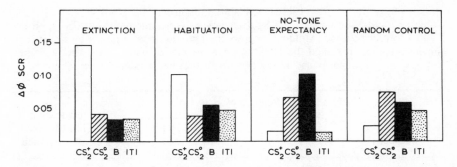

Figure 6.3 Mean ϕ SCR values for all four groups during phase 4 of Experiment II. Means are calculated from the two presentations of $CS_2{}^+$ and $CS_2{}^0$ and the four presentations of the blank slides (B). ITI values are a mean of two 6-sec. samples taken during this phase ($\triangle\phi$ SCR = change in SCR (range-corrected micromho))

they believed the instructions they were given about the non-occurrence of the tone in phase 4. Finally, for Group R, Figure 6.3 shows that $CS_2^{\pm}$ responding was no greater than responding to other stimuli during this phase. *Discussion.* The results from Group E clearly confirm the finding from Experiment I that CR_2 survives extinction of CR_1. Conversely, Group $\bar{T}$ also clearly shows that informing the S that there will be no more UCS presentations eliminates CR_2. I will come back to this finding in a moment.

The results for Group H are somewhat less clear. Although the group mean ϕ SCR to $CS_2^{\pm}$ is still higher than that to the other control stimuli, these differences are not significant. However, a breakdown of the results for Ss in Group H can perhaps throw some light on the effects of this procedure.

Table 6.1 shows individual response levels to $CS_2^{\pm}$ in phases 2 and 4, and the effect of the habituation procedure on each subject's revaluation of the UCS on the 9 point scale. These data suggest that the habituation procedure may have been successful in producing UCS revaluation only in some Ss. For instance, those Ss who show the highest levels of responding to $CS_2^{\pm}$ in phase 4 are those subjects who favorably revalue the UCS by one scale point or less. Conversely, those Ss who favorably revalued the UCS by two scale points or more show the lowest SCR levels to $CS_2^{\pm}$ in phase 4 and also exhibit an attenuation of $CR_2^{\pm}$ between phases 2 and 4 of the experiment. So, although it appears that the habituation procedure has been less than successful with some Ss the signs are that when relatively large favorable changes occur in the revaluation of the UCS, then CR_2 is substantially reduced.[6] This is an effect which (i) was not achieved solely by extinction of responding to CS_1 and (ii) which implies that responding to CS_2 is mediated by UCS cognitions.

The results from Group $\bar{T}$, though clearer than those in Group H, are

Table 6.1. Habituation group.
Columns 2 and 3 show mean $\Delta\phi$ SCR (range-corrected micromho) to CS_2^+ in phases
2 and 4 for each subject. Column 4 shows the number of scale points by which each
subject favorably revalued the UCS between the end of phase 2 and the beginning
of phase 4. See text for further elaboration

| | Mean ϕ SCR to CS_2^+ | | UCS revaluation (no. of scale points revalued) |
Subject	Phase 2	Phase 4	
A	0.01	0.0	3
B	0.28	0.35	1
C	0.24	0.23	0
D	0.03	0.08	1
E	0.05	0.02	2
F	0.05	0.01	3
G	0.12	0.12	1

consistent with the view that CR_2 is mediated by UCS cognitions. The
rationale for including this group in Experiment II was that if responding to
CS_2 had been established through S–R associations (i.e. CS_2 had become
linked with CR_1), then any subsequent information about the tone UCS
would be incapable of influencing CR_2 since a UCS representation would
play no role in mediating the response. If we assume that the results from
Group H do indicate that internal representations of the tone affect CR_2
strength, then the data from Group $\bar{T}$ are further evidence that the second-
order electrodermal responses observed in these experiments are mediated
by knowledge of the UCS and not by reflexive S–R associations.

AN ASSOCIATIVE VIEW OF HUMAN CLASSICAL CONDITIONING

The two experiments just described are more akin to the proverbial signpost
than the destination. They demonstrate that certain inferential techniques
can be useful in determining the content of human learning in a fairly simple
classical conditioning paradigm. But what are the implications of this signpost? One implication, I believe, is that a useful theory of human classical
conditioning can be constructed around an associative framework, and that
this account will also be able to address uniquely human questions related to
the effects of instructions and of conscious awareness of contingencies.

What are the implications of the present results for an associative account?
They suggest that during second-order electrodermal conditioning, human *Ss*
probably form associations between CS_2 and an internal representation of

the UCS, a result which is at variance with the learning reported during second-order conditioning in animals: animals in similar aversive situations seem to acquire CS_2–CR_1 associations (Rescorla, 1973; 1977; Rizley and Rescorla, 1972) Why this anomaly? One difference between the present human study and the animal experiments is that animals tend to receive UCSs which evoke much larger emotional reactions than those UCSs given to human Ss: the electric shock given to a rat S is considerably more traumatic than that given to humans (who also have the option to withdraw from the experiment). Since these autonomic reactions must be quite large relative to those evoked in the human conditioning laboratory, it is not unreasonable to suppose that the animal's reaction will often overshadow other more innocuous events—especially during second-order conditioning—and become associated with preceding events (thus forming S–R type associations). During second-order conditioning in the experiments reported in this chapter, human Ss had at least three contiguous associations available; (i) between CS_2 and CS_1, (ii) between CS_2 and CR_1, and (iii) between CS_2 and the internal representation (or memory) of the UCS evoked by CS_1. Since the response to CS_1 (i.e. CR_1) was relatively quite small (and indeed many Ss were unable to discriminate when an SCR was occurring and when one was not), and CS_1 itself was a fairly neutral stimulus, it is arguably the case that the most salient event would be the memory of the UCS evoked by CS_1, and it is this that is likely to become processed with CS_2.

This leads to the question of what conditions establish what associations? We have moved away from the position that particular learning paradigms (e.g. first- or second-order conditioning) result in particular associations to suggest that factors which affect whether a referent will be attended to are important determinants of the constituents of associations. Furthermore, in second-order conditioning it is not unreasonable to suppose that one could experimentally manipulate the consequence of CS_2 that enters into association with CS_2. For instance, one could increase the intensity of CS_1 or, in the case of human Ss, provide information which focuses the attention of the S on CS_1 (e.g. 'estimate the size of the triangle (CS_1) you see on the screen'). Such manipulations according to the present view, might foster CS_2–Cs_1 associations during second-order conditioning, and would imply that second-order responding is mediated through the integration of CS_2–CS_1 and CS_1–UCS associations. Secondly, it might be possible to generate S–R associations by using more intense UCSs—especially in the case of human Ss who normally receive quite mild aversive UCSs.

Finally, how does this associative account relate to the currently popular 'levels of conditioning' view of human classical conditioning? I can perhaps provide a few speculative—but pursuable—suggestions.

First, higher-level 'relational learning' in the dual-level view is one which requires evaluation of CS–UCS contingencies before conditioning occurs. This implies that learning is mediated by CS-evocation of a memory of the UCS ('retrieval of information about the significance of the CS') and an evaluation of the status of the UCS (e.g. is it 'nasty'). In other words, the CR is mediated by CS-evoked knowledge of the UCS. Such learning, as we have indicated in the experiments discussed in this chapter, is susceptible to modification by experimental alterations to the value of the UCS (e.g. habituation) and by instructions providing information about the nature and occurrence of the UCS. This being the case, the body of literature which reports the rapid and dramatic effect of instructions on autonomic CRs (cf. Brewer, 1974) may reflect the effects of instructions on CRs which are mediated by representations of the UCS. Instructions may act directly by altering the structure of knowledge about the UCS (i.e. by revaluing the UCS and its relations with other events). This proposition is consistent with a variety of findings in the literature, not just when *Ss* are informed about the relationship between CS and UCS (e.g. instructed conditioning or extinction), but also when they are given false information about the UCS. Under these latter conditions they react in accordance with this new—but spurious—evaluation of the UCS (e.g. Deane, 1969; Epstein and Clarke, 1970; Spence and Goldstein, 1961). Hence, 'cognitive relational learning' may represent stimulus–stimulus or CS–UCS learning in the associative sense.

Secondly, lower level 'primitive' or 'true' conditioning may reflect the learning of relatively reflexive S–R associations.[7] In the light of earlier discussion in this chapter, such learning might be expected to take place when the *S's* response is salient and discriminable enough to overshadow other internal or external stimulation which is contiguous with the CS. Such conditions might be provided by using an intense UCS which evokes a strong UCR, or indeed by providing the *Ss* with feedback which enables them to more readily discriminate their autonomic behavior. S–R mediated responding should be relatively insensitive to post-conditioning manipulation of UCS knowledge, since this plays no part in evoking the response. Hence, instructions involving information about the UCS should have no effect on CR strength (e.g. instructed extinction), and the few studies which have demonstrated persistent conditioned responding that was apparently contrary to *Ss'* awareness of the CS–UCS contingencies may reflect S–R mediated learning (e.g. Bridger and Mandel, 1965; Mandel and Bridger, 1967; Wickens *et al.*, 1963). It is further interesting to note in this context that the *Ss* in the Bridger and Mandel (1965) study described the UCS (a 500 msec., 1.53 ma shock to the shinbone) as intense and 'very painful'. Since most studies of human autonomic conditioning use relatively mild UCSs, we might expect relatively few instances of S–R learning to occur.

SUMMARY

This chapter has advocated the use of inferential techniques in order to determine the content of learning in human classical conditioning studies. Two preliminary experiments were described which illustrated the use of this technique. The findings suggested that during second-order electrodermal conditioning, conditioned responding was mediated by knowledge of the UCS. Although this finding is at variance with results obtained from similar animal second-order conditioning studies, it can be considered to reflect differences in the salience of elements in the conditioning procedure rather than interspecific differences in associative mechanisms.

With regard to the implications of these results for current 'cognitive' accounts of human classical conditioning, it is suggested that the two 'levels' of conditioning postulated in the dual-level view of human classical conditioning may be differentiated on the basis of the associative content of the learning. 'Cognitive relational learning' may reflect CR mediation via CS–UCS associations, whilst 'primitive' or 'true' conditioning (which is relatively insensitive to instructional variables) may reflect CR mediation through S–R associations. The fact that 'cognitive relational learning' is mediated by UCS knowledge, implies that this type of learning can be influenced by any manipulation which results in a restructuring of knowledge about the UCS, and for human Ss, this includes instructions. Conversely, since UCS knowledge plays no role in mediating learning which is generated by S–R associations, such learning might be expected to be unaffected by post-conditioning UCS revaluation (either experimental or through instructions).

NOTES

1. The author is grateful to Charles Legg, Imelda McKenna, David Oakley, and Robert Rescorla for comments on earlier drafts of this chapter.

2. For convenience throughout this chapter 'animals' is used to denote non-human animals.

3. The dual-level view is primarily a theory of human *autonomic* conditioning rather than an all-embracing account of human classical conditioning.

4. Experiment I was conducted with the help of Tabitha Arulampalam.

5. A response was considered as an upward curve of the SCR within 5 sec of the onset of a stimulus, and the magnitude of the response was calculated by measuring the distance between the trough and apex of the curve; all response changes which did not result in an upward curve of the SCR were given zero value. The vast majority of trials with responses possessed only one response peak; only a handful possessed two response peaks and when this occurred only the first response was measured.

6. In a more substantial replication of Experiment II we have confirmed the finding that loss of CR_2^+ in phase 4 is associated with a favorable revaluation of the UCS by two scale points or more (Davey and McKenna, 1982).

7. This discussion pre-empts the discovery of S–R associations in humans using

post-conditioning revaluation techniques. However, from the point of view of the present account and evidence emerging from the most recent studies in our laboratory it is not an unreasonable assumption to presume they will eventually be detected.

REFERENCES

Baer P. E., and Fuhrer, M. J. (1968) Cognitive processes during differential trace and delayed conditioning of the GSR *Journal of Experimental Psychology*, **78**, 81–88.
Baer, P. E., and Fuhrer, M. J. (1970) Cognitive processes in the differential trace conditioning of electrodermal and vasomotor activity. *Journal of Experimental Psychology*, **84**, 176–178.
Baer, P. E., and Fuhrer, M. J. (1973) Unexpected effects of masking: differential EDR conditioning without relational learning. *Psychophysiology*, **10**, 95–99.
Biferno, M. A., and Dawson, M. E. (1977) The onset of contingency awareness and electrodermal classical conditioning: an analysis of temporal relationships during acquisition and extinction. *Psychophysiology*, **14**, 164–171.
Bijou, S. W., and Baer, D. M. (1966) Operant methods in child behavior and development. In W. K. Honig (ed.) *Operant Behavior: Areas of Research and Application* New York: Appleton-Century-Crofts.
Brewer, W. F. (1974) There is no convincing evidence for operant and classical conditioning in humans. In W. B. Weimer, and D. J. Palermo (eds) *Cognition and the symbolic processes*. Lawrence Erlbaum Associates: New Jersey.
Bridger, W. H., and Mandel, I. J. (1965) Abolition of the PRE by instructions in GSR conditioning. *Journal of Experimental Psychology*, **69**, 476–482.
Breland, K., and Breland M. (1966) *Animal Behavior*, New York: Macmillan.
Buchwald, A. M. (1959) Extinction after acquisition under different verbal reinforcement combinations. *Journal of Experimental Psychology*, **57**, 43–48.
Colby, J. J., and Smith, N. F. (1977) The effect of three procedures for eliminating a conditioned taste aversion in the rat. *Learning and Motivation*, **8**, 404–413.
Colgan, D. M. (1970) Effect of instructions on the skin resistance response. *Journal of Experimental Psychology*, **86**, 108–112.
Davey, G. C. L. (1981) *Animal Learning and Conditioning*, London: Macmillan.
Davey, G. C. L., and Arulampalam, T. (1982) Second-order 'fear' conditioning in humans: persistence of CR_2 following extinction CR_1. *Behaviour Research and Therapy*, **20**, 391–396.
Davey, G. C. L., and McKenna, I. (1982) The effects of post-conditioning revaluation of CS_1 and UCS following Pavlovian second-order electrodermal conditioning in humans. *Quarterly Journal of Experimental Psychology*, in press.
Dawson, M. E. (1973) Can classical conditioning occur without contingency learning? A review and evaluation of the evidence. *Psychophysiology*, **10**, 82–86.
Dawson, M. E., and Biferno, M. A. (1973) Concurrent measurement of awareness and electrodermal classical conditioning *Journal of Experimental Psychology*, **101**, 55–62.
Dawson, M. E., Catania, J. J., Schell, A. M., and Grings, W. W. (1979) Autonomic classical conditioning as a function of awareness of stimulus contingencies. *Biological Psychology*, **9**, 23–40.
Dawson, M. E., and Furedy, J. J. (1976) The role of awareness in human differential autonomic classical conditioning. The necessary-gate hypothesis. *Psychophysiology*, **13**, 50–53.
Dawson, M. E., and Grings W. W. (1968) Comparison of Classical Conditioning and Relational Learning. *Journal of Experimental Psychology*, **76**, 227–231.

Dawson, M. E., and Reardon, P. (1969) Effects of facilitatory and inhibitory sets on GSR conditioning and extinction. *Journal of Experimental Psychology*, **82**, 462–466.

Dawson, M. E., Schell, A. M., Beers, J., and Kelly, A. (1978) Cognitive processing demands during autonomic classical conditioning: probe reaction-time results. Paper presented at the meeting of the Society for Psychophysiological Research, Madison, Wisconsin.

Deane, G. E. (1969) Cardiac activity during experimentally induced anxiety. *Psychophysiology*, **6**, 17–30.

Epstein, S., and Clarke, S. (1970) Heart rate and skin conductance during experimentally induced anxiety: Effects of anticipated intensity of noxious stimulation and experience. *Journal of Experimental Psychology*, **84**, 105–112.

Erwin, E. (1978) *Behaviour therapy: Scientific, Philosophical and Moral Foundations*, London: Cambridge University Press.

Fishbein, H. D. (1967) Effects of differential instructions, differential feedback, and UCS intensity on the conditioned eyelid response. *Journal of Experimental Psychology*, **75**, 56–65.

Fuhrer, M. J., and Baer, P. E. (1969) Cognitive processes in differential GSR conditioning: effects of a masking task. *American Journal of Psychology*, **82**, 168–180.

Fuhrer, M. J., and Baer, P. E. (1980) Cognitive factors and CS–UCS interval effects in the differential conditioning and extinction of skin conductance responses. *Biological Psychology*, **10**, 283–298.

Grings, W. W. (1965) Verbal-perceptual factors in the conditioning of autonomic responses. In W. F. Prokasy (ed.) *Classical Conditioning: A Symposium*, New York: Appleton-Century-Crofts.

Grings, W. W. (1973) Cognitive factors in electrodermal conditioning. *Psychological Bulletin*, **79**, 200–210.

Grings, W. W., and Dawson, M. E. (1973) Complex conditioning. In W. F. Prokasy and D. C. Raskin (eds) *Electrodermal Activity in Psychological Research*, New York: Academic Press.

Holland, P. C., and Rescorla, R. A. (1975) The effects of two ways of devaluing the unconditioned stimulus after first- and second-order appetitive conditioning. *Journal of Experimental Psychology: Animal Behavior Processes*, **1**, 355–363.

Holland, P. C., and Straub, J. J. (1979) Differential effects of two ways of devaluing the conditioned stimulus after Pavlovian appetitive conditioning. *Journal of Experimental Psychology: Animal Behavior Processes*, **5**, 65–78.

Katz, A., Webb, L., and Stotland, E. (1971) Cognitive influences on the rate of GSR extinction. *Journal of Experimental Research in Personality*, **5**, 208–215.

Koenig, K. P., and Castillo, D. D. (1969) False feedback and longevity of the conditioned GSR during extinction: some implications for aversion therapy. *Journal of Experimental Psychology*, **74**, 505–510.

Leyland, C. M. (1977) Higher-order autoshaping. *Quarterly Journal of Experimental Psychology*, **29**, 607–619.

Lowe, C. F. (1979) Determinants of human operant behaviour. In M. D. Zeiler and P. Harzem (eds) *Reinforcement and the Organization of Behaviour*, Vol 1. Chichester: John Wiley.

Mandel, I. J., and Bridger, W. H. (1967) Interaction between instructions and ISI in conditioning and extinction of the GSR. *Journal of Experimental Psychology*, **74**, 36–43.

McComb, D. (1969) Cognitive and learning effects in the production of GSR conditioning data. *Psychonomic Science*, **16**, 96–97.

Norris, E. B., and Grant, D. A. (1948) Eyelid conditioning as affected by verbally induced inhibitory set and counter reinforcement. *American Journal of Psychology*, **61**, 37–49.

Öhman, A. (1979) The orienting response, attention, and learning: An information-processing perspective. In H. D. Kimmel, E. H. Van Olst, and J. F. Orlebecke (eds) *The Orienting Reflex in Humans*, **87**, 532–552.

Pearce, J. M., and Hall, G. (1980) A model for Pavlovian learning: variations in the effectiveness of conditioned but not of unconditioned stimuli. *Psychological Review*, **87**, 532–553.

Prokasy, W. F., and Allen, C. K. (1969) Instructional set in human differential eyelid conditioning. *Journal of Experimental Psychology*, **80**, 271–278.

Rashotte, M. E., Griffin, R. W., and Sisk, C. L. (1977) Second-order conditioning of the pigeon's key peck. *Animal Learning and Behavior*, **5**, 25–38.

Razran, G. (1955) Conditioning and perception. *Psychological Review*, **62**, 83–95.

Razran, G. (1971) *Mind in Evolution*. New York: Houghton Mifflin.

Rescorla, R. A. (1973) Second-order conditioning: implications for theories of learning. In F. J. McGuigan and D. Lumsden (eds) *Contemporary Approaches to Learning and Conditioning*. New York: Winston.

Rescorla, R. A. (1977) Pavlovian second-order conditioning: some implications for instrumental behavior. In H. Davis and H. M. B. Hurwitz (eds) *Operant-Pavlovian Interactions*. Hillsdale, N.J.: Lawrence Erlbaum Assoc.

Rescorla, R. A. (1980) *Pavlovian Second-order Conditioning: Studies in Associative Learning*. Hillsdale, N.J.: Lawrence Erlbaum Assoc.

Rizley, R. C., and Rescorla, R. A. (1972) Associations in second-order conditioning and sensory preconditioning. *Journal of Comparative and Physiological Psychology*, **81**, 1–11.

Ross, L. E., Ferreira, M. C., and Ross, S. M. (1974) Backward masking of conditioned stimuli: Effects on differential and single-cue classical conditioning performance. *Journal of Experimental Psychology*, **103**, 603–613.

Shettleworth, S. J. (1972) Constraints on learning. *Advances in the Study of Behavior*, **4**, 1–68.

Spence, K. W., and Goldstein, H. (1961) Eyelid conditioning performance as a function of emotion-producing instructions. *Journal of Experimental Psychology*, **62**, 291–294.

Swenson, R. P., and Hill, F. A. (1970) Effects of instruction and interstimulus interval in human GSR conditioning. *Psychonomic Science*, **21**, 369–370.

Wagner, A. R. (1978) Expectancies and the priming of STM. In S. H. Hulse, H. Fowler, and W. K. Honig (eds) *Cognitive Processes in Animal Behavior*, Hillsdale, N. J.: Lawrence Erlbaum Assoc.

Wickens, D. D., Allen, C. K., and Hill, F. A. (1963) Effects of instructions and UCS strength on extinction of the conditioned GSR. *Journal of Experimental Psychology*, **66**, 235–240.

Wilson, G. D. (1968) Reversal of differential GSR conditioning by instructions. *Journal of Experimental Psychology*, **76**, 491–493.

Wilson, R. A., Fuhrer, M. J., and Baer, P. E. (1973) Differential conditioning of electrodermal responses: Effects of performing a masking task during the interstimulus and intertrial intervals. *Biological Psychology*, **2**, 33–46.

Section II

Evolutionary Aspects

Evolutionary theory provides a framework or set of principles by which we can begin to understand the behavior of organisms. They are not reductionist principles, they are functionalist. It leads to asking the question 'Why do we behave like such-and-such?' in the sense of 'what purpose does such-and-such a behavior serve?' As I have already suggested in the preface to this volume, evolutionary theory is important to extrapolation from animals to man in that it should provide general principles which at some time have governed the behavior of all living organisms; thus if we can understand the general principles by which evolution exerts its influence over behavior in one particular species, those principles should—without much modification—find application to the behavior of other species, including human beings. This section of the book deals with some of the issues raised by application of these general principles.

First, does human behavior stand the test of evolutionary biology? Do we behave the way we do because at some point in the history of our species, behaving in a particular way increased our inclusive fitness? Alternatively, do we currently exhibit behavior patterns which optimize our inclusive fitness? In the 1970s these were questions which were being asked primarily about non-human animals; more recently, however, sociobiology has been applied to many aspects of human behavior, some examples of which will follow.

Secondly, although we might feel that evolutionary theory offers significant benefits to an understanding of behavior, it is still not clear exactly *how* evolutionary theory should be interpreted in order to make comparisons between species. For instance, should we be making comparisons between species with common ancestors; or between species that have evolved similarly structured and functioning central nervous systems; or between species that share similar ecological conditions. Whichever approach one adopts can lead to quite different conclusions, and this problem is clearly one which has implications for extrapolation from animals to humans—not the least being the topic of brain function itself.

Finally, an evolutionary analysis of human behavior inevitably raises the question of whether we have evolved both psychological and social processes which nullify the effect of evolutionary variables. For instance, have we evolved a generalized intelligence which allows us to mould our own environment rather than vice versa; an intelligence which may even foster behavior which is quite contrary to the interests of our inclusive fitness? Furthermore, if it can be shown that the cultural inheritance of our species has more relevance to our current behavior patterns than, say, any talk of inclusive fitness, then does evolutionary biology have anything meaningful to contribute to an understanding of human society? This issue is at present a hotly debated one, and occurs frequently in the contributions that follow.

Animal Models of Human Behavior
Edited by G. C. L. Davey
© 1983 John Wiley & Sons Ltd

Chapter 7

The Functions of Learning and Cross-Species Comparisons

H. C. PLOTKIN

The use of animal models as a means of furthering the understanding of the behavior of man is partly an exercise in comparative analysis. That being so, a distinction should be drawn between proper comparative study and inappropriate comparative statements. The former uses methods that have a substantive and explicit conceptual framework. The framework may be subject to argument and disagreement, as for example homology and anagenetics both are, but the distinctive feature of such an approach is that the comparison is made 'with thought'. Inappropriate comparative statements are characterized by the arbitrary use of any one (or more) species and the casual extrapolation of findings to other species. In such cases a conceptual basis for comparative analysis is absent.

One should not confuse comparative analysis with the intensive study of behavior in some single species such as the rat or pigeon. A strong case can be made for the value of a deep understanding of the behavior of any one species achieved either through observation or controlled experimental procedures. However, such work should be seen for what it is and not as comparative study. It is also important to note that the distinction being drawn here between proper comparative study and inappropriate comparative statements does not rest on some common–uncommon dimension. It is not the case that work involving pigeons or rats is necessarily poor comparative science whereas that with gulls or squirrels is good. Valid as Beach's (1950) comment was, and still is, regarding the ill-considered restriction of comparative studies to a few common laboratory species, it is not the point that is being made here. To repeat: the essence of a comparative approach is a conceptual framework; the actual species used is merely a consequence of that framework.

With the exception of the classical ethologists, whose primary aim was the advancement of biology rather than the science of man, the use of proper comparative behavioral analysis has been rare. The proper comparative analysis of learning has been even more rare. Also, the function of learning raises some difficult issues. For these reasons, the principal aim of this chapter is to demonstrate that one should be wary of using animal models at the present time to understand learning processes in man. The argument will proceed as follows: first the types of permissible usage of animal models, their limitations, and their application to man will be outlined; this will be followed by a brief consideration of the function of learning and the implications of this for the comparative analysis of learning; the proper frameworks for the comparative analysis of learning will be described; and this chapter will end with a pessimistic view of the validity of currently extrapolating an understanding of learning from animals to man.

1. THE USE OF ANIMAL MODELS

Quite apart from whether comparative studies are performed within an appropriate conceptual framework or not is the question as to why anyone should wish to use animal models in order to further the understanding of human learning. There are, it seems to me, only two cases where recourse to the use of animal models is both necessary and justified. Each has severe problems associated with it.

1.1 The requirement for controlled experimental manipulation

The screening of possible pharmacological agents, and testing for the effects of potentially toxic substances such as lead, requires controlled experimental study. A related area of enquiry is the use of animal models for the construction of schemes of brain function which purport to have some generality beyond the rodents on which they are primarily based. The necessity for using animal models under these circumstances is not in doubt. What are questionable, are the animal models that are used.

Under these conditions of applied research, the behavior of both the animal models and the people to which the results are applied are relatively 'normal'. By this is meant that even under the most adverse conditions of mental abnormality or the effects of powerful drugs, the behavior of animal model or man are recognizably those characteristic of the species of the model or of *Homo sapiens* respectively, and in any individual case more like that of normal conspecifics than that of other species. Under these circumstances of relative normality, the phylogenetic distance between the model and man does become a factor—in some approaches an important factor; so too does the power of the behavioral analysis; and so too is the general conceptual framework within which the comparisons between animal models and man are made. For example, whether conditioning in the mouse has anything to do with learning in the human child is an old and unresolved debate. It none the less is a debate of real substance. In the terms being expressed here, it must be resolved around three issues. First, the relationship between man and mouse and the consideration, practical difficulties aside, as to whether some other species might not be a more appropriate model: Second, whether conditioning is present in both species, and the role and importance of conditioning to both species in terms of behavioral adaptations of individual animals to specific environmental demands: Finally, whether the comparisons are to be made in terms of phylogenetics, anagenetic grades, ecological convergence, or some other conceptual framework. In other words, any comparison that involves the mouse as model to elucidate human learning and performance must be done 'with thought'.

It is disturbing to find so little evidence of thought in this regard. If one surveys the pages of the major pharmacological and toxicological journals one finds that the use of species remains in the early 1980s what it was in the 1950s. Nor has there been any change in the kinds of behavioral testing procedures such as the use of various reinforcement schedules, one- or two-way avoidance learning, passive avoidance learning, and variations on open-field testing. It is not just the banality of these procedures that is worrying. It is the lack of serious attempts to argue about the relationships between the behavior used in these tests and the normal behavior of either model or man. It is worth noting that when such analysis is undertaken by scientists working outside of these applied areas, as for example by Bolles (1970) or Rozin and Kalat (1971), the results are not encouraging. Finally, there has certainly been no change in the cavalier extrapolation of findings across species which continues to be done without the discipline and constraint of any kind of coherent conceptual framework.

There is another way of putting all this. Whatever the merits or otherwise of biological approaches to learning, and they have been criticized (Johnston, 1981; Shettleworth, 1981; Plotkin and Odling-Smee, 1982), there has been a real increase in awareness in recent years of the need for studies of learning to satisfy the requirements of biological as well as psychological principles. It is as if the investigators who screen drugs and develop functional models of the brain have been completely passed by in the course of these developments.

The situation is of especial concern when one considers the role that the behavioral testing of animal models plays in the establishment of theoretical schemes of brain functions, including that of the human brain. Behavior in this context is the interpretative interface between the results of various kinds of neurological manipulations and competing schemes of basic psychological constructs and how the brain subserves these and generates behavior. This

means that the theoretical assumptions that the investigator makes about
these psychological constructs and how these relate to behavior become an
important determinant of the model of brain function that is constructed. It
follows that if the behavioral analysis were different (i.e. if either or both
the testing procedures and the theoretical assumptions of the investigator
were different), then so too would be the resultant schemes of brain function.
For example, if instead of a behaviorist–associationist tradition in the laboratory, a social-cognitive overview had been the prevalent mode of thought
in physiological and pharmacological psychology over the last thirty or forty
years, we would now have very different theories and models of brain function in our journals and textbooks. The consequences are not merely academic. Therapeutic measures, pharmacological, surgical and others are
directly influenced by such theoretical schemes of brain function. Yet the
rationale behind these and the form that they take are tenuous and uncertain.
They are largely the outcome of the coincidence between a particular way of
thinking by experimental psychologists and that period in the 1950s when the
unprecedented burgeoning of studies in physiological psychology occurred,
rather than the consequences of rational analysis.

1.2 Proper comparative analysis

The only other case where the use of animal models is justified is when they
are part of a proper comparative analysis to further the understanding of
human learning. The rationale for such work is the same as all other comparative study. Namely that cataloging similarities and differences between
species in terms of specified attributes will supply information about function,
about adaptedness to particular ecological demands, and possibly about
origins. In the special case of comparative studies that include human data,
the additional aim is to validate the use of specific animal models for the
purposes described in case 1.1 above.

As already indicated, there are remarkably few such studies, even when
the conventional definition of learning is extended to encompass the incor-
poration of all aspects of environmental order, thus including the learning of
motor skills, language, reasoning, and general cognitive development. It is
not intended to review such studies here, but rather to consider the merits
and demerits that different approaches have. Before doing so, however, it
is necessary to consider the function(s) of learning.

2. THE FUNCTION(S) OF LEARNING

A conceptual framework is necessary but not sufficient for comparative study.
Agreement as to what is being compared, and consistency across investigators
as to the defining criteria of what is being compared, are also necessary.

Thus whatever reason may be advanced for comparing my foot with my hand, my other foot, someone else's foot, or the foot of an ape, there must be some consensus as to what a foot is. There are only two kinds of defining criteria: structure and function. There is no denying that the use of both will often sharpen the definition of an attribute and there is no reason to consider either as exclusive of the other. But there are only the two. There is also no denying the importance of environmental interdependence for both form and function, though this is not a point at issue here. The structural definition of foot presents no problem (everything distal of the tibia and fibula), and, of course, it was structure, especially skeletal structure, that formed the basis for the development of comparative biology over the last two centuries. Function presents more problems.

I take function in this context to mean that which has been selected for. First, it is necessary to distinguish between use and function. I may, for example, kick balls with my foot, but no-one will argue for the kicking of balls as having been selected for in the evolution of the human foot. On the other hand the evolution of bipedalism has placed important functional demands on the human foot, but bipedal gait is dependent upon numerous other structural adaptations as well. This is the second problem. It is a general rule that functions and structures are related in one:many and many:one ways, and so comparative analyses based on function usually have only loose structural underpinning. That brings us to the third problem. Unless functions are tied to structures there is a strong sense of the ephemeral, the abstract and the transient about them. Atz (1970) identifies the disjunction between structure and function as the principal cause of failure in applying the concept of homology to behavior.

It is worth noting that there are exceptions. For example, hemoglobin, hemocyanin, hemerythrin, and chlorocruorin are structurally different respiratory pigments. But there is no argument as to their identity of function achieved by the same functional property of rapid association and dissociation with oxygen. Furthermore, much is known (see Steen, 1974) about variations in chemical structure of different pigments in different species and the way in which these differences relate to the pressure at which they take up or yield oxygen, which in turn relates to whether the pigment is storing or transporting oxygen. The point of this example is that the simplicity of the structure–function relationship in this instance allows for strong inferences to be made on the basis of comparative data, the strength of inference coming from the comparative physiologists knowing exactly what they are comparing, both structurally and functionally.

How does all this apply to learning? At present very little is known of learning in structural terms, neither physiologically nor neurochemically. There is certainly not enough to form a structural basis for comparative studies of learning. The whole weight of analysis must, therefore, rest on function. But what is the function of learning? Is there some single or generic function of learning, or are there many different functions? It is a remarkable fact that despite the prominence of functionalism in psychology in general, and the reflection of this in texts dealing with learning—Hilgard and Bower (1975) for example devote an entire chapter to functionalism—there have been few serious analyses of the function of learning. The treatment of function has usually been prefatory (as, for example, Skinner's (1953) excellent but all too brief discussion on the limitations of inherited behavior), rather than being seen as central to a theory of learning. Exceptions to this have been the series of essays that have attempted to derive the function of learning from the limitations of genetic and developmental information-gaining processes (Plotkin and Odling-Smee, 1979; 1981; 1982) and the work of Johnston (Johnston and Turvey, 1980; Johnston, 1981; 1982). Although Johnston's views emphasize an ecological approach to learning (see below), in so far as he sees learning as a form of 'middle term adaptation' his views on function are not seriously at variance with ours.

The position that we have tried to argue for is that the generic function of learning is a special form of phenotypic flexibility that evolves as a response to specific kinds and rates of environmental change. In itself this is not an especially original view, but it does have one real strength. This is that flexibility cannot be isolated as some abstracted quality or attribute. It has to be associated with specific traits—flexibility in sexual preference, flexibility in choice of diet, flexibility in adoption of a dialect, flexibility in moving about space, and so on. Flexibility is not an inclusive or enveloping characteristic. There are animals that are flexible in habitat choice but inflexible in vocal output. The number of possibilities is very large. The particular profile that any one species presents will be the outcome of its evolutionary history, its structural constraints and the selection pressures exerted by its ecology. In any single animal, there will also be developmental factors operating.

The significance of this view for comparative studies of learning is that cross-species comparisons must be based on the functions of learning as learning relates to specific traits whose flexibility *has been selected for*. Studies of dialect in birdsong (Marler, 1981) or imprinting (Immelmann, 1975) are examples of such specific functional flexibility.

This brings us to the issue of the learning paradigms and processes. Most psychological studies of comparative learning have used standardized laboratory procedures, the paradigms, in which experimental requirements that exploit a learning ability are imposed upon the learner by the investigator. This work is reviewed in a variety of sources (Bitterman, 1975; Corning *et al.*, 1973a; 1973b; 1975; Dewsbury, 1978; Warren, 1973; 1977). It has centered upon the use of complex procedures such as probability learning, reversal learning, and learning set formation, and on the standard classical conditioning and instrumental learning paradigms. The work on vertebrates is characterized by rigorous experimentation and high technical standards. However, a distinction was drawn earlier between use and function. The paradigms bear to learning the same relationship that kicking a ball does to bipedalism. The paradigm approach exploits a use of learning, but until such time as they can be related to the ecological functions of learning (see Johnston, 1981), their value to comparative studies of learning is limited. For the same reasons, studies of language learning in apes have little value as comparative analyses of learning.

What of the processes of learning? There are three points to be made. The first is that in the literature on learning there is much inconsistency and confusion surrounding the terms 'processes' and 'principles' (Plotkin and Odling-Smee, 1982). At an intuitive level, though, everyone would seem to be referring to 'how learning works' in the sense of how the structures underlying learning are expressed in behavioral terms. If this is correct, then in part the problem of processes will eventually be absorbed into the language of neuroscience, that is structure in the physiological, anatomical, and neurochemical sense. Second, the concentration on processes has been closely tied to the paradigms approach and its usefulness to comparative study in the form that it has been propounded is therefore doubtful. Third, it obviously cannot be argued that the study of process is not central to an understanding of learning. If, however, the arguments presented earlier about the discrete functional nature of learning is correct (that is, that learning has function only in so far as it serves specific forms of behavior and never merely as abstracted flexibility), then the study of processes also becomes a part of the study of how flexibility is locked in to these specific behavioral forms. In practical terms this means that analyses such as that of Rescorla and Wagner (1972) that are concerned with processes such as increments in the associative strength of stimulus events must be extended to show how this occurs in the context of specific forms of behavioral flexibility such as food or habitat selection that have been selected for. Work on foraging (Lea, 1981) is an excellent example of how this can begin to be done.

There is one final point to be made about the function of learning and its comparative study. Let us suppose that neuroscientists were able to present us with irrefutable evidence of a neuronal module, a kind of miniature nervous system (Jerison, 1976), that is the same in all vertebrates that learn. In other words, a learning analog of hemoglobin which is a biochemical characteristic of the subphylum. Would we then have the luxury of dealing with a simple structure-function relationship as occurs with the respiratory pigments? I think not. The reason for this pessimism is that behavior as a set of phenotypic attributes is qualitatively different from all other phenotypic attributes. The difference lies in the dynamic interrelationship that exists between behavior and the environment; this difference has found expression

in notions such as Piaget's (1971) dialectic of assimilation and accommo-
dation, and Gibson's (1977) theory of affordances; and it is the difference
between more passive phenotypic traits that are mostly the outcome of
evolutionary processes and active traits that are also causal in evolution.
Thus there is only a weak analogy between behavioral and other phenotypic
attributes. Learning serves to heighten the dynamic nature of behavior, and
thus reduces further any analogies that might be drawn between behavioral
and non-behavioral attributes of the phenotype.

3. THE CONCEPTUAL FRAMEWORKS FOR COMPARATIVE ANALYSES

The comparative method has been a cornerstone of biological science for at
least 200 years. The history of the way the method has been used reflects
changes in the paradigms of biology. Following the Darwinian revolution,
the method became coherent around the notions of homology, analogy, and
related ideas (see Ghiselin, 1969; 1976). Its contribution to that revolution
was enormous, both by way of the study of systematics as well as supplying
the necessary information on organic change in time which provided the basis
for inferences on the non-fixity of species and the operation of natural
selection. Thus the method has been central to theory construction in biology.
In the last few decades it has been partially eclipsed by more dynamic
disciplines such as ecology and development. However, cross-species comparisons continue to be a part of virtually all contemporary treatments of
evolutionary biology; if not in a central role, then in the more peripheral
one of indicating the generality of statements and the diversity of nature.
This is as true of behavioral studies as any other area (see, for example
Alcock, 1979; Immelmann, 1980). Lorenz (1974) remarked in his Nobel Prize
address that he considered his application of the comparative method to
behavior to be his 'most important contribution to science' (pp. 231).

There are, I think, three conceptual approaches to the use of the comparative method that seem to be distinctively different from one another and
for that reason I will describe each separately as it applies to learning. None,
however, is exclusive of the others and there are a number of ways by which
they may be linked.

3.1 Homology

When phenotypic traits in two different species show some similarity and
that similarity can be shown to be due to a common ancestor to the two
species, the ancestor having had an attribute that is the precursor of the traits
in the extant species, then those traits are homologous. There are a number
of related concepts such as homoplasy, homomorphy, homogeny, and iter-

ative homology (all discussed in Masterton *et al.*, 1976) which indicates how fraught with difficulty comparative analysis is. In some cases certain of these, especially homoplasy (similarity between species but where precursors in a common ancestor cannot be established) may seem to be better suited to the other kinds of comparative analyses and hence considered in the following two subsections. But the notion of homology is quite specific in that its distinctiveness is grounded in the view that comparative studies should be undertaken within a phylogenetic perspective. Comparative analysis in terms of homology is rooted in what is known about phylogenetic relatedness.

Until recently and in biology at large, homology has been at the center of most comparative studies. The European ethologists were trained as biologists and hence it was to homology that they turned in their own work. The few major comparative behavioral studies that have been carried out, such as that on courtship displays in ducks (Lorenz, 1972) and the behavior of gulls (Tinbergen, 1959), have all been based on homology. There is, however, argument as to whether the concept of homology has any real meaning (de Beer, 1958; Waddington, 1969): and if it has, whether it can be validly applied to behavior (see Atz, 1970 and Klopfer, 1973 for examples). Judgment on the first and weightier issue must wait on further evidence as to what happens at speciation to the instructions underlying phenotypic characters and on how genes are translated into those characters. My view on the latter has been summarized elsewhere (Plotkin, 1979). I believe that homology can be applied to behavior. It does, however, set certain requirements on how the analysis must proceed and these will be briefly considered as they might apply to learning.

The first of these requirements concerns the criteria of homology which, in the terms used in the previous section, define what it is one is comparing with what. These criteria are reviewed in Atz (1970). The principal ones are position, special quality, and continuity. If one retains a view of learning as some form (or forms) of abstract behavioral flexibility, then only the criterion of special quality can be applied with any certainty to comparative learning study based on homology. If continuity is used to mean ontogenetic as well as phylogenetic continuity then it might be possible to use the third criterion as well. However, as argued in the previous section, abstracted function is not a sufficient basis for comparisons of learning. The functions must be embodied in specific behaviors the flexibility of which has been selected for. In this case, there is the possibility of using all three criteria. For example, if one is concerned with the comparative analysis of learning in establishing food preferences, then the way in which food preferences change with experience can be tied firmly to developmental factors (continuity), specific foraging, and feeding patterns which are often relatively stereotyped (position), as well as whatever special qualities might be found to accompany such learning, for instance the temporal parameters relating to the observation and intake of food or the requirements for specific kinds of learning experiences such as exposure to parental or sibling feeding.

The second requirement set by homology concerns the species that must be used. Since homology is based on phylogeny it is no more than common sense that initial studies must use animals that are thought to be relatively closely related. Only with a firmly established base would one then expand the analysis to less closely related species in order to assess the systematic distribution of a particular learning trait. However, there is another issue here. A number of writers (Atz, 1970; Baerends, 1958; Lehrman, 1953; Tinbergen, 1963), sometimes representing rather different approaches to behavior, seem to agree about the acute problems set by convergent evolution of behavior and the unique difficulty posed for comparison by markedly different neurological organizations and psychological levels in widely different animals. Atz, for example, writes that 'the whole neural-behavioral organization of the bird is so unlike that of the mammal that any similarities in behavior between them must be attributed to convergence' (Atz, 1970, pp. 65). Assuming that Baerends and Tinbergen agree with Atz, which they do seem to do, then what is being said is that homology may be used as a framework for comparison but only if one respects the boundaries set by grades of organization (see next section). In other words, homology must be tempered by the additional notions of anagenesis. The significance of this is that the conceptual difficulties attaching to anagenesis are at least as great as those attaching to homology.

One last point should be made about homology. Work on imprinting and birdsong has shown how fruitful comparative studies based on closely related species can be. But the total number of learning studies done explicitly within the framework of homology is exceedingly small—certainly not enough to form an adequate basis from which to judge the approach.

3.2 Anagenesis

Comparative studies of learning have most frequently used representatives from different orders (rats, monkeys, dogs, etc.), and often different classes (mammals, reptiles, birds, etc.). Reviews of learning in various invertebrate phyla also often compare across classes, for example polychaete and oligochaete annelids, or insects and crustacea. Because so little is known of invertebrate learning, there is also a tendency to review all invertebrate work in single papers or chapters. This has the, presumably unintentional, effect of forcing the reader into comparisons across phyla. The lack of 'phylogenetic discipline' in such work is partly due to the still widespread belief that there is one or at most only a few general processes of learning present in widely different species of learners (see Plotkin and Odling-Smee, 1982 for a detailed evaluation of this assumption). Indeed the paucity of comparative learning studies can be attributed directly to the prevalence of general process theory—if your basic tenet is the identity of learning across species then the only rationale for comparative study is to invoke the learning–performance dichotomy and to claim that an identical learning process manifests itself differently as a function of species-specific performance differences. This precisely is one of Bitterman's (1975) claims: 'Since performance in learning situations is determined by a variety of processes other than learning, differences in performance may be due to differences in processes other than learning' (pp. 206). This certainly does not represent all the views that Bitterman holds on comparative learning studies. But it does, in my view, express the belief of many comparative psychologists that what they are really looking at is comparative performance not comparative learning. There is, however, an alternative way of viewing the learning of such widely disparate species. This is in terms of anagenesis and grades of organization.

The notion of anagenesis, progress in evolution, is ancient. In this century it has been championed by Huxley (1958) and Rensch (1959) and recently has found renewed and explicit support (Gould, 1976; Jerison, 1980; Yarczower and Hazlett, 1977). It has been informally and implicitly used by every psychologist who thinks of animals in terms of a phylogenetic scale, and also by biologists who frequently refer to higher and lower vertebrates. As already mentioned, the notion of levels of psychological function is an anagenetic notion even though the word is not to be found in that literature. (It should be noted that some cladists use the word anagenesis to refer to *within*-species changes over time which may lead, without 'splitting', to a new species. This, however, is idiosyncratic usage. As used here, anagenesis refers specifically to *across*-species trends, possibly taxonomically quite distantly related animals.)

The central tenet of anagenesis is that successive species in a lineage may show improvement in structures and functions that can be conceptualized as a succession of grades. 'Grades are successive levels of organization defined as stages in the improvement of an organic design for some specified function. There is nothing mystical or orthogenetic in a temporal sequence of grades in the history of a major group; to engender such a sequence, recourse needs to be had to little more than the evolutionary platitudes that: (1) better designs tend to be favored by natural selection, and (2) animals entering new adaptative zones are generally suboptimal in design because of constraints of heritage' (Gould, 1976, pp. 117). An anagenetic approach to comparative analysis, then, is one which takes representatives of different grades and compares them in terms of some particular attribute in order to assess how that attribute is altered across grades; or it selects different species occupying a single grade in order to assess how relatively unrelated species achieve the same level of organization. Thus, whereas the comparative method based on homology chooses its species on the basis of presumed phylogenetic relatedness, anagenetic analysis dictates choice of species on the basis of what grades are occupied by what species and hence may use unrelated species. Obviously it will usually be the case that the same grades are occupied by related species, but that is not necessarily the case and it is not the point of an anagenetic analysis.

Whatever merits anagenetic thinking may have and however devoid of orthogenetic content, there clearly is a potential for damaging confusion between the concepts of improvement and progress. Improvement can in theory at least be objectively defined and measured in terms of excellence of design. Progress, on the other hand, evokes the response of 'progress towards what?', and is a word heavily loaded with finalism. Most psychologists, for example, use progress to mean 'getting closer to man' which is equated with excellence. In some sense it may indeed be equated with excellence and improvement in certain dimensions. But the implication is that evolution has occurred towards a goal, namely man, and that is biological nonsense.

There are other difficulties with an anagenetic approach that relate to its practical use. Briefly, these are that though 'design' or 'engineering' criteria may be an excellent idea, in practice, especially when considering behavioral and psychological grades, they are in fact subjectively defined. Second, whatever criteria are being used they must define a *quantitative* dimension along which animals can be ordered. A third problem is knowing where the boundaries of a grade lie—where does one end and another begin. This leads to a fourth difficulty. How does one choose a representative of a grade for comparative study if one does not really know the limits of a grade? To answer that some species are clearly typical of a grade is not enough. A comparative framework must allow one to place any species and an anagenetic approach to behavior does not provide for this.

In the terms set out earlier in this chapter as to what is necessary for comparative study—knowing what species to compare and with regard to what attribute the comparisons are to be made—anagenetic analysis is a weak approach to use in comparative studies. There are, it seems to me, two possible ways of improving on matters. First, it may prove worthwhile to anchor an anagenetic analysis of behavior in grades that are not defined by behavioral dimensions. The obvious example is Jerison's (1973) encephalization quotient (EQ) which is a true dimension based upon objectively measured structural attributes. EQ is a measure of the brain size that a species actually has when compared to the brain size that would be expected on the basis of body size alone. The EQ of man and dolphin are approximately the same (about 6 or 7) and quite distinctly greater than the EQs of any other mammals. They form, that is, a separate grade. The great apes form another grade with EQs of around 1.5 to 2.5; horses, dogs, and lemurs form part of another grade, rats and mice yet another, and so on. Jerison's own assumptions are that EQ reflects information-processing capacity beyond that required to control routine bodily functions and hence that representatives from different EQ grades will differ in processing capacity; this, in turn, will show itself, amongst other cognitive differences, in differences in learning (Jerison, personal communication). Intuitively it seems that the hypothesis that different EQ grades will demonstrate different cognitive capacities must be correct. But can it be shown to comprise some kind of dimension? And can it be demonstrated with learning? The answer to these last questions is not intuitively obvious, but surely is worth attempting to answer.

The second and less promising approach is that instead of defining grades non-behaviorally (albeit in terms of a dimension that may seem to have behavioral relevance, as does EQ), may it not be possible to establish grades using behavioral dimensions themselves? Obviously if the exercise is not to be self-fulfilling then the grades must be established using a behavioral dimension that is independent, or at least partially independent, of what one may then wish to study within a comparative framework. Bitterman (1965; 1975), for example, used learning paradigms to order species of vertebrates into rat-like or fish-like learners. These grades of fish and rat are established by behavioral analysis that, in my view, is only partially dependent on valid measures of learning ability. Representatives from these grades may then be subjected to further comparative analysis of learning in terms of more valid learning measures. Alternatively, the grades may be established using quantitative behavioral measures such as amount of information-processing in unit time and thus the basis established for generating species for comparative analysis.

The difficulty with all of these strategies is that it is generally accepted that any one species will occupy different grades depending upon the crteria being used to establish them, and there are no criteria for establishing the criteria. There is, in other words, an unacceptable arbitrariness about the procedure. It seems to me that if anagenetic analysis is to have any meaning at all, the behavioral grades used must have a validity in terms of actual ecological demand. That brings us to the last comparative conceptual framework.

3.3 Ecology

Analogous properties may be found in relatively unrelated species if they live under similar ecological conditions. Thus it is generally the case that all arboreal primates are of small body size and terrestrial and semi-terrestrial primates are larger, irrespective of whether the animals are apes, monkeys, or prosimians. Also, frugiverous arboreal primates have larger home ranges than do folivores of equivalent size. Furthermore, semiterrestrial species tend to live in variable habitats and are varied feeders; they also tend to live in larger groups and to form age-graded male troops (all examples taken from Crook, 1970 and Eisenberg et al., 1972). These statements are the behavioral equivalents to those that are made in standard textbook comparisons of the wings of birds, bats, pterodactyls, and insects—homologs if the species are closely related, analogs if they are not. The important point about the analysis of analogs, and the extent to which closely related species may diverge which is the other side of the same analytical coin, is that the ecological demands that are imposed on animals become important factors in the analysis which ties the atrributes of animals, including complex behavioral attributes, in a dynamic relationship with the environment. Behavioral ecology is now a major growth area in biology; when wedded to the notions of inclusive fitness and epigenesis it becomes a part of an even more vigorous sociobiology. The hallmarks of an ecological approach to behavior are that the dynamic nature of the interaction between animals and environment is stressed; so to is development; and natural selection is central.

Behavioral ecology has influenced thinking about learning, but largely in an informal way. The famous contrast between the rat, a nocturnal feeder, and the diurnal bobwhite quail that presumably identifies food items visually, in terms of their relative facility for associating nausea with taste and visual cues respectively is a statement in behavioral ecology; as are all attempts to explain non-equivalence of reinforcement effects or associability in terms of ecological factors and natural selection. Until the recent series of papers by Johnston (1981; 1982; Johnston and Turvey, 1980), however, there has not been any attempt to systematize an ecological approach to the study of learning.

Johnston argues for an ecology of learning as proceeding in three stages. The first is to follow the old ethological adage of 'know thy animal', especially in pinpointing where learning is operating in natural animal–environment interactions. The second stage comprises the forming of 'local principles of adaptation'. These are statements as to how learning occurs in response to specific ecological contexts and covers not merely questions of learning processes but many broader issues such as whether the learning in question is subject to a sensitive period and how early learning constrains later learning. The third stage, establishing 'global principles of adaptation', is the formulation of general principles of learning that are abstracted from the more specific local principles and by which learning is seen to be a part of the coimplicative, dynamic interaction between animals and their natural environment. Sommerhoff's (1950) analytical biology is powerfully employed in describing the nature of these principles.

There is neither space for, nor point in, reiterating the details of Johnston's views here. Suffice it to say that he presents a rich program for research, almost all of which is yet to be done. The importance of Johnston to this chapter is that he presents an approach in which the function of learning within a larger behavioral framework is a major emphasis. If a comparative science of learning is to be built on functionally real forms of learning, habitat, and food selection rather than instrumental learning and learning set paradigms, then Johnston's approach must be an important part of future comparative studies.

It is worth repeating the earlier assertion that neither homology, anagenesis, nor ecology are exclusive approaches. Playing off similarities and differences between species in terms of phylogenetic relatedness and ecological convergence and divergence seems to be a powerful combination to use in comparative analysis. Similarly, it would be interesting to compare species that occupy the same encephalization grade but that have had to adapt to different ecological demands. All of this, however, is for the future. The number of proper comparative learning studies in the literature is astonishingly small given the prominence of learning in psychology. Studies that mix approaches in these powerful ways have not yet been done at all.

4. ANIMAL MODELS AND LEARNING IN MAN

Assuming that the three approaches described above cover all possible comparative studies, where does this leave the use of animal models in the study of man? If homology is to be one's chosen vehicle for comparison then work on man must be coupled with that on apes; if an anagenetic approach is adopted, then on present evidence the dolphin will shed more light on man's cognitive ability than any other animal; if ecology is used, then social predators such as wolves and Cape hunting dogs must be studied. These are all either rare or costly animals. They will be an important part of comparative studies that include man, but obviously are impractical as preparations for controlled experimental manipulations when looking at the effects of potentially toxic substances or mapping brain functions. On the other hand, I can see no point in adopting an optimistic and unreal stance of using inappropriate animal models and hoping that somehow they may tell us things of importance. At most they may weakly signal that something *is* important, but it is doubtful if they are able to identify even the general area at issue.

Probably the best strategy to adopt is one of pushing foward and refining the comparative analysis of learning without special regard to man and using a range of species, provided always that the work is done within that all important coherent conceptual framework. Only when the evidence and analyses are in, will we be able to judge which are the best methods. Only then might such methods be of use in furthering the understanding of man.

ACKNOWLEDGMENT

My thanks to Dorothy Einon, Celia Heyes, Harry J. Jerison, and F. J. Odling-Smee for constructive comments and criticisms of this chapter.

REFERENCES

Alcock, J. (1979) *Animal Behavior. An Evolutionary Approach.* Sunderland Mass., Sinauer.

Atz, J. W. (1970) The application of the idea of homology to behavior. In L. R. Aronson, E. Tobach, D. S. Lehrman, and J. S. Rosenblatt (eds) *The Development and Evolution of Behavior.* San Francisco, Freeman. pp. 53–74.

Baerends, G. P. (1958) Comparative methods and the concept of homology in the study of behavior. *Archives Neerlandaises de Zoologie,* **13,** 401–417.

Beach, F. A. (1950) The snark was a boojum. *American Psychologist,* **5,** 115–124.

Bitterman, M. E. (1965) Phyletic differences in learning. *American Psychologist,* **20,** 396–410.

Bitterman, M. E. (1975) The comparative analysis of learning. *Science,* **188,** 699–709.

Bolles, R. C. (1970) Species-specific defence reactions and avoidance learning. *Psychological Review,* **77,** 32–48.

Corning, W. C., Dyal, J. A., and Willows, A. O. D. (1973a) *Invertebrate Learning,* Vol. 1. New York, Plenum.

Corning, W. C., Dyal, J. A., and Willows, A. O. D. (1973b) *Invertebrate Learning,* Vol. 2. New York, Plenum.

Corning, W. C., Dyal, J. A., and Willows, A. O. D. (1975) *Invertebrate Learning,* Vol. 3. New York, Plenum.

Crook, J. H. (1970) Social organization and the environment: aspects of contemporary social ethology. *Animal Behaviour,* **18,** 197–209.

de Beer, G. (1958) *Embryos and Ancestors.* Oxford, Clarendon Press.

Dewsbury, D. A. (1978) *Comparative Animal Behavior.* New York, McGraw-Hill.

Eisenberg, J. F. Muckenhirn, N. A., and Rudran, R. (1972) The relation between ecology and social structure in primates. *Science,* **176,** 863–874.

Ghiselin, M. T. (1969) *The Triumph of the Darwinian Method.* Berkeley, University of California Press.

Ghiselin, M. T. (1976) The nomenclature of correspondence: a new look at homology and analogy. In R. B. Masterton, W. Hodos, and H. Jerison (eds) *Evolution, Brain and Behavior: Persistent Problems.* Hillsdale, New Jersey, Erlbaum. pp. 129–142.

Gibson, J. J. (1977) The theory of affordances. In R. Shaw and J. Bransford (eds) *Perceiving, Acting and Knowing: towards an Ecological Psychology.* Hillsdale, New Jersey, Erlbaum. pp. 67–82.

Gould, S. J. (1976) Grades and clades revisited. In R. B. Masterton, W. Hodos, and H. Jerison (eds) *Evolution, Brain and Behavior: Persistent Problems.* Hillsdale, New Jersey, Erlbaum. pp. 115–122.

Hilgard, E. R., and Bower, G. H. (1975) *Theories of Learning.* Englewood Cliffs, Prentice-Hall.

Huxley, J. S. (1958) Evolutionary processes and taxonomy with special reference to grades. *Uppsala Univ. Asssks,* 21–38.

Immelmann, K. (1975) Ecological significance of imprinting and early learning. *Annual Review of Ecology and Systematics,* **6,** 15–37.

Immelmann, K. (1980) *Introduction to Ethology.* New York, Plenum.

Jerison, H. J. (1973) *Evolution of Brain and Intelligence.* New York, Academic Press.

Jerison, H. J. (1976) Principles of the evolution of the brain and behaviour. In R. B. Masterton, W. Hodos, and H. Jerison (eds) *Evolution, Brain and Behavior: Persistent Problems.* Hillsdale, New Jersey, Erlbaum. pp. 23–45.

Jerison, H. J. (1980) The evolution of intelligence. *Interciencia,* **5,** 273–280.

Johnston, T. D. (1981) Contrasting approaches to a theory of learning. *Behavioural and Brain Sciences*, **4**, 125–173.

Johnston, T. D. (1982) Learning and the evolution of developmental systems. In H. C. Plotkin (ed.) *Essays in Evolutionary Epistemology*. Chichester, Wiley. Chap. 19, 411–442.

Johnston, T. D., and Turvey, M. T. (1980) A sketch of an ecological metatheory for theories of learning. *The Psychology of Learning and Motivation*, **14**, 147–205.

Klopfer, P. H. (1973) Does behavior evolve? *Annals of the New York Academy of Sciences*, **223**, 113–119.

Lea, S. E. G. (1981) Correlation and contiguity in foraging behavior. *Advances in the analysis of Behaviour*, **2**, 355–406.

Lehrman, D. S. (1953) A critique of Konrad Lorenz's theory of instinctive behaviour. *Quarterly Review of Biology*, **28**, 337–363.

Lorenz, K. (1972) Comparative studies on the behavior of Anatinae. In P. H. Klopfer, and P. Hailman (eds) *Function and Evolution of Behavior*. Reading, Mass., Addison-Wesley, pp. 231–259.

Lorenz, K. (1974) Analogy as a source of knowledge. *Science*, **185**, 229–234.

Marler, P. (1981) Birdsong: the acquisition of a learned motor skill. *Trends in Neuroscience*, **3**, 88–94.

Masterton, R. B., Hodos, W., and Jerison, H. (1976) *Evolution, Brain and Behavior: Persistent Problems*. Hillsdale, New Jersey, Erlbaum.

Piaget, J. (1971) *Biology and Knowledge*. Edinburgh, Edinburgh University Press.

Plotkin, H. C. (1979) Brain–behaviour studies and evolutionary biology. In D. A. Oakley and H. C. Plotkin (eds) *Brain, Behaviour and Evolution*. London, Methuen. pp. 52–77.

Plotkin, H. C., and Odling-Smee, F. J. (1979) Learning, change and evolution. *Advances in the Study of Behaviour*, **10**, 1–41.

Plotkin, H. C., and Odling-Smee, F. J. (1981) A multiple-level model of evolution and its implications for sociobiology. *Behavioural and Brain Sciences*, **4**, 225–268.

Plotkin, H. C., and Odling-Smee, F. J. (1982) Learning in the context of a hierarchy of knowledge gaining processes. In. H. C. Plotkin (ed.) *Essays in Evolutionary Epistemology*. Chichester, Wiley. Chap. 20, 443–471.

Rensch, B. (1959) *Evolution above the Species Level*. London, Methuen.

Rescorla, R. A., and Wagner, A. R. (1972) A theory of Pavlovian conditioning. Variations in the effectiveness of reinforcement and nonreinforcement. In A. H. Black and W. F. Prokasy (eds) *Classical Conditioning II: Current Research and Theory*. New York, Appleton-Century-Crofts. pp. 64–99.

Rozin, P., and Kalat, J. W. (1971) Specific hungers and poison avoidance as adaptive specializations of learning. *Psychological Review*, **78**, 459–486.

Shettleworth, S. J. (1983) Function and mechanism in learning. *Advances in the Analysis of Behaviour*, **3**, in press.

Skinner, B. F. (1953) *Science and Human Behavior*. New York, Macmillan.

Sommerhoff, G. (1950) *Analytical Biology*. Oxford, Clarendon Press.

Steen, J. B. (1974) *The Comparative Physiology of Respiratory Mechanisms*. New York, Academic Press.

Tinbergen, N. (1959) Comparative studies of the behaviour of gulls. *Behaviour*, **15**, 1–70.

Tinbergen, N. (1963) On the aims and methods of ethology. *Zeitschrift für Tierpsychologie*, **20**, 410–433.

Waddington, C. H. (1969) The theory of evolution today. In A. Koestler and J. R. Smythies (eds) *Beyond Reductionism*. Boston, Beacon Press, pp. 357–395.

Warren, J. M. (1973) Learning in vertebrates. In D. A. Deswbury and D. A. Rethlingshafer (eds) *Comparative Psychology*. New York, McGraw-Hill. pp. 471–509.

Warren, J. M. (1977) A phylogenetic approach to learning and intelligence. In A. Oliverio (ed.) *Genetics, Environment and Intelligence*. Amsterdam, Elsevier. pp. 37–56.

Yarczower, M., and Hazlett, L. (1977) Evolutionary scales and anagenesis. *Psychological Bulletin*, **84**, 1088–1097.

Animal Models of Human Behavior
Edited by G. C. L. Davey
© 1983 John Wiley & Sons Ltd

Chapter 8

Multiple Levels in Evolution: An Approach to the Nature–Nurture Issue via 'Applied Epistemology'

F. J. ODLING-SMEE

> *A devil, a born devil, on whose nature nurture can never stick; on whom my pains, humanely taken, are all lost, quite lost;*
> Prospero: *The Tempest*

One of the most persistent controversies in the behavioral sciences is the nature–nurture issue. How do genes relate to behavior? To what extent are certain behaviors constrained by genetic instructions? Conversely, to what extent may some behaviors act so as to offset certain underlying genetic constraints? These are complex questions which have never been properly answered.

In view of the history of this issue it might seem stupid to return to it. Dewsbury (1978) discusses one school of thought which now regards the nature–nurture issue as a pseudo question. Everyone agrees that behavior is the product of both genes and environment, so why can't we leave it at that? The trouble with this tactic is that it amounts to an evasion rather than to a solution. It might serve if the nature–nurture issue were trivial or of no human concern, but as Gottlieb (1979) points out the issue is far from trivial. Rather it remains stubbornly central to the study of behavior and to comparative psychology. Its relevance to human affairs also persists, a point currently highlighted by the sociobiology debate (Wilson, 1975; Caplan, 1978).

One reason why progress in this area has been slow may be our inability to ask the right questions. Seemingly we are repeatedly driven back to misleading clichés. Two examples must suffice. One is the tendency in the literature to contrast 'genetic information' with 'environmental information' or environmental influences (cf. Hinde, 1966). This dichotomy is frequently justifiable as shorthand, but it is nonetheless imprecise. It obscures the fact that genetic information is itself largely (if never entirely) another form of environmental information. From the point of view of an organism the interesting contrast is between information about the world which it receives as a function of its own individual 'experience', and information about the world which it receives as a function of the 'experience' of the population or species to which it belongs. The confusion goes back to Kant. Kant led us to suppose that an organism's *a priori* knowledge is 'independent of experience' (*Critique*, p. 42), but in fact it is simply dependent on the *a posteriori* experience of another 'unit of life' which is different in kind from itself (see below). A second misleading dichotomy is implicit in the phrase nature–nurture. If by nature we mean genetics, then what do we mean by nurture? Do we mean an organism's developmental experience, or its individual learning, or, in the human case especially, the transmitted 'experience' of a culture? The answer is seldom clear.

What is needed is not the abandonment of the nature–nurture issue, but rather a fresh approach and some new questions. In this chapter I want to advocate one possibility based on a multiple level model of evolution (Plotkin and Odling-Smee, 1981).

MULTIPLE LEVELS IN EVOLUTION

The model is summarized in Figure 8.1. It is based on the observation that there are several information gaining processes in nature, each of which stores information about an environment in a separate locus. Figure 8.1 shows four such processes operating at four different levels within a hierarchy of 'knowledge' gaining processes. Within this model the critical defining attribute of a level is the existence of a distinct locus of information store. Previously these separate stores were called 'referents' (Plotkin and Odling-Smee, 1979, 1981) but this word blurred the distinction between (i) the information store itself; (ii) the particular 'unit of life' which is responsible for 'experiencing' a world and for acquiring information about it; and (iii) the process which actually does the information gaining and storing at a given level. In this chapter these distinctions are vital so 'referent' will be dropped in favor of 'information store'. In addition the phrase 'unit of life' will be used to signify a category of life which is gaining information at a given level via some specified process (e.g. a population, an individual organism, or a culture). This usage is in contrast with convention which, for example, treats organisms as units of life, but populations as 'classes' of life rather than as units. Both Hull (1980) and Ghiselin (1981) have indicated that there is

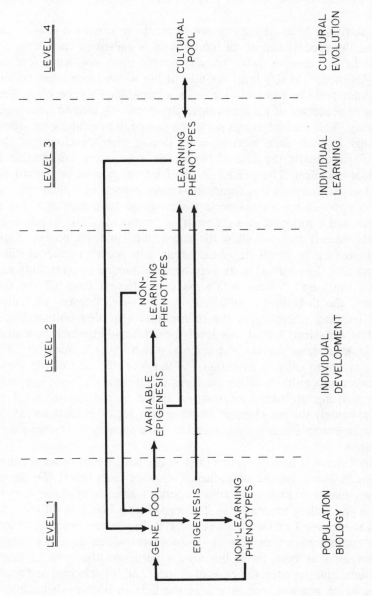

Figure 8.1. The four levels of evolution. See the original text for a fuller explanation. (Reproduced from H. C. Plotkin and F. J. Odling-Smee, *The Behavioral and Brain Sciences*, **4** (2) (1981), by permission of Cambridge University Press, Cambridge)

something seriously wrong with the way we normally categorize life. Ghiselin, for instance, argues persuasively that species (populations) should be regarded as 'individuals' and not classes. That point is of great importance here.

The particular locus of information store; the information gaining unit of life; and the process via which information is gained at each level are as follows: *Level 1* consists of the primary genetic process which is responsible for phylogenesis. At this level the unit of life which gains information is a population, and the locus of storage is a population's gene pool. *Level 2* consists of processes of plastic or open development, termed here 'variable epigenesis'. Variable epigenesis permits a degree of fine tuning by individual organisms to their local environments during their development (Mayr, 1974). Consequently the unit of life which is acquiring information is an individual organism. The precise locus of information store is hard to pin down, but preliminarily it is regarded as those aspects of a phenotype which exist, as opposed to other aspects which would have existed if the same organism had developed in a different environment. This definition is not adequate since it does not allow for 'equifinality' in development (Bateson, 1976) according to which the same result may occur in spite of different environments. In addition there may be some unique irreversibility restrictions on the Level 2 store which make it different from all the others. However, the definition is sufficient here. *Level 3* consists of individual animal learning where again the information acquiring unit of life is an individual organism; but at this level the information which it acquires is stored only in those regions of the c.n.s. which underlie 'memory'. Finally *Level 4* refers to cultural evolution. At this level the unit of life acquiring information is a culture, while the locus of information store is a 'cultural pool' consisting of shared information stored in the memories of plural animals, namely the members of a culture (Ruyle, 1973; Durham, 1976). In the human example it may also extend to extra phenotypic storage sites such as libraries.

Apart from this basic structure the model has several other features, at least one of which must be mentioned. Following Campbell (1974) the model proposes that a common algorithm operates at each of these four levels (Plotkin and Odling-Smee, 1981). The algorithm is based on different mechanisms at each level which tends to conceal it. In essence, however, it consists of the continuous alternation of (i) processes which generate variety in different units at each level, but always partly on the basis of historical constraints, and partly on the basis of chance; and (ii) selection and retention devices which winnow that variety in the light of both environmental and 'own' states, and which retain 'fit' variants in store at each level. The information in store then acts as a source of further constraint on the further generation of variety.

ADAPTATION

In addition to providing a model it is also necessary to say something about adaptation; if only because the concept has recently been under attack. Lewontin (1978; 1982); Gould and Lewontin (1979) and Gould (1980) have argued that not all traits expressed by phenotypes are adaptations; that not all adaptations are optimal; and that in any case adaptations are not simply solutions to problems imposed on organisms by a pre-existing world, but are rather solutions to problems which have, to varying extents, been self-imposed. These criticisms are well founded. They do not, however, make the concept of adaptation less important. They merely make it more difficult.

At least three points need stressing. The first is that phenotypes, like genotypes, carry redundancy. Gould and Vrba (1982) refer to this redundancy in claiming that organisms express 'exaptations' as well as 'adaptations'. Exaptations are functionless traits which may or may not turn out to be useful at some future time and place. Bock (1980) makes a similar point by differentiating between an organism's 'features' and its adaptations. A feature is only an adaptation if and when it is in a special kind of matching relationship, or 'synerg' with a specific environmental selection force. Lacking synerg a feature is just a feature. It may then be convenient to assign to it some other status (e.g. para-adaptation or perhaps exaptation) or to treat it merely as phenotypic junk, but it will not be an adaptation.

The second point refers to the widely acknowledged fact that it is no good organisms expressing adaptations on a rigid one-off basis. Organisms are confronted by constantly changing capricious worlds. An organism's task is to track a kaleidoscopic environment throughout its lifetime. In this connection change can arise from three different sources. The first is change imposed by the inorganic environment (e.g. changes of temperature or light); the second is change imposed by other organisms (e.g. by predators, or competitors); the third is self-imposed change arising from an organism's own activities in its own environment (e.g. feeding, burrowing, migration). This last source of change is of special interest because it is least well handled by current theory (Lewontin and Levins, 1978).

The third point is that in biology environments only exist relative to organisms (Lewontin, 1982, Lewontin and Levins, 1978, which means that environmental changes only exist relative to organisms too. Figure 8.2 summarizes one earlier attempt to work out some of the relationships which can occur between different kinds of organisms and different types of environmental change (Plotkin and Odling-Smee, 1979). Four types of change are shown. They are (i) directional change (e.g. the onset of an ice-age, or increasing population size); (ii) singular change (e.g. a falling tree, a volcanic eruption); (iii) periodic change (e.g. seasonal, tidal, or diurnal changes) and (iv) aperiodic changes around a regular feature (e.g. changes of temperature

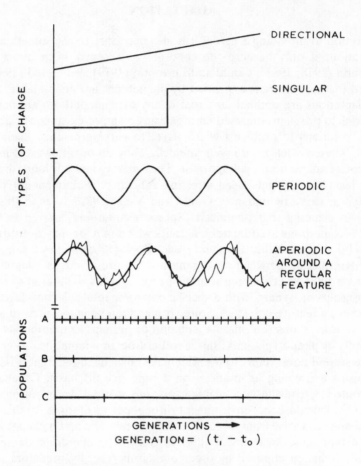

Figure 8.2. Types of environmental change related to types of
population. (Reproduced from H. C. Plotkin and F. J. Odling-
Smee, *Advances in the Study of Behaviour*, **10** (1979), by permission of Academic Press, New York)

during day and night). These changes are plotted against three species of
organisms: (i) a population (A) of short-lived organisms; (ii) a population
(B) of intermediate lived organisms, and (iii) a population (C) of long-lived
organisms. The point the figure makes is that the classification of the different
types of change depends in part on how long the organism which encounters
them lives. For example, a seasonal change which is 'objectively' periodic,
will only be encountered as periodic by organisms from population (C). The
same change will be encountered as directional by the short-lived organisms
from population (A).

In sum organisms are faced with a highly complex 'managerial' problem throughout their lifetimes. To solve it they have to be able to form and express arrays of features on a time-sharing basis which is appropriate to their changing environments. Moreover they must do this in such a way that at each moment in time enough of their features are in synerg with the selection forces they are currently encountering to ensure their overall adaptation. This is essentially how the life history tactic problem (Stearns, 1976, 1977) looks from an individual organism's point of view.

THE QUESTION

We can now rephrase the nature–nurture question. The multiple level model provokes at least two different kinds of question. The first asks: 'Why should supplementary levels of information gain ever evolve in nature, and why only in some species?' The second asks: 'Suppose an individual organism belongs to a species which has already evolved one or more supplementary levels of information gain, then which level should govern which of its adaptations relative to which selection force in its environment?' The first question relates to the origins of Levels 2, 3, and 4 and has been considered elsewhere (Plotkin and Odling-Smee, 1979). The second relates to their use. The two questions sound similar but they are different if only because there is no reason why, once a supplementary level has evolved, it should stay confined to dealing with the selection forces which originally provoked its existence. On the contrary, to the extent that a supplementary process of information gain, learning for instance, confers generalist capacity on organisms, it is likely to be used opportunistically. Of these two questions only the second really refers to the traditional nature–nurture issue, so I shall concentrate on it.

AN HYPOTHESIS

The hypothesis I want to propose is that the features (in Bock's sense) of any organism which has access to more than one information store, should be governed by whichever evolutionary level provides it with the best basis for 'predicting' the different selection forces in its environment at different times and places in its future. This does not mean that organisms are expected to be prescient, or to make predictions about their worlds in any cognitive sense, although a few may; but it does mean that organisms are seen as 'knowledge' using entities which are 'prepared' for specific worlds, and which travel into the future via inductive steps.

The rationale for this hypothesis is that it could provide a new point of entry to the nature–nurture controversy. It should be possible, by making use of epistemological criteria, to work out in advance which information store, at which level, should offer the best basis for predicting different selection forces in the environments of different organisms. Accordingly I shall argue that a key to the nature–nurture issue can be obtained from examining just three sets of variables. The first set comprises those variables which collectively determine the contents of any given information store at any given moment. I shall refer to this set as the *sampling limits* of a given information store. The second set comprises variables which collectively determine the extent to which the contents of any given store can be revised during some interval of time in the light of environmental change. I shall refer to this set as the *tracking limits* of a given information store. Finally the third set consists of those variables which collectively determine the degree to which a given organism has *access* to a given information store during its lifetime.

The argument will proceed in three stages. First, some alternative strategies will be considered (in the abstract) according to which organisms might cope with their capricious futures. The purpose of this step is not to investigate the strategies themselves but rather to derive from them the factors which are responsible for deciding the sampling limits and the tracking limits which attach to information stores in general. Second, the four particular information stores which occur in the multiple level model will be compared with respect to their different sampling and different tracking limits. At this stage the accessibility of these four stores to organisms will also be discussed. Finally, I shall consider how those organisms which do have access to plural information stores are likely to be governed in the light of these between store differences.

SOME ALTERNATIVE 'MANAGEMENT' STRATEGIES

A random strategy

Let us begin with a naive question: Why should information in store ever be of use to an organism? Consider the probable fate of an organism which had no access to any information about its world at all. Such an organism could only proceed into its future blindly. Hence as a phenotype it could do no better than form and express arrays of features on a random basis. If, by chance, enough of its features happened to be in 'synerg' with the environmental selection forces it encountered, then the organism could survive. However, if too few of its features achieved the synerg status, it could not. The one advantage of this strategy is that it minimizes an organism's 'control costs'. Any organism which depended on it would not have to pay either for acquiring or using information. The strategy's overwhelming disadvantage is that it could not work except relative to an extremely simple, near static environment. Even then it would still demand an organism which carried vast phenotypic redundancy, and which would therefore be required to pay vast 'plant costs' in lieu of its near zero control costs. In fact only organisms which, by chance, happened to be super-generalists, nearly infinitely adaptable, could have any chance of surviving. In reality contemporary environments are never that simple, while the cost of carrying sufficient phenotypic redundancy is probably always prohibitive. However, a random strategy does have some relevance, as we shall see.

A prediction strategy

A different fate awaits an organism that does have access to at least one information store, regardless of whether the store in question is one which the organism has acquired for itself, or whether it is one which has been acquired by some other unit of life (e.g. its population). Instead of proceeding into its future blindly, such an organism could proceed under the control of the information in store; meaning that its features would be governed by that information. In this case, and to the extent to which the information in the store was originally put there by a process which reflected the past states of some environment, the strategy would be equivalent to 'preparing' the organism for a future which was the same as that recorded in the past. In this sense the strategy is a 'prediction strategy', and it is based on induction (Campbell, 1974; 1979; Plotkin and Odling-Smee, 1979).

Compared to the random strategy a prediction strategy suffers from the defect of inflicting some 'control costs' on organisms. Any organism which uses information will have to pay some kind of biological price for doing so. The strategy's major advantage, however, is that it greatly reduces an organism's 'plant costs' by minimizing its need for phenotypic redundancy. In lieu of a scenario in which it is only possible for super-generalists to survive, it is now possible for an organism which is specialized in advance for a predicted future to survive too. It will do so provided the predictions turn out to be correct. There therefore ceases to be a requirement for such an organism to carry vast phenotypic redundancy. In short, there is a trade-off between an organism's control costs and its plant costs. The proviso, however, is crucial. Predictions are only useful so long as they are correct. When an organism's future ceases to correspond to the recorded past, then the organism is likely to be left worse off than it would be under a random strategy, simply because it will no longer be carrying sufficient redundancy to cope with unpredicted selection forces even by chance. Hence a pure prediction strategy could not be expected to work indefinitely. Nevertheless, it is still worth considering since some of the variables we are looking for are derived from it.

One long-standing question asks what factors determine the likelihood that predictions which are based on a history of the past will be correct relative to the future of a given organism? It is not yet possible to answer this question fully, but it is possible to indicate some key factors. Before doing this, however, it may help to reemphasize that there does not have to be an identity between the information *using* organism, and the information *gaining* unit of life which is accumulating a history, before a prediction can be correct. 'Experience' can be transferable. The history which governs a particular feature in a particular organism may therefore be the history of its population; or the organism's own history; or the history of its culture; or some combination. The following remarks are general and apply to all such cases.

The first point is that unless an inductive step is constrained by past instances of actual order in the 'objective' environment, then there can be little chance of correct predictions (Popper, 1968; 1972; Campbell, 1974; 1979). This is because, given the nature of the environment's structural texture, only events which are based on 'objective' order are likely to reoccur across environmental space and time, and so may reoccur in an organism's future. It is therefore important that any information in store should reflect environmental order, and not just 'subjective' criteria, or merely the transitory background events which constitute environmental 'noise'. But this requirement demands that the unit of life which is responsible for acquiring and storing information at a given level, should have as great a capacity as possible for demarcating between actual instances of environmental order, and environmental noise.

The problem here is that the capacity of every unit of life (e.g. a population, or an organism) for demarcating between order and noise will always be limited by its own pattern of contact with the environment. Every unit of life is localized in space and time, the actual dimensions of its localization being set by its fixed or shifting pattern of contact with its world, and so by its cumulative range across both environmental space and time. Hence a unit of life can only ever 'sample' its environment. This means that it may only store information about those samples of the environment which it happens to have encountered. To put the same point in cognitive terms, every unit of life has the status of an 'observer' with a limited 'observational horizon'. It may be able to stretch its observational horizon (e.g. an individual organism may be able to deploy distal senses) but it cannot go beyond it. So, assuming for the moment that the 'objective' environment is constant, and that it only contains reoccurrences of the same 'old' events and does not introduce any 'new' events, then the capacity of any unit of life for demarcating between environmental order and environmental noise will be limited by its own range across that environment. The greater its cumulative range across both space and time, the greater will be its capacity for sampling the environment. In which case the greater also should be its capacity for demarcating between environmental order and environmental noise. The reasoning behind this last inference is complicated, but it ultimately goes back to the fact that reoccurring instances of environmental order are more likely to be re-encountered by a unit of life with a larger capacity for sampling the environment, than by one with a smaller capacity. A larger sampling range therefore implies the highlighting of any information in store which relates to the presence of actual instances of order in the environment.

It also implies the suppression of information relating to environmental noise, since accumulating instances of environmental noise will tend to cancel themselves out.

It follows that any organism which is governed by a prediction strategy should ideally draw its information from a store which has been acquired by a unit of life with as great a 'sampling range' as possible. This should maximize the likelihood that the information in that store is statistically reliable relative to past instances of order in the 'objective' environment, which should, in turn, maximize the chances of correct predictions.

A second factor which influences the quality of prediction is the relevance of the information in a store to an organism. However reliable the information in a store may be about the presence of order in the objective environment, it will still be of little use to an organism which confronts a world which is substantially different, either 'objectively' or 'subjectively' from that upon which the information in store is based. What an organism requires is not just reliable information about the objective environment, but information which is as relevant as possible to its own particular world.

Here there are two principal variables. The first concerns the relationship between the specific environmental or 'sampling' locality of the unit of life which acquires a given information store; and the specific environmental locality of the individual organism which is using that store. The sampling locality of every information gaining unit of life inevitably imposes some biases on the information which it can store relative to the wider environment. The locality of the information using organism, on the other hand, affects the precise set of environmental events which the organism must confront. To the extent to which these two localities are similar, then the information in the store is likely to be based on relevant samples of the environment relative to the organism's own world. But to the extent to which these two localities are different, the information in store is likely to be irrelevant at best, and a source of incorrect predictions at worst.

The second variable concerns the fact, mentioned earlier, that in biology environments only exist relative to specified organisms, or more generally to specified units of life. It is therefore possible for the same 'objective' environment to act as different 'subjective' environments, and as a source of different selection forces relative to different units of life. For example, an organism belonging to Population (A) in Figure 8.2 might confront the same 'objective' environment as another organism from Population (C). However, the two organisms would not be living in the same world 'subjectively'. For this reason the degree of similarity between the particular unit of life which is responsible for acquiring a given information store, and the particular organism which is using the information in that store, becomes important. Provided the information in the store is acquired by a unit of life sensitive to the same selection forces which are important to the information using organism, then the information in the store should be relevant to the organism. If, however, the information is acquired by a unit of life which is insensitive to the selection forces which act on the organism, then the information in store will either be useless or dangerous to the organism.

We have now derived two of the principal factors which determine the likelihood that information in a store will lead to correct predictions. Together they define the 'sampling limits' of whatever unit of life is responsible for acquiring a given information store. The general point is simply that the contents of any information store will be powerfully influenced by the particular 'sampling range' and the particular 'sampling locality' of the unit of life which has been responsible for accumulating it. In turn the usefulness of any information store to an organism will depend on its contents.

A mixed strategy

This still leaves a residual problem. However sensitive a unit of life may be to environmental order, and however relevant the information which it gains may be to an organism, it is still never going to be possible for information about the past to act as a perfect basis for predicting the future. As Hume long ago pointed out, there can never be a guarantee that an organism's future will be the same as any recorded past. On the contrary pervasive environmental change guarantees that sooner or later it will be different. New changes will occur, and when they do, predictions based on the past must fail. In the long run a prediction strategy is no more viable than a random strategy. So how can organisms cope with inevitable failures of prediction?

Apparently in a capricious world the only viable solution is for organisms to depend neither on a pure prediction strategy nor on a pure random strategy, but rather on a mixture of both. Under a mixed strategy organisms can still be governed primarily by predictions based on stored information about the past, thereby permitting them to benefit from the reduced 'plant costs' which are associated with prediction. At the same time organisms can also carry sufficient phenotypic redundancy, in the form of spare features (or exaptations), to provide them with at least some chance of surviving encounters with unpredicted selection forces. Their 'plant costs' will therefore inevitably be higher than they would be under a pure prediction stategy. However, the organisms will benefit from being at least partly insured against the unpredicted. Again this does not imply prescience or preadaptation on the part of the organisms, since the redundancy will ultimately be chance based. It merely implies that only organisms which happen to carry sufficient phenotypic redundancy can have any chance of surviving.

Campbell (1979) vividly describes the essence of this mixed strategy in terms of what he calls the 'doubt–trust ratio'. Doubt corresponds to the random element; trust to the prediction element. The doubt–trust ratio may vary in value at different evolutionary levels, and relative to different units of life, but it should always be present. It accounts for both Campbell's and our own notion (Plotkin and Odling-Smee, 1981) that there is a recursive algorithm in nature which is based on a mixed strategy.

The pursuit of a mixed strategy introduces one further demand. It demands the revision of the contents of an information store in the light of errors of prediction, and therefore in the light of 'new' environmental change. Unless information in a store can regularly be brought up to date, the doubt–trust ratio will become progressively diluted in favor of doubt. Errors of prediction will accumulate, forcing organisms to depend more heavily on the random component of the mixed strategy by carrying more redundancy. Thus, to keep the doubt–trust ratio as much in favor of trust as possible, the information in store must be continually revised so that the organism's plant costs can continuously be cut back.

The capacity for revision of any information store will, however, be limited by (i) the nature of the unit of life which acquires it; (e.g. whether it is a population, an organism, or a culture), and (ii) the operating characteristics of the particular information gaining (or evolutionary) process which is responsible for feeding that store. Between them these two factors will determine the 'tracking limits' of every information store. It follows that, ideally, the management of organisms should be based on information which is as up to date as possible relative to a changing environment. The information should therefore be drawn from a store which is subject to minimal tracking delays.

One final difficulty is that to an extent a fast tracking rate is incompatible with the need for the information in a store to be acquired by a unit of life with a maximum sampling range. For example, the greater the sampling range of a unit of life, the greater will probably be the number of encounters with the environment which will end up being registered in its store. Its store may therefore become less labile, and may show greater resistance to change than will some other store accumulated by a less extended unit of life. Bayes' theorem models this point well. Paradoxically the opposite might also be true. As a unit of life tracks a changing world, it will not only gain 'new' information about 'new' events, but probably it will lose some 'old' information about 'old' events. In these circumstances it is possible that a changing environment might force too great a loss of information upon a particular information store, thereby making that store too labile. For example the gene pool of Population (A) in Figure 8.2 might not be able to retain information about every stage of the periodic change which is illustrated in the same figure, even though it might be useful for it to do so. In which case, the effect of such an over-labile information store would be to limit the effective sampling range of that population in time; and to convert what is 'objectively' an 'old' environmental event, namely the reoccurring periodic change, into a perpetually 'new' 'subjective' event.

These incompatibilities (plus a few others like them) could force compromises on organisms. They could also force different species of organisms to evolve various devices for resolving their dilemmas. One such device is for a species to evolve supplementary processes of information gain, and supplementary information stores. Provided each of several stores has different sampling limits and different tracking limits, then organisms stand to benefit from these between store differences. In practice they will benefit to the extent to which their management problems are judiciously shared out across plural information stores, gained by diverse units of life (Plotkin and Odling-Smee, 1979).

THE FOUR DIFFERENT INFORMATION STORES

We can now turn back to the four specific information stores which occur within the multiple level model of evolution shown in Figure 8.1. We will compare them with respect to their sampling and tracking limits, and their accessibility to individual organisms, and we shall do this from the point of view of an organism which is assumed to have access to all four stores. This does not mean that all organisms are supposed to have access to multiple information stores; most clearly do not; but it is simply convenient to talk about ones which do.

Level 1

To recapitulate: Level 1 comprises the primary genetic process of evolution. The unit of life which acquires information at this level is a population, and the information store is a population gene pool. The sampling range, or observational horizon upon which Level 1 information is based is therefore given by the cumulative range of a population across environmental space and time. But different populations have different ranges across space and time. Furthermore, range across space does not always imply an equivalent range across time (nor vice versa). For example, an asexual and a sexual population might both extend back in time an equal number of years and generations. Nevertheless, relative to their currently living members, the effective sampling range of the asexual population across space would be more limited than that of the sexual population during the same interval of time. This can be seen by comparing the genealogies of sexual and asexual organisms. Sexual organisms have more ancestors, which between them sample wider regions of environmental space than do the ancestors of asexual organisms (cf. Williams, 1975; Maynard Smith, 1978). Hence their populations will have different sampling ranges. The sampling locality upon which Level 1 information is based will likewise depend on the particular environmental locality which has been sampled by a particular population across both space and time. So in this case, to the extent to which the information in any Level 1 store is biased, its biases will be due to the sampling locality of a population.

The other two variables which concern us, namely the tracking limits and the accessibility of a Level 1 store to an individual organism, interrelate. An individual organism can only gain access to its population's gene pool via the mechanisms of inheritance. It can only gain access to it once, namely at the moment of its own origin; and it can only gain access to a fraction of the total genetic instructions in its population's store. Typically a genotype contains only a fraction of the total set of genes within a gene pool. Conversely the capacity of a Level 1 store for revision and updating is itself limited by the time it takes for a population to regenerate. This is because genetic evolution depends on natural selection and because natural selection can only act directly on a between-organism and between-generation basis. (It cannot act directly either within organisms or within generations.) It is true that the tracking limits of a population will also depend on its fecundity and on its capacity to produce variety, but these properties are likewise linked to generational turnover. Hence the basic tracking limits of any Level 1 information store will always be set by, or linked to the time it takes a particular population to regenerate.

In the light of these limitations we can now list the principal advantages and disadvantages which should accrue to an organism which depends on Level 1 information. First, an organism stands to benefit greatly from the relatively colossal sampling range of its population across environmental space and time compared to its own individual sampling range. The statistical reliability of the information in its Level 1 store should be high. The precise benefits which an organism gains here will, however, depend on which kind of population the organism belongs to (e.g. sexual or asexual: numerically large or small). Second, an organism may not gain advantage from the particular sampling locality of its population. Whether it does so will depend on the similarity of its individual locality to the wider, inclusive locality of its population. To the extent to which the organism's local world is typical of its population's world, then it should benefit from its Level 1 information. But to the extent to which the organism's local world is atypical of its population's world, then it should suffer a disadvantage from the same dependence. By the same token an organism should benefit from Level 1 information only if the genes in its genotype represent a typical subset of the genes of its population's gene pool, making it a typical member of its population. In this case the organism will be subject to the same selection forces as other members of its population, and it will therefore exist in the same 'subjective' as well as the same 'objective' environment. If the organism possesses an atypical genotype, however, it will probably suffer from its dependence on its population's gene pool. It could then only benefit if it happened to encounter an environment which by chance suited its particular form of deviation.

In addition, an organism may well suffer considerably from the tracking limits of its Level 1 store. The fact that an organism can only draw genes from its gene pool at the moment of its own origin, means that it cannot benefit from any updating of the gene pool which may occur during its lifetime. Its genes must program it in advance relative to its entire lifetime with no possibility of any subsequent revision. Similarly the tracking limits which apply to the gene pool may be such that the information which the organism is provided with by its genes is already out of date. In which case the organism will have been 'prepared' for the wrong world. The crucial variables here are the capriciousness of the environment and the duration of the organism's own lifetime. Thus an organism will be unlikely to survive on the basis of its genes alone if either the rate at which new change is introduced into its environment exceeds the tracking limits of its population's gene pool, or if the changes in its local environment are on too short a time base, are too inconsistent, or are too local to be able to act as coherent selection forces relative to its population as a whole.

Levels 2 and 3

Levels 2 and 3 can be taken together since the unit of life which acquires information in both these cases is an individual organism. At Level 2 an organism gains information via variable epigenesis, and it stores it in its phenotype. At Level 3 an organism acquires information via learning and it stores it in its c.n.s. (Figure 8.1).

The advantages and disadvantages of these two levels are roughly reciprocal to those which arise from Level 1. Both the sampling range and the sampling locality upon which Levels 2 and 3 are based will now be determined by the localization in the environment of the individual organism itself, rather than by the localization of its population. Hence the sampling range of both levels will be set by the organism's own 'observational horizon', while their sampling locality will be determined by the organism's particular location in environmental space and time. This means that there will be an identity between the unit of life which is gaining information, and the unit of life which is using information at both these levels, such as does not occur at Level 1.

Compared to Level 1 an organism which depends on Levels 2 and 3 stands to lose the advantage conferred on it by the very great sampling range of its population. The information in store at Levels 2 and 3 will probably be less reliable than that stored at Level 1. Conversely an organism stands to gain from an enhanced capacity for individual 'fine tuning' at both Levels 2 and 3 relative to its own local environment. This is because an organism will now be deriving its information exclusively from the particular world that it is itself contacting. However, the greatest advantage conferred by both Levels 2 and 3 probably lies in their mutual capacity to supply organisms with fresh information about the world on a within-organism, and within-lifetime basis. They thereby offer organisms some escape from the between-lifetime tracking limits of Level 1. Thus an organism which has access to information stored at either Levels 2 or 3, is not completely dependent on pre-programing by its genes with respect to every aspect of its future life. Instead certain 'decisions' can be left open (Mayr, 1974; Waddington, 1969), allowing the organism to be kept up to date relative to a rapidly changing world by within-lifetime adjustments controlled by either Levels 2 or 3.

The major difference between Levels 2 and 3 is that the domain of Level 2 is wider than the domain of Level 3. Variable epigenesis can presumably affect almost any aspect of a developing phenotype; whereas learning is apparently only capable of modifying a phenotype's behavior. Conversely the capacity for the revision of information in the Level 2 store is generally more restricted than that of Level 3. Developmental plasticity is typically tied to sensitive or critical periods relative to given phenotypic traits, and it tends to grow less, or disappear as the sensitive periods run out. The 'tuning' of cells in a kitten's visual cortex provides a good example (Freeman, 1979). Behavioral plasticity due to learning, on the other hand, is generally present throughout an organism's lifetime. For example, most animals can be conditioned at almost any age.

Level 4

Level 4 raises many problems which go beyond the scope of this chapter. In spite of this, some preliminary points can be made. Level 4 comprises cultural information gaining. The unit of life responsible for it is a culture, while the information is stored in a cultural pool (Figure 8.1). The fact that a culture consists of multiple organisms means that we are once again dealing with a between-organism rather than a within-organism process. However, it is a very different process from that which occurs at Level 1. One striking difference is that Level 4 offers organisms the possibility of a double advantage. The sampling range upon which cultural information is based depends on the range of a culture across space and time. It does not depend on the range of an individual organism. Hence any organism which belongs to a culture

should be able to benefit from advantages which are at least roughly analogous to those gained by organisms from the extensive sampling range of
their populations at Level 1. However, at Level 1 organisms have to pay a
penalty for these sampling advantages. They must submit to the potentially
severe tracking limits which arise from the character of natural selection. No
such penalty is exacted at Level 4. Unlike genetic information cultural information can be transmitted among organisms on both a within-lifetime and
a between-lifetime basis (Cavalli-Sforza and Feldman, 1981; Plotkin and
Odling-Smee, 1981). Level 4's tracking limits are therefore far less severe
than those which apply to Level 1. In some instances they may even be less
severe than those which operate at Level 3. For instance a child might learn,
via taste aversion, that a particular fruit is poisonous. But it might also pick
up the same information faster (and less painfully) by listening to its parents
(I owe this point to Plotkin).

Nevertheless two disadvantages could still accrue to an organism from
Level 4. An individual organism is unlikely to have access to more than a
fraction of the total information stored in a cultural pool. In addition there
could be a lack of correspondence between the particular environmental
events which the culture as a whole finds relevant, and those which are
important to an organism. To the extent to which an organism is a typical
member of its culture, and to the extent to which its world is typical of the
world contacted by its culture; it will probably benefit from Level 4 information. However, to the extent to which an organism is an atypical member
of its culture, or to the extent to which it is in contact with a world which is
dissimilar to that of its culture as a whole, then the organism may not benefit,
but could even suffer from its dependence on Level 4. This raises the intriguing possibility of parallels between cultural deviance at Level 4, and 'genetic deviance' at Level 1.

SHARING OUT THE ADAPTATIONAL LOAD

With these between information store comparisons in mind, we can now go
back to the nature–nurture issue and ask again: 'What are the rules which
determine the share-out of the adaptational loads of organisms who depend
for their management on plural information stores?'

One of the few attempts to answer this kind of question before, explicitly
based on evolutionary theory, came from Slobodkin and Rapoport (1974).
They proposed a scheme according to which different adaptational problems
in different organisms should be handled at different response depths. In
their scheme shallower responses consist of within-organism behavioral and
physiological changes, while deep responses are population responses involving the selective mortality of individual organisms, and population-based
genetic changes. The share-out of the adaptational load between these re-

sponse depths is determined by a general principle of economy according to which organisms are expected to 'respond to events in their environments in such a way as to minimize their stake (costs) in the reoccurrence of these events' (p. 191).

The present hypothesis differs from Slobodkin and Rapoport's in only two respects. First, it proposes that we substitute the four different information stores that occur within the multiple level model of evolution for response depth, on the grounds that an information store is both a more specific and simpler concept. Slobodkin (1981) encourages this substitution. Second, it substitutes 'maximum predictability' for Slobodkin and Rapoport's notion of a 'minimum stake'. Thus the management of an organism's features should be shared out so that each feature, and each component part of a feature, should be handled by whichever level offers the best basis for predicting the (re)occurrence of a particular selection force in an organism's environment at different times and places in the future. This general rule should maximize the chances that the features of organisms will be in synerg with the selection forces they encounter, and therefore the chances that their features will attain adaptive status. In principle the rule 'the best basis for predicting' should also incorporate some reference to the cost of predicting; but it will still differ from Slobodkin's and Rapoport's economic rule by making economic considerations subordinate to epistemological ones. Thus, as far as the share-out between levels is concerned, only if it is possible for the same adaptational problem to be handled equally well by information in more than one store on epistemological grounds, should economic criteria decide between them.

The potential advantage of this proposal is that it allows us to work out in advance which evolutionary level should govern which feature, in which organism, on the basis of a kind of 'applied epistemology'. As a first approximation this could be done by an analysis of the sampling limits; the tracking limits; and the accessibility of the various different information stores to different organisms, relative to their different environments.

One other problem concerns the fact that this approach still only deals with an already stabilized situation, and therefore with 'old' selection forces that could have been present in a species environment for many generations. It does not provide rules for describing how 'new' selection forces arising from a newly perturbed environment should be dealt with by organisms which have access to plural information stores. In what sequence, if any, should the different evolutionary levels respond to a new change? Similarly which information store will be most in need of updating given which kind of new change?

Slobodkin and Rapoport discuss three possible answers. These are (i) a completely hierarchical solution according to which deeper responses are only activated by the failure of shallower responses; (ii) a completely non-hierarchical direct response system in which new change triggers a series of response mechanisms; and (iii) a multi-linked response system which is a combination of the other two. Previously Plotkin and I proposed an hierarchical scheme relative to our own model (Plotkin and Odling-Smee, 1979, 1982) and this may still be defensible. For example, in any species which has a capacity for both variable epigenesis (Level 2) and learning (Level 3) the primary genetic Level 1 should only be activated when natural selection begins to operate among members of the species. But this is only likely to happen if enough individual organisms exhaust their capacity for coping with a new change by either Levels 3 or 2. The same hierarchical scheme, however, is less reasonable in claiming that Levels 4, 3 and 2 should operate in a strict downward sequence, rather than, for instance, simultaneously. Slobodkin and Rapoport favor their multi-linked alternative, and they may be right.

In any case we are left with the issue of how to test the hypothesis as a whole. One possibility is to proceed from three different starting points. First, it should be possible to generate preliminary predictions about which level does what, simply by a process of elimination. Epistemological criteria could be used to rule out the involvement of those information stores which should definitely be unable to handle certain kinds of selection forces relative to certain species. To give just one example of how this might be done: Consider the case of fighting in red deer (*Cervus elaphus L.*) which occurs among rutting stags in the autumn (Clutton-Brock, *et al.*, 1979). Each year every male animal grows a new set of antlers, and each year its antlers change in size and configuration with both the overall size and the number of points tending to increase (Mitchell *et al.*, 1977). Each year therefore, a stag is faced with the prospect of fighting different opponents, armed with diverse antlers. Furthermore, it must fight them with a different set of antlers of its own. In these circumstances it is possible to draw some inferences about the level of control of the animal's fighting behavior on purely epistemological grounds. The red deer, in this example, correspond to Population (C) in Figure 8.2; and the stags are confronted by an aperiodic change based on a period, namely the seasonal rut (see Figure 8.2). Because seasonal changes must have occurred with great regularity for many generations of deer; many aspects of a stag's rutting behavior and physiology are likely to be governed by Level 1 (the genetic process). Doubtless other aspects will be governed by Level 2 (variable epigenesis). However, it should *not* be possible for either Level 1 or Level 2 to govern those aspects of the animal's fighting behavior which depend on antler configuration. This is because the degree of variance associated with the antlers is too great; and the rate at which a stag's behavior must be adjusted to cope with it is too fast; to allow either Levels 1 or 2 to operate. Hence one may infer that either Level 3 (learning) or Level 4 (imitation learning) must operate at this point. In fact, much of the learning which appears to be necessary here is probably achieved in practice sessions during juvenile sparring bouts, but some further learning ought to occur during adult fights as well.

A second possibility is to tighten up these preliminary predictions, and to generate some new ones, by using computer simulation techniques. One advantage of the present hypothesis is that it makes this step easier. Thus it ought to be possible to assign different sampling and tracking limits, and different degrees of accessibility to a set of different information stores, and then let them compete, via a common algorithm, against a simulated capricious environment.

Third, and last, it also ought to be possible to use conventional nature–nurture techniques, such as those pioneered by Tinbergen (1953), Hailman (1969), and Marler (1970), to test any predictions which are generated. For example, it should be possible to test the hypothesis that stags learn how to handle their opponents' antlers, by the artificial manipulation of antlers, by staging fights, or by selectively depriving juveniles of the opportunity for sparring, or for observing fights. On the surface there might appear to be little difference between this step and many current approaches. However, it would enable current techniques to be harnessed to specific predictions, rather than to *ad hoc* explorations, and that could make a considerable difference.

CONCLUSION

A number of omissions will be evident in the preceding argument. We know, for instance, that information stores are affected by several factors apart from those discussed here. One such is the quality of the particular biological machinery which is responsible for the input, storage, and retrieval of information in any given store. This issue has been completely ignored but it obviously cannot be in reality. A second factor concerns the extent to which information in any store can be broken down into discrete and potentially separable items. In order for an information store to work properly, it must be possible for new items of information to be added to it, and for old items to be subtracted from it, without the operation of the store as a whole being interrupted. This means that the information in any store must consist of transitory agglomerates of discrete items, which however closely knit they may be in the short run, must ultimately be separable. It also means that the tracking limits of every information store will in part depend on the extent to which the information in a store can be broken down into separable sub-units. At Level 1 (the gene pool) this phenomenon has been described in terms of the Hill–Robertson effect (Hill and Robertson, 1966; Shields, in press). It is important to our understanding of sex since one crucial effect of sex is to break up genotypes into smaller sub-units, namely the genes. However, the point is a general one and it should apply to all information stores at all levels. A third factor relates to the evolution of intelligence, and to the application of deductive reasoning to information in store as a way of increasing the usefulness and potency of whatever information is in that store, perhaps very greatly. This factor is clearly not a general one. It applies to Levels 3 and 4 only and even then probably in very few species. However, it obviously does apply to human beings. Other major omissions concern between-level interactions, discussed in part elsewhere (Plotkin and Odling-Smee, 1979, 1981, 1982); and other information gaining processes which do not even appear in the present model (Figure 8.1). The most glaring example of the latter is the vertebrate immune system. Should the hypothesis start to prove successful, then all of these omissions will eventually have to be dealt with. But they should only amplify rather than negate the basic idea.

Finally, as far as human behavior is concerned, the hypothesis claims its relevance from the relevance of the nature–nurture issue in general. Given the persistence of that issue over many years, and also the omnipresent effects of our failure to understand how human behavior is either governed or self-governed, then any step which holds out some promise of increasing that understanding is probably worth pursuing. That at least is the excuse for this chapter. To end at the beginning, and therefore back with *The Tempest*: The truth is that if today's behavioral scientists were confronted by Caliban, we still would not know his identity, nor how, or if he could be educated. We might not even know if he was real, or just the stuff of dreams. Small wonder Prospero was 'vex'd'.

ACKNOWLEDGMENTS

I should like to thank Henry Plotkin and Celia Heyes for their helpful criticisms of an earlier draft.

REFERENCES

Bateson, P. P. G. (1976) Rules and reciprocity in behavioral development. In *Growing Points in Ethology*. (eds P. P. G. Bateson and R. A. Hinde). Cambridge University Press, Cambridge, pp. 401–421.

Bock, W. J. (1980) The definition and recognition of biological adaptation. *American Zoologist*, **20**, 217–227.

Campbell, D. T. (1974) Evolutionary epistemology. In *The Philosophy of Karl Popper* (ed. P. A. Schlipp). LaSalle, Ill: Open Court Publishing Co., pp. 413–463.

Campbell, D. T. (1979) *Descriptive epistemology: Psychological sociological and evolutionary*. (Preliminary draft of the William James lectures.)

Caplan, A. L. (Ed.) (1978) *The Sociobiology Debate*. Harper and Row, New York.

Cavalli-Sforza, L. L., and Feldman, M. W. (1981). *Cultural Transmission and Evolution: A Quantitative Approach*. Princeton University Press, Princeton.

Clutton-Brock, T. H., Albon, S. D., Gibson, R. M., and Guiness, F. E. (1979) The logical stag: adaptive aspects of fighting in red deer (*Cervus elaphus L.*). *Animal Behaviour*, **27**, 211–225.

Dewsbury, D. A. (1978) *Comparative Animal Behaviour*. McGraw-Hill, New York.

Durham, W. H. (1976) The adaptive significance of cultural behavior. *Human Ecology*, **4**, 89–121.

Freeman, R. D. (Ed.) (1979) *Developmental Neurobiology of Vision*, Plenum Press, New York.

Ghiselin, M. T. (1981) Categories, life and thinking. *The Behavioral and Brain Sciences*, **4**(2), 269–313.

Gottlieb, G. (1979) Comparative psychology and ethology. In *The First Century of Experimental Psychology*. (ed. E. Hearst). pp. 147–173. Erlbaum, Hillsdale, N.J.

Gould, S. J. (1980) The evolutionary biology of constraint. *Daedalus*, **109**(2), 39–52.

Gould, S. J., and Vrba, E. S. (1982) Extrapolation—a missing term in the science of thought. *Paleobiology*, **8**, (1): 4–15.

Gould, S. J., and Lewontin, R. C. (1979) The spandrels of San Marco and the Panglossian paradigm: a critique of the adaptationist program. *Proceedings of the Royal Society of London, Series B*. **205**, 581–598.

Hailman, J. P. (1969) How an instinct is learned. *Scientific American*, **221**, 98–106.

Hill, W. G., and Robertson, A. (1966) The effects of linkage on limits to artificial selection. *Genet. Res.*, **8**, 269–294.

Hinde, R. A. (1966) *Animal Behaviour: A Synthesis of Ethology and Comparative Psychology*. McGraw-Hill, London.

Hull, D. L. (1980) Individuality and selection. *Ann. Rev. Ecol. Syst.*, **11**, 311–332.

Kant, I. (1963) *Critique of Pure Reason*. Transl. by Kemp Smith, N. (1929). First published in German, 1787. (2nd ed.) Macmillan, London.

Lewontin, R. C. (1978) Adaptation. *Scientific American*, **239**, 212–230.

Lewontin, R. C. (1982 in press). Organism and environment. In *Learning, Development and Culture: Essays in Evolutionary Epistemology* (ed. H. C. Plotkin). Wiley, Chichester.

Lewontin, R. C., and Levins, R. (1978) *Evoluzione, Enciclopodia, V*. Torino: Einandi.

Marler, P. (1970) A comparative approach to vocal learning: Song development in white-crowned sparrows. *J. of Comp. Psy. Monograph.*, **71**(2), 1–25.

Maynard Smith, J. (1978) *The Evolution of Sex*. Cambridge University Press. Cambridge.

Mayr, E. (1974) Behavior programs and evolutionary strategies. *American Scientist.*, **62**, 650–659.

Mitchell, B., Staines, B. W., and Welch, D. (1977) *Ecology of Red Deer*. Institute of Terrestrial Ecology, Cambridge.

Plotkin, H. C., and Odling-Smee, F. J. (1979) Learning, change and evolution. *Advances in the study of behaviour*, **10**, 1–41.

Plotkin, H. C., and Odling-Smee, F. J. (1981) A multiple level model of evolution and its implications for sociobiology. *The Behavioral and Brain Sciences*, **4**(2), 225–268.

Plotkin, H. C., and Odling-Smee, F. J. (1982 in press) Learning in the context of a hierarchy of knowledge gaining processes. In *Learning, Development and Culture: Essays in Evolutionary Epistemology*. (ed. H. C. Plotkin) Wiley, Chichester.

Popper, K. R. (1968) *The Logic of Scientific Discovery* (revised ed.). Hutchinson, London.

Popper, K. R. (1972) *Objective Knowledge: An Evolutionary Approach*. Clarendon Press, Oxford.

Ruyle, E. E. (1973) Genetic and cultural pools: some suggestions for a unified theory of biocultural evolution. *Human Ecology*, **1**, 201–215.

Shields, W. M. (In press). Inbreeding and the paradox of sex: a resolution? *Evolutionary Theory*, in press.

Slobodkin, L. B. (1981) The meaning of 'evolutionary law'. Commentary on Plotkin, H. C. and Odling-Smee, F. J. A multiple-level model of evolution and its implications for sociobiology. *The Behavioral and Brain Sciences*, **4**(2), 252–253.

Slobodkin, L. B., and Rapoport, A. (1974) An optimal strategy of evolution. *Quarterly Rev. of Biology*, **49**, 181–200.

Stearns, S. C. (1976) Life-history tactics: a review of the ideas. *Quarterly Rev. of Biology*. **51**, 3–47.

Stearns, S. C. (1977) The evolution of life history traits: a critique of the theory and a review of the data. *Ann. Rev. Ecol. Syst.*, **8**, 145–171.

Tinbergen, N. (1953) *The Herring Gull's World*. Collins, London.

Waddington, C. H. (1969) Paradigm for an evolutionary process. In *Towards a Theoretical Biology*, **2**, Sketches (ed. C. H. Waddington). Edinburgh Univ. Press, Edinburgh, pp. 106–128.

Williams, G. C. (1975) *Sex and Evolution*. Princeton University Press, Princeton.

Wilson, E. O. (1975) *Sociobiology: The New Synthesis*. Harvard University Press, Cambridge, Mass.

Animal Models of Human Behavior
Edited by G. C. L. Davey
© 1983 John Wiley & Sons Ltd

Chapter 9

Biological, Psychological, and Historical Aspects of Reproduction and Child-care

Peter K. SMITH

Reproduction and the successful raising of young is the most crucial criterion of biological success for any animal species. For the human species it is also the means of passing on cultural traditions from one generation to the next. The topics of reproduction and child care thus provide one of the most sensitive areas for examing the interrelationships between biological, psychological, and sociocultural factors in their impact in guiding human behavior. I plan to outline here some of these interrelationships, and their implications for interdisciplinary cooperation.

I take as my starting point the sociobiology of reproduction and parental care in mammals. Sociobiological theory has had striking success in providing an explanatory framework for non-human reproduction and investment in offspring (see, for example, Gubernick and Klopfer, 1981). Not all issues are resolved by any means, but the utility of the approach is apparent.

Several attempts have also been made to apply such theorizing fairly directly to human reproduction and child-care; for example, by Van den Berghe and Barash (1977), Freedman (1979), and Alexander (1980). These attempts also appear to have had some success, but primarily in the consideration of pre-urban societies (e.g. Barkow and Burley, 1980). I shall argue that sociobiological theory is useful for the consideration of human reproduction and child-care, but only in combination with a theoretical framework which supplements biological theories of genetic transmission and evolution with interconnecting hypotheses about cultural transmission and the relative success and appeal of different cultural ideas. Such theoretical approaches have been put forward by, among others, Campbell (1975), Durham (1976), Richerson and Boyd (1978), and Lumsden and Wilson (1981).

An adequate assessment of these theoretical approaches requires a synthesis of data from a considerable variety of disciplinary sources. This chapter represents only a beginning in suggesting the kinds of data that are necessary and pointing the way for future investigation.

1. MAMMALIAN REPRODUCTION AND PARENTAL CARE: A RESUMÉ

Mammals, as an order, are characterized by high degrees of parental care and investment. This has been facilitated by the evolution of homiothermy in mammals (and birds), and the consequent high metabolic requirements of the young. The specialization of the female mammal for suckling the offspring has further favored a combination of relatively high parental investment and relatively low litter size (or 'K' selection, Horn, 1978). The greater encephalization or intelligence of many mammals, and their relatively complex social organization, would have further provided the opportunity for increased parental investment, and increased the benefits of such investment (Jerison, 1973; Wilson, 1975).

1.1. Litter size, sex ratio, and parental investment

Larger litters would potentially increase the reproductive fitness of a mammalian mother, but only if she could successfully rear them in the resource circumstances prevailing. There is thus an optimal litter size for the species, with actual litter sizes varying within a limited range around this optimum. The optimum could theoretically vary with the mother's age or condition. Sherman (1976) found, for example, that in Belding's ground squirrel, both very young and very old mothers had three to four offspring, whereas 'prime' mothers had six to eight. The optimum might also vary in unusually poor, or plentiful, resource conditions; there is some evidence for 'litter reduction' in some species, such as mice (Gandelman and Simon, 1978), hamsters (Day and Galef, 1977), and the dwarf mongoose (Rasa, 1977). These are species with relatively large litters, and in 'litter reduction' a few offspring are neglected or even killed and eaten. For species with small to moderate litter sizes, abandonment of a litter might be to the mother's interest if she can have another litter sooner, in more favorable resource circumstances. Tait (1980) has argued this possibility for the grizzly bear.

Klopfer and Klopfer (1977), working with goats, have shown that a mother goat with two kids will normally aim to give as much milk to the less vigorous kid as to the more vigorous one. If the difference in vigor exceeds a certain threshold, however, then compensation fails; Klopfer and Klopfer argue that this would be an adaptive response in a harsh environment where only one kid could be raised successfully.

Sociobiological theory has also made predictions about the sex ratio of offspring. If male and female offspring require equal investment, then a one:one sex ratio would appear to be an evolutionary stable strategy (ESS); but if (for example) male offspring require more investment, then the sex ratio should be biased towards females (Maynard Smith, 1980). Such a difference occurs in the Northern elephant seal, in which male pups are born heavier and are weaned for longer; but, unfortunately for the theory, female pups are *not* more numerous (Reiter *et al.*, 1981). Nor is it true for red deer, despite a similar differential investment in male calves (Clutton-Brock *et al.*, 1981).

Another prediction on sex ratios was made by Trivers and Willard (1973). For polygynous species, in which males have greater variance in reproductive success than females, a mother in 'prime' condition might advantageously produce high quality male offspring (investing more in them—rather than having more offspring as in the example of the ground squirrel given earlier). Conversely, a mother in poorer condition or status might advantageously produce more female offspring.

Unfortunately, for the same two species for which there is good data to test this, the prediction is not fulfilled. Reiter *et al.* (1981) found that 'prime' elephant seal mothers did not produce more male pups than other mothers. Similarly, Clutton-Brock, *et al.* (1981) did not find that 'prime' red deer mothers produced more male calves, or that very young, or old, mothers produced more female calves. Furthermore, McCracken and Bradbury (1981) found no correlation between sex of offspring and physical condition of mother, in the polygynous bat *phyllostomus hastatus*. At present, sex ratio in litters stands out as one area in which theoretical predictions and empirical data are not well in concordance.

1.2. Specificity of parental investment

Parental care in mammals tends to be highly selective, in a number of ways. First, parents usually selectively allocate resources to their own offspring. Secondly, offspring often selectively solicit resources from their own parents. Thirdly, non-parental adults may help, or exploit, other offspring, to a degree influenced by kinship relations and the social structure of the species.

It is normally advantageous for parents to allocate resources primarily to their own offspring. Specific mechanisms for this have evolved most readily for the mammalian female, who gives birth to her offspring; for the male, paternity of particular offspring can only be probabilistic. Especially for species with precocial young, or living in social groups, maternal attachment to offspring has proved selectively advantageous. For example, in ungulates, mothers spend much time rubbing and licking the newborn. It has been shown that in goats, this licking, together with nursing, serves to 'label' the newborn; mother goats will accept alien young, only if they have not been 'labeled' by another mother. For altricial or solitary species, maternal attachment may be less specifically developed; just returning to the nest site may be normally sufficient to ensure that only one's own offspring are fed (Gubernick, 1981).

Offspring may also develop attachment behaviors (such as proximity maintenance) to parents, usually the mother. If it develops, this is generally after parental attachment. Potentially, offspring could usefully solicit resources from any adult. However, it may well be the best strategy to rapidly limit solicitation to own parents, to avoid being rejected because of incorrect 'labeling' or stimulating the mother insufficiently. Mammalian maternal state is partly hormonally controlled, but also strongly influenced by infant stimulation such as suckling.

Mammalian male parental investment is more problematic. Male attachment to offspring can occur in monogamous species; here the male is very probably the father, and can fulfil all the maternal functions except nursing. In species with a very dominant male in a multi-male group, or with female-defense polygyny, males are likely to be much more well-disposed to offspring they are familiar with and thus probably the father of (Kleiman and Malcolm, 1981).

Behavior to offspring by adults who are certainly, or probably, not parents, can take a variety of forms. Such behavior when beneficial to the offspring is called alloparental care. Communal suckling is a prominent example in some mammalian species. Usually (e.g. lions, elephants, brown hyenas, banded mongooses) this occurs in small family-like social groups, where non-maternal suckling is done by aunts, siblings, or other probably close female relatives (Bertram, 1976). Some bat species may be a puzzling exception (Davis et al., 1962). In a few species, such as banded and dwarf mongooses (Rood, 1978) and black-backed jackals (Moehlmann, 1979), siblings from one year's litter may stay on and assist the parents rear future offspring, by food-getting and defense.

Actual 'adoption' of young, if mother or parents die, seems very rare in mammals. To some extent it may occur in species with communal care, as just mentioned. Lawick-Goodall (1968) observed three cases of 'adoption' in chimpanzees, all by older but inexperienced siblings; never by older but less closely related females who could have cared for the infants better.

Behavior of probably unrelated adults to young can range from indifference to hostility. In ungulates and pinnepeds, adults may chase off or reject alien young—another reason for the development of filial attachment. Mothers are aggressive to conspecific adults who approach their young in a wide range of mammalian species (Svare, 1981). Such aggression may well function to protect the young. In some species, infants may be killed by males who 'take over' a group of females from resident males, as in lion prides, and langur groups (Hrdy, 1979); this enables the males to father their own infants sooner, as the females cease suckling and conceive earlier. Male infanticide has also been observed experimentally in some rodents; it is inhibited by prior copulation with the female, and length of cohabitation (Labov, 1980). Infants may also be killed by unrelated female adults; this is a leading cause of infant mortality in Belding's ground squirrel, due to competition for nesting burrows (Sherman, in Hrdy, 1979).

In many of the social, ground-living primates, there is a considerable amount of 'aunting' or 'alloparenting', with unrelated adults or juveniles kidnaping and carrying infants for periods of time. In some cases, this seems beneficial to the mother or infant; for example, carrying by male chacma baboons who may well be the father, protecting the infant from immigrant males (Busse and Hamilton, 1981). In other cases, alloparents may take little care of infants, treating them roughly and preventing the mother from suckling. This seems to be observed more frequently when the alloparent is less closely related to the mother, or infant (Kurland, 1979; Quiatt, 1979), as would be predicted by kin selection theory.

1.3. Type and amount of parental investment

Investment in offspring by mothers, and (if applicable) fathers is primarily positive. Parents further their own reproductive success by raising healthy offspring to maturity. Such positive investment can take forms such as suckling and feeding, providing warmth and a nest site, defense against hostile conspecifics or predators, play, and providing opportunities for learning.

However, parent–offspring relations are not predicted to be entirely positive. Earlier (Section 1.1) we saw how a parent might kill or abandon an infant; this could be an example—an extreme one—of parent–offspring conflict, as envisaged by Trivers (1974), and predicated on the non-identical genetic interests of parent and offspring. Besides possible conflict over whether investment should occur at all, conflict could occur with surviving offspring over the amount and duration of investment, for example with respect to contemporary or future siblings.

Conflict over amount of suckling, and time of weaning, is a paradigm case for parent–offspring theory. In many mammals, the young try to suckle more, and longer, than the mother seems to wish (e.g. giraffe: Pratt and Anderson, 1979). Another possible example is conflict over degree of altruism to siblings. In 'helpers at the den' situations (Section 1.2) where an offspring delays its own reproductive role for at least one breeding season, some coercion from parents might conceivably be involved. Also, parents might be expected to discourage sibling rivalry.

Subsequent theoretical formulations have examined possible resolutions of parent–offspring conflict. For example, Parker and MacNair (1979) argued that in certain circumstances either an 'offspring wins' or a 'parent wins' ESS could be stable; but that a *pro rata* type ESS may be most likely, with the parent's behavior compromising between his/her own optimum and that of the offspring. The *pro rata* ESS does still imply some overt solicitation by offspring, without reward. The suckling strategy of a mother goat to two kids, studied by Klopfer and Klopfer (1977) may exemplify this type of ESS (see Section 1.1).

2. THE SOCIOBIOLOGY OF REPRODUCTION AND CHILD-CARE APPLIED TO HUMAN BEHAVIOR

In very broad terms, humans are like other mammals in that they have rather small families, usually direct much more investment to their own offspring than others, and generally behave solicitously to their own offspring though with aspects of conflict in a number of investment contexts. This is compatible with applying sociobiological predictions in a straightforward way to the human case.

However, any detailed application needs to make explicit its premises. Reproduction and care varies with species-type. A diachronic social-structural model of primate and hominid evolution could give a basis for more precise expectations of fitness-maximizing behaviors in the human case. This could lead to predictions for humans living in hunter–gatherer ecologies, which might not apply to more settled agricultural or urban communities (see chapter by Blurton Jones, p. 000). Nevertheless, we could continue to apply sociobiological reasoning to settled communities, if we assumed either that genetic adaptation to such new environments had been very rapid, or if we assumed that new cultural traditions continued to maximize genetic fitness (Lumsden and Wilson, 1981; Durham, 1976). Selective pressures characteristic of such new environments would need to be specified, and there is the added complication that most aspects of recent human environments are themselves direct results of human behavior. Furthermore, settled communities have meant larger communities, with opportunities for more organized regulation and exploitation between societal subgroups (Harris, 1977). Even in non-human species, ESS's can be complicated; the possibilities are much more so in human societies, with the likelihood of fitness-enhancing behavior of an individual being circumscribed by the attitudes and behavior of other individuals and groups, the whole being influenced by the possibly inertial effect of prior cultural traditions, and the possibly innovative effect of conscious awareness of the outcome of choices (Boehm, 1978).

Some sociobiological predictions are sufficiently robust that they come through despite a wide variety of ecological contexts. For example, the Trivers and Willard (1973) predictions on sex ratio of offspring apply whenever variance in reproductive success is greater in males than females— generally true in mammals including humans (Symons, 1979). Dickemann

(1979) has applied this to considerations of sex-biased infanticide in stratified human societies. She finds some evidence for female-biased infanticide in élite classes, though the corresponding evidence for male-biased infanticide in poorer classes is not at all satisfactory. It is ironic though that this now widely-quoted example is based on theoretical predictions which, as we saw earlier, have not yet been satisfactorily fulfilled in non-human mammalian species.

Difficulties in specifying predictions from sociobiological theory may be lessened if we know more about the mechanisms involved in any particular behavior (such as sex-biased infanticide), whether in human or non-human species. Some mechanisms may just be impossible, so that fitness cannot be maximized in the predicted direction. Some mechanisms may allow behavior to be modified according to environmental conditions (environmental scaling, Wilson, 1975), others less so, and in the latter case non fitness-maximizing behavior is more likely in new environments.

More fundamentally, the possibility that cultural beliefs and traditions can actually act against genetic fitness must be considered. A hypothetical example comes from Burley's (1979) theory of the evolution of concealed ovulation in the human female. She suggests that during hominid evolution, as the connection between ovulation, copulation and later childbirth began to be consciously realized, women started to avoid copulation near ovulation as a deliberate means of avoiding the pain and danger of childbirth and the burden of further child-rearing. If this was carried to fitness-reducing lengths, natural selection would have reduced signs of ovulation to the females themselves (as has occurred). This theory has drawbacks (Strassmann, 1981). But it does, hypothetically, illustrate how humans might have begun to act in ways contrary to biological fitness, because for example of greater knowledge, and the transmission of this knowledge in cultural tradition. Burley's example is posited well back in evolutionary history, with the genes having a decisive comeback; females whose genes did not lead to concealed ovulation, simply raised fewer successful offspring than those who did. But clearly scientifically more advanced societies could once again overcome the effect of the genes, either by improved birth control methods, or by artificial methods of detecting ovulation.

But could such an example be feasible? Strassmann (1981) argued that a large cerebrum would not have evolved if it had such maladaptive consequences. More generally, what is the relationship between cultural evolution and genetic fitness? William Durham (1976) has advanced what he calls a 'co-evolutionary' theory of biology and culture. According to Durham, it is implausible that genes can act specifically to favor or disfavor certain cultural traits. For example, it is unlikely that particular genes code for certain kinds of kinship terminology, or for more child care by mother's brother than father's brother, even though sociobiologists have advanced explanations of such phenomena in tribal societies (Greene, 1978; Kurland, 1979). However, Durham suggests that although culture acts as a separate system, cultural traits will usually be such as to maximize biological inclusive fitness. He suggests three main reasons for this. First, as our early human ancestors began to evolve the capacity for culture, natural selection would only have acted to increase this capacity if it was biologically adaptive. Secondly, although we have a general capacity to acquire culture, certain emotional biases or the ease of learning certain things may favor retention of learnt characteristics which enhance biological fitness. (These are called 'bias' by Boyd and Richerson, n.d. and 'epigenetic rules' by Lumsden and Wilson, 1981). Thirdly, the transmission of cultural traits, like the transmission of biological traits, is often from parents to offspring. (This is called 'symmetry' by Boyd and Richerson, n.d.) In such circumstances cultural traits that increase biological fitness, would lead to more offspring successfully raised, who would learn these cultural traits from their parents. Thus, these cultural traits would increase, more than other cultural traits which did not benefit biological fitness. Durham's argument, in general terms, is then that 'bias' and 'symmetry' have been sufficient to largely keep culture in harmony with biology.

Lumsden and Wilson (1981) have produced more advanced mathematical models, which incorporate patterns of individual variation (biased by epigenetic rules) and group influence on behavior, and the feedback of culture on to epigenetic rules ('culturgen assimilation'). They conclude that genes can track many cultural changes, via epigenetic rules, in the order of 1000 years or 50 generations. They see cultural conditions which contravene epigenetic rules and lower genetic fitness as probably temporary phenomena.

Donald Campbell (1975) put forward a model of explicit conflict between biological and cultural evolution. Campbell argued that complex urban societies required forms of behavior, such as increased altruism and cooperation with non-relatives, which would not be biologically optimal for the individual. He saw 'social systems preaching', which would include folk customs and religious and moral traditions, as acting to maximize sociocultural viability or success, at some expense to individual fitness. The social systems preaching might be couched in quite extreme terms, such as 'thou shalt not kill' or 'thou shalt not commit adultery', so that the resulting compromise with individually more selfish tendencies would in fact reach close to the sociocultural optimum.

Campbell's analysis was applied to complex, literate, urbanized societies. In such societies, formalized training of the young and the development of mass media from printed books onwards, would have made social systems preaching much more effective. Thus, Campbell's model of conflict may not be in opposition to Durham's model of harmony, but rather the two theories may apply primarily to different phases of human cultural evolution. In complex urban societies, cultural transmission is much more 'asymmetric' and one of Durham's main postulates is invalidated.

Richerson and Boyd (1978, Boyd and Richerson, n.d.) have produced a set of more general dual inheritance models, in which genetic and cultural transmission are seen as competing, each trying to maximize its own criterion of fitness, resulting in some compromise solution. Whether this compromise is nearer the genetic or cultural optimum is seen as being influenced by the strength of bias and symmetry in each case. Generally, the details of the transmission of cultural traits will be of great theoretical importance in these models, which can give largely gene-determined or largely culture-determined results depending on such assumptions.

Evalutation of these models has not yet proceeded very far. In the remainder of this chapter I shall suggest that data on human reproduction and child-care might be used to do so. In modern societies, compared to preliterate societies, aspects of such behavior often do not seem to maximize fitness.

2.1. Family size in human communities

From available evidence it would seem that fertility and mortality were in rough balance in prehistoric communities and in recent hunter–gatherer societies (Petersen, 1975; Short, 1976; May, 1978). A combination of physiological mechanisms and cultural traditions served to limit family size below the physiological maximum for human females, and to modulate it with respect to economic/resource considerations.

Amongst the Kalahari San, some of whom still live by hunting and gathering, births are spaced at approximately four-year intervals (Konner, 1972; Short, 1976). A mother usually has only one child under four years at any particular time. Blurton Jones and Sibly (1978) have argued that this is very likely to be maximizing the mother's fitness (see also Blurton Jones, Chapter 10). Mothers carry babies with them while gathering, and breast-feed on demand, for the first three years. The energetic costs of carrying and feeding two closely-spaced babies could be very considerable in these circumstances. In practice, completed family size seems to be about five (with perhaps three children surviving to reproductive maturity).

An important physiological mechanism here is lactational amenorrhea, or the reduction of fertility while breast-feeding. In modern communities, an extra month of breast-feeding can cause an average increase in birth interval of 0.4 months (Jain and Bongaarts, 1981). The effect may be even stronger in the San communities, where very frequent if brief nursing could particularly effectively suppress maternal gonadal function (Konner and Worthman, 1980).

Another possible physiological mechanism is nutritional infertility. If

Frisch (1978) is correct, female fertility is directly reduced when the volume of fat reserves in the body fall below a certain proportion of normal body weight. This would modulate fertility to prevailing nutritional conditions. Even if the direct effect is small (Menken *et al.*, 1981), malnourishment can reduce fertility indirectly via delayed menarche, advanced menopause, and reduced frequency of intercourse. Also, poorer food supply could mean longer weaning. Such mechanisms can produce a regulation of population (Skolnick and Cannings, 1972), without postulating mechanisms of group selection.

In addition, cultural traditions may reinforce and augment these physiological mechanisms. Amongst the San, and generally in hunter–gatherer societies, infanticide was an accepted practice in certain circumstances; if a baby was malformed, if twins were born, or if birth spacing was too close and/or the mother could not cope with another baby. In a cross-cultural study, Granzberg (1973) demonstrated that twin infanticide was likely in material circumstances in which a mother could not reasonably cope with feeding twins and with subsistence activities. Post-partum taboos on intercourse could reinforce the effects of lactational amenorrhea. Practices such as these could be considered as co-evolved cultural traits in the sense of Durham (1976), acting to maximize fitness by modulating family size to resources.

Wider aspects of cultural evolution would, however, have broken down this complex of co-evolved biological and cultural traits. A more sedentary existence could change breast-feeding habits; more spaced feeding would be likely if a mother does not carry her infant but returns periodically to feed it, perhaps with less contraceptive effect (Konner and Worthman, 1980). There would also be less obvious immediate reason to space births, as it would not create the same energetic problems of carrying two infants simultaneously.

A change to sedentarization could cause a shift in cultural traditions; would they continue to maximize fitness? Perhaps if there were strong 'bias', or 'epigenetic rules', which continued to operate adaptively; or if there remained a 'symmetry' of cultural transmission (Boyd and Richerson, n.d.; Lumsden and Wilson, 1981).

The 'bias' toward optimum family size presumably includes the sexual drive, physiological mechanisms such as lactational and nutritional amenorrhea, and a tendency to find young children attractive. With different styles of breast-feeding and better nutrition, these mechanisms could release population growth. Rational preselection (Boehm, 1978) could modulate this to anticipated resource levels. Indeed, this seems the case in some peasant societies. Thus, Nag, *et al.* (1978) argue that in Java, parents have as many children as they can afford and find useful. They write

this strategy of maximising the number of surviving children seems to serve the parents own interests . . . but it may not necessarily be the best strategy for the interests of their children or of the society as a whole.

In the absence of modern contraceptive techniques, infanticide and abandonment would, together with celibacy or delayed marriage, have become prime means of limiting family size. There is evidence that this was the case for pre-industrial Europe (Langer, 1972). In classical times, abortion and infanticide had been regarded as acceptable methods of birth control, though Christian Law, propagated in texts such as Gratian's *Decretum* of 1140 and the *Decretals* of Pope Gregory IX in 1234, regarded infanticide as a punishable offense (Helmholtz, 1975). In the Middle Ages it seems to have been regarded as a pardonable sin, which might be punished by, for example, three years penance, a lighter penalty even than for accidental homicide. Church law was stricter than secular law, and it was not until 1623 that a statute law was passed against mothers killing their own illegitimate children (Hanawalt, 1977).

It seems likely then that through the medieval and early modern period infanticide came under increasing prohibition from religious and secular sources. A high and probably increasing incidence of abandonment of infants is evidenced by the intake of foundling homes. The first were in Florence in the fourteenth and fifteenth centuries (Trexler, 1973). The Thomas Coram home was not opened in London until the eighteenth century, and similar institutions in France and Russia in the nineteenth century (Ransel, 1976; Langer, 1974). The general experience in such institutions was that the supply of babies left in the homes greatly exceeded any ability to cope, resulting in very high mortality rates—the notes sometimes left with babies often expressed regret, and the intention to return for the baby at a future time, but this very seldom happened (Trexler, 1973).

For wealthier parents, an alternative to abandonment was mercenary wet-nursing. This also seems to have been at its height in the seventeenth to nineteenth centuries. Here, a baby was 'farmed out' to a rural wet nurse, a few days after birth, either by a wealthy family, or by an urban family where both parents were working (Sussman, 1977). Since the mother did not breast-feed, we would expect her birth spacing to be reduced, and indeed the evidence is that such mothers' fertility rose by some 20 percent (Flandrin, 1979). However, the mortality rates of children put out to wet nurse were high, often twice as high as home-reared children, due to poor care and filthy conditions (Flandrin, 1979; Shorter, 1975). The consciously reported reasons for wet-nursing seem to have been various, but included pressure from husbands to resume sexual relations with their wives; at this time, it was believed that sexual relations would corrupt the mother's milk if she was breast-feeding. However, with its high mortality rates it may in practice have been an alternative to outright abandonment or infanticide as a means of family limitation.

Both abandonment and mercenary wet-nursing declined in the nineteenth century, and it is during this period that more effective contraceptive measures became widespread and acceptable. In the Paris basin, one of the earliest documented examples, census returns give evidence of increased birth intervals and therefore probably of planned families, by the early nineteenth century (Flandrin, 1979). In other regions it was later.

The demographic changes in early modern Europe have been the subject of considerable study. Besides such physiological mechanisms as discussed earlier (e.g. Lithell, 1981), we clearly have to consider the impact of religious codes, and societal sanctions, on an individual's sexual and reproductive behavior. If an individual's cultural traits are no longer strongly influenced by parents and close kin, then 'symmetry' breaks down, and one of Durham's (1976) conditions for co-evolved cultural traits is removed. In the absence of strong 'bias' factors for optimum family size, we cannot simply predict that individuals will maximize fitness. Rather, we have to consider the wider reasons for religious beliefs, the interests of different classes or subgroups, strengths of sanctions, degree of indoctrinability, knowledge of reproductive mechanisms, and many other factors. As Barkow and Burley (1980) have also argued, evolutionary biology cannot in itself explain this complex of factors. Consideration of the various earlier biocultural mechanisms, which have their ultimate explanations in evolutionary biology, will, however, provide a starting point for historical-evolutionary analysis.

2.2. Specificity of human parental investment

In all human societies, early care of and investment in offspring is primarily by mothers, or both parents. In many agricultural communities this is supplemented by care from older siblings, or grandparents (Weisner and Gallimore, 1977; Smith, 1980). In some societies investment by mother's brother exceeds that by 'father', but this is characteristically when confidence in paternal certainty is low (Gaulin and Schlegel, 1980).

A primary 'bias' or 'epigenetic rule' here is that attachment relationships tend to develop between an infant, and a caregiver who interacts with it sensitively and responsively. Attachment theorists argue that the process is developmentally channelled (Bowlby, 1969; Sroufe and Waters, 1977). Recent reviews suggest that the process need not involve just one adult caregiver (Smith, 1980), and need not depend on very early contact (i.e. first hours and days after birth) as some researchers have argued (Svejda et al., 1980).

Adoption of an unrelated child is biologically maladaptive; in normal circumstances, it does not increase one's inclusive fitness. But there is not much genetic 'bias' against it; adoptive parents and children can form attachment relationships as well as natural parents and children, especially if the adoption is at an early age. Nevertheless, in pre-industrial societies cultural traditions seem to have co-evolved to make adoption rare and, when it occurs, it is almost invariably of related children. Writing of the Kalahari San, Marshall (1965) pointed out that adoption only occurred with orphaned children, who were looked after by their grandparents, or an older sibling. In a cross-cultural review, Goody (1969) showed that in historical times and in present-day non-urban communities, adoption when it occurred was characteristically done by close relatives.

Adoption is most common in some of the Polynesian islands, where some 25 percent of children may be raised away from their parents. In her review, Silk (1980) showed that 80 percent of adoptive parents were relatives. In Tahiti, for example, men and women delay a long time in forming settled relationships. A first pregnancy may not cement a relationship, and such a child often gets a more stable environment in the home of older relatives such as grandparents. Adoption does not mean a cutting of ties with the natural mother (Levy, 1973). Silk (1980) did find that biological children still tended to be more favored in inheritance rights than adopted children.

Another common case of non-parental care is that of kinship fostering in many African societies, such as Ghana, whereby many children at around 6 to 8 years go to live with another family, usually of an aunt or uncle. The benefits seem to be in terms of getting wider skills and experience before adolescence (Goody, 1970).

Systematic adoption of unrelated children seems to have been a relatively recent practice, restricted to urbanized societies. In England, the Adoption Law dates from 1926. In general, psychological surveys find well-planned adoptions to have very successful outcomes (Tizard, 1977). An important proviso for the success of adoption and fostering is the commitment of the adoptive or foster-parent. Such a lack of commitment may explain the statistically greater risk of child abuse in step-parent households (Lenington, 1981; Daly and Wilson, 1981), as well as the high mortality of children farmed out to wet-nurses in the seventeenth to nineteenth centuries in Europe.

Contemporary adoption is generally seen as a positive act on the part of adoptive parents. Do grandparents also view it as positively? Are adopted children more likely to adopt, themselves? These are interesting questions for sociobiologists to explore. As with family size, however, it seems likely that there is little 'bias' against adoption, and that 'symmetry' has again broken down since pre-industrial times. It is unclear that sociobiological theory has very much to say about contemporary fostering and adoption.

2.3. Type of parental investment

The formation of attachment relationships would constitute a 'bias' for parents to behave in a predominantly positive fashion to their offspring. Amongst the Kalahari San, Konner (1977) has described characteristic patterns of attachment behavior, and documented levels of face-to-face interaction, smiling and reciprocal responsiveness between mothers and babies, similar to levels in modern Western societies. However, the affective tone of parental care may vary considerably. In many agricultural communities, the general tenor of anthropological observations is that there is much maternal emphasis on physical well-being, with breast-feeding on demand and much perceptual and motor stimulation, but with face-to-face social interaction being less prominent. LeVine (1974) has proposed that in such societies, where fertility controls may have weakened but where infant mortality for the under-fives is typically 30 to 60 percent, the parents' highest priority is 'the physical survival and health of the child, including the normal development of his reproductive capacity during puberty'. LeVine considers that the parental care pattern thus puts the emphasis on physical health, while postponing more intense aspects of social involvement until later when there was more confidence in a child's continued survival.

These patterns of behavior are broadly in line with what sociobiologists would predict, as is the evidence for certain pervasive types of mother–child conflict, for example over weaning. Conflict over weaning does not seem ubiquitous (e.g. Levy, 1973) but it is certainly common. However, I do not have space here to review evidence on parent–child conflict, beyond pointing out that it is normally in the context of considerable parental investment in the child.

Not only does the attachment relationship provide a 'bias' toward such positive investment; it is also true that in pre-industrial societies cultural transmission about child-rearing practices is mainly from parents (at least mothers) to offspring. To quote Whiting (1974),

> in pre-literate societies there are obviously no 'how to do it' manuals. Mothers and grandmothers teach their children how to treat infants and toddlers, and pass on homilies and advice about child rearing.

Such lines of cultural transmission would have diversified in early modern Europe, with the invention of printing, coupled with strong moral preaching from the Christian church and later from nonconformist sects. In principle, such 'asymmetric' cultural transmission and 'social systems preaching' (Campbell, 1975) could be expected to lead to cultural traits which did not maximize fitness; but in this case, the 'bias' or 'epigenetic rule' embodied in the development of attachment relationships might nevertheless prevent parents from being generally cruel or uncaring to their children.

Nevertheless, many historians argue that in early modern and early industrial Europe, parents *were* cruel and uncaring to their children. For example, Shorter (1975) wrote

> good mothering is an invention of modernisation. In traditional society, mothers viewed the development and happiness of infants younger than two with indifference . . . mothers did not love their children very much.

Similar or stronger views come from Langer (1974) and de Mause (1974). Much of the evidence for these views comes from the high incidence of infanticide, abandonment, and mercenary wet-nursing. However, as Langer (1972) also implied, these behaviors may have reflected desperate measures by parents to cope with more babies than they had resources for, rather than distorted projections of hostile feelings as postulated by de Mause (1974).

Another source of evidence comes from parent advice manuals. These often prescribed harsh or cruel punishments for disobedience. However, there is no certainty that parents followed the advice of such manuals, which may have been trying to change parental behavior (Mechling, 1975). More direct evidence comes from diaries and autobiographies kept by parents and children. In an analysis of over 400 such manuscripts, from the sixteenth to the nineteenth centuries, Pollock (in press) found no evidence that children were more harshly treated in these earlier centuries than today. The general picture was of affectionate parent–child relationships and of considerable concern and investment by parents in the health and well-being of their children. This of course is what would be expected, given contemporary psychological theories of attachment relationships.

3. CONCLUSIONS

Although it is interesting to examine predictions from evolutionary biology in the case of human behavior, in practice they cannot provide a complete explanation for contemporary societies. A detailed analysis, for example in matters of reproduction and child-care, must consider mechanisms behind behavioral choices, and the impact of wider cultural and economic issues. In a simple way, as considered here, we can examine the existence of 'bias' and 'symmetry' for particular types of behavior. Such simple analysis already suggests that family size, and specificity of parental investment, need no longer conform to predictions of fitness maximization. Type of parental care might do so more closely, in contradiction to the abiological assumptions of many psychohistorians.

As models for the interaction of biological and cultural evolution are further developed, historical data from pre-modern Europe could provide a useful source of relevant material. This period heralds a rise in social systems preaching and parenting manuals, and a very marked breakdown of the co-evolved mechanisms of biological and cultural traits which characterized prehistoric communities. Many questions could be asked of the historical data. In what ways were certain cultural or religious ideas transmitted—by whom, to whom? Why did certain cultural ideas become accepted? Were they generally accepted, or imposed by a few? Did husbands and wives agree equally on matters such as abandonment, or wet-nursing? We are looking here at changing attitudes and moralities, and their impact on human emotions and desires in relation to the biologically fundamental matters of reproduction and child-care and their interplay with other kinds of needs and satisfactions. If our theories are on the right track in conceptualizing the interaction between biological and cultural transmission systems, the anthropology, psychology, and history of reproduction and child-care should provide a rich source of material for their elaboration.

ACKNOWLEDGMENT

I am grateful to Linda Pollock for comments on an earlier draft of this manuscript.

REFERENCES

Alexander, R. D. (1980) *Darwinism and Human Affairs*. London: Pitman.

Barkow, J. H., and Burley, N. (1980) Human fertility, evolutionary biology, and the demographic transition. *Ethology and Sociobiology*, 1, 163–180.

Bertram, B. C. R. (1976) Kin selection in lions and in evolution. In P. P. G. Bateson and R. A Hinde (eds) *Growing Points in Ethology*. Cambridge: Cambridge University Press.

Blurton Jones, N., and Sibly, R. M. (1978) Testing adaptiveness of culturally determined behaviour: do Bushman women maximise their reproductive success by spacing births widely and foraging seldom? In N. Blurton Jones and V. Reynolds (eds) *Human Behaviour and Adaptation*. London: Taylor and Francis.

Boehm, C. (1978) Rational preselection from hamadryas to *homo sapiens*: the place of decisions in adaptive process. *American Anthropologist*, 80, 265–296.

Bowlby, J. (1969) *Attachment and Loss, Vol. I: Attachment*, London: Hogarth Press.

Boyd, R., and Richerson, P. J. (n.d.) Multiple parents and nonlinear cultural transmission. Unpublished manuscript.

Burley, N. (1979) The evolution of concealed ovulation. *American Naturalist*, 114, 835–858.

Busse, C., and Hamilton, W. J. III (1981) Infant carrying by male chacma baboons. *Science*, 212, 1281–1283.

Campbell, D. T. (1975) On the conflicts between biological and social evolution and between psychology and moral tradition. *American Psychologist*, 30, 1103–1126.

Clutton-Brock, T. H., Albon, S. D., and Guinness, F. E. (1981) Parental investment in male and female offspring in polygynous mammals. *Nature*, 289, 487–489.

Daly, M., and Wilson, M. I. (1981) Abuse and neglect of children in evolutionary perspective. In R. D. Alexander and D. W. Tinkle (eds) *Natural Selection and Social Behaviour*. New York: Chiron Press.

Davis, R. B., Herreid, C. F., and Short, H. L. (1962) Mexican free-tailed bats in Texas. *Ecological Monographs*, 32, 311–346.

Day, C. S. D., and Galef, B. G. (1977) Pup cannibalism: one aspect of maternal behaviour in golden hamsters. *Journal of Comparative and Physiological Psychology*, **91**, 1179–1189.

De Mause, L. (1974) The evolution of childhood. In L. De Mause (ed.) *The History of Childhood*. New York: Psychohistory Press.

Dickemann, M. (1979) The ecology of mating systems in hypergynous dowry societies. *Social Science Information*, **18**, 163–195.

Durham, W. H. (1976) The adaptive significance of cultural behaviour. *Human Ecology*, **4**, 89–121.

Flandrin, J. C. (1970) *Families in Former Times*. Cambridge: Cambridge University Press.

Freedman, D. G. (1979) *Human Sociobiology: a holistic approach*. London: Collier Macmillan.

Frisch, R. E. (1978) Population, food intake and fertility. *Science*, **199**, 22–30.

Gandelman, R., and Simon, N. G. (1978) Spontaneous pup-killing in response to large litters. *Developmental Psychology*, **11**, 235–241.

Gaulin, S. J. C., and Schlegel, A. (1980). Paternal confidence and paternal investment: a cross-cultural test of a sociobiological hypothesis. *Ethology and Sociobiology*, **1**, 301–309.

Goody, E. (1970) Kinship fostering in Gonja: deprivation or advantage? In P. Mayer (ed.) *Socialization: The Approach from Social Anthropology*. London: Tavistock.

Goody, J. (1969) Adoption in cross-cultural perspective. *Comparative Studies in Society and History*, **11**, 55–78.

Granzberg, G. (1973) Twin infanticide—a cross cultural test of a materialistic explanation. *Ethos*, **1**, 405–412.

Greene, P. J. (1978) Promiscuity, paternity and culture. *American Ethnologist*, **5**, 151–159.

Gubernick, D. J. (1981) Parent and infant attachment in mammals. In D. J. Gubernick and P. H. Klopfer (eds) *Parental Care in Mammals*. New York: Plenum.

Gubernick, D. J., and Klopfer, P. H. (1981) *Parental Care in Mammals*. New York: Plenum Press.

Hanawalt, B. A. (1977) Child rearing among lower classes of late medieval England. *Journal of Interdisciplinary History*, **8**, 1–22.

Harris, M. (1977) *Cannibals and Kings*. New York: Random House.

Helmholtz, R. H. (1975) Infanticide in the Province of Canterbury during the Fifteenth Century. *History of Childhood Quarterly*, **2**, 379–390.

Horn, H. S. (1978) Optimal tactics of reproduction and life-history. In J. R. Krebs and N. B. Davies (eds) *Behavioural Ecology: An Evolutionary Approach*. Oxford: Blackwell.

Hrdy, S. B. (1979) Infanticide among animals: a review, classification, and examination of the implications for the reproductive strategies of females. *Ethology and Sociobiology*, **1**, 13–40.

Jain, A. K., and Bongaarts, J. (1981) Breastfeeding: patterns, correlates and fertility effects. *Studies in Family Planning*, **12**, 79–99.

Jerison, H. J. (1973) *The Evolution of the Brain and Intelligence*. New York: Academic Press.

Kleiman, D. G., and Malcolm, J. R. (1981) Evolution of male parental investment in mammals. In D. J. Gubernick and P. H. Klopfer (eds), *Parental Care in Mammals*. New York: Plenum Press.

Klopfer, P., and Klopfer, M. (1977) Compensatory responses of goat mothers to their impaired young. *Animal Behaviour*, **25**, 286–291.

Konner, M. S. (1972) Aspects of the developmental ethology of a foraging people. In N. Blurton Jones (ed.) *Ethological Studies of Child Behaviour*. Cambridge: Cambridge University Press.

Konner, M. (1977) Infancy among the Kalahari Desert San. In P. H. Leiderman, S. R. Tulkin, and A. Rosenfeld (eds) *Culture and Infancy*. New York: Academic Press.

Konner, M., and Worthman, C. (1980) Nursing frequency, gonadal function, and birth spacing among !Kung hunter-gatherers. *Science*, **207**, 788–791.

Kurland, J. A. (1979) Paternity, mother's brother and human sociality. In N. A. Chagnon and W. Irons (eds) *Evolutionary Biology and Human Social Behavior*. Massachusetts: Duxbury Press.

Labov, J. B. (1980) Factors influencing infanticidal behavior in wild male house mice (*Mus musculus*). *Behavioral Ecology and Sociobiology*, **6**, 297–303.

Langer, W. L. (1972) Checks in population growth: 1750–1850. *Scientific American*, **226**, 92–99.

Langer, W. L. (1974) Infanticide: a historical survey. *History of Childhood Quarterly*, **1**, 353–365.

Lawick-Goodall, J. van. (1968) The behaviour of free-living chimpanzees in the Gombe Stream Reserve. *Animal Behaviour Monographs*, **1**, 161–311.

Lenington, S. (1981) Child abuse: the limits of sociobiology. *Ethology and Sociobiology*, **2**, 17–29.

LeVine, R. A. (1974) Parental goals: a cross cultural view. *Teachers College Record*, **76**, 226–239.

Levy, R. I. (1973) *Tahitians: mind and experience in the Society Islands*. Chicago: University of Chicago Press.

Lithell, U. B. (1981) Breastfeeding habits and their relation to infant mortality and marital fertility. *Journal of Family History*, 182–194.

Lumsden, C. J., and Wilson, E. O. (1981) *Genes, Minds and Culture*. Cambridge, Massachusetts: Harvard University Press.

Marshall, L. (1965) The !Kung Bushmen of the Kalahari desert. In J. L. Gibbs (ed.) *People of Africa*. New York: Holt, Rinehart and Winston.

May, R. M. (1978) Human reproduction reconsidered. *Nature*, **272**, 491–495.

Maynard Smith, J. (1980) A new theory of sexual investment. *Behavioral Ecology and Sociobiology*, **7**, 247–251.

McCracken, G. F., and Bradbury, J. W. (1981) Social organization and kinship in the polygynous bat *Phyllostomus hastatus*. *Behavioral Ecology and Sociobiology*, **8**, 11–34.

Mechling, J. E. (1975) Advice to historians on advice to mothers. *Journal of Social History*, **9**, 44–63.

Menken, J., Trussel, J., and Watkins, S. (1981) The nutrition fertility link: an evaluation of the evidence. *Journal of Interdisciplinary History*, **11**, 425–441.

Moehlmann, P. D. (1979) Jackal helpers and pup survival. *Nature*, **277**, 382–383.

Nag, M., White, B. N. F., and Peet, R. C. (1978) An anthropological approach to the study of the economic value of children in Java and Nepal. *Current Anthropology*, **19**, 293–306.

Parker, G. A., and MacNair, M. R. (1979) Models of parent–offspring conflict. IV. Suppression: evolutionary retaliation by the parent. *Animal Behaviour*, **27**, 1210–1235.

Petersen, W. (1975) A demographer's view of prehistoric demography. *Current Anthropology*, **16**, 227–245.

Pollock, L. Forgotten children: parent–child relations from 1600 to 1900. Cambridge: Cambridge University Press, in press.

Pratt, D. M., and Anderson, V. H. (1979) Giraffe cow–calf relationships and social development of the calf in the Serengeti. *Zeitschrift für Tierpsychologie*, **51**, 233–251.

Quiatt, D. (1979) Aunts and mothers: adoptive implications of allomaternal behavior of nonhuman primates. *American Anthropologist*, **81**, 310–319.

Ransel, D. L. (1976) Abandoned children of Imperial Russia: village fosterage. *Bulletin of the History of Medicine*, **50**, 501–510.

Rasa, O. A. E. (1977) The ethology and sociology of the dwarf mongoose (*Helogale Undulata rufula*). *Zeitschrift für Tierpsychologie*, **43**, 337–406.

Reiter, J., Panken, K. J., and Le Boeuf, B. J. (1981) Female competition and reproductive success in northern elephant seals. *Animal Behaviour*, **29**, 670–687.

Richerson, P. J., and Boyd, R. (1978) A dual inheritance model of the human evolutionary process I: basic postulates and a simple model. *Journal of Social and Biological Structures*, **I**, 127–154.

Rood, J. P. (1978) Dwarf mongoose helpers at the den. *Zeitschrift für Tierpsychologie*, **48**, 277–287.

Sherman, P. W. (1976) Natural selection among some group-living organisms. Unpublished PhD thesis, University of Michigan, Ann Arbor.

Short, R. V. (1976) The evolution of human reproduction. *Proceedings of Royal Society of London B.* **195**, 3–24.

Shorter, E. (1975) *The Making of the Modern Family*. New York: Basic Books.

Silk, J. B. (1980) Adoption and kinship in Oceania. *American Anthropologist*, **82**, 799–820.

Skolnick, M. H., and Cannings, C. (1972) Natural regulation of numbers in primitive human populations. *Nature*, **239**, 287–288.

Smith, P. K. (1980) Shared care of young children: alternative models to monotropism. *Merrill-Palmer Quarterly*, **26**, 371–389.

Sroufe, L. A., and Waters, E. (1977) Attachment as an organisational construct. *Child Development*, **48**, 1184–1199.

Strassmann, B. I. (1981) Sexual selection, parental care and concealed ovulation in humans. *Ethology and Sociobiology*, **2**, 31–40.

Sussman, G. D. (1977) Parisian infants and Norman wet nurses in the early eighteenth century: a statistical study. *Journal of Interdisciplinary History*, **7**, 637–653.

Svare, B. B. (1981) Maternal aggression in mammals. In D. J. Gubernick and P. H. Klopfer (eds) *Parental Care in Mammals*. New York: Plenum Press.

Svejda, M. J., Campos, J. J., and Emde, R. N. (1980) Mother–infant "bonding": failure to generalise. *Child Development*, **51**, 775–779.

Symons, D. (1979) *The Evolution of Human Sexuality*. New York and Oxford: Oxford University Press.

Tait, D. E. N. (1980) Abandonment as a reproductive tactic—the example of grizzly bears. *American Naturalist*, **115**, 800–808.

Tizard, B. (1977) *Adoption: A Second Chance*. London: Open Books.

Trexler, R. C. (1973) The foundlings of Florence, 1395–1455. *History of Childhood Quarterly*, **1**, 259–284.

Trivers, R. L. (1974) Parent–offspring conflict. *American Zoologist*, **14**, 249–264.

Trivers, R. L., and Willard, D. E. (1973) Natural selection of parental ability to vary the sex ratio of offspring. *Science*, **179**, 90–92.

Van den Berghe, P. L., and Barash, D. P. (1977) Inclusive fitness and human family structure. *American Anthropologist*, **79**, 869–823.

Weisner, T. S., and Gallimore, R. (1977) My brother's keeper: child and sibling caretaking. *Curent Anthropology*, **18**, 169–190.

Whiting, B. B. (1974) Folk wisdom and child rearing. *Merrill-Palmer Quarterly*, **20**, 9–19.

Wilson, E. D. (1975) *Sociobiology: The New Synthesis*. Cambridge, Massachusetts: Belknap Press.

Animal Models of Human Behavior
Edited by G. C. L. Davey
© 1983 John Wiley & Sons Ltd

Chapter 10

Two Investigations of Human Behavior Guided by Evolutionary Theory

N. G. BLURTON JONES

INTRODUCTION

The main aim of this paper is to outline two studies of human behavior which are guided by evolutionary theory. The reader can then judge whether this is as wicked, misleading, and dangerous a way to proceed as some critical writings on evolution and human behavior would suggest.

At least four different activities help us assess the value and correctness of the application of modern evolutionary theory to studying human behavioral adaptations:

1. Many people have published discussions of the theoretical basis, particularly some of the objections that have been raised. This will continue, most usefully concentrated around studies of the adaptiveness of learning.

2. One can compare the theory and its use with other theories that attempt to explain the same phenomena, in particular with other theories of cultural adaptation, which are not so slavishly based on modern evolutionary theory. (Blurton Jones, 1976; Burnham, 1973; Allard, 1975.)

3. One can make models of cultural transmission and see what they do, and see what constraints on imitation (who imitates whom, who imitates what classes of things) would have to be postulated to give similar results to natural selection acting on genetic transmission. This is now an active field (Durham 1976, 1978; Pulliam and Dunford, 1980; Richerson and Boyd, 1978). Psychologists should be interested in this field because it could direct experimental work on imitation.

4. As in animal behavior research, people are beginning to simply use the theories to guide empirical research, intending later to look back and see

how we got on. This is happening in anthropology and archeology (Alexander, 1974, 1979; Chagnon and Irons, 1979; Essock-Vitale and McGuire, 1980; Blurton Jones and Reynolds, 1978; Hawkes and Hill, in press; O'Connell and Hawkes, in press).

I wish to illustrate and discuss the last option. I will outline and discuss two studies of adaptiveness of behavior in which attempts are made to measure the costs and benefits for survival and reproduction of behaving one way or another. Ultimately from this the optimal (inclusive fitness maximizing—not optimal from any other point of view) behavior could be calculated, and compared with the observed behavior. A main attraction in trying to apply this to human behavior is the hope for predicting the result of changes in the environment or in technology. But it also offers a way of understanding variation between cultures, as it does between animal species. Knowing the adaptiveness of behavior may also set a framework for guiding direct studies of motivation and development (McFarland, 1976, 1978).

However, the optimization approaches are based totally on the theory of evolution. Natural selection will produce behavior which maximizes inclusive fitness. There is no absolute guarantee that this must also apply to culturally transmitted behavior. Some of us think that it might. But this is the central point of most of the debate. A halfway house may be found in optimal foraging studies (reviewed by Krebs, 1978) which are based on a more limited proposition, which may be more acceptable to students of human behavior, but which animal ecologists accept because it seems sensible to start with a simple proposition, so long as it is one that looks like an approximate estimate of fitness. Thus the simplest optimal foraging model proposes that animals select their food in a way that yields the greatest number of calories per unit of time spent foraging. Obviously there may be circumstances in which some other component of diet is an important benefit (e.g. Katz *et al.*, 1974), and time may be a more or less important cost for a variety of reasons e.g. to avoid predation, or to perform other beneficial behavior. But the assumption is clear, straightforward, and produces testable predictions. The predictions are often fulfilled by behavior of animals. More complicated models have also been developed and tested.

Hawkes, Hill and O'Connell (1982), and O'Connell and Hawkes (1981) have applied optimal foraging theory to the foraging of contemporary hunter gatherers. They find that the predictions of the model are largely fulfilled and that even simple optimal foraging models predict which foods are used, and the order in which foods enter or leave the diet as the environment or technology changes. Earle and Christenson (1980) describe similar, more complicated models which aim to cover subsistence agriculture and a wider range of costs. Potentially, optimal foraging models could be related to the views people express about their food preferences and taboos as well as to the observational data on foraging.

One reason why it is easier to accept the applicability of optimal foraging models to human behavior is that we can readily grasp the idea of people wanting to eat more and work less and accept this as guiding their behavior. Perhaps I should list and discuss briefly some of the commoner or more reasonable objections to using evolutionary theory to guide studies of human behavior.

1. People learn most of their behavior. So natural selection must be irrelevant. People do what they find rewarding, or what they are taught.

So do animals. All behavior has a developmental history and is more or less modifiable. Yet this does not stop animal behaviorists being interested in the adaptiveness of behavior, pursuing answers to Tinbergen's (1963) third 'why'—what is the adaptive value of this behavior.

Learning mechanisms would not have evolved if they had not given a reproductive advantage. There is a debate about whether the speed of cultural transmission implies that it could escape from the constraints of survival and reproduction, and if so how much and for how long. Durham (1976) noting that 'neutral' or 'cost free cultural messages' are conceivable has suggested that they might occur. Evolutionists will recall comparable issues, and the view that such a proposition though logical, is a 'cop out'.

2. People do not go around thinking about how many descendants they will leave. People know what they are doing, can explain what they do and can tell us what their behavior means.

As far as we can tell animals do not think about their descendants either, probably even less than people do! Since people's explanations and interpretations of their behavior differ among cultures and individuals, we have the task of explaining why they think what they think. Part of the explanation may indeed be in Tinbergen's first and second 'why's': motivation and development (e.g. they think this because their parents and others tell them to, or more likely speak of this idea as a proper kind of idea). But why do parents promote one set of ideas in one culture and another set in another culture. A third level explanation, adaptive function, may have a role. There are some genuine rival theories, discussed in detail by Harris (1979; 1968). One central issue is whether the environment and necessities of life have an influence on ideas, or whether internal mental processes govern the way ideas change. If the former, then adaptive explanations may have a place. On the other hand if internal mental processes are the governing factor (perhaps based on universal features of human brains as structuralists would claim for example) it is hard to see why these processes move at different speeds and in different directions in different cultures, unless by some interaction with their environment.

3. Showing that something is 'adaptive' does not explain why it happens. What they do turns out to be useful, why? How does it come about that the useful behavior is evoked in the right situation.

Knowing about adaptiveness enables us to know what criteria decisions are most likely to be based on and what the decision rules are. But it is not a demonstration of how those criteria evoke behavior or influence attitudes in the short term. In the framework of Tinbergen's 'four why's' adaptiveness is one explanation, to do with long-term feedback but it is distinct from short-term causal or motivational explanations, and distinct from explanations that concern influences during the individual's development.

But it is true that adaptiveness is only one of several complementary levels of explanation (see also Barkow, Chapter 11). Adaptiveness concerns long term feedback, it is an ultimate cause by virtue of the influence of motives and behavior on the subsequent abundance of individuals that think and behave that way. But suppose it is true that people (like other animals) learn adaptive behavior, and, as common sense unreliably suggests and Smith and Sluckin (1979) remind us, people can think out 'sensible' behavior (we always beg the question of the unconscious or emotional criteria for 'sensible', for instance the concept of 'rational economic man'—why is it *rational* to work for the good of one's family, or to earn more money). Then people must be able to switch rapidly from behaving adaptively in one circumstance to behaving adaptively in another circumstance. If our research goal is either predicting behavior, or intervening to promote economic development (with whatever policy target—whether from industrialization on the one hand to better fed, less diseased, still socially coherent rural societies on the other hand) then knowing the ecology properly in the adaptive framework may be quite sufficient. We may not need to know the motivational and ontogenetic reasons in order to predict or bring about acceptable change with predictable consequences that can be laid before the decision makers (whoever they may be—city politicians or rural people themselves).

4. 'The demographic transition' proves that people do not maximize their reproductive success because as they get wealthier they have fewer children.

To my mind this is the most powerful objection. But it is an empirical one. We could attempt to measure the costs of having more children than average in urban industrial society. Economists (e.g. Schultz *et al.*, 1974) have approached this in their own way, and place importance on 'quality versus quantity' decisions and on the financial cost to women of child-rearing (children cost educated women more because the woman sacrifices more earning power by having children). However, the low reproductive rate of wealthy people remains a challenge to evolutionary theory (Barkow and Burley, 1980).

Some other serious issues arise from these points: (1) what are ideas and conscious plans for, are they all good for recipients as well as proponents, when do we believe them, when don't we (see Dawkins and Krebs, 1978, and Smith and Sluckin, 1979). (2) Is adaptation about avoiding the impossible, or performing the optimal? (Sahlins, 1974). (3) How are goals and motives balanced off against each other to give rise to optimal or evolutionary stable behavior? I will return to some of these in the discussion, after describing two studies in which the behavioral ecology approach is applied to aspects of human behavior.

My first example of a use of evolutionary theory in guiding direct studies of human behavior escapes several of the objections discussed above. But it does so merely because it concerns newborn babies, and (1) because we are more at ease regarding them as comparable to animals (surely much of this depends on just how much we like animals, and babies, zoologists happen to like animals rather a lot), and (2) perhaps because in this example we accept staying alive as a near enough approximation to inclusive fitness. Actually survival fails to be a complete measure of the newborn's fitness in two ways: (1) it may be worth incurring extra costs as a newborn to reduce later costs or risks—e.g. by making mother like you more (2) there are restricted but conceivable situations in which natural selection will favor a baby that dies, e.g. if thereby it increases its mother's offspring by more than two additional full-siblings.

One can imagine a baby being so difficult to raise that the time and effort of raising it reduced greatly the number of other offspring the mother raised. Under such a circumstance one can imagine the spread of a gene that promotes the early death of such an offspring. Hartung and Ellison (1978) have shown how this theory predicts lowered reproduction by the parents of severely handicapped children, and thus a eugenic effect of keeping such children alive. This is an important proposition which runs counter to the usual suggestions about the genetic effects of medical intervention. But it also raises a point that still needs to be repeated, even after six years of sociobiology: it does not follow that if a characteristic is adaptive we have to regard it as good. Suppose one found that for some premature babies their prematurity was an adaptive response—they were designed by evolution to die. Surely it is quite clear that this does not tell us that we must let them die. That is a decision that belongs outside science. But such a finding might have medical implications, it might warn against the relatively *laissez-faire* 'help nature help itself' approach favored by some medical people and for the more directly interventionist approach favored by other members of that profession.

ADAPTIVE BEHAVIOR BY THE NEWBORN

The newborn study was devised by R. Woodson, and is being carried out by Woodson, and H. Morgan at the Institute of Obstetrics and Gynaecology under the direction of Geoffrey Chamberlain and myself, funded by the Mental Health Foundation. Following from his earlier work on the relationship between perinatal events and newborn behavior in one of our longitudinal studies, (Woodson *et al.*, 1979) and doubtless influenced by views expressed earlier by Freedman and by Chisholm (1978) (but independently from the excitingly similar outlook of G. Anderson-Shanklin (Anderson, 1977), Woodson proposed that the behavior of newborn babies should be looked at as part of the evolved homeostatic system of the baby. The function of newborn behavior would be to help the baby stay alive by aiding its physiology in getting the internal environment to normal levels, after the disruption of birth, and through the normal changes from fetal to postnatal life. If it was an evolved system it might be adapted to work only in a certain range of environments, and in particular only in a certain range of child-rearing practices.

The most obvious simple example is blood sugar levels. If low sugar makes babies cry and crying results in mother feeding baby (as it frequently does even in our culture) then sugar levels will be brought up again. Woodson argues that this sort of feedback loop goes much further than just hunger (indeed it is not even clear that hunger works as one would imagine in the first few days). The literature on newborn physiology shows that many important measures of the internal environment are linked, and suggests that several of these are influenced directly or indirectly by a feed, and differently for breast and bottle feeds. At the same time it is clear that behavior like crying has some direct and costly effects on the internal environment.

Crying may appear to be among the least useful behaviors in which a newborn who has experienced asphyxia could engage. The blood pO_2 drops dramatically during bouts of crying (Anderson, 1977). Forceful crying with increased muscular activity substantially raises oxygen consumption, in some cases resulting in a four-fold increase over the basal rate (Cross *et al.*, 1957). As well as consuming energy substrates, the increased metabolic activity associated with crying would result in the creation of metabolic acids. These outcomes could hardly be beneficial to a newborn who is already acidotic, liable to become hypoxic and whose metabolic reserves are likely to be depleted as a result of asphyxia (Shelley, 1969).

However, this conclusion is based upon observations of the newborn left alone and allowed to cry. In the natural environment, crying elicits a prompt response from the mother. The components of this response, moreover, are quite specific: the newborn who cries is very likely to be picked up, held closely and continually against the mother's body and fed (Bell and Ainsworth, 1972; Brazelton, 1977; Konner, 1977). A rather different set of consequences become apparent when crying is viewed from this perspective.

It can be inferred from the experimental evidence that contact with the mother's warm body will reduce heat loss, promote thermal stability and lessen the thermogenic demands confronting the newborn (Adamsons, 1966; Hey and Katz, 1970; Silverman *et al.*, 1966). It is known that recovery from acidosis is enhanced if the newborn is kept in a constantly warm environment

(Gandy *et al.*, 1964). Along with its contribution to acid-base regulation, the reduction in metabolic activity afforded by thermal stability would also lessen the risk of hypoglycemia (Hull, 1974).

Feeding obviously provides nutrients and fluids but two additional benefits derived from nursing at the breast warrant special mention with respect to the asphyxiated newborn. First, because its metabolism gives rise to few acid end-products, breast milk enables the newborn to obtain nourishment at a minimum additional burden to renal capacity (McCance and Widdowson, 1960; Fomon *et al.*, 1959). Secondly it has been shown that non-nutritive sucking facilitates oxygenation in transitional premature newborns (Burroughs *et al.*, 1978). Thus, the opportunity to nurse in and of itself may be beneficial for the maintenance of adequate respiratory function.

So the mother's responses to crying appear to promote adequate ventilation, assist in recovery from acidosis, and insure a balance between metabolic demands and reserves—three recognized goals in the treatment of asphyxia (Keay and Morgan, 1978). Thus to the extent that it elicits caretaking responses that promote homeostasis, crying may be viewed as a means of using the postnatal environment to compensate for the effects of previous insult.

The exact circumstances in which it would pay a baby to cry or not to cry (pay in terms of most benefit to its survival chances) will clearly differ by small and intricate margins. It is thus surprising that evidence exists (Graham, *et al.* 1957; Woodson *et al.*, 1981) that low blood pH is associated with more crying but not surprising that the clinical impression should evolve that irritable babies had been somewhat asphyxiated but that 'flat' babies had been much more badly affected. The costs of crying may outweigh the benefits in the unhealthy baby as well as in the contented baby.

Woodson *et al.*, (1982) gives a more careful analysis of this situation that illustrates the difference between his functional approach and the unidimensional approaches more typical of research on newborn behavior. Since crying lowers pO_2 one would expect it to be more risky for the baby with respiratory acidosis than for the baby whose acidosis is metabolic. For each baby many of the benefits of crying will be the same. If they are then we should predict that the babies for whom crying costs most should cry least. This is exactly what Woodson found. Babies with respiratory acidemia tended to be drowsier than good condition alert babies, while babies whose acidemia was metabolic were the group that cried most. More complicated interactions, including interactions with serum bilirubin and hematocrit will also be examined. But it is clear that one finds complex interactions among measures of the internal environment in predicting behavior. It seems possible that thinking of costs and benefits to survival of results of behavior will predict the behavior under different combinations of internal environment measures.

So Woodson is proposing that there is an intricately adapted series of links from the newborn's internal environment to its behavior, to mother's responses and from these back to its internal environment. He is not challenging the superiority of medicine's special care unit for the unwell or small baby but he is implying something very important for those of us interested in the care and development of the normal and 'well' babies. Neonatologists have shown that special care units can determine whether or not extreme low-birthweight leads to later problems. In the same way Woodson's model implies that in the normal baby, whether minor perinatal problems have later consequences will depend not only on how well the environment compensates later—see Sameroff and Chandler's review (1975) but also on how effective the newborn's behavior is at getting its internal environment on to normal values. It would thus be hard to attribute any associations that sometimes appear between perinatal events and later development of behavior, purely to the physiological events or to the mother's handling. The proposition is that baby is leading mother towards helping it sort out its internal environment. This may be an example of the self-correcting systems in development proposed by Bateson (1976). If later consequences have a physiological basis they can be avoided by mother following baby's lead. The trade-off may of course be that mother is taught some 'bad habits', which in turn influences the child. Indeed, it may be that kind of chain of interaction that determines whether or not perinatal events within the normal range have any consequences.

This is not a proposition that should be taken up too quickly by propagandist for 'natural' child care. Brazelton (1972) pointed out how in a culture where demand feeding was the norm, a baby that did not cry (perhaps because too ill or too starved) got dangerously underfed. The silent baby might be doing the best it can, merely because the other options might kill it quicker and because there is always a chance (probably growing with time!) that mother may decide you need feeding.

Woodson's theory is one that demands measurement and experiment on causes and consequences of behavior, and it could then lead to the calculation of optimal behavior for various physiological situations, followed by further observation to see if the behavior that occurs is indeed optimal. This process of quantification, hypothesis construction, and test is attractive to scientists but not conducive to instant belief and application. The beauty of Woodson's theory as a demonstration of the total interdependence of biological and social influences on child development should be obvious. Its weakest point is the assumption about the effects of baby behavior on maternal behavior in the environment of evolutionary adaptedness.

In Woodson's theory the physiological system and its relationship to behavior will have evolved to fit with the effects of baby behavior upon mother, and with the situation in which the baby was reared. So we are dealing with 'average' behavior over a long enough time for evolution to have selected the physiological system that works best with this behavior. One has little idea how long this takes. It is conceivable that natural selection would alter the system somewhat to suit one kind of child-rearing environment better than another. Freedman (1971) reports differences between leg reflexes of newborn Navajo babies and other babies, which he links to the subsequent use of the cradleboard. But the main features of the homeostatic system are likely to be adapted to the style of baby rearing predominant throughout our evolution. We are dependent primarily on the kind of quantitative extrapolation that I described in 1972 for our estimates of this (Blurton Jones, 1972). If we wish to demonstrate that the baby performs optimal behavior in its environment of evolutionary adaptedness we are entirely dependent on our evidence about this environment. On the other hand, if we are prepared to assume that the relationship between behavior and physiology is such as to maximize the baby's chance of staying alive, we can investigate the extent to which different kinds of maternal response aid or hinder that outcome.

It should also be clear that the predictions from this model about newborn behavior, and about later outcome will be more complex and subtle than predictions from the rather unidimensional models most of us use: irritable versus passive babies, at risk versus not at risk, and so on.

One implication of Woodson's model that reflects on our standard thinking in psychology concerns 'consistent stable measures of newborn behavior'. It is customary (and some effort has already been put into the task despite clinicians like Brazelton and Prechtl warning us against it) to assess the usefulness of a measure of behavior by its stability over time: if a baby who cries a lot on the first day of study also cries a lot on the second day of study then crying is a good measure. Babies are actually not very strongly consistent in this way. Woodson finds that crying relates to blood values on the day that the measurements are made, not on previous days. This is what one would expect if he is right that crying is part of the system that controls the blood values. Our psychometric custom would then demand that we lose interest in crying, it is not a 'good measure'. But to follow our custom would require us to decide to ignore (a) life and death, (b) the most important behavior from mother's point of view. This would be ridiculous. Perhaps we should think again about our criteria for good and bad measures. Undeniably we need to be able to measure crying accurately, but day-to-day variation may be what we want to measure! Day-to-day consistency seems desirable if we think we are measuring something about the baby, some enduring characteristic of the baby. But what if its only enduring characteristic is a set of mechanisms that work towards its survival in a changing internal and external environment? Although Woodson's model teaches us the futility of the quest for 'consistent measures' of newborn behavior it does not deprive us of suggestions about later consequences of perinatal events. What may count is the baby's success or failure at organizing its internal environment, not whether it has a high or low consistent score for crying.

OPTIMAL BIRTHSPACING FOR KALAHARI HUNTER–GATHERER WOMEN

Lee (1972b) has reported that Bushman women who live the traditional foraging life have gaps around four years between births, and make gathering excursions only once every two or three days. There is active research on the physiological pathway by which the wide spacing is achieved. But for the evolutionist and the behavioral ecologist there is also another question. If people behave in ways that maximize their reproductive success why do not Bushman women have babies more often, and go out collecting food more often? The evolutionary biologist immediately wonders whether if she did, she would end up with fewer not more adult offspring? Would the losses from dying babies or even from mother's premature death, outweigh the gains. Lee analyzed the situation from a different theoretical viewpoint but which none the less points the way for an evolutionist analysis. He shows how, given that women continue to carry babies with them up to two years old, shortening the inter-birth interval would lead to women carrying much greater loads on their gathering excursions. He argues that the absence of good weaning foods requires frequent suckling and therefore taking the baby with mother to a high age. Richard Sibly and I (1978) examined this situation more closely, and because of our theoretical position were forced to ask more questions: for instance if behavior maximizes reproductive success then high backloads should not deter the mother, people should only be expected to be lazy if it pays them or they have nothing to gain by working harder. In evolutionary terms the agony of carrying a high load should be worthwhile if it results in rearing more offspring. So why do they not carry heavier loads?

If we are serious about our basic question we must also ask whether Bushman women could not arrange their lives more efficiently in all sorts of other respects. Can they really not wean babies earlier? Can they find more baby-sitters after 'weaning' and thus take the baby with them less often? Could they not live in the nut groves and thereby remove the problem of carrying babies and food? Could they not make their husbands provide all the food for them and their children, perhaps by persuading them to gather nuts instead of hunting? Of course we cannot answer all these questions at once. Indeed we leave most of the questions asked but unanswered in our initial analyses.

Our analysis is based almost entirely on Lee's data. But we are concerned with the last two months of the dry season. In some respects this is probably the hardest time of year because the distance between permanent water and the staple plant foods is at its maximum. Women face a round trip of up to 12 miles to gather mongongo nuts, the staple plant food where Lee worked. So far we have not questioned Lee's argument that dry season camps are optimally placed between permanent water and the nut groves. He describes how eventually families change their strategy and go to live in the nut groves for a few days at a time (getting water from water-storing roots or tubers). Our analysis concerns the time before this when people are based near permanent water.

Lee has shown that many features of Zhun/twa Bushman society and individual behavior are readily explicable as successful adapations to surviving with a hunter–gatherer technology in the sparse habitat of Ngamiland. Most of these are clearly adaptive in almost any sense—personal survival or comfort, survival of children or group. But the observations that we argue need further 'explanation' are two which are in some ways 'counterintuitive' and may provoke more precise considerations of the way in which they are adaptive: (1) the interval between births in non-settled traditionally foraging Bushmen, approximately four years (this declines markedly when people settle); (2) women (who provide 67 per cent of the calorie 'income') only go gathering once every two or three days. Most of the time they spend talking and singing and processing food at home, and visiting or being visited by friends and relatives.

Thus there are several observed aspects of Bushman behavior, some very important, whose adaptive values we have not questioned at this stage of the investigation: (1) mothers carry children of under two years old when they go gathering, and frequently carry children under four years old. We use Lee's figures on this and for the time being assume that a woman makes the maximum possible use of babysitters; (2) men do not gather, but hunt, acquiring at unpredictable intervals an average 33 per cent of the calorie 'income' (but of course acquiring a wider range of proteins); (3) that the dry season villages are six miles from the nut groves and one mile from water and that Lee is correct in calling this optimal for the energy or thermoregulatory budgets; (4) that mongongo nuts (*Ricinodendron rautanenii*) are the most useful plant food source and the main one to consider (other plant foods provide 8.9 per cent of calorie income—Lee, 1968), although (5) they take a very long time to crack (Lee, 1969) which excludes daily gathering excursions; (6) start and end ages for having babies (19.5–45 years) (Howell, 1976); (7) that Lee is correct in arguing that although plant food is superabundant and the supply of mongongo nuts is not exhaustible by foraging, exhaustion of supplies near dry season camps is, as Konner (personal communication) and Lee (1969) suggest, a reason for the long 'six mile' journeys late in the dry season.

BIRTH-SPACING, FOOD REQUIREMENTS, AND BACK-LOADS

If a Bushman mother has a baby more often than every four years (given that as she does, she carries children up to four years old on her foraging trips) she will spend some time carrying two small children when she goes gathering and more time carrying at least one of them. This will reduce the amount of food that she can bring back, if there is some limit to the total weight that she can carry. At the same time it will increase the amount of food her family needs; there are more children to feed then and subsequently. As her payload goes down so the food requirements go up. Obviously at some point shortening the birth interval will lead to a situation where the mother would have to carry extremely high loads to feed her family. But of course there is strong selective advantage in having more children, so long as you can feed them enough for them to grow up and reproduce. If reproductive success is the criterion it would be worth great costs to the extent of risking physical integrity to have just one more baby (provided this means more babies growing up and reproducing). Since too great a level of risk cannot be worth taking there must be some optimal birth interval which maximizes reproductive success.

The first step in analyzing this situation is to work out what maximum back-loads are required to support various sized families. If we treat the number of years for which the woman reproduces as a constant, then family size and birth interval are closely correlated. Much of the relevant data is available. Lee (1972b) published weights of children of various ages, and of adults. He also calculated dietary requirements of adults (1968). We recalculated these and those of children. We have used data from the biological data handbooks for the calorie cost of lactation and requirements for babies under one year. Lee (1968, 1969) published data on food values of a given weight of both prepared and unshelled mongongo nuts. From this we have calculated the weights of nuts a mother would have to carry home to feed her family (given she provides 58.8 per cent of the calories from nuts) for a range of birth intervals (two to six years in steps of 0.1 year), for gathering one day in three and for gathering one day in two, for family sizes that do or do not assume the infant mortality reported by Howell (1979).

Our first objective was to calculate the load of food and children that on average a mother will carry if she spaces births at a particular interval. This load is derived from the probabilities that a child will survive to each age and estimates of weight and food requirements of Bushman children of different ages (as given in Table 1 in Blurton Jones and Sibly, 1978). In the computer simulation estimates were made every tenth of a year by linear interpolation between the values shown.

The weight of nuts that a mother will have to carry for each child is calculated as (expected nut requirement/child of given age, kg) = (probability that a child survives to that age) × (energy requirements of a child of that age, calories/day) × (% of Western recommended daily dietary allowance that Bushman children eat) × (% diet that is nuts) × (weight of nut needed to supply 1 calorie, kg/cal) × (number of days nuts must last). We suppose that Bushman children require 76% of the Western standards for children of that age (based on comparison of Lee's figures for adults with figures in Spector, 1956); that 58.8 per cent of the calories in their diets are from nuts (Lee, 1969), and that 0.00119 kg nuts provide 1 calorie (Lee, 1969; Wehmeyer, et al., 1969). Our conclusions are fairly insensitive to small errors in these figures.

Older children are carried progressively less and we followed Lee (1972b) in supposing that the most important parameter is the average weight carried per journey. Lee's (1972b) Table 14.2 is the source of our figure for this: weight of child is multiplied by proportion of mileage for which child is carried. Whether it is correct to consider only average weight carried depends on the relative dangers of the different catastrophes that may ensue. If the greatest risk is heat stress, or dehydration, or some consequence of fatigue then our assumption will be at least approximately true, especially if reciprocal sharing of loads between mothers' functions to even out the load of individual mothers around the average they expect to have to carry. On the other hand, if the major risk is of back injury when positioning the load before carrying it, then our assumption would be invalid. Although there is a surprising lack of evidence on this second risk, we believe, as we shall argue later, that the former is the greater risk, and so we have chosen to use the first assumption rather than the second. Our conclusions are very sensitive to which assumption is made (and so is the applicability of our model to other cultures).

In addition to these variable loads a mother has to carry a constant load, being her contribution to the three- (or two-) day food requirements (i) for herself at 1750 calories/day (calories required for lactation and for nourishing the fetus were included as child requirements, a procedure which, along with calculating age from conception, greatly simplifies the calculations), (ii) for her husband at 2250 calories/day, and (iii) possibly a contribution for a dependent relative (average requirement of say, 400 calories/day) (Lee, 1969, 1972). Working as above we calculate three-daily nut requirement for adults as $4400 \times 0.588 \times 0.0019 \times 3 = 9.24$ kg.

The weight carried by a mother for each child was combined with the constant load of food for adults in order to calculate the total load carried by a mother in different years. This load is shown for five different birth-spacings that she might adopt in Figure 10.1. It is clear that for some birth-spacings she has to carry more in some years than in others, the maximum amounts ever carried are shown in Figure 10.2.

These calculations produced two unexpected results: (1) a sharp upturn in the back-load of food plus babies when birth interval comes below four years (Figure 10.2); (2) a remarkably even level of back-load through a woman's reproductive career with birth intervals around 4 years (Figure 10.1). We had speculated that four years might allow a cycle of two easy years in which a woman could give away excess food to her friends or close relatives,

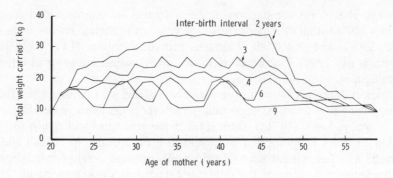

Figure 10.1

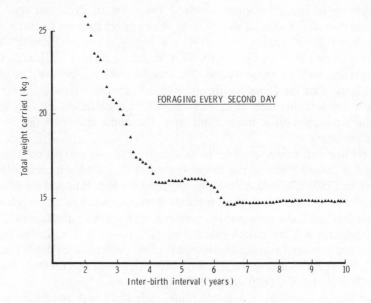

Figure 10.2

followed by two years in which they reciprocated. We do not know any data on the amount of sharing plant food between specified individuals but this contrasts with the frequent remarks in the literature on exchange of meat and the x'aro system of exchange of objects and so might suggest that the exchange of plant food between women of child-bearing age is minor and unimportant, as our model would predict.

However, the overall levels of backload that one must expect is less clear. With no infant or child mortality, gathering one day in three, and a four-year interval, some extremely high loads are predicted. Including mortality, and with gathering on alternate days, the backloads decline to near the observations reported by Lee (1968, 1969) and DeVore and Konner (1974). It is important to note that Lee's original measurements of work and food income, although taken at a very hard time of year, were, as far as we can judge from his published data, collected from a group of people with only very few small children in the entire group. People with more children may indeed carry more or go gathering more often, or have husbands who contribute more calories than average.

POSSIBLE LIMITS TO BACKLOAD

It is now clear that if we are to set any limit to family size and birth interval we must know about the limits to how much a woman can carry and how often she can go out foraging.

Bushmen are very small and we may wonder why big women do not manage to carry bigger loads and support more babies and thus why Bushmen (women, anyway) are not bigger. We have considered several restrictions on backload: the effect of exhaustion on your ability, even having shed the nut part of the load, to run away from a predator in the unlikely event of having to do so; load of water to be carried to replace sweat loss; and more probable: accidents to backs or ankles from lifting or carrying too much, which would make the mother unable to forage for a dangerously long time; and therefore badly in debt to her friends and relatives. The ergonomics literature (e.g. Davies, 1972) implies that safe limits for women are quite low, lower for smaller women, and that the observed 15–20 kg carried by Bushmen is likely to be about the safe limit. However, this evidence implies that it would be advantageous to Bushwomen to be larger. In addition there is as yet only the beginning of a documented quantitative relation of risk to back injury to load and this data is only available for men (Davis and Stubbs, 1977).

Finally, we considered the effect on the mother's heat balance of the energy liberated by carrying a load. Particularly in September and early October, the hardest months, the hot end of the dry season, there will be days when work of any kind is impossible. We can thus exclude daily gathering as a possibility on these grounds, in addition to the need to spend time processing the nuts that have been gathered, and in other domestic tasks. If we knew the number of days on which work of any kind was possible we would be able to say more about the maximum frequency of gathering excursions to which a woman can commit herself. There will be many days on which high loads cannot be carried without a good chance of collapse from heat imbalance. It is clear that there comes a point past which the more food the mother attempts to bring back the greater the risks she is taking.

A woman should not produce a family which requires her to carry heavier loads on a greater number of days than is safe. But within this limit there must always be an advantage in adjusting the backload to the weather on any day, either by changing foraging strategies as the days warm up, or by predicting midday temperatures successfully from early morning conditions.

Environmental physiologists use a number of criteria for tolerable thermal conditions, the limit to conditions in which acclimatized people can expect to work without collapse. It is important for the present discussion that once collapse has occurred the risks are severe. It would be very hard for people who collapsed from heat problems in the Kalahari in September–October to get home. If they could not get to shade their problems might worsen, and even if they did get to shade, death occurs in a substantial proportion of untreated cases of heat stroke and other forms of heat collapse (Leithead and Lind, 1964). Several ways of relating these criteria to work levels are available but one of the most appropriate and convenient, and one of the best recorded criteria of tolerable conditions is the Predicted Four Hour Sweat Rate (P4SR) (McArdle et al., 1947). This gives an equation into which one can insert energy liberated by work. Carrying loads requires more energy than walking and thus liberates more heat. Empirically established equations relating energy liberated to body size, speed of walking and load carried, give the heat produced by 41 kg ladies walking at 3 or 4 mph. carrying various loads (e.g. Durnin and Passmore, 1967, and others). Carried loads are, up to a point, similar to increased bodyweight. Thus, although increased size might allow higher maximum loads it would also unhelpfully increase heat production (Robinson, 1942 and others show that large people are at a disadvantage when working in heat). The heat produced when carrying various loads can be fed into the P4SR equations and from these the environmental conditions under which it would be possible to carry each load could be ascertained. The P4SR depends on wet-bulb, dry-bulb, and globe temperatures, air-speed, level of clothing worn, area of body surface, and metabolic rate. In calculating metabolic rate we used the regression formula suggested by Datta et al. (1973), namely (metabolic rate, kcal min^{-1}) = 0.0943 × (bodyweight + load carried, kg) − 2.183. This was based on subjects of average surface area 1.62 m^2. Details of our calculations are given in Blurton Jones and Sibly 1978.

Daily readings of globe thermometer (which assess gain in heat from radiation) or wet-bulb thermometer (both required for P4SR) do not seem to have been taken in any part of !kung Bushman land so we cannot make precise predictions. However, Wyndham (1956; 1958; 1964) mentions that GT readings 'of 140 °F in the sun . . . were recorded . . .' (1964) 'as high as 50 °C' at the cold time of year, and 'up to 60 °C in the Kalahari accompanying dry-bulb readings of 40 °C' and 'globe thermometer temperature exceeds air temperatures by some 20 °C at 2 p.m.'. Lee (1972a) gives September shade temperatures at Dobe (where he did his foraging measurements) as showing 'highs ranging from 35–43 °C'. We can thus safely assume that there are many days with globe thermometer readings of 50 °C and more. (Shade is negligible on journeys to the nut groves and we propose to leave it out of our calculations. In the habitats of other cultures it could be very important). The actual temperatures are rather critical but even a guess at the distribution of GT readings in September and the assumption of a very low wet-bulb reading (actually humidity rises steadily during September), suggests that there will be few days when 20 kg could be carried, rather more when 15 kg could be carried, very few when 30 kg could be carried. As load increases, number of safe days for foraging decreases. The exact relationship will determine the maximum amount of food that can be brought home, and hence the limits to interbirth interval. But the fragmentary information available suggests that carrying 15–20 kg around one day in two to three days may well be the best that can be done in September and October. This is in the region that Lee and others report that the women do.

DISCUSSION

This analysis is obviously very incomplete. We need more information on the temperatures during September and October to allow us to complete the examination of limits to backload and foraging frequency. We need more information about the risks of early weaning, and the relationship between undernutrition and mortality in children. There is data on both from Third World countries but we would need to demonstrate that the loss of offspring from these causes would be greater than the gain in offspring at shorter interbirth intervals. Above all, we need to know more about the potential babysitters—who are they, what else do they need to do, just how many are available. An indirect approach to this question is to check by simulation the gains to the mother from leaving behind the child over two years old more often, and to simulate strategies for grandmother (probably the most likely babysitter). The important thing is that the evolutionary approach forces us to ask these questions, and many more. It does this because we are allowed to take very little indeed for granted about what is 'reasonable' for people to do. Most other approaches allow us to smuggle in assumptions about what is 'reasonable' all over the place and thus, giving more ready answers, require us to ask fewer questions. An example is at the beginning of this section: to Lee and any normal person (but this is only a 'reasonable' assumption if we do not like heavy physical work) the effort involved in carrying heavy loads is reason enough not to do it, and thus there is no question to be asked about limits to load. But our theory forced us to look at limits to backload because carrying heavier loads had an obvious reproductive advantage. Another example, a story Sibly and I can tell against ourselves is our figure for food brought home for an elderly relative. What could be more natural? But if we are applying an evolutionary perspective we must ask on the one hand why the mother should feed this elderly relative—reducing the amount of food she can bring home for her children, and on the other hand why evolution allows this old person to stay alive while reducing the fitness of his or her younger relatives. Of course part of the answer may be that the old person more than repays his or her 'keep' by babysitting without which the mothers would be able to support a much smaller family. We are brought to notice and question our assumption about the relationship with the old person. We also gain an insight into the complexity of the babysitter issue.

Formally, the investigation of the proximal mechanisms by which the wide birth spacing is achieved is an entirely separate enterprise from this ecological level of investigation. But it is interesting to refer to the research on some of the possible mechanisms. Konner and Worthman (1980) found that interval between breastfeeds correlated with serum progesterone levels in Bushman women. The suggestion, confirming much circumstantial evidence, is that if feeding is very frequent there is a significant suppression of ovulation. Frisch and McArthur (1974) have proposed that ovulation is suppressed when mothers' fat reserves fall below a critical level. This has been contradicted by Huffman's analysis of data from Pakistan (Huffman et al., 1980). Our functional (adaptive) model ought to allow us to predict the factors to which the proximate mechanism should respond. It seems likely that it should respond both to (1) an indication of the present baby's needs from lactation (relative to the availability of other foods and its readiness to switch to eating other foods), (2) indications of mother's ability to provide for the present baby both by lactation and by substitute foods, and her ability to cope with the backloads and foraging effort that would be involved by the next pregnancy and birth. Some measures of mother's nutritional state or energy balance would seem a good candidate but it would be hard to say which.

IMPLICATIONS OF OUR APPROACH TO BUSHMAN BIRTHSPACING

This evolutionists approach to birthspacing differs radically, discomfortingly (and not so very credibly) from most approaches to human population regulation. Our proposition was that people have the number of babies that allows them to leave the largest number of descendants, in the conditions under which they live. We illustrated a situation in which having few babies might lead one to have more descendants than would having more babies. Most approaches to population regulation examine only proximate mechanisms and emic explanations. They examine people's level of education and use of contraceptives, they discover and describe social 'values of children', without too much concern about why societies have these values. There are exceptions among economists, such as Schultz, 1974; Becker and Lewis,

1974; Nerlove *et al.*, 1974. It is known that the response to provision of birth control facilities depends on a prior wish to restrict births. Should we not look at the ecological factors behind that wish?

Our efforts to demonstrate limits to the amount of food gathering that a woman can do, indeed our whole approach to behavior as a maximization of reproductive success, places us in apparent contrast to important writings on subsistence economics. It places us in disagreement, not with Lee's *observation* of the amount of leisure in Bushman lives, but with the interpretations of this that Lee and others have made. In a way our Bushman model implies that the 'leisure' observed by Lee is an important part of the strategy for maximizing reproductive success by reducing risks of heat collapse.

Our approach also puts us in opposition to Sahlins (1974) who presents a thorough review of the data showing that hunter–gatherers and peasant farmers do not maximize production or wealth in the sense that some economists might expect. Other economists would have different expectations, they might regard numbers and quality of children as likely components of an empirically derived function that is maximized (e.g. Schultz, 1974). Sahlins' argument against the *direct* application of the economic theory of industrial nations to the subsistence activities of other cultures seems absolutely convincing. This is of course a credit to the clarity and testability of economic theory, as well as to Sahlins' thoroughness and perception. But his approach is in conflict with some of the alternative interpretations of the data. For instance, our proposition is that people do not produce as much food or wealth as they can but as many descendants as they can. Thus I would argue that an economist would have the wrong costs and benefits in mind but that costs and benefits for reproduction (descendants not births) are relevant, and that these may well restrain total output.

Sahlins describes 'Chayanov's Rule', that in social or family units with more 'producers' the individuals produce less than in units with more 'dependents'. My reaction would be: (1) like Sahlins, pp. 88 and 89, we expect this if people work to support their children and relatives (a venerable economic doctrine as well as an evolutionary one), (2) but my task would be then to try to show why the units with few dependents have few dependents, why cannot they increase food production and thus have more children? (Actually Chayanov's cross-sectional data scarcely raises this question, as Sahlins implies, different families may simply be at different stages in their development when data is collected.)

Variation in economic 'success' between families, while clearly a good argument that *societies* are not maximizing output and thus that the domestic group may be the 'unit' of production is also no surprise from the evolutionists' point of view. There are good examples of enormous individual differences in reproductive success among both men and women in several societies. But again the evolutionists' approach demands that he try to explain the difference, go to the field and see why they differ—do families own different amounts or qualities of land, etc., etc.

Many authors in addition to Sahlins have been impressed by calculations of 'carrying capacity' and evidence that actual populations are usually well below 'carrying capacity'. To the biologist this is not impressive. But perhaps we have only ourselves to blame. In biology carrying capacity is best known as a theoretical concept—the population density at which population stops increasing and becomes level. Only in the simplest situations can it be calculated from available habitat (e.g. perhaps pests of grain storage bins). To calculate carrying capacity from measuring the habitat requires detailed knowledge of the way the species exploits its habitat and of the factors that limit population growth. The situation is particularly complicated in a predator–prey relationship where the prey has ways of making itself difficult to catch and where its population may be influenced by predation. Thus it comes as no surprise even from an evolutionist's perspective to find populations at a lower level than indicated by even relatively sophisticated calculations of available land and the population it could support. If one tried to calculate the carrying capacity of Ngamiland from the weight of nuts on the ground it would be many times higher than the observed population. But Sibly's and my analysis implies that population is limited not by the number of nuts but by the difficulty imposed on gathering them by the need to drink, and by the habit of carrying babies. Again, our theory makes us ask more questions: why carry babies? This question divides into two: (1) there is a well documented influence in the Third World of age of cessation of breast-feeding upon infant mortality, mortality rises sharply as age of weaning declines. Is this effect large enough to outweigh the benefits of reduced interbirth interval? Would a woman lose more children than she gains by stopping suckling and leaving them home earlier than she does? (2) could the mother find more babysitters to care for her child while she goes gathering? Who is available, do you have to feed them, and what else do they want to do?

There is a difference between a theory that forces one to ask specific empirical questions such as these, and one that in effect says: people don't maximize anything, they have ideas about what they should do, these ideas limit their economic performance, you are not required to measure anything. Such a view leaves us wondering where people's ideas come from and if they are not influenced by the necessity of survival and the consequences of reproduction what are they influenced by?

Recently anthropologists have come to realize the limitations of the early carrying capacity research: Cordell (1978) gives a detailed analysis of choice of coastal fishing sites in Bahia in Brazil which clearly shows how the result of individuals trying to maximize their catch leads to a complicated distribution of fishing effort that is remote from the result of any calculation based on the number of fish. Tide, wind, light, and distance, all influence the success of a fishing trip and therefore where people fish. Harris (1979) points out that one expects people to exploit the habitat only to the point where their costs begin to outweigh the benefits, not to exploit the habitat to its maximum. Studies of carrying capacity based on calculations from the habitat pose no threat either to cultural materialist theory or to evolutionary theories.

In the introduction I said that learning and thinking may be part of the mechanism that gives rise to adaptive behavior. How are goals and motives balanced off against each other to give rise to optimal behavior? The evolutionist hopes that his optimization studies and ESS studies will give some clues about this, sometimes with the intention of returning to study the short term mechanisms that achieve this. One reaction of fellow ethologists to my argument for closer links between animal behavioral ecology and cultural materialism (Blurton Jones, 1976) was that motivation and reinforcement was adequate to explain the same data and therefore one did not need to explore survival value or add it to the explanation. This is closely paralleled by Harris (1979) when he argues that it is enough to propose 'a minimal set of human bio-psychological selective principles' and lists four: the need to eat, the tendency to conserve energy, reinforcement from sexual intercourse, a need for love and affection. He rightly, and ambitiously claims 'the adequacy of the list must be judged by the adequacy of the theories it helps to generate. The more parsimonious we are about granting the existence of bio-psychological constants, the more powerful and elegent will be the network of theories emanating from sociocultural strategies. Our object is to explain much by little'. Evolutionary theorists (or human behavioral ecologists) must be implying some comparable motivational and reinforcing systems but perhaps because more familiar with the fate of such drive theories in the history of psychology, are less open about naming them. But in addition the evolutionist must argue that different combinations of the degree of fulfillment of these 'motives' will lead to different possible patterns of behavior in each environment. Unless we specify for example how much love equates how much work, we cannot identify optimal behavior. One might hope that the evolution-based theories would lead us towards answering such questions.

But the stumbling block will remain: do we think it correct to believe that culturally transmitted behavior maximizes inclusive fitness, rather than not quite doing so. I argue that the heuristic value of this assumption justifies making it, so long as we remember that it is an assumption and so long as people are exploring theories of cultural transmission to see whether some other assumption might be better.

ACKNOWLEDGMENT

The research described in this chapter was supported in part by the Social Science Research Council, The Harry Frank Guggenheim Foundation, The Royal Society, The Wenner Gren Foundation, The Mental Health Foundation.

REFERENCES

Adamsons, K. (1966) The role of thermal factors in fetal and neonatal life. *Pediatric Clinics of North America*, **13**, 599–619.

Alexander, R. D. (1974) The evolution of social behavior. *Annual Review of Ecology and Systematics*, **5**, 325–383.

Alexander, R. D. (1979) Darwinism and Social Affairs. Seattle, University of Washington Press.

Alland, A. (1975) Adaptation. *Annual Review of Anthropology*, **4**, 59–73.

Anderson, G. C. (1977) The mother and newborn: mutual caregivers. *Journal of Obstetric, Gynecologic and Neonatal Nursing*, **6**, 50–57.

Barkow, J. H., and Burley, N. (1980) Human fertility, evolutionary biology, and the demographic transition. *Ethology and Sociobiology*, **1**, 163–180.

Bateson, P. P. G. (1976) Rules and reciprocity in behavioral development. In Bateson, P. P. G. and Hinde, R. A. (eds). *Growing Points in Ethology*. London: Cambridge University Press.

Becker, G. and Lewis, H. G. (1974) Interaction between quantity and quality of children. In Schultz, T. (ed.) *Economics of the family*. Chicago, University of Chicago Press.

Bell, S. M., and Ainsworth, M. D. S. (1972) Infant crying and maternal responsiveness. *Child Development*, **43**, 1171–1190.

Blurton Jones, N. G. (1972) Comparative aspects of mother–child contact. In *Ethological Studies of Child Behaviour*, edited by N. G. Blurton Jones. London: Cambridge University Press.

Blurton Jones, N. (1976) Growing points in human ethology: another link between ethology and the social sciences? In Bateson, P. P. G. and Hinde, R. A. (eds). *Growing Points in Ethology*. London: Cambridge University Press.

Blurton Jones, N., and Sibly, R. M. (1978) Testing adaptiveness of culturally determined behaviour: do Bushman women maximise their reproductive success by spacing births widely and foraging seldom? In Blurton Jones, N. and Reynolds, V. (eds). *Human Behaviour and Adaptation. Symposium No. 18 of the Society for Study of Human Biology*. London, Taylor and Francis.

Blurton Jones, N. G., and Reynolds, V. (1978) *Human Behaviour and Adaptation*. Taylor and Francis, London.

Brazelton, B. (1972) Implications of infant development among the Mayan Indians of Mexico. *Human Development*, **15**, 90–111.

Brazelton, T. B. (1977) Implications of infant development among the Mayan Indians of Mexico. In Leiderman, P. H., Tulkin, S. R., and Rosenfeld, A. (eds). *Culture and Infancy: Variations in the Human Experience*. New York, Academic Press.

Burnham, P. (1973) The explanatory value of the concept of adaptation in studies of culture change. In Renfrew, C. (ed.). *The Explanation of Culture Change*. Duckworth, London.

Burroughs, A. K., Asoyne, U. O., Anderson-Shanklin, G. C., and Vidyasagar, D. (1978) The effect of non-nutritive sucking on transcutaneous oxygen tension in noncrying, preterm neonates. *Research in Nursing and Health*, **1**, 69–75.

Chagnon, N. A., and Irons, W. (1979) *Evolutionary Biology and Human Social Behavior*. Duxbury, North Scituate, Mass.

Chisholm, J. S. (1978) Developmental Ethology of the Navajo. Ph.D. Thesis, Rutgers University, New Jersey.

Cordell, J. (1978) Carrying capacity analysis of fixed-territorial fishing. *Ethnology*, **17**, 1–24.

Cross, K. W., Tizard, J. P., and Trythall, D. A. (1957) The gaseous metabolism of the newborn infant. *Acta Paediatrica*, **46**, 265–285.

Datta, S. R., Chatterjee, B. B., and Roy, B. N. (1973) The relationship between energy expenditure and pulse rates with body weight and the load carried during load carrying on the level. *Ergonomics*, **16**, 507–513.

Davies, B. T. (1972) Moving loads manually. *Applied Ergonomics*, **34**, 190–194.

Davis, P. R., and Stubbs, D. A. (1977) Safe levels of manual forces for young males. *Applied Ergonomics*, **8**, 141–150.

Dawkins, C. R. and Krebs, J. R. (1978) Animal signals: information or manipulation? In Krebs, J. R. and Davies, N. B. (eds.) Behavioural Ecology. Oxford, Blackwell Scientific Publications.

Durham, W. H. (1976) The adaptive significance of cultural behavior. *Human Ecology*, **4**, 89–121.

Durham, W. H. (1978) The coevolution of human biology and culture. In Blurton Jones, N. and Reynolds, V. (eds). *Human Behaviour and Adaptation. Symposium No. 18 of the Society for Study of Human Biology*. London, Taylor and Francis.

Durnin, J. V. G. A., and Passmore, R. (1967) *Energy, Work and Leisure*. Heinemann, London.

DeVore, I., and Konner, M. J. (1974) Infancy in hunter–gatherer life; an ethological perspective. In White, N. F. (ed). *Ethology and Psychiatry*. University of Toronto Press, Toronto.

Earle, T. K., and Christenson, A. L. (1980) *Modeling Change in Prehistoric Subsistence Economies*. Academic Press, New York and London.

Essock-Vitale, S. M., and McGuire, M. T. (1980) Predictions derived from the theories of kin selection and reciprocation assessed by anthropological data. *Ethology and Sociobiology*, **1**, 233–244.

Fomon, S. J., Harris, D. M., and Jensen, R. L. (1959) Acidification of the urine by infants fed human milk and whole cow's milk. *Paediatrics*, **23**, 113–119.

Freedman, D. G. (1971) Genetic influences on development of behavior. In: Stoelinga, G. B. A. and Werff ten Bosch, J. J. (eds). *Normal and Abnormal Development of Brain and Behaviour*. Leiden: Leiden University Press and Baltimore: Williams and Wilkins.

Frisch, R. E., and McArthur, J. W. (1974) Menstrual cycle: fatness as a determinant of minimum weight for height necessary for their maintenance or onset. *Science*, **185**, 949–951.

Gandy, G. M., Adamsons, K., Cunningham, N., Silverman, W., and James, L. S. (1964) Thermal environment and acid–base homeostasis in human infants during the first few hours of life. *Journal of Clinical Investigations*, **43**, 751–758.

Graham, F. K., Pennoyev, M. M., Caldwell, B. M., Greenman, M., and Hartman, A. F. (1957) Relationship between clinical status and behavior test performance in a newborn group with histories suggesting anoxia. *Journal of Pediatrics*, **50**, 177.

Harris, M. (1968) *The Rise of Anthropological Theory. A History of Theories of Culture*. New York; Crowell.

Harris, M. (1979) *Cultural Materialism*. New York, Random House.

Hartung, J., and Ellison, P. (1978) A eugenic effect of medical care. *Social Biology*, **24**, 192–199.

Hawkes, K., Hill, K. and O'Connell, J. (1982) Why hunters gather: optimal foraging and the Ache of eastern Paraguay. *American Ethnologist*, **9**, 379–398.

Hey, E. N., and Katz, G. (1970) The optimum thermal environment for naked babies. *Archives of Diseases in Childhood*, **45**, 328–334.

Howell, N. (1979) *Demography of the Dobe !kung*. New York and London, Academic Press.

Huffman, S. L., Chowdhury, A. K. M. A., Chakroborty, J., and Simpson, N. K. (1980) Breastfeeding patterns in rural Bangladesh. *American J. of Clinical Nutrition*, **33**, 144–154.

Hull, D. (1974) The function and development of adipose tissue. In Davis, J. A. and Dobbing, J. (eds). *Scientific Foundations of Paediatrics*, London: Heinemann.

Katz, S. H., Hediger, M. L., and Valleroy, L. A. (1974) Traditional maize processing techniques in the New World. *Science*, **184**, 765–773.

Keay, A. J., and Morgan, D. M. (1978) *Craig's Care of the Newly Born Infant* (Sixth Edition), London: Churchill, Livingstone.

Konner, M. J. (1977) Infancy among the Kalahari Desert San. In Leiderman, P. H., Tulkin, S. R., and Rosenfeld, A. (eds). *Culture and Infancy: Variations in the Human Experience*. New York: Academic Press.

Konner, M. J., and Worthman, C. (1980) Nursing frequency, gonadal function, and birth-spacing among !kung hunter–gatherers. *Science*, **207**, 788–791.

Krebs, J. R. (1978) Optimal foraging: decision rules for predators. In Krebs, J. R. and Davies, N. B. (eds). *Behavioural Ecology*. Blackwell, Oxford.

Lee, R. B. (1968) What hunters do for a living, or, how to make out on scarce resources. In *Man the Hunter*. Ed. R. B. Lee and I. DeVore. Aldine, Chicago.

Lee, R. B. (1969) !kung Bushman subsistence: an infant-output analysis. In Vayda, A. P. (ed.). *Environment and Cultural Behavior*. Natural History Press, Garden City, New York.

Lee, R. B. (1972a) The !kung Bushmen of Botswana. In Bicchieri, M. G. (ed). *Hunters and Gatherers Today*. Holt, Rinehart and Winston, New York.

Lee, R. B. (1972b) Population growth and the beginnings of sedentary life among the !kung Bushmen. In Spooner, B. (ed). *Population Growth: Anthropological Implications*. Cambridge, Mass., M.I.T. Press.

Leithead, C. S., and Lind, A. R. (1964) *Heat Stress and Heat Disorders*. Cassell, London.

McArdle, B., Dunham, W., Holling, H. E., Ladell, W. S. S., Scott, J. W., Thomson, M. L. and Weiner, J. S. (1947) The prediction of the physiological effects of warm and hot environments: the P4SR index. Medical Research Council (London), R.N.P. Report, 47/391.

McCance, R. A., and Widdowson, E. M. (1960) Renal aspects of acid-base control in the newly born. *Acta Paediatrica*, **49**, 409–420.

McFarland, D. J. (1976) Form and function in the temporal organisation of behavior. In Bateson, P. P. G. and Hinde, R. A. (eds). *Growing Points in Ethology*. Cambridge University Press, London.

McFarland, D. (1978) Optimality considerations in human behaviour. In Blurton Jones, N. and Reynolds, V. (eds). *Human Behaviour and Adaptation. Symposium No. 18 of the Society for Study of Human Biology*. London; Taylor and Francis.

Nerlove, M. (1974) Toward a new theory of population and economic growth. In Schultz, T. W. (ed.). *Economics of the Family*. Chicago and London, University of Chicago.

O'Connell, J. F., and Hawkes K. (1981) Alyawara plant use and optimal foraging theory. In Winterhalder B., and Smith, E. A. (eds) *Hunter–gatherer foraging strategies*. University of Chicago Press, Chicago and London.

Pulliam, H. R., and Dunford, C. (1980) *Programmed to Learn: An Essay on the Evolution of Culture*. Columbia University Press, New York.

Richerson, P. J., and Boyd, R. (1978) A dual inheritance model of the human evolutionary process I: basic postulates and a simple model. *J. Social Biol. Struct.*, 1, 127–154.

Robinson, S. (1942) The effect of body size upon energy exchanges in work. *Amer. J. Physiol.*, 136, 363–368.

Sahlins, M. (1974) *Stone Age Economics*. Tavistock, London.

Sameroff, A. J., and Chandler, M. J. (1975) Reproductive risk and the continuum of caretaking casualty. In *Review of Child Development Research*. (eds). F. D. Horowitz, M. Hetherington, S. Scarr-Salapatek, and G. Sregel, Vol 4. Chicago. University of Chicago Press.

Schultz, T. W. (1974) *Economics of the Family*. Chicago and London, University of Chicago.

Shelley, H. J. (1969) The metabolic responses of the foetus to hypoxia. *Journal of Obstetrics and Gynaecology of the British Commonwealth*, 76, 1–15.

Sibly, R., and McFarland, D. (1976) On the fitness of behavior sequences. *The American Naturalist*, 110, 601–617.

Silverman, W. A., Sinclair, J. C., and Agate, F. J. (1966) The oxygen cost of minor changes in the heat balance of small newborn infants. *Acta Paediatrica Scandinavica*, 55, 294–300.

Smith, P. K., and Sluckin, A. M. (1979) Ethology, ethogeny, etics, emics, biology, culture: on the limitations of dichotomies. *European J. of Social Psychology*, 9, 297–415.

Spector, W. S. (1956) *Handbook of Biological Data*. Saunders; London and Philadelphia.

Tinbergen, N. (1963) On aims and methods of ethology. *Z. Tierpsychol.*, 20, 410–433.

Wehmeyer, A. S., Lee, R. B., and Whiting, Marjorie (1969) The nutrient composition and dietary importance of some vegetable foods eaten by the !kung Bushmen. *South African Med. J.*, 43, 1529–1530.

Winterholder, B., and Smith, E. A. (1981). *Hunter–gatherer foraging strategies*. University of Chicago.

Woodson, R. H., Blurton Jones, N. G., da Costa Woodson, E., Pollock, S., and Evans, M. (1979) Fetal mediators of the relationships between increased pregnancy and labour blood pressure and newborn irritability. *Early Human Development*, 3, 127–139.

Woodson, R. H. (1980) *Antecedents of Individual Differences in the Behaviour of Human Newborns*. PhD Thesis. University of London.

Woodson, R. H., Reader, F., Shepherd, J., and Chamberlain, G. (1981) Blood pH and crying in the newborn infant. Infant Behaviour and Development, 4, 41–46.

Woodson, R. H., Morgan, H., Blurton Jones, N., and Chamberlain, G. (1982) Blood acid-base regulation and behavioural state responses in the newborn infant. In Lipsitt, L. P. and Field, T. M. (eds.) *Infant behaviour and development: perinatal risk and newborn behaviour*. Norwood, New Jersey, Ablex Publishing Corp.

Wyndham, C. H., and Morrison, J. F. (1956) Heat regulation of MaSarwa (Bushmen). *Nature*, 178, 869–870.

Wyndham, C. H., and Morrison, J. F. (1958) Adjustment to cold of Bushmen in the Kalahari Desert. *J. Applied Physiol.*, **13**, 219–225.
Wyndham, C. H., Strydom, N. B., Ward, J. S., Morrison, J. F., Williams, C. G., Bredell, G. A. G., Von Rahden, M. J. E., Holdsworth, L. D., Van Graan, C. H., Van Rensburg, A. J., and Munro, A. (1964). Physiological reactions to heat of Bushmen and of unacclimatised and acclimatised Bantu. *J. Applied Physiol.*, **19**, 885–888.

Animal Models of Human Behavior
Edited by G. C. L. Davey
© 1983 John Wiley & Sons Ltd

Chapter 11

Begged Questions in Behavior and Evolution

Jerome H. BARKOW

'Beg questions or get bogged down' could be the motto of the social-behavioral sciences. We advance by avoiding the swampy issues and getting on with the more workable. But here are some questions often slighted in discussions of brain, behavior, and biological evolution. Here, too, are some very tentative answers, a framework to put them in, and why we should ask them in the first place.

1. WHY IS OUR RATIONAL HUMAN INTELLIGENCE SO INEFFICIENT IN OPTIMIZING BIOLOGICAL FITNESS?

Human beings are dreadfully inefficient maximizers of inclusive fitness. Evolutionary biologists agree that selection should favor behaviors which tend to increase the individual's genetic representation in the next generation (Hamilton, 1964). But we human beings gorge on junk food, fight wars against strangers in the interests of other strangers, often favor genetic outsiders over kin, and are currently flirting with zero population growth. How does this make biological sense?

The easiest way to solve this problem is to deny the premiss and argue that human beings *do* tend to optimize biological fitness, and do it rather efficiently at that. This denial can be made at the levels of both the individual and the cultural pattern. At the individual level, for example, perhaps it is our *physiological* rather than our *biological* fitness which we damage with our junk food. Dental caries are rarely fatal, after all, and obesity hardly precludes sexuality (and in some cultures is actually considered to be attractive). Even the soldier who goes to war may be enhancing his fitness— perhaps the consequences of staying at home would risk his fitness even more than would war. So perhaps even a sugar-eating soldier is optimizing his biological fitness. But is he really doing it with the intelligence and efficiency we would expect from a space-going species?

To belabor the obvious, physiological and biological fitness are intimately linked. Junk food and sub-optimal diets in general may not destroy all possibility of reproductive success but they do lower the probability. A poorly nourished mother is less likely to carry her offspring to term than a well-nourished mother. A man whose diet has led to dental caries is likely to be less attractive then he would otherwise be, and toothache is hardly likely to aid him in competing with other men. Even our patriotic soldier, were he to use his rational intelligence in the service of inclusive fitness, might well devise alternative paths to prestige and women. At war he might succeed in winning glory, he might even directly increase his reproductive success through rape: but he might also be killed. Despite our intelligence, as individuals we seem to be quite inefficient in seeking biological fitness.

Do cultural patterns, however, succeed where individual intelligence fails? Do our cultures somehow automatically channel our behavior along fitness-enhancing paths? Some of the anthropologist contributors to Chagnon and Irons' (1979) reader on sociobiology and the social sciences argue that cultural patterns tend to *be* inclusive fitness strategies. They interpret such cultural patterns as destroying some of one's female offspring or investing more in sister's children than in wife's as fitness strategies.

Such arguments result from a confusion of levels. Sociobiologists postulate that *individuals* follow strategies which enhance their biological or 'inclusive' fitness. *Cultural* patterns are historical phenomena resulting from individuals interacting with one another over generations. Why should the resulting cultural pattern be the amplified equivalent of a single individual's fitness strategy? A 'tragedy of the commons' situation in which similar individual fitness strategies actually reduce the fitness of the population sharing the cultural pattern is at least as likely. We might also expect cultural patterns to favor the fitness of the élite over the fitness of others. The actual relationship between culture and biological fitness is an extremely complex one (cf. Barkow, 1978b; 1980c; 1982; Lumsden and Wilson, 1981) and both more data and more theory are needed. It is safe enough, however, to conclude that there is no reason to expect any particular pattern to be fitness-enhancing. We are left, then, with the original question of why our rational intelligence does not appear to be particularly efficient in aiding us to strive for improved biological fitness.

The answer to the inefficiency problem seems to be that we did not evolve *de novo* as 'perfect biological machines' (Barkow and Burley, 1980). Our intelligence and volition were added to a behavioral organization which today often appears to militate against the optimization of biological fitness. This is because the behavior of our distant ancestors must have been organized *ethologically* rather than in terms of the rational intelligence to which we now aspire.

One way to conceptualize ethological behavior is as a series of links composing a chain whose final outcome entails a likely increase in biological fitness (Barkow and Burley, 1980). For example, we flirt, we court, we copulate, we bond, we bear offspring, we act parentally toward them and, eventually, our young themselves become parents. If all goes well, in this complex sequence, our inclusive fitness is enhanced. From the perspective of evolution, the entire series of behaviors was a means toward that end. We could analyze each of these links as itself a complex chain, and continue our analysis by descending levels of hierarchical organization until we reached the neurophysiological level, and beyond. But let us not.

Instead, let us note the varied nature of the links. Some are stereotyped or even reflexive motoric responses—a dilation of the pupil, a flash of the eyebrow in greeting or a look of 'coyness' (Eibl-Eibesfeldt, 1975). Some links involve learning, but a learning that the individual is predisposed to accomplish because his sensory apparatus and CNS are so structured as to cause him to attend to certain types of stimuli—the wobbly gait of a youngster or the curving lines of hip and breasts of a female, for example. Other links involve hormonal preparation—the hormones associated with lactation, or the increased androgen production of puberty. In the normal environment of the species, the various kinds of links form behavioral chains which integrate themselves into fitness-enhancing activities. The organism mates, reproduces, and nurtures its offspring. It hunts and flees from predators. Some links may involve intelligence and planning but the chain itself is not a product of ratiocination: The wisdom of the organism's acts are those of natural selection, which has so designed the species that, in its normal environment, adaptive behaviors will be generated. This is neither a matter of nature nor of nurture but of the complex interactions of both, at all levels.[1]

What happens when we add a self-conscious and rational intelligence to such a system? A problem arises because some of the old ethological links are intrinsically rewarding in themselves—copulation and sweetness, for example. The one was part of the behavioral chain we label 'reproduction,' the other, 'nutrition.' They were a means to fitness-enhancing ends, but our self-aware and intelligent creatures make them ends in themselves. Ethology's intermediate links become our ultimate goals, in themselves functionally autonomous. So, we copulate while using contraceptives and damage teeth and health with refined sugar. Imagine a species of rational and intelligent moles, maximizing not their biological fitness but the opportunity to dig holes. Imagine a civilization of intelligent wolves, maximizing the hunt and the chase while slighting animal husbandry. It is rational intelligence and volition which lead us to lower our biological fitness by pursuing reinforcing but fitness-reducing or adaptively neutral stimuli. Intelligent volition can destroy ethologically organized behavior.[2] The net effect of self-awareness and intelligence has no doubt been fitness-enhancing but the costs have been great. We often optimize formerly instrumental goals rather than the ultimate goal of fitness itself.

Our symbolic ability makes matters worse, for what we find reinforcing we may have only learned to *associate* with one of evolution's intrinsically rewarding links. So we seek (for example) symbolic prestige rather than the actual deference of those around us. We hope for the recognition of an unknowable posterity while neglecting our own children. We enter professions high in honor but low in salary. Between the pursuit of self-rewarding links for their own sake, and the pursuit of symbols associated with them, we unwittingly neglect our biological adaptedness. Inclusive fitness theory, then, cannot substitute for theories of human motivation. We do *not* necessarily optimize fitness.

2. HOW COULD INTELLIGENCE AND VOLITION HAVE EVOLVED, IF IT LEADS TO SUCH INEFFICIENT FITNESS-ENHANCING BEHAVIOR?

The easy answer is that its adaptive advantages must have outweighed its maladaptive consequences. But this response, while undoubtedly true enough, substitutes a 'why' for a 'how.' Here is an educated guess—a reconstruction—of how intelligence and volition may have evolved, in our species.

Volition (the philosopher's 'intentionality') necessarily implies a theory of an acting self—a theory of intelligence which neglects volition is only a theory of data-processing.[3] But even for a discussion of volition, data processing or computer analogies can be useful, at least for beginning. I am going to assume that what we call 'intelligence' involves a sort of computer simulation model, a model of adaptation-relevant aspects of the physical and social environments. Selection has so 'wired' the CNS that we tend to pay attention ontogenetically to those aspects of reality which phylogenetically had adaptive or maladaptive consequences.

Our (pre-structured) attention causes us to include certain phenomena in our mental models. A rat attends to geography, for example. Its cognitive map is a geographic model which permits it to predict the shortest path between two points (Tolman, 1948)—adaptive behavior indeed, for a rat fleeing a predator. Our early ancestors were probably rather rat-like in their cognitive maps. Since they were foragers and (presumably) the prey of other species, detailed cognitive maps of their ranges would have had obvious adaptive advantage. Later, as they became social hunters as well as foragers, selection would have caused the maps to grow still more elaborate. As Peters (1978) points out, wolves have intricate and detailed cognitive maps of their ranges: the similar ecological adaptation of our later, hunting and gathering ancestors, would have produced similar selection pressures.

But the word 'map' has an erroneously static connotation. Geographic landmarks change with the seasons, while each kill brings a newly noteworthy site to be remembered. One must locate oneself on a map, and this physical location changes constantly. Position must be continually computed, as well. A 'cognitive map' is already closer to being a computer simulation model than it is a piece of flat paper.

Our ancestors were social primates, and a social animal's world includes more than the geographic. Adaptively salient features of the social as well as physical environment must be represented. Not just rocks and trees, but internal representations of one's troop members—and one's particular relationship with each of them—are part of the model. Our ancestors, like our ape and monkey cousins, must certainly have had personal relationships with one another.

The resulting cognitive model might be analogous to a sociometric plotting of the social surround, but that is still too static and simple. Trivers' (1971) theory of reciprocal altruism, for example, suggests that the internal models of social relationships included who did and who did not tend to reciprocate a favor. Hamilton's (1964) idea of kin selection emphasizes the adaptive value of being able to distinguish (behaviorally, not cognitively) kin from non-kin. Esser and Deutsch (1977, p. 131) have rightly emphasized the selection advantage in being able 'to differentiate clearly between group members' strengths and weaknesses' and to be 'able to gauge the reactions of others.' Just as the geographic part of the model must be updated frequently to reflect changes in environment and location, so too must the social aspect. Social position and relationships change frequently. Our ancestors' cognitive models of physical and social reality, then, grew to be elaborate indeed.

What of their internal representations of themselves, within these models? Is the organism ill or strong, in estrus or not? Does it have allies or 'reciprocity partners' in the vicinity? Where, within its geographic map, is it physically located? Such factors affect behavior and therefore biological fitness, and so would be included in the organism's cognitive model. They could not be included as part of the organism's internal representation of someone else: they would have to be part of the organism's internal representation of *itself*.

An internal representation can be thought of as a locus in a data-processing system. The internal representation of the organism's fellow band member Tom is the locus involved with processing certain categories of data about Tom—where he is, whether he is an ally of the organism, and so on. The organism's internal representation of itself includes similar data, but about itself. It is a hypothetical locus involved with information about the organism:

its physical health and condition, the state of its social relationships, and its geographic location.

Note that this internal representation of the organism itself is not a homunculus, not a little man hiding in the mind. Nor is it a scale model, complete in every detail. The internal representation of self is limited to mapping the three classes of information already mentioned—the organism's physical condition and health, its geographic location and movement, and the state of its social relationships. Only such data, relevant to biological fitness, are included in the organism's internal representation of itself. The body's homeostatic, autonomically regulated systems, are not. What is relevant for adaptation is whether the organism is physically capable of fighting or foraging or mating—not what its precise bilirubin count is.

I am here asserting that an organism with this kind of internal representation experiences, phenomenologically, self-consciousness, a sense of self-awareness. Regardless of the neuroanatomy, and regardless of whether we are discussing our own species or one visiting from Betelgeuse, it is difficult to conceive of any alternative way in which self-consciousness could have evolved as a product of biological evolution.[4]

I suspect that self-consciousness—the presence of an internal representation of self in the organism's cognitive model—is very widespread among animal species (cf. Gallup, 1975; 1979; Griffin, 1976; Premack and Woodruff, 1978). Individual recognition of conspecifics implies internal representations of them. A species with internal representations of others is very likely to have internal representation of self, and therefore, self-awareness. Of course, this self—the internal representation of the organism itself—must be quite rudimentary, in many species, perhaps limited only to position in a social hierarchy and present physical strength and condition. Self-awareness would be correspondingly limited.

More interesting is the question of whether human beings differ in the *elaborateness* of their internal representation of self, of self-concept. The answer here is probably yes. Unfortunately, following this line would take us away from the thrust of the present paper, which is evolutionary. It must suffice to note that the ontogenesis and content of the self is taken up elsewhere. The approach outlined here turns out to be quite compatible with a number of theories of the self, including the symbolic interactionist approach of G. H. Mead (1934).[5]

So far the self has been presented as the rather passive recipient of information furnished by the organism (or at least by the CNS) as a whole. But if the self is merely a sort of dynamic token in a model, what of our phenomenological experience of self as will, as a controlling, guiding agent with volition? If certain neurophysiological processes in the CNS are identical to our phenomenological sense of awareness, is volition epiphenomenal? The computer simulation analogy certainly makes it look that way, contradicting our everyday experience.

Volition turns out to be a characteristic of the CNS and its cognitive model as a whole, rather than of its internal representation of itself. To a considerable extent, our subjective feeling of '*I* have made a decision' is illusory—unless by '*I*' is meant the entire CNS. These conclusions stem from the approach developed by Miller, Galanter, and Pribram (1969) and by John Bowlby (1969).[6]

Imagine the organism as having a number of goals built-in by biological evolution. Some of these goals are the obvious ones such as a requirement for water when the body is dehydrated, or food when blood sugar is low; but others are more subtle. The goals are not necessarily endpoints but are often *states*, states to be maintained within certain limits. The system can switch among goals, optimizing now some and now others, while the level of goal attainment required can also vary (we do not always drink large quantities of water, for example). One goal for a child is that of attachment to its mother. Bowlby (1969) suggests that this 'goal-state' involves maintaining a certain proximity to mother. The actual distance required is affected by many factors—the presence of strangers, or the child's past experience of separation, for example—but there is always a state to be maintained. As the child grows older, the limits to the permitted distance and the length of time during which separation is tolerable both increase, and attachment ultimately takes a form more symbolic than geographic.

The means by which we strive to attain goals involves a hierarchical array of plans, sub-plans, sub-sub-plans, and so on (Miller *et al.*, 1960). These plans are the human equivalent of ethological behavior chains, though the identity is not exact. The ethologically 'rewarding' links, for example, are likely to be goals in the Miller, Galanter, and Pribram framework. 'Plans' are far more flexible than ethological behavior 'chains', and often far more complex as well—any individual piece of behavior is likely to be a tactic in the service of several goals at once. There is constant feedback from the outcome of behavior to the goal(s) it is servicing, and unsuccessful plans are quickly dropped. All goals either directly maximized the inclusive fitness of our ancestors, are symbolic (learned) derivatives of such goals, or (back in ethological days) once formed part of fitness-enhancing chains. A few examples of goals would be the obvious ones of food and drink, sexual bonding and copulation; less obvious goals involve access to information to keep cognitive maps current,[7] playing at skills as children we are likely to find useful as adults, and controlling or hoarding resources. The strategies we follow in seeking goals are culturally ordered and wonderfully flexible (due to end-testing feedback).

The self, it will be recalled, is the locus of CNS processes monitoring geographic location, state of social relationships, and physical condition of the organism. It would seem inevitable that it also be the locus of evaluation of progress towards a goal. By 'locus' is meant only that these processes directly alter the organism's internal representation of itself—its self.

This self is not a homunculus—*it* is not 'guiding' or deciding—but it is being altered by the CNS processes involved in plan behavior, including the processes of evaluating the priorities among goals and switching from one to another, or from one plan to another. Phenomenologically, though, as these processes take place we *experience* having made a decision, or realizing that a given tactic will be unsuccessful so another one must be used.

What we experience as 'emotions', though their precise role lies beyond the scope of this paper, are an integral part of the evaluation of the state-of-the-organism and progress-towards-a-goal processes. It remains accurate to say that 'I' make decisions and feel emotions, because 'I' refers to the entire organism. It is *not* accurate to say that 'the self decides' or 'the self feels.' The self merely reflects the computations of the brain; as our internal representation of ourself is continuously altered, we experience being, feeling, and 'making up our minds.' Conscious experience, then, is only a limited aspect of CNS processes, the tip of an iceberg.

We are aware only of data likely to alter the self, particularly data pertaining to our physical location, condition, state of our social relationships, progress toward a goal and contingencies likely to affect such progress. It is as if the CNS screened data according to these criteria and automatically kept out of awareness that which does not fit. Much CNS activity, such as that involved in habitual activity, remains out of awareness unless it is likely to result in an altering or updating of the organism's internal representation of itself, the self. On the other hand, awareness is intensified when data are likely to drastically affect the organism (and therefore its internal representation of itself). To return to an earlier theme, natural selection has so ordered our attention that data which are likely to affect our inclusive fitness are precisely the kind of information to which we are drawn.

3. HOW DOES ALL THIS SOLVE THE MIND–BODY PROBLEM?

The mind–body (more properly, following Pribram [1976], the 'brain–body') problem is the who-done-it question of the ultimate cause of behavior. Am *I* pressing the keys of this typewriter, or is the motion of my fingers the results of complex neurophysiological processes, and my subjective experience of will merely epiphenomenon? Can thought cause, or just biochemistry? The idea that consciousness is biologically adaptive is common enough (e.g. Blakemore, 1976, p. 37), but does it really fit into a biological, evolutionary framework? Is it not 'causally redundant' (Popper and Eccles, 1977)? Evolution affects gene frequencies and genes are responsible for the structure of my neuroanatomy, which in turn determines my behavior. How, in the name of biology, can the self be anything more than an explanatory red herring, unless we are to invoke mystic notions of 'soul' or 'mind.'? Yet, if the contents of self-consciousness are merely epiphenomena, how can Wilson (1978), among others, argue that evolution has 'preprogrammed' much of that content? Hampshire (1978) rightly points out that to ignore the problem posed by Descartes is to be incoherent.

The most tempting solution to this mind–body confusion goes by the name of 'duality'. It holds that thought and the neurophysiological processes which underlie it are identical, and the entire problem is simply a linguistic artifact: brain versus mind is a false dichotomy. How can this be, though, when there is abundant evidence for there being no conscious correlates of most of our detectable neurophysiological activity (Popper and Eccles, 1977, 81–91; Pribram, 1976; Thorpe, 1978)? Awareness cannot be another name for CNS processes, for it is associated with only a small proportion of what is happening in our brains.

The evolutionary conception of self presented earlier neatly avoids this difficulty. An information-processing system or computer simulation model of sufficient complexity to include a detailed internal representation of itself and its own state, as well as of external physical and social reality, has the property we experience phenomenologically as consciousness or awareness. (It would be confusing to say that the internal representation, the self, is itself aware. Awareness is here presented as a passive trait, lest we risk making the self rather than the CNS the active agent.) This awareness is identical to *some* but not *all* CNS processes. To repeat, it is identical to those processes actually or potentially altering the internal representation. It is not identical to others, such as habitual actions, or the computations determining priorities among goals (decision-making). The CNS carries out these processes and if they ultimately alter the state of the organism the self may eventually be altered accordingly (meaning that the individual will become aware of having driven home by force of habit, or of having come to a decision).

Our experienced self-awareness is neither a guiding agent homunculus nor an epiphenomenon. Awareness is *not* the decision-maker, the actor. Deciding or ordering priorities is a function of the CNS as a whole, and volition, while real, belongs to no one part of it. In particular, it does not belong to the one part of it we experience, our awareness. Western culture, with its values of personal responsibility, 'will-power', and rational and logical decision-making leads us to grossly exaggerate the extent to which our conscious awareness controls our behavior. Other cultural traditions, which explain many actions as the result of outside agents (e.g., possession by spirits), or which view human beings as irrational and readily controlled by strong emotions, are not as subject as we to this distorted perception of the power of 'I'.

None of this means that our conscious thoughts and ideas—or unconscious, out-of-awareness at the moment thoughts, too, for that matter—are irrelevant to our behavior. It is far easier to follow the operation of a computer from the flow-charts of its programs than from watching each one of its hundreds of thousands of sequential machine operations. In the same way, it is far easier to understand human behavior in terms of desires and motives and self-images than it is to discuss the firing of neurons—even though many of these desires and motives are not always part of conscious awareness (as we shall see).

4. WHY IS SELF-CONSCIOUSNESS SO LIMITED? WHY IS SELF-DECEPTION POSSIBLE?

There are sharp limits to consciousness. As we have seen, only information relevant to biological fitness is likely to enter awareness. But there are additional limits, and distortions, too, and these also have to do with biological fitness.

There is no evolutionary requirement for an internal representation to be accurate. The requirement is only that it serve to enhance inclusive fitness. The withholding of data from awareness and distortion of the self arise from the same selection pressures which favor our deceiving others. We deceive ourselves and each other for the same reasons (Trivers, 1976).

Deception arises because the biological fitness interests of individuals differ, so that selection will frequently favor their deceiving one another. Trivers (1971), for example, discusses how reciprocal altruism involves individuals being selected for the ability to predict accurately whether or not the recipient of an altruistic act will return the favor. This selection pressure has resulted in our being far readier to act altruistically toward intimates than toward strangers.

But selection is also favoring the 'confidence man,' who can persuade others that he will reciprocate when in fact he will not. Evolution, in short, favors the successfully deceitful. In similar fashion, Trivers (1972), in his discussion of sex differences in fitness interests, suggests that males should often attempt to impress females with false information about relative strength and health, control over resources, and willingness to invest in offspring.[8] Since females must choose among males, in many species (including our own), selection favors those males who can give the impression of being the best fitness bets available—in effect, of having the 'best' genes (as evidenced by their apparently superior phenotypes) and of being (apparently) most willing to share in the care of young. The point of all this, then, is that deceit often is biologically adaptive.

How do I lie non-verbally? One form of self-deceit arises from selection for *efficiently* deceiving others. Human beings constantly broadcast and pick up information on several non-verbal 'bands'. Much of the neurological underpinning of this 'broadcasting' behavior is phylogenetically ancient, perhaps going all the way back to our reptilian ancestors (MacLean, 1973). Given the competitiveness engendered by our differing fitness interests, selection favors much deceitful broadcasting—for example, about our physical abilities, commitment to a sexual bond, willingness to reciprocate aid, and so on. Evolution seems to have hit upon a remarkably efficient way of permitting us to deceive non-verbally: in order to deceive others, we deceive ourselves. Rather than cutting the links between our display patterns and the internal states with which they have for so long (phylogenetically) been associated, the evaluation of state processes centered in and on the self-representation have been distorted. We deceive ourselves constantly about our physical condition, inner state and motivation, sincerity and commitment to others, and intentions and goals. We were selected for unconscious hypocrisy in the service of our own fitness interests and this tendency, disapprove of it though we may (hypocritically?) profess to, is a genuine species trait and not just a moral failing.

Social status provides a good example of adaptive distortion and manipulation of information.[9] High social rank is one of our goals as primates, presumably because it was once, at least, associated with enhanced biological fitness. Non-verbal communication of high status—confidence and poise—are sexually attractive. While young human beings, like other primates, rely heavily on agonism to establish rank, as adults we rank and evaluate each other in symbolic terms. Rather than thinking, 'I'm tougher than you are,' we say, 'I have naturally curly hair,' or 'I have more publications than you have.' Culturally provided symbolic standards of relative rank replace pure agonism. But which standards, since even in low-technology societies, multiple sets of criteria of relative status are often available? The answer is, the standards in terms of which we can rank ourselves highest.

Our particular skills, accomplishments, physical attributes, control over resources, ancestry, and so on, provide the criteria in terms of which we decide that we rank high indeed. Even today, it may well be that the non-verbal communication of our self-evaluated 'high rank' confers various benefits, possibly including enhanced fitness (presumably by permitting more ready access to the most fit mates). It is clear that a nursery school child's confident stance and expression (his 'win face') accurately predict his winning an agonistic encounter with another child (Zivin, 1975).

Other forms of biologically adaptive self-deception may be less subtle. For example, we find it quite easy to suppress our knowledge of our failure to meet obligations to others, while demanding that the obligations of others to ourselves be met. When we fail, it is the fault of others, and only rarely our own. It is possible to develop a theory of unconscious motivation based not on pathology but on the idea that self-deception is often in the service of biological fitness (though not necessarily in the service of any of our *conscious* goals). Such an effort would require a new chapter, however (if not an entire book).

One final example of self-deception, this time one related to physical violence. It seems remarkably easy, cross-culturally, to convince warriors of their invulnerability in battle, or in the existence of a desirable after-life should they fall. Were it possible to have a representative sample of warriors rate themselves on 'toughness' just before combat began, they would undoubtedly rank themselves near the 'invincible' end of the mortality scale. This is because physical violence is much more often in the service of maximizing inclusive fitness than it is pure survival. Running away from all combat might be the best strategy for mere survival, but in the environment in which we evolved, such 'cowardice' would probably have meant losing in the competition for resources and mates and so leaving few or no progeny. Thus, we were selected for the cognitive distortions and deceptions involved in 'bravery,' not only because they permitted us to communicate non-verbally to our opponents that we were likely to win, but because they permitted us to engage in combat or rivalry in the first place. Adrenalin in conflict situations may have interesting effects on self-assessment.

Note that this picture of self-deception and 'unconscious motivation' is quite consistent with the locus-of-evaluation model of the self drawn earlier. Awareness is strictly limited, in this conception, and the internal representation of the self concerned only with adaptively salient aspects of the organism. But there is no reason to expect that internal representation to be accurate, only adaptive. This means that part of the CNS must have accurate information, while another part—the conscious part—does not.

Such a conclusion accords well with the findings of Sackheim and Gur (1978), who report experimental evidence of self-deception and suggest that it may be linked to the Freudian defense mechanism of repression. These authors and the researchers whom they cite find that we self-deceive about our voice and appearance. Given the tip-of-the-iceberg image of awareness presented here, and the conception of the self as being more in the service of inclusive fitness than of accuracy, these findings are not surprising.

5. WHY SHOULD WE BE CONCERNED ABOUT THESE ABSTRACT QUESTIONS?

'Vague', 'general', 'untestable,' and 'so what' summarizes the reaction of many social and behavioral scientists to the kinds of abstract questions and answers provided in this sketch. The building of grand theoretical structures has long been out of vogue. Micro-theories dealing with a handful of concretely ('operationally') defined and easily manipulated variables are the norm. Students who repeatedly ask how it all fits together, students with a high need for closure and with advanced synthetic abilities, these are the students who drop out or are forced out in response to the four adjectives with which this paragraph begins. Experimental method, quantification, operationalism, tests of statistical significance, parsimony—and perhaps selective recruitment to (non-clinical) psychology of individuals with a limited range of cognitive styles—these have combined to create psychological theories like oddly shaped bricks, no two fitting together, building nothing no matter how cunningly fashioned in themselves. Is it not time to try to fit all these varied research findings into a single framework? Do we not owe it to the undergraduate, who takes an introductory course expecting a discipline and finds a congeries of ideas and findings and perspectives and no unity?

There is, of course, a conceptual framework available, that of biological evolution. No scientific psychological system incompatible with evolutionary biology can be possible, just as no chemistry incompatible with the laws of physics is conceivable, or a biology incompatible with chemistry (Barkow, 1980b). Each level has its own laws and properties, of course, but these must be compatible with the laws of the lower level or else they (or perhaps the lower level itself) are in error.

But the relationship between evolutionary biology and psychology is a good deal closer than that between, say, physics and chemistry. Evolution provides not just principles to which psychological explanations must conform (e.g., the ethogram of a species must be biologically adaptive in the environment in which the species evolved, or else you do not understand that ethogram): evolution provides an explanatory *framework* as well.

This is hardly new. One thinks, for example, of Bowlby (1969), and of Freedman (1974), who make proper use of evolution's spacious frame, and do not force data into the procrustean bed of limited logical systems. Most recently, several biologists—Edward Wilson, Robert Trivers, and Richard Alexander in particular—have attempted to rethink the social-behavioral sciences in terms of evolutionary theory. Their approach suffers from several drawbacks, including a lack of sufficient concern with the mechanisms mediating the selection pressures with which they deal, and a slighting of those selection pressures deriving from environment rather than from pure theory—but they do successfully demonstrate the enormous synthetic power of evolutionary thought and its ability to 'make sense of' behavior (Barkow, 1978a; 1980b).

Place some basic questions about awareness, self-deception, and the mind–body problem in an evolutionary frame. This sketch results. It is overly abstract, deliberately ignoring current research on neurophysiology because the details of that research would distract from the larger frame under construction. Few specific, testable hypotheses have resulted, yet much seems to 'make sense,' to fit together. Is the resulting structure falsifiable?

Why should it be? Falsifiability is a useful rule-of-thumb in evaluating small hypotheses dealing with a limited number of variables. It is inappropriate when we are concerned with larger structures similar to Kuhn's (1962) paradigms. Either such frameworks order existing data and some small-scale theories, or else they do not and are discarded when better ones come along. Here are some evaluation criteria in terms of which the present effort will be maintained, revised, or junked:

(1) Is it logically consistent?
(2) Are there any data pertaining to neurophysiology or behavior incompatible with it?
(3) Is it consistent with evolutionary biology?
(4) Is there any alternative evolutionary interpretation of awareness and self more powerful (in the sense of ordering more data) than the present offering?

The perspective of this sketch has been that mind and body are one, and that they are a single product of the extraordinarily convoluted process of human phylogenesis. Numerous selection pressures, often at odds with one another and acting on mechanisms originally serving old purposes, built by accretion a three-layer Rube Goldberg of a CNS in which the parts, too, are often at odds with one another, and serve old purposes.

ACKNOWLEDGMENTS

The author wishes to thank the Harry Frank Guggenheim Foundation for providing support during the initial preparation of this chapter. He also wishes to thank Professor Roland Puccetti of Dalhousie University's Department of Philosophy for his useful comments on an early draft of this work. Responsibility for errors remains ineluctably with the author.

NOTES

1. As Bateson (1979, p. 350) puts it in his dismissal of the nature–nurture question, 'Sources of variability in behavior are treated as though they were components of fully developed behavior—which is about as sensible as arguing that 20 percent of bread is due to the cooking.' At no level, from molecular biology to parental behavior, is environment–biology interaction lacking.
2. See Barkow and Burley (1980) for a discussion of this topic in the context of human fertility trends and the demographic transition.
3. See, for example, Stenhouse's (1973) useful theory of intelligence as having evolved in terms of three components: a central 'memory store'; an 'abstracting and generalizing factor'; a 'postponement factor' permitting the delay of an 'instinctual' response so that thinking can take place; and a 'sensorimotor efficiency factor' which has to do with the choice of mode of expression of an action. Stenhouse's argument that selection would have favored such abilities is beyond dispute. He is not, however, concerned with self, consciousness, volition, the maladaptive consequences of intelligence, or the mind–body problem.

For a very readable popular account of the evolution of human intelligence, see Sagan (1977).

4. Consciousness is a pillow-fight of a topic, with plenty of feathers but nothing very concrete. Izard (1977, pp. 131–160) offers a useful overview of various theories.

Granit (1977) argues that consciousness is the highest level of a hierarchical organization, so that 'conscious man makes use of neurophysiological mechanisms without being governed by them' (p. 73), thereby begging the question of just how the 'governing' is taking place. To make of consciousness an emergent top level of a hierarchical organization, as Granit does, seems to obfuscate with the aid of systems theory rather than to enlighten. Descartes solved the problem of consciousness and mind by invoking an immaterial soul which interacted with the body at the pineal gland. Popper and Eccles (1977) solve the problem in similar fashion by invoking a 'mind' which interacts with the brain via the pyramidal cells of the vertical columnar arrangements of the sensory cortex of the dominant hemisphere. They hypothesize (and apparently conclude as well) that

> the self-conscious mind is an independent entity that is actively engaged in reading out from the multitude of active centres in the modules of the liaison areas of the dominant cerebral hemisphere. The self-conscious mind selects from these centres in accord with its attention and its interests and integrates its selection to give the unity of conscious experience from moment to moment. It also acts back on the neural centres (p. 355).

Pribram (1976) presents similar details of neuroanatomical functioning but, while recognizing the inadequacy of the various proposed solutions to the problem of mind, provides none of his own. None of the treatments of consciousness seems particularly germane to the present discussion, but Izard's overview and Popper and Eccles' bibliography will supply the interested reader with a variety of conjectures, ranging from the entirely philosophical to the relentlessly neuroanatomical.

Readers wishing further discussion of consciousness and mind–body problems should consult any of the above, or perhaps Ryle's (1949) attack on Cartesian thinking and Koestler's (1967) response.

5. Since this paper is largely concerned with putting self-awareness and volition in an evolutionary context, it omits discussion of the actual contents and structure of consciousness, except in outline form. For a discussion of the role of attention and attention structure in relation both to the self and to human evolution, see Barkow (1976, 1977). For a discussion of the self and social norms, see Barkow (1978a). For recent research and theory pertaining to consciousness, see Schwartz and Shapiro (1978).

6. This discussion is summarized from Barkow (1973; 1975a; 1976).

7. Hence the human fascination with gossip, discussed by Gluckman (1963). To gossip about someone is to include him or her in our group—gossip about total outsiders strikes us as pointless, presumably because it would have no adaptive value.

8. For further discussion of human sexual behavior and Trivers' parental investment theory, see Barkow (1981), Larsen (1978), and Daly and Wilson (1978).

9. The following argument is summarized from Barkow (1975b; 1980a).

REFERENCES

Barkow, J. H. (1973) Darwinian psychological anthropology: a biosocial approach, *Current Anthropology*, **14**, 373–388.

Barkow, J. H. (1975a) Strategies of self-esteem in Maradi (Niger Republic). In *World Congress: Psychological Anthropology* (ed. T. R. Williams), Mouton, The Hague.

Barkow, J. H. (1975b) Prestige and culture: a biosocial interpretation, *Current Anthropology*, **16**, 553–572.

Barkow, J. H. (1976) Attention structure and internal representations. In *The Social Structure of Attention* (eds M. R. A. Chance and R. R. Larsen), Wiley, London.

Barkow, J. H. (1977) Human ethology and intra-individual systems, *Social Science Information*, **16**, 133–145.

Barkow, J. H. (1978a) Social norms, the self, and sociobiology: building on the ideas of A. I. Hallowell, *Current Anthropology*, **19**, 99–118.

Barkow, J. H. (1978b) Culture and sociobiology, *American Anthropologist*, **80**, 5–20.

Barkow, J. H. (1980a) Prestige and self-esteem: a biosocial interpretation. In *Dominance Relations: An Ethological View of Human Conflict and Social Interaction* (eds D. R. Omark, F. F. Strayer, and D. G. Freedman), Garland Publishing Company, New York.

Barkow, J. H. (1980b) Sociobiology: Is this the new theory of human nature? In *Sociobiology Examined* (ed. Montagu), pp. 171–197, Oxford University Press, New York.

Barkow, J. H. (1980c) Biological evolution of culturally patterned behavior. In *The Evolution of Human Social Behavior* (ed. J. Lockard), pp. 277–296, Elsevier North Holland, New York.

Barkow, J. H. (1981) Evolution et sexualité. In *Sexologie Contemporaine* (eds C. Crépault, J. J. Lévy, and H. Gratton), pp. 103–118, Les Presses de l'Université du Québec, Québec.

Barkow, J. H. (1982) Return to nepotism: the collapse of a Nigerian gerontocracy, *International Political Science Review*, **3**, 33–49.

Barkow, J. H., and Burley, N. (1980) Evolutionary biology, human fertility, and the demographic transition, *Ethology and Sociobiology*, **1**, 163–180.

Bateson, P. (1979) Review of *The Development of Behavior* (eds G. M. Burkhardt and M. Bekoff), *Science* (26 Jan., vol. 203, no. 4378, p. 350).

Blakemore, C. (1976) *Mechanics of the Mind*. Cambridge University Press, Cambridge.

Bowlby, J. A. (1969) *Attachment and Loss. Vol. 1: Attachment*. Basic Books, New York.

Chagnon, N. A., and Irons, W. (eds) (1979) *Evolutionary Biology and the Social Sciences*. Duxbury, North Scituate, Massachusetts.

Daly, M., and Wilson, M. (1978) *Sex, Evolution and Behavior*. Duxbury, North Scituate, Massachusetts.

Eibl-Eibesfeldt, I. (1975) *Ethology: The Biology of Behavior* (2nd ed.). Holt, Rinehart and Winston, New York.

Esser, A. H., and Deutsch, R. D. (1977) Private interaction territories on psychiatric wards: studies on nonverbal communication of spatial needs. In *Ethological Psychiatry* (eds M. T. McGuire and L. A. Fairbanks), Grune and Stratton, New York.

Freedman, D. G. (1974) *Human Infancy: An Evolutionary Perspective*. Lawrence Erlbaum, Hillsdale, N.J.

Gallup, G. G., Jr. (1975) Toward an operational definition of self-awareness. In *Socioecology and Psychology of Primates* (ed. R. H. Tuttle), Mouton, The Hague.

Gallup, G. G., Jr. (1979) Self-awareness in primates, *American Scientist*, **67**, 417–421.

Gluckman, M. (1963) Gossip and scandal, *Current Anthropology*, **4**, 307–316.

Granit, R. (1977) *The Purposive Brain*, MIT Press, Cambridge, Massachusetts.

Griffin, D. R. (1976) *The Question of Animal Awareness: Evolutionary Continuity of Mental Experience*, Rockefeller University Press, New York.

Hamilton, W. D. (1964) The genetical evolution of social behavior, *Journal of Theoretical Biology*, **7**, 1–51.

Hampshire, S. (1978) The illusion of sociobiology (Review of E. O. Wilson, *On Human Nature*), *New York Review*, Oct. 12, **25**(15), 64–69.

Izard, C. E. (1977) *Human Emotions*, Plenum, New York.

Koestler, A. (1967) *The Ghost in the Machine*, Hutchinson, London.

Kuhn, T. S. (1962) *The Structure of Scientific Revolutions*, University of Chicago Press, Chicago.

Larsen, R. R. (1978) Les fondements évolutionnistes des différences entre les sexes. In *Le fait féminin* (ed. E. Sullerot), Fayard, Paris.

Lumsden, C. J., and E. O. Wilson (1981) *Genes, Mind, and Culture: the Coevolutionary Process*, Harvard University Press, Cambridge, Massachusetts.

MacLean, P. D. (1973) *A Triune Concept of the Brain and Behavior*, University of Toronto Press, Toronto.

Mead, G. H. (1934) *Mind, Self, and Society*, University of Chicago Press, Chicago.

Miller, G. A., Galanter, E. and Pribram, K. H. (1960) *Plans and the Structure of Behavior*, Holt, New York.

Peters, R. (1978) Communication, cognitive mapping, and strategy. In *Wolf and Man: Evolution in Parallel* (eds R. L. Hall and H. S. Sharp), Academic Press, New York.

Popper, K. R., and Eccles, J. C. (1977) *The Self and Its Brain*, Springer-Verlag, Berlin.

Premack, D., and Woodruff, G. (1978) Does the chimpanzee have a theory of mind?, *Behavioral and Brain Sciences*, **1**, 515–526.

Pribram, K. H. (1976) Self-consciousness and intentionality. In *Consciousness and Self-regulation. Advances in Research, vol. 1* (eds G. E. Schwartz and D. Shapiro), Plenum, New York.

Ryle, G. (1949) *The Concept of Mind*, Hutchinson, London.

Sackheim, H. A., and Gur, R. C. (1978) Self-deception, self-confrontation, and consciousness. In *Consciousness and Self-regulation. Advances in Research, vol. 2* (eds G. E. Schwartz and D. Shapiro), Plenum, New York.

Sagan, C. (1977) *The Dragons of Eden. Speculations on the Evolution of Human Intelligence*, Random House, New York.

Schwartz, G. E., and Shapiro, D. (eds) (1978) *Consciousness and Self-regulation. Advances in Research, vol. 2*, Plenum, New York.

Stenhouse, D. (1973) *The Evolution of Intelligence*, Allen and Unwin, London.

Thorpe, W. H. (1978) *Purpose in a World of Chance*, Oxford University Press, Oxford.

Tolman, E. (1948) Cognitive maps in rats and men, *Psychological Review*, **55**, 189–208.

Trivers, R. L. (1971) The evolution of reciprocal altruism, *Quarterly Review of Biology*, **46**, 35–57.

Trivers, R. L. (1972) Parental investment and sexual selection, In *Sexual Selection and the Descent of Man*, Aldine, Chicago.

Trivers, R. L. (1976) Foreword (to *The Selfish Gene*, by Richard Dawkins), Oxford University Press, New York.

Wilson, E. O. (1978) *On Human Nature*, Harvard University Press, Cambridge, Massachusetts.

Zivin, Gail (1975) Preschoolers' facial-postural status messages. Paper presented at the 3rd International Human Ethology Workshop, Sheffield, England.

Section III

Neurobiological Aspects

Potentially one of the areas where extrapolation from animals to humans could prove to be most useful is brain research. Clearly, one can carry out systematic experimental research in human neurobiology only in very limited circumstances—usually where the subject requires necessary clinical treatment for related problems. So to possess animal models which can be shown to have some relevance to human functioning is invaluable. They would prove to be invaluable not only to an understanding of normal human brain functioning, but also to an understanding of human pathological problems which stem from central nervous system dysfunction. To date, however, there has been a conspicuous dearth of such animal models—particularly so in the case of psychopathy. The problems encountered by extrapolation in this particular region of psychology are numerous. In the case of psychopathy, we not only have the problems of deciding *how* to extrapolate, we also encounter the problem of defining what the original phenomenon itself is. For instance, animal models of psychoses may have played only a minor role in understanding human psychoses because we are still arguing about the behavioral attributes that define the various psychoses. Even when there is some general consensus as to these attributes they are often couched in ways which are predominantly 'human' (e.g. as thought disorders, paranoia, etc.) and hence difficult to translate into the psychological world of the non-human animal.

A second problem which has beset comparative studies of brain–behavior relationships has been the problem of setting different species behavioral tasks which are functionally similar. For instance, most tests of perception in non-human animals involve discriminated responses to biologically important events such as food or electric shock. The particular effects of brain lesion studies may well depend on the natural relationship between the appetitive or aversive reinforcer used and the modality being tested. For instance, if a species is predominantly an olfactory feeder the behavioral effects of lesions to visual centers of the brain may be less apparent than with species that are largely visual feeders. This could lead one to erroneous conclusions about the function of those brain centers in the two species: in this hypothetical example the difference between the species is in the ethological implications of the task set, not necessarily in the function of specific brain structures. The problem is at its gravest when we try to make comparisons between humans and animals (at any level of analysis—behavioral, cognitive, or brain function). In our study of psychological processes in humans we rarely involve biologically salient events such as food whilst in a state of hunger, or intensive electric shock. Most often the experimental technique involves a fairly mundane problem-solving task with more social than strictly biological implications.

This final section of the book discusses issues concerning what might properly constitute correct interspecific brain–behavior analyses, and also makes some attempt to review the current state of affairs on animal models of psychopathy—including the attendant clinical implications of such extrapolation.

Animal Models of Human Behavior
Edited by G. C. L. Davey
© 1983 John Wiley & Sons Ltd

Chapter 12

Interspecific Comparisons and the Hypothetico-Deductive Approach

C. R. LEGG

INTRODUCTION

For years neuropsychologists have attempted to build up a picture of brain function by studying the effects of localized brain injury, either intentional or accidental. While many types of study are possible on humans they are, of necessity, crude with respect to anatomical localization so that although the neuropsychologist can describe in exquisite detail the cognitive, perceptual and emotional disturbances suffered by his patients he is unable to specify accurately the nature of the injuries producing them. Procedures like the computerized axial tomography have vastly improved the degree of localization possible but until the technique is refined to the point at which the cytoarchitecture of individual regions becomes visible it leaves a lot to be desired. Even if it is possible to specify the location of an injury it remains impossible to be definitive about the connectivity of the area damaged if we are forced to rely upon data from human neuroanatomical studies alone. Our understanding of the human brain clearly depends upon our understanding of those of other species but there are practical and theoretical difficulties in extending the knowledge gained from non-human species to the human. The practical difficulties are that when researchers have looked for similarities between the effects of damage to supposedly homologous areas in man and other species they have failed to materialize. For example, it would be a brave person who attempted to predict the known effects of frontal lobe damage in man from their effects in primates or rodents (Nauta, 1971). The theoretical difficulty is the 'psychophysical assumption' operating at evolutionary level: if behavior is deterministically controlled by brain processes

225

and behavioral adaptations are genetically determined then there are bound to be interspecific differences in brain function.

To extrapolate from animals to man we need a set of rules that enable us to develop models of brain function on non-human species and extend them to man by making due allowance for the differences between man and the other species. The only way to solve this problem is to recognize that, formally speaking, the status of extrapolating from, say, a rhesus monkey to man is indistinguishable from extrapolating from a rabbit to a rhesus monkey and that extrapolating from animals to man is part of a wider problem of systematizing species differences in brain structure and function. Empiricism alone cannot solve this problem; active hypothesis formation is required, hence the title of the chapter.

It would be improper to say that neuropsychology lacks extrapolation rules but the two most widely used concepts, 'encephalization' and the principle of conservation, are largely inadequate. My aim in this chapter is, therefore, to review both of these positions and consider their shortcomings as extrapolation rules, as opposed to their value as heuristic devices or as means of *post hoc* systematization of species differences. This will be followed by the development of a third position which emphasizes ecological trends as the main determinants of differences in brain and behavior relationships, an approach which will be illustrated by a discussion of recent views of the visual functions of the superior colliculus.

ENCEPHALIZATION

It should be superfluous to repeat the already well rehearsed arguments against 'encephalization' (Hodos and Campbell, 1969; Jerison, 1976; Weiskrantz, 1961) but the fact that contemporary authorities (e.g. Goldberg and Robinson, 1978) can appeal to such a process to account for species differences in brain function suggests that the main points are worth repeating, albeit briefly. The encephalization hypothesis holds that during mammalian phylogenesis functions that were originally represented in the brain-stems of ancestral reptilian forms have been translated to the neocortex, with corresponding changes in the functions of both regions, and that mammalian species may be ranked on an independent scale from 'primitive' to 'advanced' on morphological grounds which is monotonically related to the degree to which encephalization has occurred. Central to the objections to this approach is the recognition of evolution as a process of radiation rather than a progression. For example, all of the major orders of mammals emerged about 70 million years ago and since that time have been undergoing further divergence and convergence. Thus no species can be said to be more 'advanced' than any other and the only realistic way of ordering animals is in terms of the closeness of their relationship to a target species. However, a measure of closeness of relationship is of no use in predicting the degreee of encephalization of function as different degrees of relatedness are confounded with the dimensions along which the differences exist. Two species may be equally closely related to a third but distantly related to each other.

Recognizing these problems some recent workers have restricted their search for such phylogenetic trends to within lineages (Diamond, 1976). In this work the approach is to attempt to reconstruct lineages by searching for representatives of common ancestral types and determining the presence of systematic changes as one progresses from primitive to advanced forms. Using this approach Diamond and his colleagues (Diamond, 1976; 1979) have reported a systematic change in the organization of the visual cortex as one progresses from primitive insectivores (represented by the hedgehog), through primitive prosimians (represented by the tree shrew) to the true prosimian (the bushbaby) and the old world monkey (the rhesus macaque). As Campbell (1976) points out this reconstruction is compromised because we can no longer sustain the classification of the tree shrew as a primate. Even if the inclusion of the tree shrew is accepted this approach only accounts for some twenty, out of a total of about seventy, million years of primate evolution, the major primate lines having been undergoing progressive divergence for the last fifty million years. If one wishes to reconstruct primate evolution this may be the only viable approach but as a basis for formulating phylogenetic trends that can allow reasonable cross-species extrapolations it is inadequate. It is inadequate for two reasons. First, because it only takes account of a small part of the variance within the primate family tree and second because reasons of experimental convenience dictate that we select species that come from different lineages.

THE PRINCIPLE OF CONSERVATION

Is it reasonable to presuppose that evolution has involved the progressive alteration of function of homologous brain areas, asks Jerison (1976). From his review of brain organization in fossil and living mammals (see also Jerison, 1973) he concludes that it is not and that evolution has, in fact, involved the addition of new brain systems rather than the modification of old ones. For example, he maintains that the significant feature of the evolution of mammalian brains was the development of a neocortex containing a system for representing objects independently of a specific stimulus event, a view recently elaborated with experimental evidence by Whitfield (1979). Jerison takes the view that homologous brain structures have comparable functions in different species, explaining species differences in terms of the relative contributions of specific systems. This is the 'principle of conservation', one that allows ready generalizations from one species to another, providing one is dealing with homologous systems, and one that has informed a large body of recent work in comparative neuropsychology (see Chapter 13). As an heuristic device the principle of conservation is unsurpassed. As an extrapolation rule it fails miserably because of the inherent circularity in the way in which it is applied.

Let us take two examples from the realm of visual system neuropsychology to inspect the issues in more detail. The first concerns the behavioral analysis of the functions of the visual cortex, the second the analysis of the superior colliculus. In the nineteenth century there was considerable debate about whether removal of the primary visual cortex did, or did not, impair visual function (James, 1890; Polyak, 1957) which ended with an affirmative answer when trouble was taken to ensure that the entire primary visual cortex was removed. Nevertheless, the next generation of researchers managed to demonstrate a range of residual functions in such animals as rats and monkeys (Lashley, 1930; 1935; Kluver, 1941) to which subsequent investigators have added more (Pasik and Pasik, 1971; Keating, 1979; Weiskrantz, 1979). In humans the position appears different, primary visual cortex damage producing dense blindness in those parts of the visual field represented by the missing cortex (Teuber et al., 1960). Since the subcortical visual pathways in man are presumed to be homologous with those in other species the fact that residual visual capacity, which must depend upon these pathways, is poorer in man than in other species is a direct challenge to the principle of conservation, as Weiskrantz (1961) recognized. The solution to this dilemma has been to argue that in humans visual function is assessed in terms of subjective reports of conscious experience whereas non-human species learn visual discriminations without the intervention of consciousness. This proposal has received considerable support from studies of vision in scotomata using non-verbal indices of performance. Getting humans with visual field defects to make responses to visual stimuli, of which they were not aware, by pointing (Perenin and Jeannerod, 1978), moving the eyes (Poppel et al., 1973) or making guesses (Weiskrantz et al., 1974) has proved an experimental gold-mine, revealing a range of visual functions in scotomata that were previously unsuspected. Whether the conditions under which the capacities were demonstrated could be said to have been predicted from the studies on non-human species is another matter since it is hard to see why one set of voluntary actions, making verbal utterances, requires conscious intervention while another set, pointing the hand or moving the eyes, does not. Furthermore, the main reason for believing that the performance of non-human animals does not always require consciousness is that extensive training procedures, involving reinforcements for correct stimulus choices, are used and these may generate visuomotor reactions at a quasi-reflex level. No such formal training procedures are used with humans hence the analogy between the non-verbal choice reactions of animals and those of humans is superficial at best. A simpler interpretation of the human 'blindsight' literature is that non-verbal responses do not enjoy higher visual sensitivity than verbal ones but that the associated response criteria are much lower.

It could be argued that it is the lowering of the response criterion, either through training or appropriate verbal instructions, that links 'blindsight' to residual vision in non-human species but such an argument, by virtue of being *post hoc*, does little more than illustrate the circularity frequently present in the application of the principle of conservation. Furthermore, neither a lowering of the response criterion nor the absence of a need for conscious intervention can explain the wide, within and between species, differences in residual visual function that obtain in non-human species. Primary visual cortex removal in the rat produces a severe depression in spatial vision, leaving intact the ability to orientate towards light sources (Lashley, 1930; Horel *et al.*, 1966) and to detect the presence of contours (Cowey and Weiskrantz, 1971; Dean, 1978). Tree shrews, in contrast, are capable of sophisticated form discrimination after comparable lesions and can orientate towards the locations of specific forms (Killackey *et al.*, 1971). The same is true of the cat (Spear, 1979). With monkeys form identification has been claimed (Pasik and Pasik, 1971) but the use of extensive training and reinforced transfer trials in the assessment of the animals' ability to identify form independently of modifications that would affect flux cues leaves this conclusion open to doubt. Otherwise rhesus monkeys deprived of striate cortex behave very much like posterior neodecorticate rats in that the most prominent form of visually guided behavior is the ability to respond to and orientate towards light sources (Humphrey, 1970; Kluver, 1941; Weiskrantz *et al.*, 1977). Since the structures implicated in residual vision (Doty, 1973) are all brain-stem regions the principle of conservation would lead us to expect that they should operate similarly in all mammals, but this assumption is directly contradicted by the data.

Problems with the principle of conservation may also be seen in attempts to explore the functions of brain-stem regions by direct means, bearing in mind that the principle predicts a constancy of function across species. For example, the superior colliculus appears in all mammals (Goldberg and Robinson, 1978; Ingle and Sprague, 1977) and is claimed to be homologous with the optic tectum of avians, reptiles, amphibians, and fishes (Ingle and Sprague, 1977). However, direct investigation of the functions of the colliculus reveals a far from constant function across species. For example, lesions in cats and tree shrews interfere with discrimination learning (Berlucchi *et al.*, 1972; Casagrande and Diamond, 1974; Tunkl and Berkley, 1977) but in rats, hamsters, and rhesus monkeys they do not (Legg and Cowey, 1977; Rosvold *et al.*, 1958; Schneider, 1969). Stimulation in the cat yields eye and head movements but in the monkey only eye-movements occur reliably (Roucoux *et al.*, 1980; Schiller and Stryker, 1972; Schiller *et al.*, 1979). Lesions also interfere with spontaneous visumotor reactions but the nature of the interference varies from species to species. In cats, tree shrews, and hamsters the most obvious loss is of orientating movements of the head while in the rhesus monkey saccadic eye-movements are depressed but not eliminated (Goldberg and Robinson, 1978; Schiller *et al.*, 1980). Rats typically fail to exhibit any of these orientating movements in the first place but manifest colliculus damage in terms of a loss of inhibitory reactions to sudden stimuli (Goodale and Murison, 1975). Curiously, it is difficult to demonstrate this form of behavioral inhibition in intact cats (Winterkorn and Meikle, 1981). Attempts to apply the principle of conservation to this work has lead to the claim that the colliculus is involved in the 'visual grasp reflex' (Ingle, 1977) or visumotor orientation (Schneider, 1969) but the manifestation of these reactions in different species is so varied that one is tempted to conclude that the visual grasp reflex, or a visual orientation movement, is any piece of behavior under the control of the colliculus.

THE PRINCIPLE OF PROPER MASS

Jerison (1976) resolves the issue of persisting species differences by proposing a second principle, that of 'proper mass', which holds that homologous structures vary in extent according to the amount of information that they have to process and by arguing that phylogeny has led to the development of structures and systems novel to particular groups, the operation of which modify the operation of structures having homologues in all species. Either may be invoked to explain species differences in the effects of manipulations of the superior colliculus whereas the principle of proper mass is most relevant to the issue of why surviving subcortical systems operate differently after visual cortex ablation in different species. One of the explanations of the devastating effects of superior colliculus ablation upon visual discrimination learning in the tree shrew (Casagrande and Diamond, 1974) is that since it is so massive, relative to the geniculostriate system, its loss must produce a significant loss of visual information processing capacity. There are two ways of viewing this imbalance. One is to hold that the principle of proper mass is operating and the colliculus is large because there is much information to process, the other being that the visual cortex is too small, relative to the amount of visual information being extracted at the retina so the modification of visual function attributable to the visual cortex is less in the tree shrew than in the rhesus monkey. Following this line of argument it may be suggested that species differences in the effects of visual cortex ablation may be attributed to variations in the extent of the subcortical visual system.

One cannot take exception to the idea that structures unique to a species, or group of species, will modify the operation of more widespread systems but the principle of proper mass faces two objections. The first is that as it stands there is no means of predicting how proper mass will be distributed between different components of a system. The second is that we presently lack an algorithm for calculating proper mass. Let us consider these in turn.

It is generally acknowledged that the amount of visual information available in the retinal image is determined by two factors, ambient light intensity and the light gathering power of the eye so it is reasonable to presuppose that the extent of the visual nervous system will vary from species to species according to the impact of these two variables (but see below). Nevertheless the nature of the retinal image alone cannot account for the way in which visual information is distributed within the central nervous system. For example, both tree shrews and many species of monkeys are diurnal tree dwellers living in very similar environments, yet in one group the bulk of the optic nerve distributes to the superior colliculus while in the other it reaches the lateral geniculate nucleus. Clearly, if we are to avoid postulating an already discredited phylogenetic trend we must find some other explanation of these differences.

This point is linked to the second problem, that of calculating 'proper' mass in the first instance. While the proper mass of many central nervous system structures may be impossible to calculate at this stage it is possible to essay some predictions concerning the early stages of sensory systems and it is worthwhile looking at these to illustrate the problems involved. Once again the visual system makes a convenient model. Most authorities agree that the density of ganglion cells in the retina reflects the quantity of spatial information in the retinal image (Lythgoe, 1979; Rodieck, 1973) and within a single species the amount of visual cortex allocated to processing any single part of the retina is proportional to the ganglion cell density at that retinal locus (Daniel and Whitteridge, 1961), suggesting that within species there is a proper mass of cortex to be allocated to each ganglion cell. For example, Drasdo (1977) reports that in humans each retinal ganglion cell requires 4 $\times$ 10^{-3} mm^2 of visual cortex, a figure which requires correction for the fact that ocular dominance columns (Hubel and Wiesel, 1968) effectively half the area of cortex available for each eye, giving a value of 2 $\times$ 10^{-3} mm^2 (Rovamo, 1978). If we apply Drasdo's procedure to the rat visual system using estimates of around 120 000 ganglion cells in the retina (Fukuda, 1977; Hughes, 1977) and a primary visual cortex of area 9.88 mm^2 (Adams and Forrester, 1968) we get a figure of around 8.5 $\times$ 10^{-5} mm^2 of visual cortex per ganglion cell. Similar calculations on data for the rabbit (450 000 ganglion cells and 82.3 mm^2 of visual cortex; figures from Hughes, 1977, and Polyak, 1957) gives 1.85 $\times$ 10^{-4} mm^2 of visual cortex per ganglion cell. Evidently the allocation of visual cortex to ganglion cell inputs is not constant across species. Lennie (1977) has already pointed out two reasons why this approach is likely to fail: the possibility of parallel access to the visual cortex by different populations of ganglion cells and variations in the distribution of ganglion cell fibers to subcortical visual relays. However, these arguments simply serve to reinforce the point being made here that it is impossible, in practice, to calculate the proper mass of the visual cortex of any species.

FURTHER SHORTCOMINGS OF THE PRINCIPLES OF CONSERVATION AND PROPER MASS

Even if we accept that the principle of proper mass does operate and that proper mass can be calculated it is still far from clear that it can account for species differences in the operation of homologous structures in the way intended. The problem is that there is now an extensive body of evidence showing that there are species differences in the internal circuitry and external connections of homologous structures, a point which becomes clear when one considers the results of single unit recording studies and the effects of electrical stimulation on the superior colliculus (Goldberg and Robinson, 1978). According to these authors the mammalian tectum contains cells that have large visual receptive fields and which respond best to moving stimuli but this is as far as one can take cross-species generalization. For example, although there is frequently a preference for moving stimuli in some species there is an additional requirement for stimuli moving in an horizontal plane on a naso-temporal trajectory while in the mouse the preference is for stimuli moving in an upward and nasal direction. Rhesus monkeys on the other hand possess colliculi showing very little directional selectivity but directional selectivity is quite prominent in other monkey species such as the squirrel and cebus monkey. Stimulation studies have been largely restricted to cats and rhesus monkeys but even here there is a distinct difference in effect. In monkeys stimulation of the colliculus yields saccadic eye-movements of an amplitude and direction that is determined solely by the location of the stimulation site (Schiller and Stryker, 1972). Head movements may also be evoked but this is an unreliable phenomenon and their amplitude and direction is a function of the position of the eye in the orbit rather than of the location of the stimulation site, suggesting that head movements are secondary to eye deviation (Stryker and Schiller, 1975). In contrast electrical stimulation of the colliculus in the cat will yield either eye or head movements with a direction and amplitude predictable from the location of the stimulation site (Roucoux et al., 1980), suggesting that both eye and head movements are under direct control of the colliculus in this species.

AT WHAT LEVEL COULD FUNCTION BE CONSERVED?

Clearly the internal organization of the superior colliculus is not constant across species. This does not disprove the suggestion that function is conserved but does raise the important question of the level at which this conservation is occurring. Jerison (1976), for example, talks of the conservation of 'input–output relationship(s)' but for this principle to be applied to the colliculus 'input–output relationship(s)' need to be defined either at a level of generality that destroys the predictive power of the concept of conservation or in a new way that is independent of the specific motor connections or patterns of sensory input to a structure.

Most authors have adopted the former approach. For example Goldberg and Robinson (1978) conclude their review of the colliculus with the suggestion that one way to make sense of it is to suggest that it acts, in all species, to reorientate the eyes to ensure that salient parts of the environment are brought to bear upon the area of the retina with the highest receptor density. The actual nature of the movements involved then depend upon the 'evolutionary status' of the organism, 'primitive' animals using head movements and 'advanced' ones using eye movements. If the reader takes exception to the concepts of 'primitive' and 'advanced' for the purposes of Goldberg and Robinson's argument they can be redefined in terms of the degree of divergence of the optic axes (Hughes, 1977) but that leaves the question of whether this level of generalization is predictive, there being differences in visuomotor function between closely related species possessing similar levels of divergence of the optic axes.

This point is well illustrated by a comparison between the effects of tectal lesions in hamsters and rats. According to Schneider (1969) hamsters with undercut colliculi are incapable of orientating towards a stimuli in the peripheral visual field and make approach errors on two choice visual discrimination tasks, although they do not push open the incorrect response door more often than controls. Rats, on the other hand appear indistinguishable from controls on such tasks but this is largely by virtue of the fact that normal rats fail to make the relevant responses in the first instance. For example, they do not orientate towards food pellets introduced into the peripheral visual field and on visual discrimination tasks they run right up to the stimuli before making their choices unless steps are taken to discourage this behavior. Goodale and his colleagues (Goodale and Murison, 1975; Goodale et al., 1978) have sought to rectify this 'methodological' problem by devising a task in which visumotor orientation would be more prominent, the animals being trained to run across a large arena to one of an array of widely separated stimuli. In order to assess spontaneous reactivity to visual stimuli lights were introduced at different points around the walls of the arena while the animals were in motion. According to these authors rats with collicular lesions take routes to the goal which are even shorter than those taken by controls but fail to respond like controls to stimuli introduced on the sides of the arena, results which they take to mean that the colliculus controls spontaneous visumotor reactions (the 'orientation reaction') but not visually guided locomotion. Therefore, in both rats and hamsters the colliculus may be seen as being involved in visuomotor orientation but there is a problem with this conclusion. When tested in an apparatus similar to that used by Goodale and colleagues hamsters with colliculus lesions do not behave like similarly treated rats (Mort *et al.*, 1980) but show good levels of orientation to peripherally presented stimuli. Furthermore, although Goodale and colleagues describe the behavior of normal rats in terms of visuomotor orientation their protocols suggest something very different, the most common reactions being rearing and sniffing, freezing or turning around and running away, none of which can be considered to involve bringing visual stimuli to bear on to appropriate parts of the retinae. It is possible to reconcile the literature on the rat and the hamster colliculus only by glossing over significant differences between the data on the two species which leads this author to question whether they are simply 'methodological' as much of the literature would have us believe.

In addition to the difficulty of predicting how visuomotor orientation will manifest itself in a particular species there is the problem of whether 'orientation' is an adequate description of the behaviors involved. We have already seen that in the rat a large number of reactions, most of which can be seen as defensive, are dependent on the colliculus. In the rabbit there is evidence of a similar state of affairs according to Schaeffer and his colleagues (Schaeffer, 1972), this group having shown that electrical stimulation of the colliculus in this species can produce head movements away from the region of visual field corresponding to the stimulation site as well as orientation towards it.

CONSERVATION OF INFORMATION TRANSFORMATION CHARACTERISTICS

A sensible alternative to the all pervading vagueness of the 'principle of conservation' as currently applied in the literature is to re-evaluate 'input–output relationship(s)' by emphasizing the nature of the transformation of input by the system under study rather than seeking to identify common features of the behavior sequences under its control in different species. This leaves the problem of explaining how the particular implementation of these transfer characteristics in a given species is determined. We have already seen the problems with appealing to a phylogenetic trend such as encephalization and rather than tread that barren ground once more it is suggested that more attention should be paid to ecological factors, with the proviso that a serious attempt be made to identify ecological principles determining brain and behavior relationships that transcend their implementation in a single species. This skeleton of a notion can be given flesh by considering how it applies to work on the superior colliculus.

We have two problems: to demonstrate that the transfer characteristics of the superior colliculus are invariant across species and to derive acceptable ecological rules for predicting their implementation in a given species. Let us consider them in turn. Few would now dispute that the colliculus forms a center for visuomotor integration so a useful starting point is to consider the constraints imposed on the operation of such a system as a result of the nature of the visual environment. If one considers the environment outside the laboratory the first point that becomes apparent is that discrete stimuli are nowhere to be found. Instead each organism is faced with a constant barrage of information and under these circumstances the major difficulty is not one of detecting stimuli but of filtering out noise. Decisions of this sort must be made rapidly if the behavior is to be successful. Predators have to orientate to pursue and seize their prey with speed and prey are under a corresponding pressure to detect and evade predators with similar alacrity. The need for speed is not restricted to predator–prey relationships since the established selection pressure for reducing time and energy spent in feeding to a minimum (McCleery, 1978) favors all visually guided feeders, even well protected fructivores and herbivores, that can select food items rapidly. Finally, there needs to be an element of adaptability in the system. Little is to be gained from orientating towards a food source if one is not hungry. Similarly, emitting defensive reactions to events that have never previously been associated with danger is immensely wasteful of energy.

These constraints suggest a system that has a discriminative capacity, involves a short pathway between sensory input and motor output (with few synapses), and which can be modulated by both the internal state of the organism and the results of prior experience. How does the colliculus match up to these requirements? With respect to the first point, data are largely lacking owing to the tendency to persue the secrets of the colliculus using the same types of elementary shapes (bars, edges, and spots) as have been used to investigate the retina and visual cortex. Most of the supporting evidence therefore comes from studies of non-mammalian vertebrates the tecta of which contain units with remarkably precise requirements concerning the size, contrast, and direction of movement of objects in the visual field (Ingle and Sprague, 1977). Recently Rizzolatti (1978) has demonstrated a similar degree of stimulus specificity for units in the intermediate layers of the primate tectum, suggesting that complex trigger features are a feature of mammals as well.

Although the colliculus lacks direct outputs to the oculomotor system there are a number of projections to regions within the mesencephalic and pontine tegmentum that themselves project to the oculomotor system (Goldberg and Robinson, 1978). In addition there is a projection to the extrapyramidal motor system, via the pons, and a direct projection on to motorneurons in the cervical spinal cord, via the tectospinal tract. All of these projections derive from the deep laminae. Since vertical distances within the colliculus are short and the maximum number of synapses imposed between retinal input and the motor output fibers is five visual input gains rapid, if not direct, output to motor centers.

Activating retinorecipient cells in the colliculus is far from a sufficient condition for the generation of a motor reaction. This is shown both by the fact that many stimuli that are sufficient to activate cells in the superficial, retinorecipient, layer fail to drive cells in the deeper layers and by the fact that the threshold for eliciting movements by direct electrical stimulation is far higher in the superficial than in the deep layers (Schiller and Stryker, 1972; Roucoux and Crommelinck, 1976). Part of the problem may be that the trigger features of the intermiediate and deep layers are far more precise than those of the superficial layers so that, for example, diffuse excitation of a small region in the superficial layers may not generate the right pattern of input to the deeper layers to activate the cells there but there are a number of observations that suggest additional modulation of tectal transmission. They are: (1) the rapid habituation of cells in the intermediate layers to stimuli that reliably drive cells in the superficial. (2) The 'Sprague effect', which involves the depression of visuomotor reactiveness produced by unilateral ablation of the visual cortex being reversed by destruction of the contralateral colliculus (Sprague, 1966), a phenomenon indicative of inhibitory control by one colliculus over the other. (3) The 'remote effect' whereby the introduction of a second stimulus into the visual field reduces the level of response to an initial stimulus even though the second stimulus is so far outside the receptive field of the cell under study to be unable to influence it in any other way (Buchtel *et al.*, 1979). (4) The 'enhancement effect' (Wurtz and Mohler, 1976) in which the visual responses of cells in the superficial layers of the colliculi of alert monkeys are augmented if the stimuli are used repeatedly as targets for saccades. (5) In frogs and toads destruction of the caudal thalamus leads to a release of prey-catching reactions and a failure of these reactions to habituate that is paralleled by an absence of habituation at the single unit level (Muntz, 1977).

In all species studied to date the unifying features of tectal operation are that highly selective trigger features may be observed, it has direct connections with the motor system and is subject to modulation by a variety of internal and external influences that give it a considerable degree of plasticity of operation. It is these characteristics, not the possession of specific motor outputs, that are conserved across species. This leaves us with the challenge of specifying how ecological factors determine the application of these properties in a given species.

ECOLOGY AND TECTAL FUNCTION

The two most prominent selection pressures derive from the nature of the food source exploited and the degree of predation danger so it will be instructive to explore how far they can be used as a framework for organizing the data on species differences in tectal function. Let us start with the nature of the food source. Classical ecology views food sources from the point of view of the organism's place in the food chain and thus distinguishes between carnivores, herbivores, insectivores, ominvores, and fructivores but for the purposes of visual ecology a more fundamental distinction needs to be made. That is one between animals that exploit food sources in which individual elements possess a low level of spatial uncertainty and those exploiting foods that are spatially unpredictable. Of the species commonly used for the study of tectal functions the cat, monkey, hamster, tree shrew, frog, and toad all use spatially unpredictable food sources, some, like the cat, tree shrew, frog, and toad because they are of a predatory nature, the rest, like monkey and hamster, because the vegetable matter they feed on comes in small packets (individual seeds or pieces of fruit) distributed about the environment. In contrast the rat uses massed food sources the elements of which have a high degree of spatial predictability. Similarly, the pigeon searches for food within areas in which it is likely to be of a high density. Animals in the first group reliably make orientating movements to circumscribed stimuli introduced into the visual field, those in the latter do so only rarely. Unfortunately it is impossible to explore this point further because there has been a tendency to select for studies of the colliculus only those species that yield reliable orientating movements. This, in turn, has biased researchers to animals that have specific feeding habits. Within the species exploiting spatially uncertain foods mode of praxis then becomes the major determinant of the visuomotor processes under the control of the colliculus. Animals that seize food with their mouths make prominent head movements (e.g. cats, tree shrews, and hamsters) whereas in those using hands obvious short latency head movements are less apparent and saccadic eye-movements occur (e.g. the rhesus monkey). The obvious objection is that mode of praxis is confounded with 'phylogenetic status' but it may be unconfounded by considering non-mammalian species like the frog in which praxis involves tongue movements (Ingle and Sprague, 1977). It is therefore possible to make pronouncements about the visuomotor functions of the tectum on the basis of knowledge about the feeding habits of an organism.

Can the same be said for the impact of predation pressure? The problem is that while food sources are many and varied predators tend to offer a uniform set of constraints, the essence of a successful predator being that of surprise. Furthermore, most species, except the very largest and most well protected, have to deal with predators so that the selection pressure is likely to be similar across species. Nevertheless, predation pressure can influence visuomotor function in two ways. First, there is the question of how the species copes with predators, whether they flee or freeze. Unfortunately this dimension of anti-predator behavior has not been explored with respect to tectal involvement. Second, the less the visual system is involved in food gathering behavior the more likely it is that the most obvious visuomotor reactions will be of a defensive nature. Thus Schaeffer and his colleages (see Ingle and Sprague, 1977) have shown that electrical stimulation of the superior colliculus in the rabbit only very unreliably generates contralateral head movements whereas increasing the stimulation intensity to a point at which reliable movements occur results in ipsilateral movements of a defensive kind. Similarly, although rats rarely orientate their eyes towards visual stimuli (although they may raise their heads and sniff) the introduction of a sudden stimulus will induce them to freeze or turn and run away (Goodale and Murison, 1975).

The preceding paragraphs may not be sufficient to convince the reader that the model of tectal function is correct in all details but it does give the essence of the approach to interspecific comparisons favored by this author. In addition to being a useful device for providing *post hoc* accounts of brain and behavior relationships the marriage between the restricted view of the principle of conservation and the application of ecological principles also carries implications for how future research should be conducted. Before considering these issues, however, it is worthwhile assessing the extent to which it is possible to apply these ecological principles to the analysis of human brain and behavior relationships.

HUMAN ECOLOGY AND HUMAN BRAIN FUNCTION

Given the diversity of habitats occupied by human beings and the range of social structures erected by them to enable them to live together, the reader might be forgiven for thinking that what makes human beings unique as a species is the absence of a classically defined ecology. In reality contemporary anthropology shows us that man has a very distinct ecology and a distinct reaction to variations in ecological circumstances. *Homo sapiens* are terrestrial, diurnal, omnivores living within complex social frameworks and interacting with the physical environment through the medium of tools. Body surface temperature has to be maintained within a narrow band, a minimum average daily caloric intake is necessary for normal health, and water balance has to be maintained by frequent consumption of fluids (McNaughton and Wolf, 1973). The patterning of individual behavior and the organization of social structures is then a product of how these basic capacities and limitations interact with a specific habitat.

Specific sensorimotor reaction patterns (reflexes and fixed action patterns) play a small (but possibly important) part in human behavior, behavioral adaptation being based on learning ability and the adoption of behavioral strategies (McNaughton and Wolf, 1973).

Many previous authors have explored the question of how these ecological factors have molded unique features of the human nervous system, such as the disproportionate brain/bodyweight ratio (Jerison, 1973) and the production of language (Premack, 1975) but few have considered ways in which these same factors would have altered the manifestation of the functions of other brain systems. Exceptions to this are Geschwind (1965) and Rozin (1976) who have discussed human brain evolution in terms of increasing levels of connectedness between different brain regions, the result of which being that brain mechanisms initially at the disposal of only a small range of behaviors become accessible to the mechanism controlling a much wider range. A change like this could be viewed as part of a phylogenetic trend towards increasing brain complexity but a more sensible attitude is to consider it as a reaction to strong ecological pressures for highly adaptable behavior (McNaughton and Wolf, 1973; Hardesty, 1978).

With respect to using animal models of human brain function the main implication of this interpretation is that in humans the information processing capacities of specific regions will be far less rigidly tied to particular actions. Consequently the fact that a focal brain injury in a non-human species produces a defined behavioral deficit in no way guarantees that damage to an homologous area in the human brain will have comparable effects. It is equally possible that more extreme effects will occur, either taking the form of the expected deficit being absent because other brain systems are capable of substituting for the damaged one or of the deficits being more widespread because more brain regions connect into the damaged area. These problems can be illustrated by extending the discussion in tectal function, presented in the previous section, to an account of its role in human visually guided behavior.

To recap, the superior colliculus is most meaningfully viewed as a device for carrying out rapid parallel analyses of the visual field with the aim of selecting relevant targets for species typical reaction. Similar reasoning may be applied to tectal operations in human, the main difference being that in *Homo sapiens* the operation of the tectum is integrated with higher lvel behavioral control systems. Perhaps the most prominent species typical visuomotor reaction is that of moving the eyes to fixate peripherally located targets. The significant feature of this behavior is that it is not reflex but is exquisitely tuned to the information processing demands of the immediate situation (Mackworth, 1976; Gould, 1976; Hochberg, 1976). Therefore the operation of the human colliculus is most likely to be manifested in skilled visual information processing. The validity of this account can be tested against the information about human tectal function currently available. This is not a particularly demanding test because there is hardly any data on patients with ablation of the colliculi and, consequently, most of the work has relied on indirect sources of evidence.

Heywood and Ratcliff (1975) have described deficits in saccade control in a patient who underwent removal of the right superior colliculus. This took the form of a reduced tendency to make spontaneous saccades to the contralateral visual field, small alterations in the timing and accuracy of saccades to individual targets and abnormal movement patterns when attempting saccades of defined size in the dark. While establishing that the colliculus is necessary for normal human oculomotor function the subtlety of the results in this study suggests that it was only obliquely tapping tectal function. Turning to the indirect studies of tectal function few of them have established that the phenomena concerned involved the tectum *per se*. Both the demonstrations of interocular transfer of various forms of visual information after section of the forebrain commissures (Trevarthen, 1970) and of residual vision after primary visual cortex lesions (Weiskrantz, 1978; Poppel, 1979) are reduced in value by the fact that brain structures other than the colliculus might be involved (Blochert *et al.*, 1976; Gray *et al.*, 1979; Horel, 1968). Poppel (1979) describes a more sophisticated approach looking for phenomena in normal human perception that correspond to the known properties of tectal but not non-tectal systems in non-human species. Two of these are habituation and the 'remote effect'. The latter refers to the capacity of a second stimulus introduced into one visual field to inhibit the response to an initial stimulus presented in the other (Buchtel *et al.*, 1979). Habituation was demonstrated by obtaining an increase in absolute visual threshold by means of repeated stimulation in the peripheral visual field. The remote effect was explored by reversing the habituation by presenting a second stimulus in the mirror symmetrical position in the contralateral field. However, the parallel is not exact because the behavioral effect obtained by Singer *et al.* (1977) only works if the second stimulus is presented in the mirror symmetrical position to the first while the remote effect occurs with a wider range of stimulus locations. Since the behavioral 'remote effect' was only obtained if the subjects switched their attention to the second target this, if we accept we are dealing with tectal function, is the nearest evidence for integration of tectal function with ongoing behavior.

SUMMARY

Neuropsychologists who wish to use animal models of human brain and behavior relationships have been faced with the problem of species differences in behavior and the associated variations in brain organization implied by these differences. Generally they have employed one of two extrapolation rules to get round this problem: phylogenetic trends like 'encephalization' or the 'principle of conservation' (Jerison, 1976). Detailed examination of these principles show them to be either devoid of predictive power or already invalidated by currently available data. An alternative is therefore proposed which incorporates the principle of conservation but which maintains that what are conserved are not specific brain/behavior relationships but the information transforming properties of individual systems. How these properties are translated into behavior is then a function of the ecology of the species concerned. The value of this approach can be seen in an exploration of the functions of the superior colliculus in man and other animals. From the point of view of making prescriptions for future research there are two important conclusions. The first is that comparative neuropsychologists should shift from using one or two species as convenient substitutes for man towards a more detailed exploration of the ecological determinants of brain/ behavior relationships. The second is that test procedures used by experimental neuropsychologists should have a higher degree of 'ecological validity' than many in current use.

REFERENCES

Adams, A. D., and Forrester, J. M. (1968) The projection of the rat's visual field on the cerebral cortex, *Quart. J. Exp. Physiol.*, **53**, 327–336.

Berlucchi, G., Sprague, J. M., Levy, J., and Di Berardino, A. C. (1972) Pretectum and superior colliculus in visually guided behaviour and in flux and form discrimination in the cat, *J. Comp. Physiol. Psychol.*, **78**, Monogr. Suppl. 1, 123–172.

Blochert, P. K., Ferrier, R. J., and Cooper, R. M. (1976) Effects of pretectal lesions on rats wearing light diffusing occluders, *Brain Res.*, **104**, 121–128.

Buchtel, H. A., Carmarda, R., Rizzolatti, G., and Scandolara, C. (1979) The effect of hemidecortication on the inhibitory interactions in the superior colliculus of the cat. *J. Comp. Neurol.*, **184**, 795–810.

Campbell, C. B. G. (1976) What animals should we compare?, in *Evolution, Brain and Behaviour: Persistent Problems* (eds W. Hodos and H. Jerison), Erlbaum, Hillsdale.

Casagrande, V. A., and Diamond, I. T. (1974) Ablation study of the superior colliculus in the tree shrew (*Tupaia glis*), *J. Comp. Neurol.*, **156**, 207–238.

Cowey, A., and Weiskrantz, L. (1971) Contour discrimination in rats after frontal and striate cortical ablations, *Brain Res.*, **30**, 241–252.

Daniel, P. M., and Whitteridge, D. (1961) The representation of the visual field on the cerebral cortex in monkeys, *J. Physiol. (London)*, **159**, 203–221.

Dean, P. (1978) Visual acuity in hooded rats: effects of superior collicular or posterior neocortical lesions, *Brain Res.*, **156**, 17–31.

Diamond, I. T. (1976) Organisation of the visual cortex: comparative anatomical and behavioural studies, *Fed. Proc.*, **35**, 60–67.

Diamond, I. T. (1979) The subdivisions of the neocortex: a proposal to revise the traditional view of sensory, motor and association areas, in *Progress in Psychobiology and Physiological Psychology, vol. 8* (eds J. M. Sprague and A. N. Epstein), Academic Press, New York, 2–43.

Doty, R. W. (1973) Ablation of visual areas in the central nervous system, in *Handbook of Sensory Physiology, vol. VII 3B Central Processing of Visual Information* (ed. R. Jung), 483–541, Springer-Verlag, Berlin.

Drasdo, N. (1977) The neural representation of visual space, *Nature*, **266**, 554–556.

Fukuda, Y. (1977) A three group classification of rat retinal ganglion cells: histological and physiological studies, *Brain Res.*, **119**, 327–344.

Geschwind, N. (1965) Disconnexion synchromes in animals and man I, *Brain Res.*, **88**, 237–294.

Goldberg, M. E., and Robinson, D. L. (1978) Visual system: superior colliculus, in *Handbook of Behavioural Neurobiology, vol. 1, Sensory Integration* (ed. R. B. Masterton), 119–164, Plenum, New York.

Goodale, M. A., and Murison, R. C. C. (1975) The effects of lesions of the superior colliculus on locomotor orientation and the orienting reflex in the rat, *Brain Res.*, **88**, 243–261.

Goodale, M. A., Foreman, N. P., and Milner, A. D. (1978) Visual orientation in the rat: a dissociation of deficits following cortical and collicular lesions, *Exp. Brain Res.*, **31**, 445–457.

Gould, J. A. (1976) Looking at pictures, in *Eye Movements and Psychological Processes* (eds R. A. Monty and J. W. Senders), 323–345, Erlbaum, Hillsdale.

Gray, T. S., Lavond, D. G., Meyer, P. M., and Meyer, D. R. (1979) Comparative significance of pretectal and ventral lateral geniculate systems in functional recoveries after injuries to the posterior cortex, *Physiol. Psychol.*, **7**, 22–28.

Hardesty, D. L. (1978) Human evolutionary ecology, in *Human Evolution: Readings for Physical Anthropology*, 234–244, Holt, Rinehart and Winston, New York.

Heywood, S., and Ratcliff, G. (1975) Long term oculomotor consequences of unilateral colliculectomy in man, in *Basic Mechnaisms of Ocular Motility* (eds G. Lennerstrand and P. Bach-y-Rita), 561–564, Pergamon, Oxford.

Hochberg, J. (1976) Toward a speech-plan-eye-movement model of reading, in *Eye Movements and Psychological Processes* (eds R. A. Monty and J. W. Senders), 397–416, Erlbaum, Hillsdale.

Hodos, W., and Campbell, C. B. G. (1969) Scala naturae: why there is no theory in comparative psychology; *Psychol. Rev.*, **76**, 337–350.

Horel, J. A. (1968) Effects of subcortical lesions on brightness discrimination acquired by rats without visual cortex, *J. Comp. Physiol. Psychol.*, **65**, 103–109.

Horel, J. A., Bettinger, L. A., Royce, G. J., and Meyer, D. R. (1966) Role of neocortex in the learning and relearning of two visual habits by the rat, *J. Comp. Physiol. Psychol.*, **61**, 66–78.

Hubel, D. H., and Wiesel, T. N. (1968) Receptive fields and functional architecture of monkey striate cortex, *J. Physiol.*, **195**, 215–243.

Hughes, A. (1977) The topography of vision in mammals of contrasting life styles: comparative optics and retinal organization, in *Handbook of Sensory Physiology, vol. VII/5, The Visual System in Vertebrates* (ed. F. Crescitelli), 613–756, Springer-Verlag, Berlin.

Humphrey, N. K. (1970) What the frog's eye tells the monkey's brain, *Brain, Behav., Evol.*, **3**, 324–337.

Ingle, D., and Sprague, J. M. (1977) Sensorimotor function of the midbrain tectum, *Neurosci Res. Prog. Bull.*, **13**, 167–288, MIT Press, Cambridge.

Ingle, D. (1977) Classes of visually guided behaviour, *Neurosci Res. Prog. Bull.*, **13**, 180–185.

James, W. (1890) *The Principles of Psychology, vol. 1*, Dover, New York.

Jerison, H. J. (1973) *Evolution of the Brain and Intelligence*, Academic Press, New York.

Jerison, H. J. (1976) Principles of the evolution of the brain and behaviour, in *Evolution, Brain and Behaviour: Persistent Problems* (eds R. B. Masterton, W. Hodos, and H. Jerison), Erlbaum, Hillsdale.

Keating, E. G. (1979) Rudimentary colour vision in the monkey after removal of striate and preoccipital cortex, *Brain Res.*, **179**, 379–384.

Killackey, H., Snyder, M., and Diamond, I. T. (1971) Function of striate and temporal cortex in the tree shrew, *J. Comp. Physiol. Psychol.*, **74**, Monogr. Suppl. 1.

Kluver, H. (1941) Visual functions after removal of the occipital lobes, *J. Psychol.*, **11**, 23–45.

Lashley, K. S. (1980) The mechanism of vision. II. The influence of cerebral lesions upon the threshold of discrimination for brightness in the rat, *J. Genet. Psychol.*, **37**, 461–480.

Lashley, K. S. (1935) The mechanism of vision XII. Nervous structures concerned in the acquisition and retention of habits based on reactions to light, *Comp. Psychol. Monogr.*, **11**, 43–79.

Legg, C. R. and Cowey, A. (1977) The roles of the ventral lateral geniculate nucleus and posterior thalamus in intensity discrimination in rats, *Brain Res.*, **123**, 261–273.

Lennie, P. (1977) Neuroanatomy of visual acuity, *Nature*, **266**, 496.

Lythgoe, J. W. (1979) *Ecology and Vision*, Clarendon, Oxford.

Mackworth, N. H. (1976) Stimulus density limits of the useful field of view, in *Eye Movements and Psychological Processes* (eds R. A. Monty and J. W. Senders), 307–322, Erlbaum, Hillsdale.

McCleery, R. H. (1978) Optimal behaviour sequences and decision making, in *Behavioural Ecology: an evolutionary approach* (eds J. R. Krebs and N. B. Davies), 377–410, Blackwell, Oxford.

McNaughton, S. J., and Wolf, L. L. (1973) *General Ecology*, Holt, Rinehart and Winston, New York.

Mort, E., Cairns, S., Hersch, H., and Finlay, B. (1980) The role of the superior colliculus in visually guided locomotion and visually guided orienting in the hamster, *Physiol. Psychol.*, **8**, 20–28.

Muntz, W. R. A. (1977) The visual world of the amphibia, in *Handbook of Sensory Physiology, vol. VII/5, The Visual System in Vertebrates* (ed. F. Crescitelli), 275–308, Springer-Verlag, Berlin.

Nauta, W. J. H. (1971) The problem of the frontal lobe: a reinterpretation, *J. Psychiat. Res.*, **8**, 167–187.

Pasik, P., and Pasik, T. (1971) The visual world of monkeys deprived of striate cortex: effective stimulus parameters and importance of the accessory optic system, *Vision Res., Suppl. 3*, 419–435.

Perenin, M. T., and Jeannerod, M. (1978) Visual function within the hemianopic field following early cerebral hemidecortication in man. I. Spatial localization, *Neuropsychologia*, **16**, 1–13.

Polyak, S. (1957) *The Vertebrate Visual System*, University of Chicago Press, Chicago.

Poppel, E. (1979) Midbrain mechanisms in human vision, in *Neuronal Mechanisms in Visual Perception, Neurosci Res. Prog. Bull. vol. 15*, (eds E. Poppel, R. Held, and J. E. Dowling), 335–343, MIT Press, Cambridge.

Poppel, E., Held, R., and Frost, D. (1973) Residual visual function after brain wounds involving the central visual pathways in man, *Nature*, **243**, 295–296.

Premack, D. (1975) On the origins of language in *Handbook of Psychobiology* (eds M. S. Gazzaniga and C. Blakemore), 591–606, Academic Press, New York.

Rizzolatti, G. (1978) Two functional types of neurons in the superficial layers of monkey superior colliculus, *Arch. Ital. Biol.*, **116**, 235–240.

Rodieck, R. W. (1973) *The Vertebrate Retina*, Freeman, San Francisco.

Rosvold, H. E., Mishkin, M., and Szwarzbart, M. K. (1958) Effects of subcortical lesions in monkeys on visual discrimination and single alternation performance, *J. Comp. Physiol. Psychol.*, **51**, 437–444.

Roucoux, A., and Crommelinck, M. (1976) Eye movements evoked by superior colliculus stimuation in the alert cat, *Brain Res.*, **106**, 349–363.

Roucoux, A., Guitton, P., and Crommelinck, M. (1980) Stimulation of the superior colliculus in the alert cat II: Eye and head movements evoked when the head is unrestrained, *Exp. Brain Res.*, **39**, 75–85.

Rovamo, J. (1978) Receptive field density of retinal ganglion cells and cortical magnification factors in man, *Med. Biol.*, **56**, 97–102.

Rozin, P. (1976) The evolution of intelligence and access to the cognitive unconscious, in *Progress in Psychobiology and Physiological Psychology, vol. 6* (eds J. M. Sprague and A. N. Epstein), 245–280, Academic Press, New York.

Schaeffer, K. P. (1972) Neuronal elements of the orienting response: microrecordings and stimulation experiments in rabbits', *Bibl. Opthalmol.*, **82**, 139–148.

Schiller, P. H., and Stryker, M. (1972) Single unit recording in superior colliculus of the alert rhesus monkey, *J. Neurophysiol.*, **35**, 915–924.

Schiller, P. H., True, S. D., and Conway, J. L. (1979) Paired stimulation of the frontal eye fields and the superior colliculus of the rhesus monkey, *Brain Res.*, **179**, 162–164.

Schiller, P. H., True, S. D., and Conway, J. L. (1980) Deficits in eye movements following frontal eye field and superior colliculus ablations, *J. Neurophysiol.*, **44**, 1175–1189.

Schneider, G. E. (1969) Two visual systems, *Science*, **163**, 895–902.

Singer, W., Zihl, J., and Poppel, E. (1977) Subcortical control of visual thresholds in humans—evidence for modality specific and retinotopically organized mechanisms of selective attention. *Exp. Brain Res.*, **29**, 173–190.

Spear, P. D. (1979) Behavioural and neurophysiological consequences of visual cortex damage: mechanisms of recovery, in *Progress in Psychobiology and Physiological Psychology, vol. 8* (eds J. M. Sprague and A. N. Epstein), 45–90, Academic Press, New York.

Sprague, J. M. (1966) Interaction of cortex and superior colliculus in mediation of visually guided behaviour in the cat, *Science*, **153**, 1544–1547.

Stryker, M. P., and Schiller, P. H. (1975) Eye and head movements evoked by electrical stimulation of monkey superior colliculus, *Exp. Brain Res.*, **23**, 103–112.

Teuber, H. L., Battersby, W. S., and Bender, M. B. (1960) *Visual Field Defects after Penetrating Missile Wounds of the Brain*, Harvard University Press, Cambridge.

Trevarthen, C. (1970) Experimental evidence for a brain stem contribution to visual perception in man, *Brain Behav. Evol.*, **3**, 338–352.

Tunkl, J. E., and Berkley, M. A. (1977) The role of the superior colliculus in vision: visual form discrimination in cats with superior colliculus ablations, *J. Comp. Neurol.*, **176**, 575–588.

Weiskrantz, L. (1961) Encephalization and the scotoma, in *Current Problems in Animal Behaviour* (eds W. H. Thorpe and O. L. Zangwill), 30–58, Cambridge University Press, Cambridge.

Weiskrantz, L. (1979) Some aspects of visual capacity in monkeys and man following striate cortex lesions, *Arch. Ital. Biol.*, **16**, 318–323.

Weiskrantz, L., Warrington, E. K., Sanders, M. D., and Marshall, J. (1974) Visual capacity in the hemianopic field following a restricted occipital ablation, *Brain*, **97**, 709–728.

Weiskrantz, L., Cowey, A., and Passingham, C. (1977) Spatial responses to brief stimuli by monkeys with striate cortex ablations, *Brain*, **100**, 655–670.

Whitfield, I. C. (1979) The object of the sensory cortex, *Brain Behav. Evol.*, **16**, 129–154.

Winterkorn, J. M. S., and Meikle, T. H. (1981) Distractibility of cats with lesions of the superior colliculus pretectum during performance of a 4-choice visual discrimination, *Brain Res.*, **206**, 345–360.

Wurtz, W. H., and Mohler, C. W. (1976) Organization of the superior colliculus: enhanced visual responses of superficial layer cells, *J. Neurophysiol.*, **39**, 745–765.

Animal Models of Human Behavior
Edited by G. C. L. Davey
© 1983 John Wiley & Sons Ltd

Chapter 13

Learning Capacity Outside Neocortex in Animals and Man: Implications for Therapy after Brain-Injury

David A. OAKLEY

The vertebrate central nervous system, and in particular the mammalian central nervous system, shows a continuous development over evolutionary time but retains a common and easily recognizable ground-plan. A conservative view of the evolutionary process might favor the assumption that despite progressive elaboration of central nervous system structures there remains an essential constancy of structural/functional relationships across species. Indeed, extrapolations in neuropsychology depend on this being more or less true (see, for example, Weiskrantz, 1977). Basic brain processes should not be expected to flit from structure to structure like errant sparrows on the branches of an evolutionary tree. Against this, however, must be set the very real probability that new or more elaborate functions may be added by the evolution of new neural substrates and that existing functions may be modified in the details of their expression to meet new and changing environmental conditions.

Warren and Kolb (1978), referring specifically to mammals, have suggested a very useful distinction between species-typical behaviors, with their specialized neural counterparts, and class-common behaviors, which depend on class-common neural mechanisms. I will not repeat their evidence here, but they suggest at least four potentially class-common abilities with common neural mechanisms. These are the ability to localize visual and auditory stimuli in space, the use of limbs for locomotion and forepaws (or hands) for precise manipulations, control over intake and deployment of food resources and, finally, the hind-limb scratch reflex. I would like to add associative learning to the list of class-common behaviors and will argue later that not only is its substrate common in mammals but that it is primarily subcortical.

Before expanding this point, however, I think it is necessary to consider briefly the fact that the above plea for conservatism in comparative neuropsychology is counter to the ancient but still revered belief in encephalization, or in mammals corticalization, of function. This principle of evolutionary progress held that, with the expansion and differentiation of the nervous system during phylogeny, existing functions were progressively taken over by the newer structures; a process of neuroanatomical asset-stripping with the neopallium as the main beneficiary. Recently a number of voices have been raised against the encephalization view, presenting arguments which are of course similar to those offered in favor of class-common neural mechanisms (Oakley, 1979a; 1981a; Russell, 1980; Warren and Kolb, 1978; Weiskrantz, 1977). To take vision as an example, the encephalization view held that with the evolution of neocortex, one area, the striate cortex, progressively took over visual function from its earlier midbrain sites. The evidence for this was that removal of striate cortex in rats left considerable visual ability intact whereas in dogs and cats a similar lesion appeared to cause far more profound visual deficits. In primates even the ability to distinguish brightness was thought to be lost with striate cortex removal and in the neurological clinic, destriate man declared himself to be totally blind. It now seems evident from the use of comparable testing procedures across species that all mammals with striate cortex removed show similar visual abilities. The most dramatic evidence in favor of this has come from studies of monkeys and humans. With good post-operative care and opportunity for practice, a destriated monkey in one particular study has been shown to guide her behavior visually with such skill as to be able to catch live cockroaches, pick up currants, and to avoid obstacles (Humphrey, 1974). Similarly, humans with striate cortex removal or damage, whilst continuing to profess their blindness, are able to perform very accurately in forced-choice visual discriminations between horizontal and vertical lines and circles versus crosses (Weiskrantz, 1977; 1980). The human patients are, moreover, also apparently able to improve the level of function in their blind visual fields, particularly if they are given intensive, systematic training in forced-choice tasks (Weiskrantz, 1980). The residual visual ability, or 'blindsight', which is evident in humans and other primates without striate cortex now seems to be very similar indeed to that of rats without striate cortex, though that is not to deny that humans are far more severely incapacitated by their loss than is the rat.

A comparable case can be made for similarity across species in residual motor control in the absence of motor areas of neocortex. The evidence for this conclusion can again be found in Warren and Kolb (1978) but I would like to add one more study to their list as it is of particular relevance to the present discussion. In opposition to the then prevailing view that primates suffer permanent loss of all useful motor function after removal of cortical areas 4 and 6 (motor cortex), Travis and Woolsey (1956) reported an extensive surgical series which demonstrated that both righting and walking were possible not only after removal of motor areas but also in totally neodecorticated monkeys. Recovery to this stage of motor competence appeared to depend on the institution postoperatively of a program of passive exercise (manipulation of limbs, neck, and trunk for 15–20 minutes, 10–14 times each day) followed by assisted practice in the appropriate stepping and walking movements with the animal's body suspended in a horizontal position. Travis and Woolsey's rehabilitation program has certain interesting parallels to that advocated by Doman (1974) for use with brain-injured human infants.

The encephalization view of changes in sensory and motor functions during phylogeny is part of a more general tendency to overestimate the role of neocortex, or at least to underestimate the functional ability of the rest of the mammalian brain. In a similar way it is often overlooked that the relative expansion of the primate brain involves all its structures, with the possible exception of the olfactory bulbs, and not just neocortex (see Russell, 1979). A corticocentric attitude has been particularly evident where adaptive behaviors seeming to require a high level of plasticity are concerned and is well illustrated by the case of associative learning (Oakley, 1979a; 1979b). The idea that Pavlovian conditioning takes place within the neocortex stemmed in large part from Pavlov himself (Pavlov, 1927). Opinion on the role of neocortex slowly changed with respect to that type of associative learning but the view that instrumental learning depended on neocortex seemed well founded until quite recently and was supported in reviews (e.g. Russell, 1966) and in experimental studies (e.g. DiCara et al., 1970). The newer evidence that all types of associative learning are possible without neocortex in mammals comes primarily from rats and rabbits in which all neocortex has been surgically removed (neodecorticated). To give some idea of the tissue loss involved in this procedure Figure 13.1 (middle) shows a normal rat brain and below that a neodecorticated rat brain. The average lesion size in the studies reported below is in the region of 98 percent of all neocortical tissue removed and post-operative recovery ranged from at least two months to up to twelve months or more.

Where Pavlovian conditioning is concerned neodecorticated rabbits acquire conditional responses of the nictitating membrane with a slight delay in the onset of acquisition, suggesting an attentional deficit, but show normal learning curves once the first conditional response has emerged. Where the conditional stimuli are a light *versus* a tone the neodecorticates show a much clearer differentiation than the normal animals and their reversal of responding between the two stimuli is both more rapid and more complete. Not only is Pavlovian nictitating membrane conditioning more clearly expressed in the

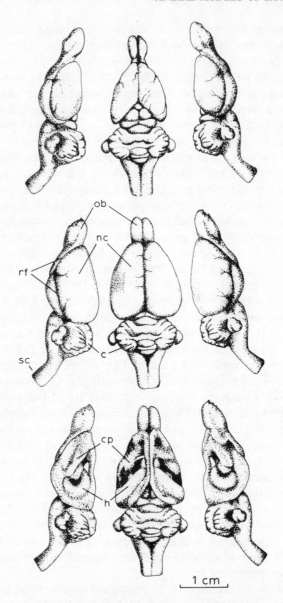

Figure 13.1 Microcephalic (top), normal (middle) and
neodecorticated (bottom) rat brains[1]

absence of neocortex but conditional responses are retained if neocortex is
removed subsequent to training, suggesting that this type of learning occurs
outside neocortex even in the normal brain (Oakley and Russell, 1977). A
somewhat different type of Pavlovian conditioning procedure has been used

with neodecorticated rats, with very similar results. The procedure was autoshaping, in which either the movement of a retractable lever or the illumination of a static lever served as a conditional stimulus predicting the delivery of food. With both types of conditional stimulus neodecorticated rats autoshaped, that is contacted the predictive lever, more readily than normal animals. They also showed a greater tendency than normals to differentiate between predictive and non-predictive stimuli and to reverse their differentiation when the relative predictiveness of the two stimuli changed (Oakley et al., 1981).

In a simple instrumental learning situation where the animal was required to push a food-tray door on a fixed ratio schedule for food, neodecorticated rats produced response patterns which were very similar to those of normals. The lesioned animals were also significantly faster than normals when running a straight alleyway for food as well as in a more complicated 'chicane' alleyway, which involved following a Z-shaped path, for water reward. In the case of the straight alleyway, however, none of the neodecorticates were able to learn the same running behavior to avoid foot-shock. They all produced excessive defensive behaviors at a variety of shock levels and these interfered with learning the appropriate response (Oakley, 1979c). The latter in fact seems to explain earlier failures to find instrumental learning in the absence of neocortex as previous workers had used shock-avoidance procedures. Where operant tasks with spatially separated manipulanda and food-trays have been used neodecorticates have shown slow acquisition, a low response ceiling and a tendency to intermix manipulandum related and food-tray related behaviors instead of restricting them to different parts of the interreinforcement period. These deficits can be overcome, however, by the use of relatively simple instrumental pretraining procedures intended to focus the animals attention on to the relevant manipulandum (Oakley, 1979d; 1980). Preliminary observations also suggest that autoshaping with lever movement as the predictive stimulus is an effective pretraining procedure for fixed ratio schedules in the lesioned animals in standard operant chambers. Recent work with fixed interval schedules has shown that a neodecorticate will develop very similar response patterns to normal rats, with appropriate post-reinforcement pauses and a clear response scallop (Jaldow et al., 1981).

The capacity for residual associative learning ability in fact is not limited to neodecorticates. If due allowance is made for sensory and motor limitations both Pavlovian conditioning and instrumental learning can be demonstrated in brain-stem and isolated spinal cord preparations (see Oakley, 1979a for a brief review). Reductions in cerebral mass and particularly in the development of neocortex can be brought about by exposing the developing rat fetus to X-irradiation or methylazoxymethanol at the fifteenth day of gestation. Figure 13.1 (top) shows a microcephalic rat brain, produced by the second of these methods. Behavioral testing of microcephalic rats has shown no evidence of impairment on associative learning tasks (see Oakley, 1981a for a summary of these data). Exposure to alcohol *in utero* due to maternal alcohol consumption results in a complex of abnormalities of the face, heart, and brain (amounting to anencephaly in some cases) accompanied by mental retardation in humans (Abel, 1980). Identification of this so-called fetal alcohol syndrome (FAS) in man has resulted in a number of animal studies which confirm the teratogenic effects of both fetal and postnatal alcohol exposure (Abel, 1980). Postnatal ingestion of alcohol (days 4–7) in particular, causes reduced brain sizes in rats (31% by volume) with the major effects on the cerebellum and cerebral hemispheres (Diaz and Samson, 1980). Behavioral testing of rats exposed to alcohol postnatally has shown, as in neodecorticates, an impairment on a shock-avoidance task (Bond, 1980) but not on a Hebb–Williams or a Krechevsky 4-choice maze for food reward (Bond, 1980; Gray, Potts and Means, 1981). Interestingly rats whose mothers drank only wine (chablis) during pregnancy and lactation showed a small but significant impairment in forming a learning set over a series of oddity problems (Phillips and Stainbrook, 1976). Learning set formation, however, is an example of a cognitive process (abstract learning—see below) and is also impaired by removal of neocortex (Kolb and Whishaw, 1981; Oakley, 1979d; 1981a).

The conclusion I would wish to draw from what has been said so far is that associative learning is not neocortical but seems to represent a rather fundamental property of the central nervous system which can be expressed at even its lowest levels. Such impairments that are seen after neodecortication in Pavlovian and instrumental tasks are not due to failures of associative learning but to changes in such processes as attention and to the disruptive effects of aversive stimulation. This of course raises the question of what sorts of information gain the neocortex *is* involved in. I have suggested elsewhere (Oakley, 1981a,b) that the adult mammalian brain is involved in at least three types of information gaining process. One of these is associative learning. The others are representational learning and abstract learning, which are concerned respectively with the formation of spatial and temporal representations of the external world, including linguistic representations, and with the extraction of general information, rules, or 'knowledge' independently of spatial and temporal context. This is not the place to expand upon these other types of information gain and for the purposes of this chapter I would like to combine them under the blanket label of 'cognitive processes'. Representational and abstract systems, then, are a cognitive overlay to association systems. They are seen as primarily dependent upon neocortical and older cortical structures such as the hippocampus.

It would follow from this that the neodecorticated mammal is an ideal preparation for studying associative learning. Stripped of its cognitive overlay it can behave in a purely Pavlovian or thoroughly Thorndikean manner as the situation demands. The normal mammal is at least tolerably Tolmanian in its approach. The straight alleyway, Skinner box, and Pavlovian chamber are not ideal places for thinking animals to display their cognitive skills and this may be the reason why the neodecorticate has so often outshone his normal counterpart in these situations. One might in fact go further and suggest that the Pavlovian chamber and the Skinner box were designed to eliminate so far as possible cortical processes from analysis. If this were the case, though, it would have to be admitted that the usual arrangement within a Skinner box is not quite perfect as it still allows a slight advantage to the normal animal over the neodecorticate. The converse of this argument should be that if cognitive overlay were to be increased then performance on associative tasks would become less predictable both within and across species. This is certainly true if autoshaping in humans (Wilcove and Miller, 1974) and squirrel monkeys (Gamzu and Schwam, 1974), or operant tasks in humans (Lowe, 1979 and this volume, Chapter 5) are considered.[2] The regular and predictable relationships which are seen between performance and the reinforcement schedules in the majority of subprimates founder in human studies in particular as behavior increasingly comes under the influence of personal hypothesis formation and verbal self-instruction. Avoiding cognitive overlay and in particular verbal self-instruction by testing humans on fixed interval schedules at a very early stage of their development (9–10 months post-partum) has the predicted effect of returning control to already matured association systems and results in regular, rat-like cumulative records (Lowe et al., 1980). There is some evidence also that reliable autoshaping can be produced in 4–5-year-old human infants by pairing a lighted key with the delivery of a piece of candy (Zeiler, 1972). A less happy way in which human brains can be stripped of cognitive overlay is through developmental abnormalities which result in microcephaly or anencephaly and through direct physical traumata which can occur at all stages of development and adult life, commonly destroying differentially the more rostral portions of the central nervous system and in particular neocortical tissue. The implications of what has been said above for the treatment and rehabilitation of such individuals is the subject of the remainder of this chapter.

If associative learning is a class-common behavior, with a class-common neural substrate, it should be possible to extrapolate the information already obtained with rats and rabbits to other mammals, including man. We should expect, as with the 'blindsight' data, to find similar residual associative capacities outside neocortex in humans as have now been described for rat and rabbit. In other words if we were presented by some convenient mishap with a totally neodecorticated human with a long postoperative recovery we would expect to find a massive, if not total, loss of cognitive functions; the retention of associative learning ability; attentional deficits, which might delay the onset of both Pavlovian and instrumental learning; and the release of defensive reactions, which may disrupt learning. We would also expect that attention-enhancing pretraining programs would improve instrumental performance in some situations. Autoshaping procedures would be expected to serve as a useful method for attentional pretraining and as a very powerful way of eliciting operant-like responses for subsequent reinforcement and shaping by instrumental means. This might be useful if a particular subject had a very low baseline of spontaneous and/or acceptable behaviors.

Some of these predictions can be evaluated on the basis of observations deriving from work with brain-damaged humans. What follows in the next few paragraphs has emerged from conversations with Peter Eames and Rodger Wood on the basis of their experience in running a behavior modification unit for brain injured adults (the Kemsley Unit) at St Andrew's Hospital, Northampton, UK and from Wood and Eames (1981). A major problem in extrapolation emerges immediately in that none of the patients' injuries conform to the ideal of an uncomplicated neodecortication. Etiologies are varied and in those with closed-head injuries diffuse damage, particularly to lower brain-stem structures, complicates the picture of neocortical loss. In others a combination of direct cortical damage and cortical disconnection caused by shearing of fibers subcortically corresponds more closely to neodecortication, though in all cases the effective lesion is a partial one. In view of the small group size and the difficulty in determining the exact extent and distribution of damage in living brains, no attempt has been made at this stage to subdivide patients on the basis of their injuries. Taking the group as a whole, however, they can all be characterized as having massive neocortical damage. They are all, not surprisingly, also characterized by varying degrees of cognitive disability. The question of associative learning in these patients can be approached on two fronts. First, it would appear that many of the behavioral problems seen in these patients are not primary consequences of the damage to their brains, but are acquired post-traumatically, possibly as a consequence of attention-seeking in the institutional situations in which they recover. This in itself implies the intactness of learning mechanisms. The second piece of evidence, which is the corollary to the first, is that the systematic application of operant techniques of behavior modification is a very effective way of removing the undesirable behaviors in the brain-injured patients and of replacing them with more socially acceptable ones. Successful techniques in controlling temper tantrums, spitting, swearing, and other inappropriate patterns of speech range from the use of a token economy, through time-out, to direct punishment with ammonia vapor. A number of specific cases are described in Wood and Eames (1981). It seems reasonable to conclude that associative mechanisms are intact in these patients and that they operate independently of cognitive functioning in the sense that there seems to be no correlation between the success of the behavior modification program and level of residual cognitive ability.

In addition to taking part in the behavior modification program eight of the brain-injured patients have been tested on a two-color discrimination (yellow and blue; squares and circles—with shape as an irrelevant dimension) using Smarties as reinforcement for correct choices. The majority showed delayed onset of acquisition but very rapid consolidation of the correct response once it had appeared. This was particularly evident in three subjects who were shown on independent tests of vigilance to have marked attentional deficits. Also interesting is the fact that despite their eventual 100 percent level of correct performance none of these three patients could verbalize the solution. One interpretation of these data is that the primary deficit in all eight subjects was one of attention and not of associational learning. This observation and the suggested interpretation have clear parallels in the work of Zeaman and House (1963) who used a similar color discrimination task in young human retardates. Zeaman and House noted that their retardates produced normal acquisition functions preceded by abnormally long pre-solution stages and concluded from this that the deficits 'do not seem to lie in the area of instrumental learning but rather in that of attention'. A recent attempt to describe the mechanisms underlying the apparent attentional deficit in human retardates in terms of situational expectancies has been forwarded by Mageean (1981). A group backward learning curve based on Zeaman and House's data is shown in Figure 13.2(a). Figure 13.2(b) and 13.2(c) show the discrimination data for the eight brain injured subjects plotted separately as a group of three with independently established severe attentional difficulties and a group of five with less marked attentional problems. The extended pre-solution phase is particularly marked in the subjects with the attentional deficit. I have already noted that Oakley and Russell (1976) interpreted the delayed acquisition of a Pavlovian light/tone discrimination in their neodecorticated rabbits as evidence of an attentional deficit and deficits in the performance of nedoecorticated rats in operant situations have been ascribed to a failure to attend to or to identify the manipulandum and other relevant aspects of the training situation (Oakley, 1979d, 1980; Oakley and Russell, 1978). In a similar vein Lashley (1935) described his neocortically lesioned rats in latch-box problems as lacking in exploratory activity, failing to react with normal vigor to irregularities, projections, corners, and so forth in their environment and lacking in aggressiveness in investigating the elements of the problem. Normal rats rapidly appeared to dissociate the latch from other parts of the apparatus and to react to it as an object to be manipulated in a particular way. The neocortically damaged animals did not do this and even on latch tests which they passed in as few trials as normals on the basis of associative mechanisms, Lashley described their behavior as deficient in 'attention, insight, and initiative', though he

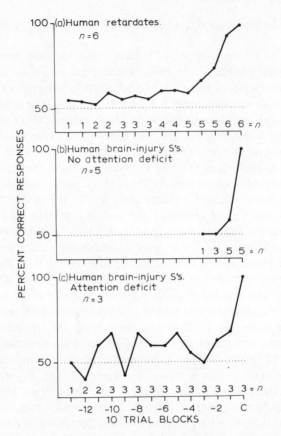

Figure 13.2 Discrimination learning in retarded and
brain-injured humans.[3] (a) Top. Backward learning
curve showing percent correct responses in a group of
six human retardates on a color/form discrimination
task. Based on Zeaman and House (1963). (b) Middle.
Backward learning curve for five brain-injured adult
humans on a color discrimination with two stimulus
dimensions. (c) Bottom. Backward learning curve for
three brain-injured adult humans with marked attentional deficits on a color discrimination with two stimulus dimensions

apologized for his lapse into 'pseudoscientific . . . psychological interpretations of behavior'.

A recent study (Oakley, 1981c) involved training neodecorticated rats in
a two-choice visual discrimination (horizontal *versus* vertical stripes) for food
reward, which has obvious similarities to the procedures employed by both
Zeaman and House and Wood and Eames. The data from the neodecorti-

cated and the normal rats in the pattern discrimination study have been reworked as backward learning curves and are presented as Figure 13.3. Once more it seems clear that the brain-injured group has a normal acquisition function preceded by a longer than normal stage of responding at around chance level. Again an attentional deficit rather than an associative deficit seems to be the most reasonable interpretation.

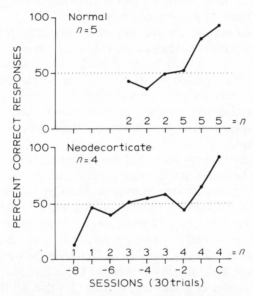

Figure 13.3 Backward learning curves showing performance on a horizontal/vertical stripes discrimination in normal and neodecorticate rats[4]

Associative learning mechanisms thus seem to survive the neurological defects leading to mental retardation in humans as well as those resulting from direct brain injury to give much the same pattern of learning in discrimination tasks as that seen in neodecorticated rats and rabbits in comparable test situations. By extrapolation from the animal work, attentional pretraining would be expected to enhance the onset of instrumental learning in human brain-injury patients as well as improving its efficiency. Given the very powerful effects of Pavlovian conditioning in the neodecorticate it would further be predicted that autoshaping would be equally effective in brain-injured humans both as an attentional pretraining device and as a means of eliciting responses for further shaping by other means. The effectiveness of autoshaping in eliciting responses to a lever, the illumination of which predicted the delivery of a piece of chocolate, has already been demonstrated for a group of human retardates (mean IQ = 35) by Ragain *et al.* (1976). The same study also showed that response levels subsequent to the first autoshaped response were highest when a response–reinforcement contingency was added to the stimulus–reinforcement contingency, intermediate when only the stimulus–reinforcement contingency was present and least, but still above zero, when a negative response–reinforcement contingency was present alongside the stimulus–reinforcer contingency (negative auto-maintenance). The same relative response strengths are generated under these three conditions in pigeons and rats.

There are, as far as I am aware, no parallel data from retarded or brain-damaged humans which correspond to the use of negative reinforcement (shock avoidance) in alleyway running in the rat. Eames and Wood do report, however, that 'explosive' behaviors, both spontaneous and elicited, are a problem in behavior management with their brain-damaged patients. It seems possible that shock escape or avoidance procedures would be as ineffective in eliciting controlled behaviors in these patients as they were in the neodecorticates.

In addition to looking for animal to human parallels there are a number of aspects of the behavior modification program which have no counterpart as yet in the literature on neodecorticate learning and which thus raise questions of human to animal extrapolation. Success with the behavior modification program in brain-injured humans suggests that token reinforcements, time-out procedures as well as direct punishment are effective in behavioral control. In so far as there is no clear relationship between the extent of neocortical damage and the effectiveness of these procedures they may be mediated subcortically. It would follow from this that all three procedures would be effective in behavioral control in the neodecorticated rat or rabbit and a research program has recently been initiated to investigate this possibility.

Before leaving the area of traumatic head injury in humans I would like to mention some recent work by E. Miller at Addenbrooke's Hospital in Cambridge, which serves as a further demonstration of the considerable residual learning capacity which can be demonstrated using performance measures in such cases (Miller, 1980). Miller trained a group of eight severely head-injured patients on a moderately difficult psychomotor task involving four Formboards taken from the Minnesota Spatial Relations Test. The subjects were required to fit 58 different shapes into the 58 holes in each board, with five daily trials allowed on any given board before the next one was attempted. Despite very low initial levels of performance the head-injured subjects showed rapid improvement from trial to trial and good transfer of training from one board to the next. On completion of the fourth board these subjects were still improving their performance and had almost closed the gap between themselves and a normal control group. Poor initial levels of performance on tests of psychomotor skills in the head-injured should not therefore be taken as an indication that little improvement is possible and, as with associative learning paradigms, impressive residual capacities may be revealed by appropriate training procedures. In this context it is worth noting that neodecorticated rats are also able to acquire and retain motor skills such as those required to negotiate the non-retrace doors fitted in alleyways and two-choice apparatuses or to operate a suspended chain manipulandum in a Skinner box. Clearly the types of skill involved in the human and animal cases are not identical, but both sets of data are consistent with a significant potential for the mediation of skilled performance by subcortical systems.

There is a small amount of work on human microcephalics which is also worth mentioning here in so far as it confirms the general picture of residual ability in areas of associative learning despite massive neocortical reduction and gross intellectual loss. Beritashvili and Dzidzishvili (1934—cited by Beritashvili, 1971), for example, describe the case of a severely microcephalic girl, thought to be around 10 years of age, who when she entered the psychiatric clinic was unable to utter or understand speech, was uncontrollably aggressive and did not seem able to cope with even such simple problems as reaching a piece of food from behind a grating with a stick even though her sensory and motor abilities appeared normal. Food placed beneath a plate no longer existed for her. So primitive were the child's reactions that she earned for herself the name Pita, from Pithecanthropus. Over a period of one year, however, by a mixture of demonstration, imitation, and trial and error Pita was able to learn to use sticks to retrieve food, though with no apparent insight as to the length of stick which was appropriate in any given situation, and would retrieve food from beneath a plate if she had seen it placed there. Her general behavior also improved, she became friendly and could respond to a small number of verbal commands. When she died at the age of 13 the cortical suface of Pita's cerebral hemispheres was found to be some 4.3 times smaller than that of a normal child. Pita evidently lacked all but the crudest cognitive skills and appears to have progressed on the basis of a residual capacity for imitation and associative learning.

A more recent case of microcephaly was that of a 17-year-old male who had been institutionalized since the age of 6 (Jacobson et al., 1973). He too was unable to speak or to follow even the simplest instructions unless they were accompanied by a demonstration of the action required. He failed to display any ability to sustain attention or even to point his finger at an object. Medical and psychological assessment concurred in offering no hope of behavioral, intellectual, or social development. After an initial five hours of attentional and motor skill training, however, Jacobson et al. were able to test their microcephalic patient on a series of 34 two-choice visual discrimination problems using social reinforcement and frosted cereal as rewards for correct performance. The series commenced with 14 simple one-dimensional problems (e.g. red stimuli correct), followed by 10 two-dimenstional problems (e.g. blue squares correct), and finally 10 three-dimensional problems (e.g. small yellow triangles correct). The patient proved able to solve all 34 problems in about as many trials as normal preschool children and improved as the series progressed, indicating the development of a learning set. There were a number of unexpected bonuses to the training program in that the patient spoke his first words whilst it was in progress and in a 20-minute test at the end of discrimination training (after a total of 50 hours on the program) he verbalized 45 one- or two-syllable words. This patient had been untestable on standard intelligence scales but by the end of the program he was able to demonstrate a mental age of 3.2 years on the Stanford–Binet test. A follow-up study nine months after original training showed not only that the progress which had been achieved was maintained but that the patient could benefit further from a specific language acquisition program during which he added a further 7 months to his mental age (Bernal *et al.*, 1975). There were doubtless many reasons for this particular microcephalic's poor performance prior to the initiation of the behavioral program, not the least of which was the consensus of ineducability which institutionalized him at an early age. What the data do support, nevertheless, is first the sparing of an impressive associative learning capacity in human microcephaly and secondly, the utility of tapping this ability for associative learning as a first step in behavioral programs aimed at maximizing the damaged brain's residual conceptual and cognitive potential.

Hydranencephaly is a condition in which the cerebral hemispheres fail to develop for a variety of reasons and the cranial vault, which may remain of normal size, is filled with clear cerebrospinal fluid. Lorber (1965) has described one case in which anencephaly was identified postnatally by transillumination of the skull, needle biopsy, and air encephalography and was confirmed at 12 months of age. In none of the tests was there any evidence of brain tissue anterior to the level of the tentorium (the boundary between the cerebellum and the cerebral hemispheres). Despite so unpromising a neurological picture the child progressed normally and at 21 months of age he was alert, playful, and able to say many words. He liked to look at picture-books and could name some of the pictures. He played with toy cars and building toys and was able to feed himself with a spoon and fork. No more formal tests were reported nor was there any assessment of associative learning ability, though in view of the child's progress in other fields it would have been surprising if any deficit in associative learning was present. One interpretation, which I will resist, is that all the capacities displayed by the child, including linguistic skills, are capable of subcortical mediation. I shall content myself with the more conservative conclusion that normal human function, at least to a 21 month level, can be sustained by a brain in which the cerebral hemispheres are either so small or so displaced as to evade detection by normal clinical methods. This particular patient is still alive and well, with no physical handicap and only moderate mental retardation (J. Lorber personal communication 1981).

In hydrocephalus the skull is typically enlarged as the brain is distorted and the cerebral mantle is stretched by the enlargement of the lateral ventricles. This is due to an internal accumulation of cerebrospinal fluid and the progress of the enlargement can be controlled by the insertion of a ventriculo-atrial shunt. Despite thinning of the cerebral mantle to 10 mm or less over the expanded ventricles, normal intellectual development after treatment is possible, even to the attainment of IQs in the region of 120–129 (Lorber, 1968). More recent observations using computerized tomography (CT scanning) to assess the hydrocephalus have revealed that in shunt-treated cases, in which the head need not be abnormally large, normal intellectual achievement is possible despite sustained ventricular enlargement to the extent that 95 percent of the supratentorial part of the cranial cavity appears to be fluid filled. The most remarkable, and widely reported, case in the latter category at the time of assessment had a first-class honours degree in economics, mathematics, and computer studies (see Paterson, 1980). The implication that the CT scans indicate 'virtually no brain' has been challenged, especially as it is not backed by histological verification (see Bower, 1980; Oakley 1981a). In particular, CT scans may underestimate the thickness of the residual cortical mantle, which appears to contain well preserved cortex and some white matter in hydrocephalics, and are not a good way of visualizing parts of the brain lying close to the base of the skull (Janota, 1980).

Both the hydranencephaly and hydrocephaly data are challenging and have been widely reported in the media and I have considered them in some detail here for that reason. In the absence of histological verification, however, they do not allow any precise conclusions to be drawn with respect to cortical versus subcortical functioning. What they do show is that the human brain is capable of functioning apparently normally despite gross displacement, compression, and distortion of the cerebral hemispheres, accompanied by an unknown degree of neocortical loss. Perhaps their most important outcome, however, is to encourage clinicians and therapists not to give up too soon when faced with what appears on a conventional assessment to be a hopeless case in neuroanatomical terms.

IN CONCLUSION

There are obviously severe problems with the type of extrapolation attempted in this chapter, not the least of which is that no control can be exercised over brain lesions in humans. I would submit, however, that the parallels between human brain-injury patients and brain damaged, and in particular neodecorticated, rats and rabbits are sufficiently close as to be worth taking seriously. All the observations reported in this chapter are consistent with the view that associative learning, as exemplified by the major paradigms of Pavlovian conditioning and instrumental learning, is a class-common behavior which may be subcortically mediated in humans just as in rats and rabbits. Perhaps though, the reader would be happier with the less precise, but still useful, conclusion that associative learning is a very robust form of information gain which survives massive injury to the brain in both humans and other mammals. In this way it contrasts with what I have called 'cognitive processes' which appear to be rather more sensitive to cerebral insult, though even here the human brain appears to be able to withstand considerable abuse before abandoning its role. At a practical level it seems possible that the sorts of procedures which assist in the development of learned behaviors in neodecorticates may also assist in the rehabilitation of human patients following massive neocortical damage, particularly in the early stages of the therapeutic process. Irrespective of the scientific merits or demerits of what I have attempted here, there is I believe a real message of hope for all those actively engaged in remedial care in cases of human brain abnormality or injury. It is that the mammalian brain has far greater potential for behavioral adaptation after injury than has previously been supposed. In particular the dissociation between the neural substrates of associative learning and cognitive processes means that a poor profile of intellectual functions is not a good guide to the extent of residual associative abilities or to the likely outcome of behavior modification programs. Therapeutic programs based on Pavlovian and instrumental learning principles can thus be contemplated, possibly as a first resort, in the face of massive cerebral injury or abnormality with the expectation that the capacity to benefit from such a program will be one of the last functions to be lost. Behavior modification programs used in this way may then provide a behavioral baseline upon which to build later cognitive therapies. If we accept that associative learning is possible in mammalian brain-stems and spinal cords (see Oakley, 1979a) and extrapolate this to humans it may not be an exaggeration to suggest as a practical therapeutic rule that if sufficient brain tissue remains to sustain independent life then there is sufficient brain to sustain associative learning. In this light the successes claimed in brain-injured infants for various 'intensive stimulation' therapies which build upon whatever residual function is present without presuming limits to eventual function may not be unreasonable. Certainly the optimistic approach to therapy pioneered by Doman and Delacato and practiced by the Institutes for the Achievement of Human Potential in the USA and in a modified form by the British Institute for Brain Injured Children in the UK is consistent with the spirit of what has been proposed in this chapter, though historically the rationales are very different (Beasley and Hegarty, 1976; Doman, 1974).

Perhaps I could end with a footnote to learning theorists. The fact that learning within the two major types of learning situation appears to depend on only a small proportion of the neural apparatus available to an intact mammal implies that association learning itself represents only a small proportion of behavioral adaptiveness even in the rat. Cognitive processes such as those involved in reasoning, detours, hypotheses, and the integration of information may, on this analysis, be more important than animal psychology has tended to assume (see Oakley, 1979a; 1981a,b). Perhaps unwittingly experimenters involved in Pavlovian conditioning and instrumental learning have been carefully plotting the operating characteristics primarily of subcortex—not that that is necessarily a bad thing in itself. It may, however, be time to attend more to what neocortex might be doing in behavioral terms in the rat and other mammals and to stop filtering out its contribution by insisting on training procedures developed in an associationist framework, as exemplified by traditional Pavlovian and instrumental paradigms.

ACKNOWLEDGMENTS

I am grateful to Peter Eames and Rodger Wood for the opportunity to discuss their work on brain-damaged adults, to Keith Pennock and Alan Morgan for discussing their approach to therapy in brain-injured children and to Lesley Eames and Laura Goldstein for first drawing my attention to much of the experimental work referred to in this chapter.

NOTES

1. The top drawing is based on material supplied by S. Pereira and I. S. Russell of the MRC Unit on Neural Mechanisms of Behaviour and the other two drawings on material from the author's laboratory. c—cerebellum; cp—caudate/putamen; h—hippocampus; nc—neocortex; ob—olfactory bulb; rf—rhinal fissure; sc—spinal cord. The neocortex extends from the midline over the entire dorsal surface of the cerebral hemispheres and is bounded laterally by the rhinal fissure.

2. See Chapter 6, 'An associative view of human classical conditioning', p. 95, G. C. L. Davey: for a discussion of a distinction between 'primitive' conditioning and 'cognitive relational learning', either of which may occur in the Pavlovian paradigm with human subjects.

3. Graphs b and c are based on previously unpublished data collected by R. Ll. Wood and I am grateful for permission to present them here. In all three parts of the figure and in Figure 13.3 individual data were plotted backward from the block or session in which the discrimination criterion (c) was reached prior to the calculation of group means. Numbers with a minus sign identify blocks or sessions prior to criterion. The numbers immediately above the horizontal axis of each graph show the number (N) of subjects contributing to each data point.

4. These graphs are based on data originally reported in a different form in Oakley (1981c).

REFERENCES

Abel, E. L. (1980) Fetal alcohol syndrome: Behavioral teratology. *Psychological Bulletin*, **87**, 29–50.

Beasley, N., and Hegarty, J. (1976) *The Doman–Delacato Treatment: Methods and Results*. Published by the Department of Psychology, University of Keele, Staffordshire.

Beritashvili, I. S. (1971) *Vertebrate Memory: Characteristics and Origin*. New York: Plenum Press.

Bernal, G., Jacobson, L. I., and Lopez, G. N. (1975) Do the effects of behaviour modification programmes endure? *Behavioural Research and Therapy*, **13**, 61–64.

Bond, N. W. (1980) Postnatal alcohol exposure in the rat: its effects on avoidance conditioning, Hebb-Williams maze performance, maternal behavior and pup development. *Physiological Psychology*, **8**, 437–443.

Bower, A. J. (1980) Is your brain really necessary? A comment. *World Medicine*, **15**, 21, 25–27.

Diaz, J., and Samson, H. H. (1980) Impaired brain growth in neonatal rats exposed to ethanol. *Science*, **208**, 751–753.

DiCara, L. V., Braun, J. J., and Pappas, B. A. (1970) Classical conditioning and instrumental learning of cardiac and gastrointestinal responses following removal of neocortex in the rat. *Journal of Comparative and Physiological Psychology*, **73**, 208–216.

Doman, G. (1974) *What to do about your Brain-injured Child*. London: Jonathan Cape.

Gamzu, E., and Schwam, E. (1974) Autoshaping and automaintenance of a key-press response in squirrel monkeys. *Journal of the Experimental Analysis of Behavior*, **21**, 361–371.

Gray, S. L., Potts, F. L., and Means, L. W. (1981) Failure of neonatal ethanol exposure to impair maze acquisition in rats. *IRCS, Medical Science*, **9**, 16.

Humphrey, N. K. (1974) Vision in a monkey without striate cortex: A case study. *Perception*, **3**, 241–255.

Jacobson, L. I., Bernal, G., and Lopez, G. N. (1973) Effects of behavioral training on the functioning of a profoundly retarded microcephalic teenager with cerebral palsy and without language or verbal comprehension. *Behavioral Research and Therapy*, **11**, 143–145.

Jaldow, E. J., Oakley, D. A., and Davey, G. C. L. (1981) Temporal control in the absence of neocortex. In Press.

Janota, I. (1980) Letters: Is your brain really necessary? *World Medicine*, **15**, 18, 59.

Kolb, B., and Whishaw, I. Q. (1981) Decortication of rats in infancy or adulthood produced comparable functional losses on learned and species-typical behaviors. *Journal of Comparative and Physiological Psychology*, **95**, 468–483.

Lashley, K. (1935) Studies of cerebral function in learning. XI. The behavior of the rat in latch-box situations. *Comparative Psychology Monographs*, **11**, 5–40.

Lorber, J. (1965) Hydranencephaly with normal development. *Developmental Medicine and Child Neurology*, **7**, 628–633.

Lorber, J. (1968) The results of early treatment of extreme hydrocephalus. *Developmental Medicine and Child Neurology. Supplement 16*, pp. 21–29.

Lowe, C. F. (1979) Determinants of human operant behaviour. In M. D. Zeiler and P. Harzem (eds) *Advances in Analysis of Behaviour, Vol. 1: Reinforcement and the Organization of Behaviour*. Chichester, England: Wiley. pp. 159–192.

Lowe, C. F., Beasty, A., and Bentall, R. P. (1980) Operant conditioning in infants:

Evidence for the generality of learning principles? Paper presented at a meeting of the Experimental Analysis of Behaviour Group held in London, December 1980.

Mageean, B. (1981) The form of the information and selective counting by ESN(M) pupils. *Quarterly Journal of Experimental Psychology*, **33A**, 61–76.

Miller, E. (1980) The training characteristics of severely head-injured patients: a preliminary study. *Journal of Neurology, Neurosurgery and Psychiatry*, **43**, 525–528.

Oakley, D. A. (1979a) Cerebral cortex and adaptive behaviour. In D. A. Oakley and H. C. Plotkin (eds) *Brain, Behaviour and Evolution*. London: Methuen. pp. 154–188.

Oakley, D. A. (1979b) Neocortex and learning. *Trends in NeuroSciences*, **2**, 149–152.

Oakley, D. A. (1979c) Learning with food reward and shock avoidance in neodecorticate rats. *Experimental Neurology*, **63**, 627–642.

Oakley, D. A. (1979d) Instrumental reversal learning and subsequent fixed ratio performance on simple and go/nogo schedules in neodecorticate rabbits. *Physiological Psychology*, **7**, 29–42.

Oakley, D. A. (1980) Improved instrumental learning in neodecorticate rats. *Physiology and Behavior*, **24**, 357–366.

Oakley, D. A. (1981a) Brain mechanisms of mammalian memory. *British Medical Bulletin*, **37**, 175–180.

Oakley, D. A. (1981b) The varieties of memory: A phylogenetic approach. In A. Mayes (ed.) *Memory in Animals and Man*. London: Van Nostrand. In Press.

Oakley, D. A. (1981c) Performance of decorticated rats in a two-choice visual discrimination apparatus. *Behavioural Brain Research*, **3**, 55–69.

Oakley, D. A., Eames, L. C., Jacobs, J. L., Davey, G. C. L., and Cleland, G. C. (1981) Signal-centered action patterns in rats without neocortex in a Pavlovian conditioning situation. *Physiological Psychology*, **9**, 135–144.

Oakley, D. A., and Russell, I. S. (1976) Subcortical nature of Pavlovian differentiation in the rabbit. *Physiology and Behavior*, **17**, 947–954.

Oakley, D. A., and Russell, I. S. (1977) Subcortical storage of Pavlovian conditioning in the rabbit. *Physiology and Behavior*, **18**, 931–937.

Oakley, D. A., and Russell, I. S. (1978) Manipulandum identification in operant behaviour in neodecorticate rabbits. *Physiology and Behavior*, **21**, 943–950.

Paterson, D. (1980) Is your brain really necessary? *World Medicine*, **15**, 15, 21–24.

Pavlov, I. P. (1927) *Conditioned Reflexes*. Translated by G. V. Anrep. New York: Dover Publications.

Phillips, D. S., and Stainbrook, G. L. (1976) Effects of early alcohol exposure upon adult learning ability and taste preferences. *Physiological Psychology*, **4**, 473–475.

Ragain, R. D., Anson, J. E., and Sperber, R. D. (1976) Autoshaping and maintenance of a lever-press response in mentally retarded children. *The Psychological Record*, **26**, 105–109.

Russell, I. S. (1966) Animal learning and memory. In D. Richter (ed.) *Aspects of Learning and Memory*, London: Heinemann. pp. 121–171.

Russell, I. S. (1979) Brain size and intelligence: A comparative perspective. In D. A. Oakley and H. C. Plotkin (eds) *Brain, Behaviour and Evolution*, London: Methuen. pp. 126–153.

Russell, I. S. (1980) Encephalisation and neural mechanisms of learning. In M. A. Jeeves (ed.) *Psychology Survey No. 3*, London: George Allen & Unwin. pp. 92–114.

Travis, A. M., and Woolsey, C. N. (1956) Motor performance of monkeys after bilateral partial and total cerebral decortications. *American Journal of Physical Medicine*, **35**, 273–310.

Warren, J. M., and Kolb, B. (1978) Generalizations in neuropsychology. In S. Finger (ed.) *Recovery from Brain Damage*, New York: Plenum Press. pp. 35–48.

Weiskrantz, L. (1977) Trying to bridge some neuropsychological gaps between monkey and man. *British Journal of Psychology*, **68**, 431–445.

Weiskrantz, L. (1980) Varieties of residual experience. *Quarterly Journal of Experimental Psychology*, **32**, 365–386.

Wilcove, W. G., and Miller, J. C. (1974) CS–UCS presentations and a lever: human autoshaping. *Journal of Experimental Psychology*, **103**, 868–877.

Wood, R. Ll., and Eames, P. (1981) Application of behaviour modification in the rehabilitation of traumatically brain-injured patients. In G. C. L. Davey (ed.) *Applications of Conditioning Theory*, London: Methuen. pp. 81–101.

Zeaman, D., and House, B. J. (1963) The role of attention in retardate discrimination learning. In N. R. Ellis (ed.) *Handbook of Mental Deficienty*, New York: McGraw-Hill. pp. 159–223.

Zeiler, M. D. (1972) Superstitious behavior in children: an experimental analysis. *Advances in Child Development and Behavior*, **7**, 1–29.

Chapter 14

In Search of a Retarded Rat

J. T. RICK

At first sight it would appear to be a relatively simple task to create an animal model of mental deficit or retardation. Lashley, in 1929, demonstrated that the coping ability of the rat depended upon the amount of cortical tissue the animal had available: the rat's ability decreasing as more tissue was destroyed. But the gross anatomical features of the brains of the vast majority of mentally retarded patients fall well within the normal ranges of weight, size, and general morphology. Thus, models based simply on ablation are unlikely to serve much purpose, and until recently no satisfactory model of mental deficit did exist. Another sort of seemingly simple task is how to recognize a retarded rat. But as we shall see, changes in behavioral attributes other than just performance decrements have to be taken into account.

This chapter will first describe the two main approaches to the study of behavior in psychobiology, that is by means of behavioral *change* or behavioral *difference*. An argument, based on this methodological dichotomy, will then be presented for the need to extrapolate from animals to man. Following this, an animal model will be described that has been proposed for hitherto unclassified congenital encephalopathies, in general and mental retardation in particular. The model makes use of antibodies raised against various brain antigens. These are administered either to pregnant or newborn rats; the aim of the former procedure being to create behavioral deficits in the offspring and thus provide a preparation that has not experienced any invasive techniques from birth. After a brief review of the area, counter-intuitive results from some of the research will be compared to other work where abuses to the central nervous sytem have led to incremental, rather than decremental, effects on performance; these data having been drawn from work on insects as well as rats and man. Finally, a hypothesis based on signal detection theory will be proposed to account for all these counter-intuitive results.

1. METHODOLOGICAL CONSIDERATIONS

In psychobiology we can study behavior experimentally in one of two fundamental ways. These essentially are studies based on behavioral *change* within one individual either acting as his own control or measured against a matched control and those studies that make use of behavioral *difference* between two or more individuals. Behavioral change, being a function of both environmental manipulation and the passage of time, is of its nature an unstable state. For example, the administration of certain drugs to subjects will bring about temporary changes in behavior which will then revert to the pre-drug state after a period of time. Since the types of manipulation employed in experiments of behavioral change result in unstable and temporary states it is this approach which is normally used with human subjects. Behavioral difference, on the other hand, has the characteristics of stability and permanence, individuals act differently to the same environment and such differences do not disappear with the passage of time. Individual differences that are studied in human subjects are not the outcome of experimental manipulation but are due to a combination of genetic and experiential dissimilarities already existing within the population. It is the fact that behavioral differences are stable that precludes the use of manipulative techniques with humans for experimental purposes that would result in irreversible states. At the same time a stable difference in behavior is obviously a very desirable attribute in many instances, especially when the behavior studied is to be related to its biological substrata. Behavior, like its biochemical or physiological counterparts, is a dynamic process, a set of 'events' not 'things'. But stable differences between individuals in one domain are likely to reflect a similar state of affairs in another. It is this stability that provides adequate control of the dynamic character of the two systems to be related. The inhibitory neurotransmitter gamma-aminobutyric acid in cortex, for example, has been shown to be inversely associated with a behavioral dimension of learning and activity in an experiment exploiting the stability of inherited differences between animal strains (Rick *et al.*, 1971). Behavioral differences can be brought about in animals in numerous ways that are not available when working with humans. Apart from direct genetic manipulation, stable behavioral differences may be created by irreversible brain lesions, differential early experience, or emotive trauma. It is because such experimental manipulation is not ethically possible with human subjects that extrapolation from animal studies becomes an important means of attempting to understand human behavior and the mechanisms that underly it. Extrapolation of the concepts formed from a study of animal behavior to hypotheses concerning man involves moving from the attributes of a simpler to a more complex nervous system and it is this differential complexity of nervous systems that is the major problem in attempting to form any valid, comparative relationship in psychology. Some workers claim that the problem is insurmountable, but to take this stance is to deny the possibility of asking a whole range of questions based on techniques which exploit experimentally created differences in behavior.

2. ANIMAL MODELS OF PSYCHOPATHOLOGY

The need to establish behavioral differences is most clearly seen in attempts to create animal models of psychopathology. Viable models of psychopathology in the animal laboratory have proved somewhat elusive in the past (Abramson and Seligman, 1977), but one lesson that emerges from a study of such endeavors is the need for greater sophistication in modelling based first on a clear definition of the target psychopathology. One of the areas where this can clearly be accomplished is in mental retardation. Unlike the diagnostic disputes associated with other psychopathologies, such as minimal brain dysfunction, schizophrenia, or depression, patients suffering from mental retardation are readily recognized and assessed by reliable psychometric procedures. This ability to clearly define the group allows the investigator to establish the occasions upon which the state is the result of genetic, congenital, or postnatal influences. The model that will be described here is one of mental retardation due to congenital factors. Secondly, for a model to be valid the need is not so much for a similarity in symptomatology but rather for a common anatomical, physiological, or biochemical base between the human pathology and its animal model. Mental retardation has been associated with morphological deficits in dendritic arborization and synaptogenesis during development (Huttenlocher, 1975; Purpura, 1974) and more recently Karpiak and his co-workers have demonstrated similar structural changes in neonate rats exposed to antibodies to ganglioside (Kasarskis et al., 1981). Gangliosides are a group of sialic acid containing glycosphingolipids found predominantly in the grey matter of mammalian brain, and they are concentrated in the subcellular fraction of brain that contains pinched off nerve endings (Wiegandt, 1967). In other words, gangliosides are constituents of that part of the nerve membrane which is involved in synaptic transmission and exposure to antibodies specific to such molecules results in anatomical abnormalities in the developing mammalian brain which are similar to those reported to occur in mental retardation. It is on this basis that we have attempted to create a model for mental retardation in the rat.

In 1973, Kirman, in considering the causes of hitherto unclassified congenital encephalopathies and mental retardation, suggested that some of these conditions could be ascribed to the presence of maternal antibodies against brain antigens (Kirman, 1975). The instances of mental retardation thought to be congenital are those occurring with neither a familial history of the disease nor any untoward events at birth or postnatally that might cause retardation. Further, the hypothetical etiology is supported in that the presence of such antibodies would not be expected to affect the mother adversely, which is also the case. Women enjoying normal health and uneventful pregnancies do give birth to mentally retarded offspring. Kirman's hypothesis is based on the assumption that although the concentration of antibodies in the maternal circulation is too low to affect the mother's mature brain, the antibodies should reach the more sensitive developing brain via the fetal circulation. The two major objections to this role that such antibodies may play—namely the presence of a complete blood–brain barrier to plasma proteins during fetal and perinatal life and the widely accepted view that the intercellular clefts between nerve cells and neuroglia are not open to the diffusion of large molecules—have now been removed. In fact, studies in man and experimental animals have shown that during fetal and perinatal life several plasma proteins, including immunoglobulins, can cross the blood–cerebrospinal fluid (CSF) barrier (Adinolfi, 1979). Furthermore, evidence has been produced that a number of substances of different molecular weights can enter the intercellular spaces of the brain from the CSF even in adult animals (Brightman and Reese, 1969; Kuffler and Nicholls, 1976). It is not surprising therefore that the suggestion that maternal antibodies against brain antigens reach fetal brain and affect its development has received experimental support from a number of laboratories, nor that in the last few years behavioral data have been obtained that indicate that brain antibodies, injected into newborn or adult animals, may affect certain functions of the CNS (Adinolfi et al., 1982).

It is only recently that antibodies to specific antigens have become readily available. But in the earlier studies to be described the crude, non-specific extracts used would have contained, amongst other things, antiganglioside antibodies. Perturbations of the capacity to learn were observed by Auroux and collaborators (1968) in the offspring of rats injected with a crude brain extract. In 1975 Karpiak and Rapport injected immune sera against synaptic endings into 19-day pregnant rats and noted that male offspring manifested behavioral deficits in tests of avoidance conditioning at two months of age. Similarly, in my laboratory, immature rats born to mothers injected interperitoneally with antiganglioside antibodies between days 16 and 19 of their pregnancies, took longer to learn a sequence maze when no overt cues were provided. However, they did perform as well as their controls when the way through the maze was cued—see Table 14.1 (Rick et al., 1981). Kasarskis et al. (1981) have also reported that a behavioral deficit in adult rats after neonatal administration of antibodies to ganglioside only occurred in more demanding learning situations. They trained adult animals, who at five days of age had received either a single injection of antiserum to ganglioside or antiserum which had been absorbed with pure ganglioside to remove the specific antibodies, to pause between bar presses for food reinforcement.

Table 14.1: Maze learning in young rats: the effects of pre-natal exposure to antiganglioside antibodies (reproduced from Rick *et al.*, 1981, by permission of Elsevier Biomedical Press B.V.)

	N	Trials to criterion		
		Learning	Memory	Reversal
Uncued				
Antiganglioside	14	63.7 ± 5.2*	19.7 ± 2.3	46.5 ± 3.7**
Control	5	38.2 ± 2.3	18.6 ± 1.5	22.8 ± 2.1
Cued				
Antiganglioside	15	32.7 ± 2.3	9.9 ± 1.5	13.7 ± 2.0
Control	6	26.3 ± 1.9	9.0 ± 0.9	13.3 ± 1.8

Numbers represent mean ± s.e.m.
$*p<0.05$, $**p<0.01$, antiganglioside >control

Rats, at 35 days of age, ran a five-door straight-alley runway for food reward to a criterion of four faultless trials in five. Twenty-four hours later they were tested for their memory of the maze then immediately trained with the sequence reversed. When the correct door was not cued the rats, exposed prenatally to the antibody, were significantly inferior to their controls during initial learning and in reversal. These deficits disappeared when the correct path through the maze was cued.

Only when the imposed pause exceeded seven seconds did the performance of the experimental rats become significantly inferior to that of the control animals. This particular schedule, differential reinforcement at low rates (DRL), is not at first sight a simple task for the rat. Shaping the behavior and the training procedure takes a considerable amount of time, yet at a response–response interval of five seconds the treated group's performance was indistinguishable from that of the control. Furthermore, in a number of studies of the effects of anti-brain antibodies, experimental animals have had normal rates of body growth and general activity (Hofstein *et al.*, 1980; Kasarskis, *et al.*, 1981). So, although numerous performance deficits have been reported in animals subjected to anti-brain antibodies in perinatal life, in some learning situations the extent of the deficit would seem less than might be expected. In fact, in three studies of discrimination learning, animals exposed to antibodies were apparently superior to their controls and it is to these counter-intuitive results that we will now turn.

BRAIN ABUSE: INCREMENTS IN PERFORMANCE

MacPherson and Shek (1970) first trained mature rats on a visual discrimination task and then immunized them with a crude microsomal fraction from rat brain. When the discrimination was reversed the immunized animals were found to require fewer trials to the criterion than their controls. This result is similar to our own findings using antiganglioside (Rick *et al.*, 1980). Briefly, adult male rats were first trained to press a lever for food reinforcement in a standard two-lever chamber, the 'correct' lever being cued with a light. At the end of training the animals were matched for performance and one of each pair received rabbit serum containing a high concentration of antiganglioside antibody, and the other received normal serum under double-blind conditions. After five days the animals were tested daily on the same schedule as during training but now at every reinforcement the light-cue switched from one lever to the other with a probability of 0.5. The animals injected with antiganglioside showed a significantly superior adaptation to this task of random alternation over the first two days of testing (Figure 14.1). This transient superiority was again observed when the significance of the light

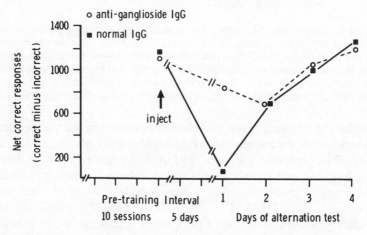

Figure 14.1 Effect of antiganglioside injected into rats, tested by alternation of bar-pressing response. (From Rick *et al.*, 1980; copyright 1980 by Spastics International Medical Publications. Reprinted by permission of the Editors of *Developmental Medicine and Child Neurology*)

cue was reversed and subsequently with the same pairs of animals in another discrimination test using an elevated eight-arm maze (Figure 14.2). Recently these results have been substantiated in another random alternation experiment in which adult rats were used that had been born to mothers injected during pregnancy. On this occasion the superiority of the antiganglioside animals persisted for seven days (Rick *et al.*, 1981). In these experiments the animals' behavior regulated either by a specific stimulus, the light cue in random alternation of the lever or with the elevated eight-arm by visual cues in the immediate environment of the maze which enable the rat to identify the un-entered arms (Olton and Samuelson, 1976). Thus, under both conditions, the rat copes by recognizing the significance of some stimuli to the exclusion of others and it is perhaps at this level of analysis that these apparently counter-intuitive results may be explained.

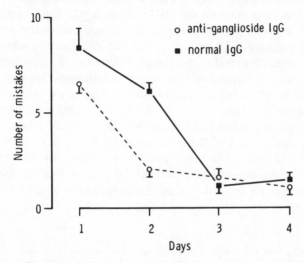

Figure 14.2 Effect of antiganglioside injected into rats, tested by an eight-arm maze for food reward. Bars show standard errors of means. (From Rick *et al.*, 1980; copyright 1980 by Spastics International Medical Publications. Reprinted by permission of the Editors of *Developmental Medicine and Child Neurology*)

In any discrimination task, relevant stimuli must be sorted out from the rest and the greater the signal-to-noise (S/N) ratio the more rapidly will a subject acquire the learned response (Sutherland, 1964). Any treatment which diminishes the 'noise' levels, while leaving the signal strength unaffected, would increase the S/N ratio and thus enhance acquisition. Noise in this context is associated with the complexity of the central nervous system. The more complex the nervous system the greater will be the neuronal activity and the depth of processing that occurs to any incoming stimuli. In fact, the complexity of the system may, in certain circumstances, obscure the immediate relevance of a stimulus. As an example take an imaginary experiment. Two groups of subjects are asked to find the next letter in the series A, E, F, H, I. One group is composed of normal adults, the other of eight-year-old children. Whereas the adults are likely to indulge in counting exercises or attempts to impose arithmetic or geometric progressions on the series before taking into account the stimuli *per se*, the children, incapable of such complex processing, can only take the letters at face value and therefore are likely to reach the correct solution, K, more quickly. If one result of exposing rats to antiganglioside antibodies is to make them retarded in the sense that their processing of information is diminished then on some tasks, as we have seen, they might be expected to acquire a transient superiority. But as tasks become more complex, and presumably the depth of processing required much greater, their inability to cope becomes evident as seen with the uncued maze or the DRL schedule with long pauses.

How general is this phenomenon of diminished processing giving rise to improved performance? There are a number of examples where lesioned animals have been observed to discriminate more rapidly than their controls. Cockroaches can be trained to keep their metathoracic leg out of a saline solution in order to avoid an electric shock. Figure 14.3 shows data from such an experiment (Rick *et al.*, 1972). In the acquisition phase isolated metathoracic ganglia learn faster than headless animals which in turn are quicker than intact animals. Whereas the extinction and reacquisition times did not differ between the latter two preparations, the time needed for reacquisition by the isolated ganglion was the same as that needed for acquisition, and it may be argued that in this preparation a passive mechanism

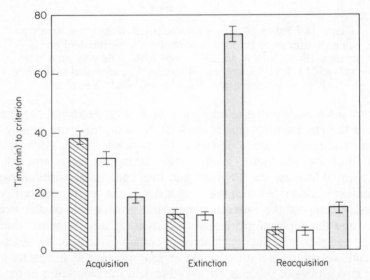

Figure 14.3 Times of acquisition, extinction, and reacquisition of a learnt response in three cockroach preparations. ▧ = intact, ▢ = headless, ▢ = isolated. The *N* for each group was 15 and each bar represents the mean and standard error. Note that the less nervous system available to a preparation, the faster it learns the initial acquisition. (From Rick *et al.*, 1972; reproduced by permission of The Experimental Psychology Society)

akin to forgetting took place during the extinction phase rather than an active suppression of the acquired response. Such an argument would be consistent with the relatively long period needed for extinction by the isolated ganglion. What is of interest in the present context is that by successively decreasing the extent of the nervous system, and hence the 'noise' or depth of processing, the rate of acquisition of the discrimination increases in a stepwise manner while, on the basis of the extinction and reacquisition data, the quality of the learning diminishes considerably when the ganglion alone is involved.

Stevens and Cowey, in 1973, reported a series of experiments which studied the effects of hippocampal lesions in rats on a number of behavioral tasks. In the main, the experimental animals' performances were inferior to the controls, but on a probability learning task, rats with dorsal hippocampal lesions were indistinguishable from controls, and when tested on lever alternation these lesioned rats were significantly superior. In an attempt to replicate this last result, but using the random lever-alternation task, we have recently tested adult animals that had had hippocampal lesions, cortical lesions, or sham operations shortly after birth (Rick, Foreman and Robinson, unpublished results). The training procedure employed was the same as that described earlier (Rick *et al.*, 1980) and Figure 14.4 gives the results. Over the eight days of testing the hippocampal animals were superior to the other two groups, which did not differ significantly from each other. Thus, hippocampal lesions produced much the same effect on this task as antiganglioside exposure.

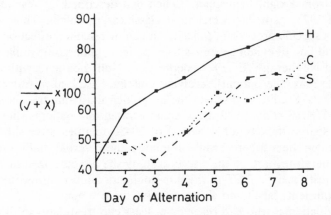

Figure 14.4 The percent correct responses of three groups of rats in a two-lever random alternation task, tested daily for 8 days. H = hippocampal lesion; C = cortical lesion, and S = sham-operated controls. The *N* for each group was 6

The third example of an incremental effect of brain abuse on discrimination of relevant stimuli has been reported in a cognitive experiment with humans. The study made use of the Four-Card Problem (Wason, 1966). This problem can take numerous forms from which concrete examples have to be considered in relation to a test sentence. The subject has to determine which practical instances would allow a valid inference to be made in relation to the test sentence. It is usually carried out using cards on each of which is a shape (a circle or a diamond) and a color (yellow or green). Top and bottom halves of the cards are balanced for shapes and colors, such that a color is in the top half in four instances, resulting in eight possible combinations. Having inspected all eight cards, a subject is shown four with the top half masked and with the four possibilities, of shape or color, visible in the bottom half. A test sentence of the form 'Whenever there is a circle on one half of the card there is yellow on the other half' is then read. The subject is to name *only* those cards of the four shown one would need to unmask to test the truth of the sentence. Earlier work using this procedure (Golding *et al.*, 1974) had indicated that once an incorrect selection had been made it is highly resistant to correction and that this is due to the visual aspects of the task interfering with the verbal reasoning. It was postulated that visual skills, known to be lateralized to the right hemisphere, inhibited the left hemisphere's verbal skills of inference thus preventing insight into the problem. A recent report (Golding, 1980) confirmed this prediction in two ways.

The first study was with unilateral cerebral lesioned patients and it was found that right hemisphere cerebral lesions facilitated insight into the problem. In particular, the problem was completely solved by all the patients suffering from a right hemisphere deficit first described by Warrington and Taylor in 1973, namely a perceptual classification deficit. Thus, a known deficit in a specific processing capacity had an incremental effect on the task. The second line of evidence comes from patients undergoing unilateral electro-convulsive therapy (ECT) for depression. Unlike patients with unilateral cerebral lesions, the patients receiving unilateral ECT have transitory cognitive deficits. Studies to discover the neurological asymmetries immediately after ECT (Kriss *et al.*, 1978) have demonstrated that patients show perceptual and spatial deficits for a period of 20–30 minutes after shock to the non-dominant hemisphere, while retaining their verbal skills during this period. Therefore, in Golding's second study she hypothesized that patients who had just received ECT to the non-dominant hemisphere would demonstrate a transient, facilitated ability to solve the problem.

Twenty patients, who had received at least two treatments in their course of therapy, were given the four-card problem. Ten patients were given the task for the first time immediately after ECT and an equivalent second version of the problem just prior to their next treatment. The other ten patients were presented with the two versions of the problem in the reverse order, on the first occasion before ECT, and the second time immediately after ECT. The two versions of the problem were counter-balanced for presentation and in this way each patient acted as his own control. The selections were analyzed according to the theoretical analysis of Johnson-Laird and Watson (1970) such that a subject scores for complete insight, partial insight, or failure.

Five patients gained complete insight immediately after ECT while eight gained at least partial insight. No patient achieved either level of insight under the control condition. Following ECT, patients showed a deficit of perceptual classification, performing at a significantly poorer level than under the control condition. In particular, seven of the eight patients who gained at least partial insight following ECT demonstrated non-dominant hemisphere cognitive dysfunction while only one of the remaining twelve patients did so.

Incremental effects on performance following abuse to the central nervous systems are obviously exceptional. Normally one would expect, and find, performance decrements after the disruption of nervous function. None the less, the examples from work with the cockroach, rat and man, strengthen the feasibility of the model put forward for mental retardation in demonstrating that the enhanced performance of rats exposed to antiganglioside antibodies on certain tasks is but one of a number of instances where brain dysfunction can lead to apparent improvements in coping behavior. The improvements are only apparent since they do not persist across a variety of tasks nor are they sustained when the difficulty of those tasks where they do occur is increased.

4. NOISE AND THE CNS

To account for these various incremental effects on performance following a diversity of invasive procedures to nervous systems it was indicated earlier that a solution might be found in the context of signal detection theory. A number of types of 'noise' in the nervous system have been cited. For example, Treisman (1964) suggested three sources: (a) the irreducible physical variability of the stimulus, (b) the spontaneous neural background activity to which a stimulus is added, and (c) the neural noise arising from variation in the pathways transmitting the message centrally. Hebb (1961) identified noise as random activity in redundant neurons. Pinneo (1966) suggested that the various types of background activity, such as those identified by Hebb and Treisman, constitute the functional substrate of the brain. He distinguishes between phasic activity which is a transient variation in neuronal firing rates and time-locked to a particular stimulus, and tonic activity which is non-transient, or continuous, where the average firing rate is constant and not time-locked to stimulation. Whether background activity has a function or not, it is what is normally equated with noise in the system and has two main characteristics—a constant firing rate and a temporal independence from input. When attempting to explain the counter-intuitive results presented in this chapter, 'noise' is defined in a diametrical opposite manner in that it does change and is time-locked to the stimulus. Noise in this context is the level or amount of stimulus processing. By stimulus processing is meant the depth, elaborateness, or extensiveness of the encoding induced at input (Craik, 1979). The extent to which stimulus input is processed is dependent on the complexity of the nervous system; the greater the complexity, the more sophisticated the processing. One result of any form of lesioning is a decrease in the complexity of the system and hence some loss of stimulus processing. Following such treatment, an individual's performance on the vast majority of tasks is diminished. However, as we have seen, in a number of situations, performance is facilitated and it is on these occasions that the processing of the stimulus is equated to noise in the system. If the level of processing required to complete a given task is less than that normally induced, it might well be disruptive and thus could constitute noise. This was seen to be intuitively the case in the imaginary experiment described earlier with adults and children solving an alphabetic series. And, finally, decreasing the capability of an individual to process information could facilitate performance in some circumstances, and it is argued that this is what is occurring when an increment in performance is observed following the various forms of brain abuse described above.

Two questions were posed at the start of this chapter and it is to these that we will now return. How can one create a model of mental retardation in the rat? It was argued that any animal model must be based on two criteria. First, the target psychopathology must be clearly defined, and secondly, the model and the pathological state should exhibit common abnormalities rather than simply have a superficial similarity in symptomatology. The model described here is of congenital mental retardation and does share with this condition an abnormal morphology in dendritic structure. Thus, it does meet the two criteria. Exposing rats prenatally to antiganglioside antibodies, via the maternal vascular system, creates behavioral deficits during their neonatal and adult life. But such treatment also results in an improved performance, compared to controls, on certain tasks. So in attempting to answer the second question, 'How would one recognize a retarded rat?', these unexpected results have to be taken into account. In doing this, similar results from a number of other studies were first described to demonstrate that the phenomenon of incremental performance following brain abuse was not confined to the model, and an explanation in terms of stimulus processing was given to account for all these data.

Much work has to be done with humans as well as their putative animal models before Kirman's hypothetical etiology of congenital mental retardation is substantiated. Meanwhile, the first-fruits of extrapolating from the model may occur if some regard is paid to the involvement of stimulus processing when choosing tasks to be included in training programs for the mentally retarded.

ACKNOWLEDGMENT

Some of the original work described in this chapter was supported by a grant to the author from the Spastics Society.

REFERENCES

Abramson, L. Y., and Seligman, M. E. P. (1977) Modelling psychopathology in the laboratory: history and rationale, in *Psychopathology: Experimental Models* (eds J. D. Maser and M. E. P. Seligman), pp. 1–26, Freeman, San Francisco.

Adinolfi, M. (1979) The permeability of the blood–CSF barrier during fetal life in man and rat and the effect of brain antibodies on the development of the CNS, in *Protein Transmission Through Living Membranes* (ed. W. A. Hemmings), pp. 349–364, Elsevier–North Holland, Amsterdam.

Adinolfi, M., Rick, J. T., Leibowitz, S., and Gregson, A. N. (1982) Effects of brain antibodies during development and in mature animals, in *Pädiatrische Fortbildungskurse für die Praxis* (ed. E. Köng), Karger, Basel, 178–186.

Auroux, M., and Alnot, M. O. (1968) Perturbations tardines du système nerveux central compatibles avec la vie. II. Etude de la récupération aprés altération chez le rat de la capacité d'apprentissage, *Comptes Rendus de la Societe de Biologie*, **162**, 1261–1264.

Brightman, M. W., and Reese, T. S. (1969) Junctions between intimately opposed cell membranes in the vertebrate brain, *J. cell. Biol.*, **40**, 648–677.

Craik, F. I. M. (1979) Human memory, *Ann. Rev. Psychol.*, **30**, 63–102.

Golding, E. (1980) Non-dominant hemisphere ECT and reasoning, *Bull. Brit. Psychol. Soc.*, **33**, 184.

Golding, E. G., Reich, S. S., and Wason, P. C. (1974) Inter-hemispheric differences in problem solving, *Perception*, **3**, 231–235.

Hebb, D. O. (1961) Distinctive features of learning in the higher animal, in *Brain Mechanisms and Learning* (eds A. Fessard, R. W. Gerard, J. Konorski, and J. F. Delafresnaye), pp. 37–51, Thomas, Springfield Ill.

Hofstein, R., Segal, M. and Samuel, D. (1980) Antibodies to synaptosomal membranes of rat hippocampus and caudate nucleus: immunological and behavioral characteristics, *Exp. Neurol.*, **70**, 307–320.

Huttenlocher, P. R. (1975) Synaptic and dendritic development and mental defect, in *Brain Mechanisms in Mental Retardation* (eds N. A. Buchwald and M. A. B. Brazier), pp. 123–140, Academic Press, New York.

Johnson-Laird, P. N., and Wason, P. C. (1970) A theoretical analysis of insight into a reasoning task, *Cogn. Psychol.*, **1**, 134–148.

Karpiak, S. E., and Rapport, M. M. (1975) Behavioral changes in 2-month-old rats following prenatal exposure to antibodies against synaptic membranes, *Brain Res.*, **92**, 405–413.

Kasarskis, E. J., Karpiak, S. E., Rapport, M. M., Yu, R. K., and Bass, N. H. (1981) Abnormal maturation of cerebral cortex and behavioral deficit in adult rats after neonatal administration of antibodies to ganglioside, *Devel. Brain Res.*, **1**, 25–35.

Kirman, B. H. (1975) Immune reactions as a possible cause of hitherto unclassified encephalopathy and mental retardation, in *Proceedings of the 3rd congress of the International Association for the Scientific Study of Mental Deficiency* (ed. D. Primrose), p. 675, Polish Medical Publishers, Warsaw.

Kriss, A., Blumhardt, L. D., Halliday, A. M., and Pratt, R. T. C. (1978) Neurological asymmetries immediately after unilateral ECT, *J. Neurol. Neurosurg. Psychiat.*, **41**, 1135–1144.

Kuffler, S. W., and Nicholls, J. G. (1976) *From Neuron to Brain*, Sinaver, Sunderland.

Lashley, K. S. (1929) *Brain Mechanisms and Intelligence*, Univ. of Chicago Press, Chicago.

MacPherson, C. F. C., and Shek, R. P. N. (1970) Effect of brain isoantibodies on learning and memory in the rat, *Exp. Neurol.*, **29**, 1–15.

Olton, D. S., and Samuelson, R. J. (1976) Remembrance of places passed: spatial memory in rats, *J. exp. Psychol.*, **2**, 97–116.

Pinneo, L. R. (1966) On noise in the nervous system, *Psychol. Rev.*, **73**, 242–247.

Purpura, D. (1974) Dendriticspine 'dysgenesis' and mental retardation, *Science*, **186**, 1126–1128.

Rick, J. T., Gregson, A., Adinolfo, M., and Leibowitz, S. (1981) The behaviour of immature and mature rats exposed prenatally to antiganglioside antibodies, *J. Neuroimmunol*, 413–419.

Rick, J. T., Gregson, A. N., Leibowitz, S., and Adinolfo, M. (1980) Behavioural changes in adult rats following administration of antibodies against brain gangliosides, *Develop. Med. Child Neurol.*, **22**, 719–724.

Rick, J. T., Oliver, G. W. O., and Kerkut, G. A. (1972) Acquisition, extinction and reacquisition of a conditioned response in the cockroach: the effects of orotic acid, *Quart. J. exp. Psychol.*, **24**, 282–286.

Rick, J. T., Tunnicliff, G., Kerkut, G. A., Fulker, D. W., Wilcock, J., and Broadhurst, P. L. (1971) GABA production in brain cortex related to activity and avoidance behaviour in eight strains of rat, *Brain Res*, **32**, 234–238.

Stevens, R., and Cowey, A. (1973) Effects of dorsal and ventral hippocampal lesions on spontaneous alternation, learned alternation and probability learning in rats, *Brain Res.*, **52**, 203–224.

Sutherland, N. S. (1964) The learning of discriminations by animals, *Endeavour*, **23**, 148–152.

Treisman, M. (1964) Noise and Weber's law: the discrimination of brightness and other dimensions, *Psychol. Rev.*, **71**, 314–330.

Warrington, E. K., and Taylor, A. M. (1973) The contribution of the right temporal lobe in object recognition, *Cortex*, **9**, 152–164.

Wason, P. C. (1966) Reasoning, in *New Horizons in Psychology* (ed. B. M. Foss), Penguin Books, Harmondsworth.

Wiegandt, H. (1967) The subcellular localization of gangliosides in the brain, *J. Neurochem*, **14**, 671–674.

Animal Models of Human Behavior
Edited by G. C. L. Davey
© 1983 John Wiley & Sons Ltd

Chapter 15

Do Animal Studies Tell Us Anything About the Relationship Between Testosterone and Human Aggression?

David BENTON

1. INTRODUCTION

Much of our understanding of human biology has been acquired directly from animal experimentation, or has involved the study of humans using techniques and ideas derived from research using non-human animals. Researchers turn to animals to obtain a variety of advantages; laboratory animals are generally small, cheap, and hardy; they have short life-spans and reproductive cycles that permit a more rapid testing of a hypothesis than would be possible in a human population. Experimentation is more easily controlled when using laboratory animals; the genetic input, pre-natal and post-natal environments can be prescribed; in addition surgical intervention, the use of drugs, and the taking of biological samples is possible. In general the well controlled and designed experimentation typical in animal studies leads to relatively unequivocal results; an outcome frequently precluded in human studies as ethical considerations prevent a satisfactory experimental design.

The role of animal research in the behavioral sciences is more controversial. For example very different views have been taken of the relevance of animal models to our understanding of human aggression. On one hand workers such as Lorenz (1966) draw direct analogies from animals to man, and clearly see the insights derived as important; a position that has been widely criticized (Montagu, 1973). Conversely other workers, who see cultural and social factors as predominant in determing man's behavior, doubt if animal research will tell us much of relevance to the human condition (Tedeschi *et al.*, 1974).

The aim of this chapter is to look at animal and human studies that have examined one representative topic, the importance of androgens in aggression. The objective is to contrast research using different species, using this example to point out some general problems in extrapolating from animals to man.

2. DIFFERENCES AND SIMILARITIES BETWEEN SPECIES

It is vitally important to remember the complexity of human behavior when compared with non-human animals: both similarities and differences between species must be considered if one is to correctly interpret comparative data. One problem that arises is that phenomena that are superficially similar in both man and other animals may not necessarily reflect similar mechanisms, a point that will be illustrated by looking at the early influences of androgens.

It is well accepted that the sexual differentiation of the genitalia in the fetus is controlled by androgens; the absence of androgens leads to the development of the female genitalia; the presence of male hormone stimulates the differentiation of male genitalia (Johnson and Everitt, 1980). Normally only a genetic male is exposed to an early burst of androgens produced by the testes, although in animal studies hormone levels can be manipulated during sensitive periods of development. In the human, aberrant conditions may parallel these phenomena. A more recent, and in the human a more controversial suggestion, is that during development androgens not only produce changes in the genitalia, but, may also lead to changes in the structure of the brain and thus alter the predisposition for characteristically male and female behavior.

2.1. Animal studies

In mice and rats, unlike mammals who have a long gestation period (e.g. primates), the process of differentiation into the male phenotype continues into the first week of post-natal life; thus rodents are susceptible to manipulation of androgens during this first week. As well as controlling the differentiation of genitalia, exposure to androgen during both the prenatal and neonatal periods influences sex-related behavior patterns later in life (Johnson and Everitt, 1980). In mice numerous investigators have reported that males castrated at birth and treated with testosterone in adulthood show reduced inter-male aggression, a normal masculine characteristic (e.g. Edwards, 1969). Equally, the neo-natal exposure of genetic female mice to androgens produces a more masculine response to androgens in adulthood, they respond by becoming aggressive. Thus it seems that during a sensitive period, the presence of androgens change the structure of the brain, predisposing the rodent to act aggressively.

The classical experiment on the behavior of non-human primates was carried out by Goy (1968) who injected pregnant rhesus monkeys with testosterone propionate. As expected, the prenatally administered androgen masculinized the external genitalia of genetic female offspring, although the internal reproductive structures were of normal female type. The behavior of juvenile male monkeys differs from females in particular ways. Male monkeys typically display more rough-and-tumble and chasing play, and threaten more frequently. Those females that had been subjected to prenatal androgen tended to display the more typically masculine behaviors. In addition, the mounting frequencies of the prenatally androgenized females were similar to those produced by male controls and exceeded those of female controls. As these behaviors were observed in juveniles subjected to only the low levels of testosterone produced by the adrenals, it is suggested that the central nervous system had been functionally modified. Eaton et al. (1973) extended the work by looking at the behavior of the adult animals. The pre-natally androgenized females were ovariectomized, and when their behavior was recorded they displayed a higher number of potentially injurious attacks than control animals. The further administration of testosterone in adulthood induced overt aggression, threat, sexual exploration and display only in those females prenatally androgenized. These workers concluded that the administration of testosterone to the pregnant rhesus monkey predisposes the genetic female to acquire predominantly masculine patterns of behavior, by modifying the brain during development.

2.2. Human studies

Ethical considerations often preclude the possibility of human experimentation in this area. There are, however, a number of clinical syndromes that in some ways parallel the early androgenization data in animals. These include the adrenogenital syndrome (AGS), progestin-induced hermaphroditism, and the androgen-insensitivity syndrome. In the first two cases the female fetus is exposed to male hormones with a consequent masculinization of the genitalia; the effect varies from a mildly enlarged clitoris to an empty scrotum and normally-appearing penis. The adrenogenital syndrome results from a recessive gene that induces the adrenal gland to produce abnormally high levels of male hormone (Lee et al., 1977). The prescription of progestins to prevent a miscarriage produces the second syndrome, masculinization being a side-effect. Treatment includes the surgical removal of the male genitalia from the genetic female and in addition those suffering from the adrenogenital syndrome will have cortisone administered over the rest of their lifetime.

Most of the data concerning the behavioral concomitants of the early androgenization of the human female come from two research programs. Money at Johns Hopkins University studied 15 girls with AGS who were diagnosed and treated early in life and were compared with matched controls (Money and Ehrhardt, 1968). Another set of 17 girls were studied in Buffalo; they were compared with unaffected siblings (Ehrhardt and Baker, 1974). The AGS samples preferred boys' toys and had little interest in dolls, they liked active outdoor sports and wore boys' clothes. The AGS girls showed little interest in infants, something not typical of the control subjects; marriage and motherhood were less frequently seen as important whereas a career was often stressed. Fifty-nine percent of the Buffalo sample were identified as tomboys, something not said of any of the unaffected siblings.

Although the AGS was associated with a tendency to display behavior and express attitudes more usual of male children, there was no evidence that sexual identity was a problem, none of the subjects wished to change their gender. In later life the AGS patients did not display higher levels of aggression, they were not more likely to be leaders or to be dominant over others (Money and Schwartz, 1976). The conclusion of Money and Ehrhardt was that there may well be a hormonal influence in the fetus but it is limited in scope, and does not approach a complete psychosexual reversal of the genetic female.

It is always possible that any differences associated with the AGS are mediated via some mechanism other than hormones. For this reason the parallels between AGS and progestin-induced hermaphroditism are important. To prevent spontaneous abortion some mothers have been given progestins that sometimes have androgenic properties. The behavior of these progestin-masculinized girls is very similar to the AGS; they were also tomboys, preferring boys' toys and clothes, perceiving careers rather than marriage as important (Ehrhardt and Money, 1967).

Genetic males suffering from the androgen insensitivity syndrome are born with a normal female appearance. It may be a failure to menstruate that produces the first clue that the syndrome exists; this will occur despite the normal development of breasts and feminine secondary sexual characteristics. The condition is associated with a defective androgen-binding protein molecule that means the androgen, although present, is not recognized by the body. Money and his colleagues have studied 18 of these cases, 15 raised as women and three as men. Those patients raised as women conform to the female gender role; they preferred dolls to other toys and enjoyed caring for infants (Money and Ehrhardt, 1972). They repeatedly had dreams and fantasies about raising children and strongly desired marriage. Their intellectual abilities followed a female pattern, they displayed higher scores on verbal than non-verbal intelligence tests (Masica et al., 1969).

2.3. The similarities and differences in the androgenization of humans and sub-humans

As the hypothesis that early androgenization may influence later behavior was derived from animal studies and only later examined in humans, there is a natural tendency to look for similarities between the results obtained from different species. For those predisposed to find them there are clear parallels between the perinatal androgenization studies in rodents, humans, and non-human primates. In all these species the fetal differentiation of genitalia is androgen dependent; the addition of these hormones to genetic females masculinizes the genitalia; the removal of androgens from genetic males produces a female structure. There are also parallels in the resulting behavior: at least during childhood the human female subjected to prenatal androgens is tomboyish; the rhesus monkey similarly treated displays the rough-and-tumble play more typical of the juvenile male.

It can be argued, however, that it is not only the similarities between species that should be examined but also the differences. The drawing of simple analogies from man and other animals ignores the added complexities that characterize man. These differences between human and other animals have led Scott (1970) to conclude that '. . . no direct analogies (of agonistic behaviors) from any other species to man are justified'.

It is difficult to exclude non-hormonal mechanisms when examining the human data in this area. Will parents bringing up a daughter born with a phallus treat her in a similar way to a normal daughter? Will the masculine appearance produce the expectation that the daughter will become a tomboy, something that becomes a self-fulfilling prophecy? Will the child's self-image be altered by her abnormal anatomy? Ehrhardt and Baker (1974) examined 17 AGS females, of whom six received surgery in the first year of life, seven between one and three years of age, and four later in life. In the cases in which surgery was carried out relatively late in life it is likely that there is some psychological reaction to the abnormality.

Parental attitudes are difficult to discount in these studies particularly when examining interview data. In these studies the measures used are often not based on observed behavior, rather the opinions of the parent are examined in an interview. The human data are essentially that AGS patients are perceived by their parents as more tomboyish. The question remains as to the origin of the perception of these children. Are they displaying altered behavior, or is it the parent's perception that is altered? If the behavior is different, is this due to the style of parental upbringing, or to hormonal mediated changes of the brain?

An argument in favor of a hormonal explanation of the human behavioral changes that follow androgenization is provided by Lloyd Morgan's canon. He proposed that 'in no case may we interpret an action as the outcome of the exercise of a higher psychical faculty if it can be interpreted as the outcome of the exercise of one that stands lower in the psychological scale': complex mentalistic explanations should be avoided where simpler explanations can suffice. Should we then explain the androgenization data in biological terms because this is a simpler explanation? Does the consistency of cross-species data demand the simpler biological explanation? The clinical nature of the human data precludes any definite conclusion, the uncontrolled nature of studies makes it impossible to decide between biological or psychological explanations (or some combination). The possibility of an unequivocal conclusion is prevented by the ethical problems associated with designing well controlled experiments. However, the general impression that man is largely a product of his culture makes it unlikely that a hormonal influence is the only mechanism in this instance.

A further problem arises from the distinguishing of characteristically male and female behaviors. It may be reasonable to distinguish characteristic sexual and aggressive behavior patterns in rodents but the existence of such stereotyped behaviors are not typical of man. Even in the rodent aggression is not an unitary phenomenon (Moyer, 1968). Is it reasonable to describe any human behavior as characteristically male? Cultural factors are vital in determining the form of particular aggressive acts. Differences between the sexes, to a large extent, reflect differences in children's rearing patterns and the resulting sex-role they take in society.

3. THE REDUCTIONIST APPROACH

Another problem in looking at animals and their biology and extending the findings to humans results from the implied model of man. To what extent is it useful to view humans as biological machines; can psychological processes be adequately identified with biological mechanisms? If human behavior so largely reflects experience, is it sensible to seek biological explanations based on animals that differ from man in terms of their linguistic and cognitive powers?

Infra-human species transmit threat through a relatively limited range of facial expressions, postures, or vocalizations. The ritualized threat, attack, and submissive behavior can be identified; these often occur in specific contexts. The species characteristic nature of these aggressive behaviors facilitate any study of their biological concomitants. It seems possible that species-characteristic threat postures, for example, may be hard-wired into the brain and they may respond to particular neurochemicals; thus study at a biological level becomes possible.

The added complexities of the human need to be recognized. Man's behavior is not so stereotyped; he has invented tools such as swords, guns,

bombs, and missiles; he fights over symbolic goals such as religion or freedom; by language he can convey an infinite range of wishes and intentions
to others; he can see insult or innuendo where others do not; he may hold
a grudge or take revenge long after a triggering event. The cognitive, cultural,
and linguistic developments that are so characteristic of man suggest that
purely biological approaches to his behavior may prove untenable.

The question is whether human psychological processes can be adequately
identified with biological mechanisms? A particular set of problems are
associated with the relationship betwen different levels of explanation. It is
usual to refer to these latter problems as the problem of reductionism. Within
psychology it is possible to distinguish two diametrically opposed viewpoints.
Some argue that any real explanation is psychology must be reductionist in
nature. The opposite is also argued, that all reductionist explanations are in
principle impossible.

Jessor (1958) describes the essence of reductionism in four related
propositions:

(1) That several disciplines can be ordered in a hierarchy; for example
    physics would appear at the bottom followed at higher levels by chem-
    istry, biology, psychology, and sociology. Other discriminations could
    be made, for example social psychology could be added, although in fact
    there are no sharp breaks between sciences.
(2) The terms, laws and concepts of one discipline can be translated into
    those of another without loss of meaning.
(3) These deductions proceed in one direction, from lower to higher levels
    in the hierarchy. Thus the term 'reductionism' implies that the laws of
    the higher discipline are 'reduced' to those of a lower one. In the present
    example, one may understand human aggression in terms of biology; the
    role of testosterone being one of many biological factors involved.
(4) The final proposition is that lower level explanations give a more
    fundamental or basic explanation of the phenomenon in question.

Naturally not everybody who wishes to take a reductionist position would
subscribe to all the propositions; they do however serve as a useful definition
for the purpose of discussion.

3.1. In favor of reductionism

Krech (1950) discussed the nature and role of hypothetical constructs in
psychological theory. By a hypothetical construct he meant something that
was centrally located and actually existed. Krech argues that a purely psychological approach cannot produce hypothetical constructs. Psychological con-

structs such as expectations, tensions, or aggressiveness can be studied only by psychological analysis. Such theorists will deny that psychological constructs are only shorthand terms for certain behavior patterns, rather they are using them as hypothetical constructs; the theorists deny that they refer to conscious experiences, rather they refer to processes that lie behind the experience; they will deny that they are names for neurological activities. If these are the characteristics of psychological constructs then how, Krech (1950) asks, can they be empirically investigated? The acceptance of a purely psychological psychology seemingly places the constructs in a domain that is inaccessible to scientific inquiry. This approach offers no way of going beyond the correlating of stimulus and response. Many psychologists are content to use this descriptive, operational approach, but many others go further to postulate hypothetical constructs.

The physiological psychologist behaves very similarly to the psychological psychologist except he seeks an alliance with biology in locating his construct. If we say that aggressiveness or sexual motivation is related to the presence of testosterone, Krech (1950) would argue that we are saying that the behavior is both a biological and psychological event, and he would ask why we cannot be content with the former alone. The answer usually given is that there is more to sex and aggression than purely biological events. But what is this something more that we seek? Does a hypothetical construct need the attributes of the events it controls? There has been a tendency in psychology to assume that it does but it is not necessarily the case. For example, the genetic code for blue eyes contains no element of blueness, therefore does the biological mechanism that leads to aggression need to have all aspects usually associated with that behavior? This seems to be a critical difference between those who do and do not advocate reductionist approaches. Those who attempt reductionistic solutions describe behavior using the language of biology; they would not see an inability to describe all behavioral concepts in terms of biology as being crucial. They would say that we are our brains and thus the study of the brain (necessarily at a biological level) is adequate for a complete study of behavior.

When posed in its extreme form the reductionist argument leads to an infinite regression. If psychology should be reduced to biology then in turn this should be reduced to chemistry and physics. The alternative to this absurd procedure is the arbitrary claim that explanations should be sought at a level one lower than the phenomena under study. This solution creates the strange position in which sociologists are happy with psychological explanations but psychologists are forced to a biological level. Miller (1981) takes up a slightly less extreme position, he believes that the 'laws of psychology can in principle be translated into a reductionist form involving a lower level of explanation but that this by no means ensures that such a reduction is either desirable or useful within a given context'.

3.2. The problems of reductionism

Both Jessor (1958) and Bannister (1968) take a very different view, they argue that in principle reductionist explanations are impossible. A central argument is that a psychological view of behavior reflects an organism–environment interaction. Psychology requires the specification of particular environmental contexts and therefore excludes physiological study as there are no terms in biology with which to describe the external environment. The languages of physiology and psychology are different; they deal with different phenomena. If you ask the question why somebody was aggressively punched by another then very different answers can be given. A biological explanation could be given in terms of nerve impulses and muscle contractions. A psychological explanation may involve terms such as insult, grudge, or defense. It is argued that the latter type of explanation cannot be stated in terms of the former, the language is inappropriate.

Bannister (1968) tries to explain why physiological psychology seems so popular an area of research when he considers that the results are so unscientific and meaningless. He suggests that many psychologists behave as if carrying out experiments itself constitutes a science. Popper (1959) suggests that the purpose of an experiment for a scientist is to demonstrate a point in an integrated argument. Bannister questions whether experiments in physiological psychology can be said to satisfy the purpose described by Popper. Frequently both psychological and physiological concepts are defined operationally and then a correlation is demonstrated. The problem with this procedure is that it omits the necessary stage of discussing the logical relationship between the concepts. The finding of a logical relationship is precluded by the different languages of the biology and psychology. The approach of physiological psychology confuses technology with science. The finding of a significant relationship does not itself have intrinsic merit, it must provide a contribution to an ongoing theoretical argument. There is little point in demonstrating a statistical significance that lacks logical significance (Bannister, 1968).

3.3. The example of androgens and aggression

How useful are the above comments to our understanding of studies on androgens and aggression? Some examples may help answer this question. Having derived from animal studies the hypothesis that testosterone levels and aggression are related, similar phenomena have been sought in humans. One strategy is to examine individuals who have displayed an unusually high level of aggression, usually prisoners or mentally ill patients.

Kreuz and Rose (1972) took blood samples and related the level of plasma testosterone to both prison and past criminal behavior. Incidents of fighting and verbal aggression while in prison did not relate to testosterone. However, those men with high levels of testosterone tended to have committed violent crimes during adolescence. Persky *et al.* (1978) reported a positive correlation between androgen production, as estimated by urinary 17-ketosteroids, and aggression as assessed by medical staff. Kendenberg *et al.* (1973) reported a similar relationship, a positive correlation between testosterone and 'ethologically' observed non-verbal behavior in psychiatric patients. Rada *et al.* (1976) distinguished rapists in terms of the degree of violence they used; those who were 'brutally violent' had significantly higher levels of circulating testosterone than those who only used threats.

A different approach was taken by Mazur and Lamb (1980) who found that human males who had won a tennis match or received medical degrees had raised levels of testosterone. There are analogies with non-human primates (Rose *et al.*, 1975) and rodents (Schuurman, 1980) in which a rise in social status is associated with higher levels of circulating testosterone.

The above approaches have used Bannister's model (1968); androgen activity must be seen as having been operationally defined, the majority of studies have taken a single or relatively few hormone samples. As it is known that there are substantial fluctuations over time this is a risky procedure (Doering *et al.*, 1974). In addition only a small amount of circulating testosterone is free, the majority is bound to protein. It may be that rather than measuring testosterone, other metabolites or ratios of metabolites may be more appropriate. The term aggression is operationalized by taking some limited measure of criminal or psychiatric behavior. It is instructive that hormone levels were related to some of these measures of aggression and not others; it is clear that we are not dealing with an unitary phenomenon.

Is it true that the correlations between testosterone and these measures of aggression are significant only in terms of statistics and they lack any logical or theoretical importance as Bannister (1968) suggests? There is a sense in which this statement contains an element of truth but to say that the correlation is of no interest is perhaps an overstatement of the case. Man is to such a large extent a social, cultural, and political animal that much of his behavior can only be understood at this level of analysis. For example, a biologist may be able to tell us little about a Palestinian terrorist who shoots somebody while hijacking a plane. On the other hand, a study of history and politics will give considerable insight into this terrorist's actions. Jessor's (1958) propositions that underlie reductionism include the statement that a higher level of analysis can be understood in terms of a lower level; should we, in theory at least, be able to understand the history of Palestine in terms of biology? If we assume that memory involves a structural change in neuronal pathways is it in theory at least possible to map that terrorist's view of the history of his people? It is obvious that because of the complexity and dynamics of the electrical and chemical characteristics of the brain, that we would not choose this approach for pragmatic reasons, yet is it theoretically possible? For those who argue against reductionism one problem they point to is that the language we use to describe behavior is not translatable without loss of meaning into chemical and neurophysiological terms. To say that the terrorist took part in the hijacking because of his level of testosterone (if it is true) or because of the action of neuronal pathways, immediately looses the considerable insight that comes from the historical, social, and political analysis. As Bannister (1968) suggests, it is impossible to logically integrate the biology and behavior; the differences in language preclude a statement that involve both types of language.

Another problem is that the concepts used by the historian to describe the Palestinian may not exist in the brain of the terrorist himself. The terms we use to describe the behavior of another are simplified abstractions that we as human beings use to classify and understand a complex world. As an analogy, if my car is old and I need a new one, a policeman may see me as a potential traffic hazard; a car salesman may see me as a potential customer; and my bank manager as a poor credit risk. There is no center in the brain or hormone that relates to being a traffic hazard, potential customer, or credit risk. The term aggression can be seen in the human in a similar way, as a crude abstraction that does not reflect basic biology but rather the simple minded way we force the world into categories in an attempt to understand.

A further problem about the reductionist approach is summarized in the statement 'the whole is greater than the sum of the parts'. As another analogy, a man from Mars may take a 'biological' approach to the study of a motor car and look at nuts, bolts, and sparking plugs. No matter how long the Martian studied the car he would not predict the need for a traffic warden or understand the status associated with owning a Rolls-Royce. Not only would predictions from a lower to a higher level be impossible but the reductionist proposal that one could understand a higher level of analysis in terms of a lower level is untenable. How could you describe status or a traffic warden in the 'biological terms' of nuts and bolts?

However, those who wish to suggest that a reductionist approach can tell us nothing may be overstating the case. The impact of the motor car on society may not be understandable in terms of nuts and bolts but it would not take place without them. It may be that on occasions the nuts and bolts approach is the appropriate one. A traffic jam may be the result of the mechanical failure of one car, or it may be the consequence of a social phenomenon, for example a public holiday when many people drive to the beach. In the former case the full social consequences of the traffic jam will be ignored if you only look at the engine, but those wishing to solve the problem will do well to take such an approach. If you can demonstrate that tumors in particular areas of the brain or a hormonal imbalance results in extreme violent and irrational behavior then there is place for the reductionist approach. It is, however, questionable whether much of man's behavior that can be labeled aggressive is best examined at this level. His social and cultural nature suggests that the nuances of behavior are best understood at higher level of analysis in the majority of situations.

3.4. Human castration: a successful reductionist approach?

In animal studies the usual way of demonstrating a causal relationship between androgens and behavior is by castration and subsequent replacement of the hormone. Following castration the decline in behavior is monitored; the implanting of a source of hormone will typically result in the reappearance of the particular behavior (Benton, 1981). The importance of androgens in the genesis of intermale aggression is not disputed, castration decreases intermale aggression in a wide range of submammalian vertebrates (Beach, 1948). However, even in rodents hormones are not uniquely important, Lee and Narango (1974) found that the social status of a mouse was important in determining the effect of replacing testosterone following castration.

Obvious ethical considerations preclude the use of castration in a human experimental design; however, interesting data has resulted from its use in the treatment of violent sex offenders. More recently various hormone analogs that produce a 'chemical castration' have been the method of choice. Sturup (1968) summarizes the results from six European countries, where a total of 3186 rapists have been treated by castration. When followed up the rate of recidivism was only 2.2 percent. There are, however, problems associated with these data. It is not clear to what extent a placebo effect may be involved, the replacing of testosterone is not ethically possible as it may result in assaults on women or children. The diminished sexual drive reported in follow-up interviews may be only the socially expected response of an ex-prisoner who does not want to return to jail. Heim and Hursch (1979) have cast doubt on the assumption that castration decreases libido and that it is this mechanism that leads to a decrease in sexual violence. Many workers in this area fail to remove subjects who were sexually inactive prior to castration from their sample. Bremer (1959) was one researcher who did remove such a group and found they accounted for almost 20 percent of his sample. Other workers have reported that 10 percent (Cornu, 1973) and 18 percent (Langeluddeke, 1963) of the castrates reported no adverse influence on their sex drives. The increasing age of the subjects could itself be expected to produce a decline in sexual interest.

In sub-human animals castration very clearly decreases both sexual and aggressive behavior; however, it seems that as one goes higher up the evolutionary scale, the influence of hormones decreases. The argument for castrating humans who have committed sexual crimes is derived from animal studies. The prediction was that castration would decrease both sexual and aggressive behavior. Yet, the evidence that in the human male castration destroys sexual drive has not been conclusively demonstrated (Heim and Hursch, 1979). Relatively little attention has been given to aggression of a non-sexual nature but Bremer (1959), one of the few workers to comment on this matter, concluded that although castration had beneficial effects on aberrant sexual behavior it should not be used when the desired effect was the reduction of aggressive or anti-social behavior.

The difficulty of the reductionist approach to human behavior is clearly illustrated by this example. It is impossible to keep the argument to one level of analysis. Man's cognitive nature interacts with any biological manipulation. The sex offender who is castrated knows why it has been carried out, he expects certain changes; these expectations can become self-fulfilling prophecies, part of a placebo effect. This inevitability of dealing with more than one level of analysis when dealing with biological manipulations of humans brings us back to the problems associated with trying to integrate two autonomous languages, one associated with behavior and one associated with biology. There is no way of integrating statements about testosterone and the placebo phenomenon.

It seems a safe generalization that the nearer to humans you get in an evolutionary sense, then the influence of hormones become smaller. For this reason alone it is unsafe to generalize from sub-human animals. The animal studies may suggest hypotheses but it is not safe to assume that the effect will be observed in humans. Only human experimentation would allow that conclusion but then one is limited for ethical reasons to relatively ill-designed and poorly controlled studies.

3.5. The way forward?

Jahoda (1981) commented that the 'statement "everything is reducible" is in the end a metaphysical statement. I do not have anything against metaphysical statements—indeed I believe that they are at the root of all our various approaches to psychology—but they cannot be "argued" '. It is unlikely that philosophers will stop debating the merits of a reductionist approach but practicing scientists tend to take up a position that reflects their training and interests. Rose (1981) has summarized a number of possible approaches.

(1) Each discipline could stick to questions appropriate to its own level of analysis. This type of solution would be favored by those who believe that human behavior can only be understood at a psychological level of analysis (Bannister, 1968). A side-effect of accepting this answer is that all physiological psychologists and many biologists would become unemployed; for this reason alone (but also for philosophical reasons and because of their own perception of the success of the approach) they will find this unacceptable.

This solution precludes the study of the biological basis of behavior as different levels of analysis are necessarily interrelated. The very clear evidence in studies of male rodents that the removal and subsequent replacement of testosterone produces characteristic changes in some measures of aggression, reinforces the view that the hormone and behavior can be meaningfully studied. The hypothesis that a similar relationship may exist in man is thus suggested, although it awaits further study before we can be sure of the conclusion.

(2) A second approach is to allow causal relationships to run both ways through the hierarchy of sciences. Thus molecular events can be seen to 'cause' behavior, and behavioral events can 'cause' molecular events. Rose (1981) summarizes this as 'an Anglo-Saxon pragmatic solution which binds all the contradictions with a dash of common sense and a hearty reef knot— hoping no-one will notice it is really a granny'. Certainly this solution ignores the problems of characteristic languages that are associated with particular levels of explanation. To say that testosterone 'causes' aggressive behavior confuses a biological and a behavioral concept. Few workers would wish to argue that testosterone has such a mechanistic role in behavior.

(3) A third alternative is to classify phenomena as *either* biological *or* behavioral, as with the distinction between organic and functional psychoses. Thus one decides the level of analysis that is appropriate for a particular type of phenomenon. We have already seen that in rodents prior successful fighting, and in man general expectation, can influence the role of testosterone. It seems impossible to choose only one level of analysis to understand the role of testosterone in aggressive behavior.

(4) The final solution offered by Rose is to see each level as offering a different description of the same phenomenon. Thus biochemical events do not 'cause' behavioral events but are synonymous with them, in a different language system. Rose (1981) proposes that the word 'cause' can only be properly applied within a given level. It seems wise to see testosterone as not 'causing' aggression but as modulating certain biological phenomena both centrally and peripherally.

One problem is that there seems to be an inevitability that levels of analysis will be confused; Rose suggested that a biological description is an alternative to a behavioral description; however with humans this alternative has repeatedly proved impossible. The adrenogenital syndrome data involved not only the discussion of perinatal hormones but also the attitudes of child and parents to the resulting effects. It was impossible to distinguish the hormonal effects that followed human castration from previous experience and expectations. Even in rodents prior experience was important (Lee and Naranjo, 1974). The argument that you are confusing different types of language seems reasonable yet unavoidable.

4. WHAT IS THE ROLE OF ANIMAL STUDIES?

Hinde (1974) concluded that animal studies can help the understanding of human behavior only to a limited extent, but suggested three possible roles. First, animal studies can help in the development of scientific methods that may later be adapted for human use. This is the norm in many areas of medical science and much of our knowledge of endocrinology has been gained in this way. Secondly, animals can be used in particular experiments where ethical considerations preclude the use of humans. A clear example is the study of the early influence of androgens on adult behavior. The human studies are often limited to chance abnormalities such as the adrenogenital syndrome. These chance occurrences are extremely interesting but lack the precision of experimental design that allows an unequivocal conclusion to be drawn. In contrast well controlled animal studies clearly demonstrate that early hormones do influence adult behavior. Unfortunately the added complexity associated with human cognitive powers suggest that superficially similar results in animals and humans may not reflect identical mechanisms. It was clear that in the case of the adrenogenital syndrome one cannot necessarily conclude that the tomboyish behavior that results reflects only hormonal modulation or a hormonal mechanism at all.

Finally, Hinde (1974) suggests that the study of animal behavior can provide principles or generalizations whose relevance to man can be subsequently assessed. More specifically the hypothesis that testosterone may have a role in human aggressive behavior was derived from animal studies. The findings concerning the role of testosterone in animals demanded that the hypothesis be examined in humans.

The enormous gap between animals and humans makes the drawing of analogies a dangerous process. Scott (1979) concluded that it is highly probable that biological bases of human aggressive behavior exist, but it is equally probable that because of the unique human genetic composition no direct analogies from other species are justified. The animal data suggest the hypotheses, but it is human data that is critical when drawing implications for man. Paradoxically, it is the same relative simplicity of animals that makes it so difficult to draw analogies to man that is is one of the major strengths of animal studies. Because non-human animals are more simple than humans it is easier to see the importance of particular mechanisms, to derive hypotheses: they can then be tested in human studies. The impossibility of carrying out well controlled experiments using humans inevitably leaves us unable to draw firm conclusions.

5. SUMMARY

Some general problems associated with the extrapolation of data from animals to man are discussed using for illustrative purposes the relationship between testosterone and aggression. Although there are some superficial similarities between the human and animal data, it is concluded that it is unwise to generalize between species. Animal studies have the important role of suggesting possible relationships between biological mechanisms and behavior; however, the cognitive and cultural nature of the human race makes it essential to study them before commenting on their condition.

REFERENCES

Bannister, D. (1968) The myth of physiological psychology. *Bull. Brit. Psychol. Soc.*, **21**, 229–231.

Beach, F. A. (1948) *Hormones and Behavior*. Hoeber, New York.

Benton, D. (1981) The extrapolation from animals to man: The example of testosterone and aggression. In *Multidisciplinary Approaches to Aggression Research* (eds P. F. Brain and D. Benton). pp. 402–418, Elsevier/North Holland, Amsterdam.

Brain, P. F. (1981) Differentiating types of attack and defense in rodents. In *Multidisciplinary Approaches to Aggression Research* (eds P. F. Brain and D. Benton). pp. 54–78, Elsevier/North Holland, Amsterdam.

Bremer, J. (1959) *Sexualization: A Follow-up Study of 244 Cases*. Macmillan, New York.

Cornu, F. (1973) *Catamnestic studies on castrated sex delinquents from a forensic-psychiatric viewpoint*. Karger, Basel.

Doering, C. H., Brodie, H. K. H., Kraemer, H., Becker, H., and Hamburg, D. A. (1974) Plasma testosterone levels and psychologic measures in men over a two-month period. In *Sex Differences in Behavior* (eds R. L. Friedman, R. M. Richart, and R. L. Van de Wiele). pp. 413–431, John Wiley, New York.

Eaton, G. G., Goy, R. W., and Phoenix, C. H. (1973) Effects of testosterone treatment in adulthood on sexual behavior of female pseudohermaphrodite rhesus monkeys. *Nature New Biol.*, **242**, 119–120.

Edwards, D. A. (1969) Early androgen stimulation and aggressive bahavior in male and female mice. *Physiol. Behav.*, **18**, 539–543.

Ehrhardt, A. A., and Baker, S. W. (1974) Fetal androgens, human central nervous system differentiation and behavior sex differences. In *Sex Differences in Behavior* (eds R. L. Friedman, R. M. Richart, and R. L. Van de Wiele). pp. 33–51, John Wiley, New York.

Ehrhardt, A. A., and Money, J. (1967) Progestin-induced hermaphroditism: I.Q. and psychosexual identity in a study of ten girls. *J. Sex Res.*, **3**, 83–100.

Goy, R. W. (1968) Organizing effects of androgen on the behaviour of rhesus monkeys. In *Endocrinology and Human Behaviour* (ed. R. P. Michael). pp. 12–31, Oxford University Press, London.

Heim, N., and Hursch, C. J. (1979) Castration for sex offenders: Treatment or punishment? A review and critique of recent European literature. *Arch. Sex. Behav.*, **8**, 281–304.

Hinde, R. A. (1974) *Biological bases of human social behavior*. McGraw-Hill, New York.

Jahoda, M. (1981) Discussion of Miller E., Neuropsychology and the relationship between brain and behaviour. In *Models of Man* (eds A. J. Chapman and D. M. Jones). British Psychological Society, Leicester.

Jessor, R. (1958) The problem of reductionism in psychology. *Psychol. Rev.*, **65**, 170–178.

Johnson, M., and Everitt, B. (1980) *Essential Reproduction*. Blackwell, Oxford.

Kendenberg, D., Kendenberg, N., and Kling, A. (1973) An ethological study in a patient group. Unpublished work described by Kling, A. (1975). Testosterone and aggressive behavior in man and non-human primates. In *Hormonal Correlates of Behavior*, Vol. I (eds B. E. Eleftheriou, and R. L. Sprott). pp. 305–323, Plenum Press, New York.

Krech, D. (1950) Dynamic systems, psychological fields, and hypothetical constructs. *Psychol. Rev.*, **57**, 283–290.

Kreuz, L. E. and Rose, R. M. (1972) Assessment of aggressive behavior and plasma testosterone in a young criminal population. *Psychosom. Med.*, **34**, 321–332.

Langeluddeke, A. (1963) *Castration of Sexual Criminals*. deGruyter, Berlin.

Lee, L. T., and Naranjo, N. (1974) Effects of castration and androgen on the social dominance of BALB/cJ mice. *Physiol. Psychol.*, **2**, 93–98.

Lee, P. A., Plotnick, L. P., and Migeon, L. J. (eds). (1977) *Congenital Adrenal Hyperphasia*. University Park Press, Baltimore, MD.

Lorenz, K. (1966) *On Aggression*. Harcourt, Brace and World, New York.

Masica, D. N., Money, J., Ehrhardt, A. A., and Lewis, U. G. (1969) I.Q., fetal sex hormones and cognitive patterns: Studies in testicular feminizing syndrome of androgen insensitivity. *Johns Hopkins Med. J.*, **124**, 34–43.

Mazur, A., and Lamb, T. A. (1980) Testosterone status and mood in human males. *Horm. Behav.*, **14**, 236–246.

Miller, E. (1981) Neuropsychology and the relationship between brain and behavior. In *Models of Man* (eds A. J. Chapman and D. M. Jones). pp. 75–83, British Psychological Society, Leicester.

Money, J., and Ehrhardt, A. A. (1968) Prenatal hormonal exposure: Possible effects on behaviour in man. In *Endocrinology and Human Behaviour* (ed. R. P. Michael). pp. 32–48, Oxford University Press, London.

Money, J., and Ehrhardt, A. A. (1972) *Man and Woman, Boy and Girl*. Johns Hopkins University Press, Baltimore, MD.

Money, J., and Schwartz, M. (1976) Fetal androgens in the early treated adrenogenital syndrome of 46, XX hermaphroditism: Influence on assertive and aggressive types of behavior. *Aggressive Behav.*, **2**, 19–30.

Montagu, A. (1973) *Man and Aggression*, 2nd edition. Oxford University Press, London.

Moyer, K. E. (1968) Kinds of aggression and their physiological basis. *Commun. Behav. Biol.*, **2**, 65–87.

Persky, H., Zuckerman, M., and Curtis, G. C. (1978) Endocrine function in emotionally disturbed and normal men. *J. Nerv. Ment. Dis.*, **146**, 488–497.

Popper, K. R. (1959) *The Logic of Scientific Discovery*. Hutchinson, London.

Rada, R. T., Laws, D. R., and Kellner, R. (1976) Plasma testosterone in the rapist. *Psychosom. Med.*, **38**, 257–268.

Rose, S. P. R. (1981) From causations to translations: What biochemists can contribute to the study of behavior. In *Perspectives in Ethology*, Vol. 4. pp. 157–177, Plenum, New York.

Rose, R., Bernstein, I., and Gordon, T. (1975) Consequences of social conflict on plasma testosterone levels in rhesus monkeys. *Psychosom. Med.*, **37**, 50–61.

Scott, J. P. (1970) Biology and human aggression. *Am. J. Orthopsychiat.*, **40**, 568–576.

Schuurman, T. (1980) Hormonal correlates of agonistic behavior in adult male rats. In *Adaptive Capabilities of the Nervous System, Progress in Brain Research*, Vol. 53 (eds P. S. McConnell, G. J. Boer, H. J. Romijn, N. E. van de Poll, and M. A. Corner). Elsevier/North Holland, Amsterdam.

Sturup, G. K. (1968) Treatment of sexual offenders in Herstedvester Denmark: The rapist. *Acta Psychiatrica Scand.*, **44**, Suppl. 204.

Tedeschi, J. T., Smith, R. B., and Brown, R. C. (1974) A reinterpretation of research on aggression. *Psychol. Bull.*, **81**, 540–562.

Chapter 16

Psychosurgery and Brain–behavior Relationships in Animals

Douglas CARROLL and Mark A. J. O'CALLAGHAN

1. INTRODUCTION

Students of human brain–behavior relationships have frequently resorted to the study of non-human species. There are sound practical and ethical grounds for such recourse and data of considerable interest and significance can be exhibited. Kolb and Wilshaw (1980) indicated three broad areas of inquiry where lessons have been drawn from the examination of non-human subjects. First of all, in the elucidation of fundamental neurophysiological principles and mechanisms, animal research has proved particularly informative. Secondly, the investigation of selected non-human species has permitted insight into the phylogenetic context of human cerebral organization. Thirdly, animal research has inspired models of human pathology and disorder.

Although only the last of these will occupy us here, it is generally the case that all cross-species extrapolation hinges on the assumption of essential continuity among species. However, while this is undoubtedly a quite proper assumption in the context of basic neurophysiological processes, it may be much less so when dealing with pathological states, particularly those characterized mainly or exclusively by complex behavioral adjustments. It would seem reasonable to expect a deal of caution when animals are allowed to stand for humans in matters of behavioral pathology. Not only are the assumptions of continuity likely, as indicated, to be less reliable, but the decidedly more direct implications for therapeutic intervention substantially aggravate the consequences of error.

With this in mind let us examine in some detail the background and validity of one particular therapeutic intervention—psychosurgery. It hardly needs stating that in matters of therapeutic validity two areas of information require close scrutiny. One relates to the effectiveness of the therapy. Here the questions are essentially empirical. Does the therapy work? The other concerns the theoretical underpinnings of the therapy. It is the latter which will primarily concern us, and in particular the role played by animal brain–behavior research in the development of psychosurgery and the scientific rationales that have attended its practice. Reference to efficacy, though, can hardly be avoided, and data from an extensive and detailed analysis of psychosurgical studies will be summarized later in this presentation.

2. DEFINING PSYCHOSURGERY

However, at the outset it is necessary to clarify the activities subsumed under the term psychosurgery. Since the whole area remains the subject of considerable controversy and contention, it is hardly surprising to find that the boundaries of the interventions properly characterized as psychosurgery do not attract consensus. Mark and Ordia (1976), for example, argued that psychosurgery has become 'a catchword intended to stir up emotions and produce irrational and harmful obstruction in the path of patients seeking treatment' (p. 725). For present purposes we shall largely abide by the definition given by Stone (1975), in the Massachusetts Task Force Report on psychosurgery. Stone defined psychosurgery as 'any procedure which, by direct or indirect access to the brain, removes or destroys or interrupts the continuity of brain tissue that is histologically normal (i.e., tissue that is normal as seen under the microscope, though its physiological functions or properties might obviously be abnormal) for the purpose of altering behavior or treating a psychiatric illness' (p. 27). Stone went on to catalog some exclusions, 'we do not include neurosurgical procedures designed to diagnose or treat intractable physical pain or epilepsy where these conditions are clearly demonstrable. Nor do we include any other neurosurgical procedures used to diagnose or treat organic brain conditions even though such procedures may also involve destruction of normal brain tissue' (p. 28).

Stone's definition is adopted because it is clear and explicit and because it proved acceptable to all shades of opinion represented by the Task Force. However, it must be conceded that some outsiders would not accept Stone's exclusions. The use of surgery for the treatment of intractable pain has been designated as neurosurgery by some but as psychosurgery by others. Finally, it is important to note that it is not the techniques and physiological foci of surgical exercises *per se* which qualify them as examples of psychosurgery. The same procedures and foci characterize neurosurgery. It is the explicit intention of the surgery to promote behavioral change that is crucial.

3. ANIMAL RESEARCH AND THE GENERAL PERSPECTIVE UNDERLYING PSYCHOSURGERY

Before reviewing the theoretical basis of psychosurgery, it ought to be emphasized that psychosurgeons have, on the whole, tended to rely more on practical and empirical arguments. The atheoretical flavor of early psychosurgical endeavors was clearly conveyed by Fulton in 1951. 'In 1935–36, when the lobotomy operation was first proposed, knowledge of frontal function both in man and in animals was limited, and the procedure which gained wide acceptance was in large measure empirical and paid little heed of the broader problem of functional localization in the human brain' (p. 100).

Willett (1960) indicated that little had changed in the intervening decade: a decade which witnessed the emergence of many new operative procedures and modifications. 'Surgeons appear to have been prompted by hunches and empirical experience rather than by clearly formulated hypotheses when proposing their various modifications' (p. 569). As recently as 1977, Valenstein was asserting the same point. Comparing the empirical and physiological rationale forwarded for psychosurgery, he commented that the 'physiological rationale for psychosurgery is based on much more indirect, heterogeneous and often tortured sets of arguments' (pp. 9–10). It is difficult to attribute the consistency of these comments to chance.

Clearly visible in the rationales that have been offered are extrapolations from animal brain–behavior research. In fact, the influence of animal research would seem to be twofold. First of all, it helped forge a conceptualization of brain functional organization conducive to psychosurgical initiatives, and secondly, it provided the direct inspiration for specific psychosurgical operations. Let us consider these in turn.

Burckhardt (1891) is credited with the first published account of psychosurgery. Burckhardt was clearly convinced that psychological functions are precisely and permanently localized in circumscribed areas of the brain. This emerging concept of narrow localization had its roots in nineteenth century phrenology, but unlike phrenology could draw upon the apparently direct evidence from investigations with brain damaged humans and from early animal lesion and stimulation studies. It was this commitment to the narrow localization perspective that guided Burckhardt's extirpations. 'Whoever sees in psychoses only diffuse illness of the cortex . . . for him there would naturally be no point in excising relatively small portions of the cortex in the hope of influencing a psychosis favourably by it. One, therefore, has to be, as I am, of a different opinion, namely that our psychological existence is also made up of single elements, which are localised in separate areas of the brain and keep their places for life' (p. 544). Burckhardt's initiative was critically received. His call to colleagues to 'tread the path of cortical extirpation with even better and more satisfactory results' yielded no immediate recruits. The prevailing climate of ideas about brain functional organization was unfavorable. Phrenology still had a bad press. Some fifty years later when Moniz reported the results of frontal lobe surgery, the climate was noticeably better. Narrow localization still afforded the guiding logic, but by the 1930s the concept of precise cerebral specificity was widely respected and so psychosurgery could now expect a more positive reception. The following statement by Hoch (1949) indicates the continued allegiance to the narrow localization view. 'Those who thought that intellectual function and especially certain emotional behaviour patterns are localized in certain parts of the frontal lobe began to operate from the point of view of localization of function' (p. 23).

The concept of narrow localization, then, features strikingly in the emergence of psychosurgery. Few present day brain scientists would advocate precise specificity, preferring a model that acknowledges the complexity of psychological functions and their dependency on a variety of cerebral structures working in a concerted and dynamic fashion (see Luria, 1973). Few would defend the simplistic inferential logic applied to the early animal brain research by the proponents of narrow localization. However, theoretical commitments are never recklessly discarded. So it should be no surprise to find the notion of a highly specific brain persisting in contemporary psychosurgery. Admittedly, its influence is less explicit. Nevertheless, as recently as 1977, Dagi couched the rationale for psychosurgery in the following simple terms: 'A syllogism may be proposed: (i) All function has some anatomical basis. (ii) Behavior is a function. (iii) Therefore, behavior has some anatomical basis. When this syllogism is followed with two possible corollaries, complexity is gained: (iiia) All behavior has specific locus; therefore pathological behavior has some specific locus; or (iiib) Pathological behavior has a specifically pathological locus. It is on these bases that one obtains philosophical justification for the ablation of focal areas. The presumption remains that these ablations will mitigate symptomatology or eliminate disease' (pp. 518–19). This continuing allegiance to an anachronistic model of brain functional organization has prompted one critic to dismiss psychosurgery as nothing more than a 'phrenological mistake' (Chorover, 1976).

4. THE DIRECT INFLUENCE OF SPECIFIC ANIMAL RESEARCH

The second sort of influence from animal research is much more specific. Particular psychosurgical procedures have taken their cue from the outcome of particular animal lesion studies (Valenstein, 1973). While some doubt surrounds Moniz's motivation it is apparent that a conference paper presented by Fulton and Jacobsen in 1935 on the behavioral changes that followed bilateral frontal lesions in chimpanzees was a key factor in the development of frontal lobotomy; certainly Fulton was convinced of its influence. In 1951, he wrote: 'The story of how he (*Moniz*) came to induce his colleague Almeida Lima to undertake the procedure has been often told and need not be repeated here beyond stating the fact that the impulse to undertake the procedure stemmed, as in the case of Burckhardt, from a report on behavioural changes in animals which had been subjected to a cerebral ablation' (p. 98). Fulton and Jacobsen's delayed response deficit studies are obviously well-known. Nevertheless, it is important to emphasize here that the main burden of their paper was that serious intellectual deficits followed frontal ablations in chimpanzees. What apparently caught Moniz's attention however, was their aside that one of the animals displayed a marked postoperative reduction in the frustration or experimental neurosis generated by the delayed response task. The animal, Becky by name, was subsequently described by Jacobsen *et al.* (1935) in the following poetic manner. 'It was as if the animal had joined the "happiness cult of Elder Micheaux" and had placed it burdens on the Lord' (p. 10). Freeman and Watts' (1950) described Moniz's reaction. 'He (*Moniz*) compared in his own mind the querulous, the deluded, the agitated and the obsessed with these apes of Fulton and Jacobsen' (p. xvi). Moniz, indeed, enquired about possible extrapolation to human psychiatric patients. Jacobsen, however, was at some pains to point out that the rather restricted phenomenon of 'experimental neuroses' should be carefully distinguished from the equivalent label applied in a psychiatric setting. Subsequent events indicate that Moniz was not to be deterred.

The first psychosurgery addressed at the frontal lobes was conducted on November 12, 1935. In all 20 operations were performed. Moniz noted that all 20 survived. Seven were considered to have recovered completely and a further seven improved. The results were interpreted as very encouraging, both by Moniz and by later supporters of psychosurgery. Moniz's acitivities in this area were curtailed though in 1944, when he was shot by a lobotomized patient.

It fell to Walter Freeman to take over the role of 'Father of Psychosurgery'. Moniz's technique was modified by Freeman and Watts and introduced into the United States in 1936. Their modifications rapidly gained popularity. Psychosurgery had truly arrived. Its arrival is illustrated by Freeman's (1971) post-retirement claim that he had been 'personally concerned' (p. 622) with some 3500 operations. Valenstein (1973) estimated that some 40 000 (p. 55) of the older type of operations had been carried out in the United States. Less conservatively, Breggin (1972) reckoned that some 50 000 patients received psychosurgical treatment in this 'first wave'. Sargant and Slater (1962) estimated that the figure for the United Kingdom was some 15 000.

However, the 1940s and early 1950s proved to be the apex of psychosurgery. By the late 1950s, frontal operations were on the wane. Various reasons have been offered for the decline: fewer customers; increasingly visible adverse sequelae; the growing opposition lobby; the synthesis of major tranquillizers. However, even as the decline in frontal lobe psychosurgery was beginning, new emphases within animal lesion research and commensurate technological developments were kindling psychosurgical interest in a different set of structures: the limbic system. A major structure in the limbic 'circuit of emotion' described by Papez, as early as 1937, is the cingulate gyrus.

The development of cingulectomy was an important factor in the revival of psychosurgery in the late 1960s. It is now one of the most frequently performed psychosurgical operations and is considered appropriate for a variety of psychiatric disorders. As with its frontal predecessors, the impetus for cingulectomy came initially from animal brain research. The experiments of Smith (1945) and Ward (1948) are considered crucial. Fulton (1951) recalled how three years earlier he had made the connection. 'In my Withering Lectures I raised the question of whether a lesion in the cingulate area might not be chiefly responsible for the behavioral changes which occur in man after radical frontal lobotomy. This suggestion was based largely on behavioural changes reported in monkeys by Wilbur Smith and Arthur Ward' (pp. 82–83). Smith and Ward both reported that following cingulectomy their animals appeared much tamer towards both their cage mates and their human handlers. It was this increased tameness that impressed psychosurgeons. However, there is more to the behavior of cingulectomized monkeys than simple pacificity. Ward's (1948) own account patently illustrates that 'tameness' provides an utterly inadequate description of the behavior of operated animals. The complex character of disturbances produced by cingulate surgery can be intimated by citing some of Ward's description. The cingulectomized monkey showed 'no grooming behavior or acts of affection towards its companions' and seemed as though it had lost its 'social conscience' (p. 440). With regard to its cage mates, the operated animal 'treats them as it treats inanimate objects and will walk on them, bump into them if they happen to be in the way and will even sit on them'; and 'will openly eat food in the hand of a companion without being prepared to do battle and appears surprised when it is rebuffed'; and 'never shows actual hostility to its fellows' (p. 440). Ward concluded by asserting that such monkeys 'lose the ability to forecast accurately the social repercussions of their own actions' (p. 440). So, as in the development of frontal operations, a degree of selective attention is evident in the interpretation of animal data.

The more recent procedures that characterize psychosurgery's 'second wave' have also leaned heavily for justification on the results of animal experiments. The research prompted by Klüver and Bucy's initiative was markedly influential. Klüver and Bucy (1938) detailed a syndrome of behavioral changes in monkeys following bilateral temporal lobotomy. The effects included: recognition problems, hyperorality, distractability, hypersexuality, deficits in avoidance behavior, and docility. They are similar in some respects to the changes observed by Smith and Ward to follow anterior cingulate lesions. Subsequent research has revealed that much of this Klüver–Bucy syndrome could be produced by lesions restricted to the amygdaloid nuclei. As in the case of cingulate lesions, it was primarily the taming effects of amygdala surgery that attracted the interest of psychosurgeons.

Narabayashi (cf. Narabayashi et al., 1963; Narabayashi and Uno, 1966) was a pioneer with stereotaxic amygdalectomy in 1958 and the number of individuals subjected to the operation has been increasing slowly but continuously ever since (e.g. Balasubramanian and Kanaka, 1975; Hitchcock et al., 1973; Mark and Ervin, 1970). The usual behavioral indications for surgical referral are behaviors designated as 'aggressive', 'violent', and 'uncontrollably explosive'. The aim of surgery is presented as sedation.

Some practitioners have advocated limiting amygdalectomy to aggressive and violent patients with symptoms of temporal lobe epilepsy (e.g. Mark and Ordia, 1976; Vaernet, 1972). This could be considered as elevating the operation to the status of neurosurgery, given that neuropathological indices of epilepsy provided the grounds for surgery. However, it is difficult to discern the primary surgical indications with such patients. Opponents of amygdala surgery (e.g. Breggin, 1973; Chorover, 1974) contend that even with epileptic patients the main impetus for surgery is aggressive behavior. This interpretation is not without foundation. For example, Mark et al. (1972) stated that: 'When present, interictal episodes of uncontrolled violent behavior are usually a more disabling symptom to the victims of temporal lobe epilepsy than the seizures themselves. Thus the treatment of this aspect of the disorder is of prime importance' (p. 140). In addition, while an orderly relationship between episodic aggressive behavior and temporal lobe epilepsy has been postulated (cf. Mark and Ordia, 1976; Mark and Sweet, 1974), many authorities remain unconvinced (cf. Goldstein, 1974; Rodin, 1973). Caution would seem appropriate.

However, for psychosurgeons such as Narabayashi, these sort of considerations would appear to be largely cosmetic, since stereotaxic destruction of the amygdala is conducted explicitly for the control of violent behavior. Here the complexities of temporal lobe epilepsy are not permitted to cloud the metaphor provided by Klüver and Bucy's monkeys.

Once again we find a highly selective evaluation of animal research. Fortunately, in the case of the amygdala, many of the major deficits that characterize the Klüver–Bucy syndrome, such as hypersexuality and compulsive orality rarely result from human surgery. (Mark et al., 1972; Narabayashi, 1972). A literal application of the early animal research would have predicted otherwise. In a sense, the absence of some of the Klüver–Bucy deficits following human amygdalectomies serves to re-emphasize the general problems of simple animal analogies. Further, psychosurgeons operating on the human amygdala had no independent grounds for suspecting only fractional

Klüver–Bucy effects. As Valenstein (1973) emphasized: 'There is no theoretical way at present of predicting the consequences of destruction of a particular structure within the limbic system because almost all the structures are interconnected by many anatomical pathways. Knowledge of the details of how the limbic system regulates the emotions is very general at best . . .' (p. 276).

More recent research by Kling and his associates (see for example, Kling, 1972) on the effects of amygdala lesions on monkeys in non-laboratory, free-ranging settings is exceptionally revealing. It clearly demonstrates the crucial influence that post-operative social context has on the behavioral effects observed following ablations. The implications of this result has not, as yet, been explicitly represented in psychosurgical theory. In this research amygdalectomies were performed on monkeys selected from large free-ranging and semi-free-ranging colonies. The pre-operative behavior of these animals was subject to careful observation. They were then isolated from the colony, lesioned and, following a short period of post-operative recovery and laboratory-based observation, returned to the colony where their behavior was again closely scrutinized. Kling's results are of major significance. First of all, they throw some light on the absence of hypersexuality and increased orality in human amygdalectomized patients. These components of the Klüver–Bucy syndrome were observed by Kling to be present only in a restricted post-operative environment. Secondly, Kling's research reveals a dramatic pattern of post-operative deficits in social behavior apparent only when the monkeys rejoin the colony. Nothing in the usual post-operative laboratory behavior directly intimates such striking social maladjustment. Essentially, amygdalectomized animals in the monkey colony seemed no longer to comprehend the established social norms. They failed to respond appropriately to social communications and continuously appeared confused and fearful. Frequently, when approached by a monkey in a non-threatening way they would respond by cowering or fleeing. Alternatively, operated animals would, on occasion, react provocatively when threatened by a dominant colony member. A severe beating was the price of such social incompetence. In adult monkeys the failure to resocialize post-operatively was total. Complete social isolation was invariably followed by death from starvation or from attacks by predators. Recent observations also suggest that a similar lack of resocialization follows cingulate lesions (see for example, Meyers and Sweet, 1970 cited by Kling, 1972).

Kling's observations and conclusions offer little encouragement to those committed to surgical experiments on the human amygdala. To the prospect of taming aggressive behaviors, gleaned from the early animal research, it is necessary to graft on the likelihood of doing untold damage to complex social behavior, as revealed by subsequent animal research. Thomas R., one of

Mark and Ervin's patients, would seem to illustrate the dangers (see Breggin, 1973; Chorover, 1974; Scheflin and Opton, 1978).

Finally, the rationale offered by Roeder and his colleagues (Roeder and Müller, 1969; Roeder et al., 1972) for ventromedial hypothalamic surgery as a treatment for pedophilic homosexuality provides perhaps the most striking recent example of the application of animal research by psychosurgeons. We can do no better than allow these psychosurgeons to largely speak for themselves.

Their account opens with a confession of ignorance, but goes on to indicate that an important clue to the cerebral organization of 'perverse' sexual motivations is afforded by the animal research of Schreiner and Kling. Roeder et al. (1972) viewed a film of the research and clearly found it most instructive. Briefly, the film portrayed amygdalectomized cats and monkeys engaged in the sexual acrobatics characteristic of the laboratory Klüver–Bucy syndrome. This hypersexuality was subsequently excised by further surgery addressed at the ventromedial nuclei of the hypothalamus. Roeder and his associates were patently excited by the portrayal. They stated that: 'This film . . . was a mine of information for human sexual pathology. Without going into details, much of what was observed in the behavior of male cats after lesions in the region of the amygdaloid nucleus resembles human perversions. Already this film convinced us that there were solid reasons for undertaking a therapeutic stereotaxic procedure' (pp. 87). The hormonal experiments of Dörner were regarded as providing supplementary evidence. Roeder et al. (1972) acknowledged this influence, stating that: 'Synchronous with our work, Dörner reported on experimental homosexuality through hormonal influence. He showed a very instructive film . . . in 1969. Male cats castrated on the first day of life displayed homosexual behavior after implantation of testes or injections of androgen when grown up. The lack of androgen during the first days of life seemed to cause faulty programing of the hypothalamalic "sex behavior center". Electrolytic lesion of the nucleus ventromedialis hypothalami could abolish neuroendocrine male homosexuality in the rat' (pp. 87–8). These researches, then, provided the theoretical inspiration for the application of stereotaxic surgery in matters of human sexual 'deviance'.

Several points should be made here. First of all, as indicated previously, hypersexuality appears as a consequence of amygdalectomy only in confined post-operative environments. Consequently, its validity as a metaphor for human sexual perversions would seem questionable. Secondly, there is evidence to implicate the ventromedial hypothalamus in a wide range of behavioral and biological functions in addition to sex. Thirdly, as their own account indicated, Roeder and his colleagues derived support from Dörner's deduction of a separate male and female sex center in the brains of their laboratory rats. In the usual cerebral arrangement one of these centers is considered to dominate, depending on the sex of the animal. The destruction of one center results in a change of dominance. Thus, if the female sex center (localized in the ventromedial hypothalamus) is destroyed, male sexual behavior should dominate and any male homosexual tendencies would be abolished. However, Dörner's views are not shared by most of the mainstream scholars of sexual biology. Few consider that single and separate sex centers regulating the behavior of each sex represents an acceptable characterization of available evidence. Finally, there is a compelling body of argument to commend the view that, while structural and hormonal influences may dominate with regard to the intensity of sexual interest, in higher animals, especially humans, learning plays a crucial role in the mode of expression of that interest, i.e., its direction (see, for example, Zuckerman, 1972). Finally, given Roeder's susceptibility to movies, it is only to be hoped that he has not yet seen 'M.A.S.H.' and 'Young Frankenstein'.

In summary, then, the foundations of various psychosurgical procedures can be traced to particular animal brain–behavior studies. However, in extrapolating from the animal research, neither caution nor sophistication has been much in evidence. Rather than elaborate psychophysiological models of disorder and dysfunction, the lessons extracted amount to little more than simple-minded similes that betray both a striking impulsiveness and a selectivity of perception bordering on the bizarre. In fact, investigations of brain–behavior relationships in animals affords psychosurgery little in the way of real theoretical comfort.

5. THERAPEUTIC EFFICACY

Let us now turn briefly to the matter of efficacy. The two main methods of assessing the efficacy of psychosurgical interventions have been 'hospital discharge rates' and 'improvement rates'. The latter has been preferred in more recent studies and is accordingly adopted for our overview. It consists simply of assigning operatees to one of a number of categories of 'improvement'. For our assessment four such categories were employed:

1. Substantial improvement. Patient has either completely recovered or markedly improved; is on little or no medication; only occasionally or never consults psychiatrists; generally functions at 75–100 per cent of ability.
2. Marginal improvement. Patient has shown some improvement; takes medication regularly; consults psychiatrists regularly; functions at 25–75 per cent of ability.
3. No improvement. Patient's condition is not improved; is under constant psychiatric care; generally functions at below 25 per cent of ability.
4. Worse. Patient's psychiatric disorder has worsened or general condition has deteriorated due to adverse operative sequelae; includes patients

whose deaths can in some way be attributed to the operation and also suicides.

Obviously, such categories are somewhat arbitrary. They do not represent objective divisions along a continuum of outcome. However, we have adopted this particular system because it seems to be the most popular one with psychosurgeons. Inevitably, categorization schemes vary somewhat across studies and the exact matching of original categories and present classification occasionally proved difficult. In all anomalous cases, the initial descriptor listed for each category in the present system was regarded as primary in determining an operatee's status.

Our scheme was then applied to the results for a selected sample of psychosurgical studies, allowing us to assess and compare the percentage of patients in each improvement category across different studies. Some words regarding selection criteria are in order. Clearly, as indicated, only those studies whose data could be readily accommodated by our assessment scheme have been included. In addition, we have favored large scale studies, and those most frequently cited, where possible. Finally, when a particular surgeon's work is examined, there is often a considerable overlap of patients from report to report. In such cases, the fullest (almost invariably the most recent) account has been chosen. Overall, our analysis encompasses data from some 15 000 patients.

Table 16.1 summarizes the percentage of patients reported as showing substantial improvement. In the first column the rates are expressed relative to the procedure performed; in the second column they are arranged relative to diagnostic classification.

Several points need to be made. First of all, these data are wholly derived from uncontrolled studies and are the product of non-independent sources of assessment. The poor quality of psychosurgical studies is widely conceded. Valenstein (1977), for example, judged the scientific status of English language reports published between 1970–1976. Studies were assigned to one of six categories of scientific merit. The categories containing studies with the highest scientific merit (ie., 1 and 2) would include reports with adequately matched controls, objective tests, independent assessors, and long-term follow-up. The lowest category would include anecdotal case reports. According to Valenstein, none of the studies warranted a category 1 classification. Over 90 per cent of them were allocated to categories 4 to 6, with exactly half overall being relegated to the lowest scientific category of all. Valenstein indicated that a category 4 allocation '. . . would be given only to articles of low scientific value. It is unlikely, for example, that an animal study with such a low rating would be accepted for publications by the editors of a respected experimental journal' (p. 60).

Secondly, given the range of probable biases in work of such low caliber

Table 16.1 Efficacy of psychosurgical procedures: percentage of operatees showing
substantial improvement, i.e. category 1

Operation	Total no. rec. operation	Improved (%)	Disorder	Total no. rec. diagnosis*	Improved (%)
Capsulotomy	92	72	Sexual 'deviation'	30	72
Cingulectomy	789	66	Obsessional neurosis	562	62
Bimedial	85	58	Manic-depression	372	59
Mesoloviotomy	38	58	Depression	441	57
Hypothalamotomy	182	55	Anxiety/tension	268	51
Tractotomy	284	53	Aggression/hyperkinesis ('behavior disorders')	385	43
Limbic	66	50			
Orbital	304	47	Schizophrenia	1949	30
Transorbital	704	45			
Amygdalectomy	185	40			
Prefrontal	11 205	39			
Rostral	304	32			
Thalamotomy	81	25			

* Those individuals with mixed or ambiguous diagnoses, or with diagnoses that
did not fit readily into these categories were excluded for the purposes of this
analysis.

and control, many of the procedures attract alarmingly small percentages of
substantial improvement. Only capsulotomy (lesion of fibers connecting the
frontal lobes and the thalamus in the internal capsule) and cingulectomy
would seem to yield anything like respectable rates of improvement. Further,
it is worth noting that the figure for capsulotomy is based on a very small
pool of operatees. The figure for cingulectomy would appear to be based on
somewhat firmer grounds, given the relatively large number of studies available for analysis. With regard to disorders, 'sexual deviants' would appear
to attract the best result. However, it should be noted that this assessment
is again based on very few patients and it is highly unlikely that the effects
of hypothalamotomy in such cases are specific (O'Callaghan and Carroll,
1982; Valenstein, 1973). Many psychiatric conditions, such as schizophrenia,
are clearly very poorly indicated.

Thirdly, rates of improvement must be placed against patients' probable
untreated prognoses. Staudt and Zubin (1957) have gauged that the untreated
symptom remission rate in the psychiatric population from which the earlier
psychosurgical candidates were drawn lay around 40 per cent. While no

estimates are available for more recent operatees, given the shift in emphasis from more to less chronically disturbed individuals, the increasing application of surgery to so-called 'behavior disorders', and the expressed preference for patients with relatively favorable prognoses, the figure is unlikely to be lower than 40 per cent.

Fourthly, in this context it is worth considering the handful of studies that have been conducted using contemporary no-treatment control groups. These have almost exclusively been directed at the older prefrontal and transorbital procedures. In addition, even a cursory examination of these studies uncovers a range of flaws. There are good reasons for believing that many of the control and surgery groups were inadequately matched in a high proportion of instances; systematic biases in favor of the psychosurgery group in terms of length of hospitalization, duration of disturbance, and general prognostic indications are usual. Patients who were selected for surgery but for whom permission was not forthcoming have commonly served as controls. However, it is highly likely that the reasons for withholding permission are not independent of the patient's psychiatric status, the family's attitude, and expectation of eventual outcome. Such initial biases are likely to be enhanced when the two groups are, as has happened, subsequently exposed to markedly different rehabilitation regimes. All such factors conspire to favor the surgery group at the expense of their controls. It is perhaps not surprising, therefore, that many of the investigators reported much lower rates of symptom remission in untreated controls than has been traditionally observed. Other design weaknesses exist; the most salient, lack of sophisticated and independent assessment and reliance on only short-term follow-up, have already been mentioned in the context of the explicitly uncontrolled studies. Thus, where differential improvement rates have been observed, it is always possible to account for such differences by recourse to variables other than the lesion itself.

One fairly clear message does emerge from examination of the controlled studies: the better the study in terms of control and design, the less the results commend psychosurgery. The better controlled studies (see O'Callaghan and Carroll, 1982) either show no differential improvement rates for treatment and control or data which only marginally favor psychosurgery.

Finally, it must be emphasized that no investigation to date has adequately confronted the possible placebo component of psychosurgical treatment. The evidence from both other areas of surgery (Beecher, 1961) and other modes of behavioral intervention (Rosenthal, 1966) indicates that it is likely to be substantial.

In any assessment of efficacy, it is necessary to establish the specificity of treatment effects and the risk of adverse sequelae. In the context of psychosurgery, it is now generally acknowledged that the early surgical adventures were associated with a range of undesirable neurological and behavioral side-effects. However, proponents of the psychosurgical approach contend that with the improved technology and operative caution characteristic of more recent endeavors, risk has been largely eliminated. Although there would seem to be a reduction in the incidence of the more dramatic side-effects, our analysis reveals that misfortune and misadventure are still part of the contemporary psychosurgery scene. Furthermore, there is little compelling evidence that even the most circumscribed lesions achieve changes only in the designated symptoms and leave other behavioral functions unaltered. In this regard, it is also worth noting that contemporary psychosurgical studies are even less rigorous than their predecessors in the evaluation of possible adverse operative sequelae. Thus any claimed improvement in specificity or risk could simply reflect less conscientious and comprehensive investigation.

6. CONCLUSION

Two varieties of conclusion can be drawn from our consideration of psychosurgery. The first concerns the status of psychosurgery itself. Along with other reviewers we are forced to conclude that psychosurgical procedures are still without acceptable rationale. Instead of sound and sophisticated physiological theory, we find only loose and tenuous metaphors from animal brain–behavior research. The empirical evidence of efficacy is no more compelling; the frequency of operatees reported as showing substantial improvement is dismally low for a large number of procedures, and even where higher rates of improvement can be discerned, obvious shortcomings in experimental design and assessment completely compromise any claims of success. Without theoretical and empirical basis psychosurgery remains a highly experimental and, accordingly, ethically suspect enterprise.

The second sort of conclusion that can be drawn from our narrative extends beyond the boundaries of this particular therapeutic adventure. In the absence of convergent indications from human study, animal research should not, we contend, constitute a sufficient basis for psychiatric intervention. Admittedly, psychosurgeons have imposed quite idiosyncratic and obtuse interpretations on the available animal data. It is clear that these data, in fact, afford little support to the psychosurgical perspective. However, it is extremely difficult, if not impossible, to legislate for caution in this context, and simply urging it will always prove insufficient. There will always be someone, pressured by the demands of a particular clinical problem, willing to draw analogies where none really exist. Our only recourse, then, it seems, is to insist that evidence provided by the study of non-human subjects is, by itself, insufficient justification for intervening in matters of human psychological and psychophysiological disturbance.

REFERENCES

Balasubramanian, V., and Kanaka, T. S. (1975) Amygdalotomy and hypothalamotomy—A comparative study. *Con. Neurol.*, **37**, 195–201.

Beecher, H. K. (1961) Surgery as placebo: a quantitative study of bias. *J. Am. Med. Ass.*, **176**, 1102–1107.

Breggin, P. R. (1972) Lobotomies: an alert. *Am. J. Psychiat.*, **129**, 97–98.

Breggin, P. R. (1973) The psychosurgery of Thomas R.: a follow-up study. *Iss. Rad. Ther.*, **1**, 3–5.

Burckhardt, G. (1891) Ueber Rindenexcisionen, als Beitrag zur operativen Therapie der Psychosen. *All. Z. Psychiat.*, **47**, 463–548.

Chorover, S. L. (1974) Psychosurgery: a neuropsychological perspective. *Bost. Un. Law. Rev.*, **54**, 231–248.

Chorover, S. L. (1976) The pacification of the brain: from phrenology to psychosurgery, in *Current Controversies in Neurosurgery* (ed. T. P. Morley), W. B. Saunders, Philadelphia.

Dagi, T. F. (1977) Psychiatric surgery and the ethics of uncertainty, in *Neurosurgical Treatment in Psychiatry* (eds W. H. Sweet, S. Obrador, and J. G. Martin-Rodriguez), University Park Press, Baltimore, Maryland.

Freeman, W. (1971) Frontal lobotomy in early schizophrenia: Long follow-up in 415 cases. *Br. J. Psychiat.*, **119**, 621–624.

Freeman, W., and Watts, J. W. (1950) *Psychosurgery* (2nd ed.), Blackwell, Oxford.

Fulton, J. F. (1951) *Frontal Lobotomy and Affective Behaviour: A Neurophysiological Analysis*. Chapman and Hall, London.

Goldstein, M. (1974) Brain research and violent behavior: a summary and evaluation of the status of biomedical research on brain and aggressive violent behavior. *Arch. Neurol.*, **30**, 1–35.

Hitchcock, E. R., Ashcroft, G. W., Cairns, V. M., and Murray, L. G. (1973) Observations on the development of an assessment scheme for amygdalotomy, in *Surgical Approaches in Psychiatry* (eds C. V. Laitinen, and K. E. Livingston), Medical Technical Publishing Co., Lancaster.

Hoch, P. H. (1949) Theoretical aspects of frontal lobotomy and similar brain operations. *Proc. R. Soc. Med.*, **42**, 23–28.

Jacobsen, C. F., Wolfe, J. B., and Jackson, T. A. (1935) An experimental analysis of the functions of the frontal association areas in primates. *J. nerv. ment. Dis.*, **82**, 1–14.

Kling, A. (1972) Effects of amygdalectomy on social-effective behavior in nonhuman primates, in *The Neurobiology of the Amygdala* (ed. B. E. Eleftheriou), Plenum, New York.

Klüver, H., and Bucy, P. C. (1938) An analysis of certain effects of bilateral temporal lobectomy in the rhesus monkey with special reference to 'psychic blindness'. *J. Psychol.*, **5**, 33–54.

Kolb, B., and Whishaw, I. Q. (1980) *Fundamentals of Human Neuropsychology*. W. H. Freeman, San Francisco.

Luria, A. R. (1973) *The Working Brain*. Penguin, Harmondsworth.

Mark, V. H., and Ervin, F. R. (1970) *Violence and the Brain*, Harper and Row, New York.

Mark, V. H., and Ordia, I. J. (1976) The controversies over the use of neurosurgery in aggressive states and an assessment of the critics of this kind of surgery, in *Current Controversies in Neurosurgery* (ed. T. P. Morley), W. B. Saunders, Philadelphia.

Mark, V. H., and Sweet, W. H. (1974) The role of limbic brain dysfunction in aggression. *Res. nerv. ment. Dis.*, **52**, 186–200.

Mark, V. H., Sweet, W. H., and Ervin, F. R. (1972) The effect of amygdakotomy on violent behavior in patients with temporal lobe epilepsy, in *Psychosurgery* (eds E. Hitchcock, L. Laitinen, and K. Vaernet), Charles Thomas, Springfield, Illinois.

Narabayashi, H. (1972) Stereotaxic amygdalotomy, in *The Neurobiology of the Amygdala* (ed. B. E. Eleftheriou), Plenum, New York.

Narabayashi, H., and Uno, M. (1966) Long range results of stereotaxic amygdalotomy for behavior disorders. *Con. Neurol.*, **27**, 168–171.

Narabayashi, H., Nagao, T., Saito, Y., Yoshida, M., and Nagahata, M. (1963) Stereotaxic amygdalotomy for behavior disorders. *Arch. Neurol.*, **9**, 1–25.

O'Callaghan, M. A. J., and Carroll, D. (1982) *Psychosurgery: A Scientific Analysis*, M. T. P., Lancaster.

Papez, J. W. (1937) A proposed mechanism of emotion. *Arch. Neurol. Psychiat.*, **38**, 725–743.

Rodin, E. A. (1973) Psychomotor epilepsy and aggressive behavior. *Arch. Gen. Psychiat.*, **28**, 210–213.

Roeder, F., and Müller, D. (1969) The stereotaxic treatment of paedophilic homosexuality. *Ger. Med. Mon.*, **14**, 265–271.

Roeder, F., Orthner, H., and Müller, D. (1972) The stereotaxic treatment of paedophilic homosexuality and other sexual deviations, in *Psychosurgery* (eds E. Hitchcock, L. Laitinen, and K. Vaernet), Charles Thomas, Springfield, Illinois.

Rosenthal, R. (1966) *Experimenter Effects in Behavioral Research*. Appleton-Century-Crofts, New York.

Sargant, W., and Slater, E. (1972) *An Introduction to Physical Methods of Treatment in Psychiatry (5th ed.)*, Churchill Livingstone, London.

Scheflin, A. W., and Opton, E. M. Jr. (1978) *The Mind Manipulators*, Paddington Press, New York.

Smith, W. K. (1945) The functional significance of the rostral cingular cortex as revealed by its responses to electrical excitation. *J. Neurophysiol.*, **8**, 241–255.

Staudt, V. M., and Zubin, J. (1957) A biometric evaluation of the somatotherapies in schizophrenia. *Psychol. Bull*, **54**, 171–196.

Stone, A. A. (1975) Psychosurgery in Massachusetts: A task force report. *Mass. J. ment. hlth.*, **5**, 26–46.

Vaernet, K. (1972) Stereotaxic amygdalotomy in temporal lobe epilepsy. *Con. Neurol.*, **34**, 176–180.

Valenstein, E. S. (1973) *Brain Stimulation and Motivation: Research and Commentary*, Scott, Foresman, Glenview, Illinois.

Valenstein, E. S. (1977) The practice of psychosurgery: A survey of the literature (1971–1976), in *National Commission for the Protection of Subjects of Biomedical and Behavioral Research: Appendix*. US Department of Health, Education and Welfare, Washington.

Ward, A. A. Jr. (1948) The anterior cingulategyrus and personality. *Res. Publ. Ass. nerv. ment. Dis.*, **27**, 438–445.

Willett, R. A. (1960) The effects of psychosurgical procedures on behaviour, in *Handbook of Abnormal Psychology* (ed. H. J. Eysenck), Pitman, London.

Zuckerman, M. (1972) Physiological measures of sexual arousal in the human, in *Handbook of Psychophysiology* (eds N. S. Greenfield, and R. A. Sternbach) Holt, Rinehart and Winston, New York.

Animal Models of Human Behavior
Edited by G. C. L. Davey
© 1983 John Wiley & Sons Ltd

Chapter 17

Animal Models in Schizophrenia Research

Simon GREEN

'In well-run hospitals catatonic stupor or excitement lasting for years is rare, and patients learn to control their mannerisms and utterances. One catatonic who used to stand for hours in a corner answering his hallucinations with bellowing noises lost this habit entirely after he was allowed to go to the neighboring town entrusted with shopping errands. Only when he returns on winter evenings in the dark, he can sometimes be heard bellowing on the lonely road' (Mayer-Gross *et al.*, 1977).

This single example of schizophrenic behavior illustrates, dramatically, that it would be impossible to produce an animal model that is completely isomorphic with schizophrenic symptomatology. Although attempts have been made to establish an identity between single symptoms and superficially similar behavior in animals, the predominant use of animal models has been to illuminate the possible neuroanatomical and neurochemical bases of schizophrenia, with the specific aim of developing new therapies.

If a biochemical dysfunction basic to schizophrenia were identified, and then produced in animals, it would not lead to schizophrenic thought disorder and auditory hallucinations as seen in the human subject. It could, however, respond appropriately to drug intervention. Thus we would have a valuable animal model for the 'cause' and therapy of schizophrenia, but without behavioral isomorphism. We would, however, hope that the abnormal behavior shown by the animal reflected a breakdown in a fundamental behavioral process, a breakdown which, in humans, would result in schizophrenic symptomatology. This would be the maximally useful animal model, and in the following sections I shall review the use of animal models in schizophrenic research and assess how close we are to this 'ideal'.

1. DIAGNOSIS AND CLASSIFICATION OF SCHIZOPHRENIA

In an ideal world, diagnosis would have immediate implications for the etiology, course, treatment, and outcome of a psychiatric disorder (Blashfield and Draguns, 1976). Such a nosology does not exist for schizophrenia, or indeed for other categories such as manic-depressive psychosis or the depressive states (Akiskal and McKinney, 1975; Kendell, 1976). The earliest descriptions of dementia praecox emphasized chronicity, a deteriorating course, and negative symptoms such as affective flattening and poverty of speech (Kraepelin, 1919). Bleuler's modifications were less phenomenological and more bound up with his view of schizophrenia as a disease of the brain (Bleuler, 1950). Certain fundamental symptoms were inevitable corollaries of the disease process, while others were accessory in the sense that they need not be specific to schizophrenia (Table 17.1).

Table 17.1 Bleuler's fundamental and accessory symptoms of schizophrenia (Bleuler, 1950)

Fundamental Symptoms	Accessory Symptoms
Disturbances of affect	Delusions
Disturbances of associations	Hallucinations
Autism	Catatonia
Ambivalence	

Clinically, the fundamental symptoms might be present but too attenuated to be identifiable. Bleuler therefore proposed a second dichotomy which would have more clinical validity. Primary symptoms, of which thought disorder was emphasized, were seen as proceeding directly from the disease process, while secondary symptoms, such as affective disturbances, were not.

Langfeldt (1937) introduced a further subclassification by separating 'true' schizophrenia from schizophreniform psychoses. Following Kraepelin, the 'true' schizophrenic has a poor premorbid adjustment and poor prognosis, while for the schizophreniform patient, who has an underlying neurotic or personality disturbance with good premorbid adjustment, the prognosis is more optimistic. Both categories can display symptoms of emotional blunting, delusions of influence, catatonia, and hallucinations, all in the absence of organic brain damage.

Kraepelin, Bleuler, and Langfeldt emphasize chronicity and poor outcome. In fact the argument verges on the completely circular, with recovery implying that the patient was not truly schizophrenic in the first place; an assertion which fits in quite neatly with recent developments to the dopamine hypothesis of schizophrenia.

Schneider (1959) does not attempt to relate his diagnostic system to any physiological or psychological framework. Based on his clinical experience, he divides the symptoms of schizophrenia on the basis of their utility in diagnosing the disorder, and this purely phenomenological approach has become one of the more popular in current use. Symptoms are divided into those of the first rank, the presence of one or more of which is diagnostic of schizophrenia, and those of the second rank, which are of less importance. First rank symptoms are listed in Table 17.2 (Mellor, 1970).

Table 17.2 Schneiderian first-rank symptoms of schizophrenia (Mellor, 1970)

1. Audible thoughts	7. Thought broadcasting
2. Voices arguing	8. 'Made' feelings
3. Voices commenting	9. 'Made' impulses
4. Influence playing on the body	10. 'Made' volitional acts
5. Thought withdrawal	11. Delusional perception
6. Thought insertion	

The emphasis is upon auditory hallucinations and delusions of control i.e., feelings, impulses, and actions being influenced by outside agencies. Second rank symptoms include loosening of associations and flattened affect.

Since schizophrenia was introduced as a diagnostic category, the immediate outcome for a patient so categorized has been the application of the treatment then in vogue. This has ranged from insulin coma therapy and frontal lobotomies in the early days, to the antipsychotic phenothiazine and butyrophenone drugs of the last thirty years. Although the relationship between diagnosis and treatment has been predictable, the relationship between treatment and outcome has not. Some schizophrenics improve and some do not; Klein and Davis (1969), in an exhaustive review, conclude that while around 70 per cent of schizophrenics respond positively to phenothiazine medication, 30 per cent do not, while 25 per cent also respond to placebo drugs.

This problem has always been recognized, and recent developments in diagnostic systems have attempted to incorporate factors which enable the response to treatment to be predicted. To do this they have had to move away from the Schneiderian phenomenological approach to incorporate some assessment of environmental factors. The St Louis diagnostic criteria of Feighner *et al.* (1972) is such a system (Table 17.3), which has greatly influenced the most recent revision of the *American Diagnostic and Statistical Manual of Mental Disorders* (DSM–III) (Fox, 1981).

In a direct comparison of the Schneiderian and St Louis approaches to the prediction of outcome in schizophrenia, Bland and Orn (1979) found that severity of schizophrenia rated by the number of first rank symptoms did not identify a poor prognosis group, while ratings on the St Louis scale did.

Table 17.3 St Louis criteria for diagnosis of schizophrenia (Feighner *et al.*, 1972)

A. Presence of both	(i) Chronic illness (over 6 months).
	(ii) Absence of depressive or manic symptoms.
B. Presence of one out of	(i) Delusions or hallucinations without disorientation.
	(ii) Disorganized verbal production.
C. Presence of three out of	(i) Single.
	(ii) Poor premorbid social adjustment or work history.
	(iii) Family history of schizophrenia.
	(iv) Absence of alcoholism or drug abuse.
	(v) Onset before age 40.

A later study by Bland and Orn (1980) did suggest that some individual first rank symptoms correlated positively with outcome, while others correlated negatively. Carpenter *et al.* (1978), as part of the International Pilot Study on Schizophrenia (IPSS), reported that, of a range of individual signs and symptoms, only flattened affect (a Schneiderian second rank symptom) predicted a poor outcome group. As part of the same study, Hawk *et al.* (1975) compared three systems (Langfeldt, Schneider, and Carpenter *et al.*, 1976), and found none to be useful in identifying schizophrenics with a poor prognosis, although their application of Langfeldt's system has been criticized (Singh and Kay, 1978).

There is a general trend back towards the original Kraepelin emphasis upon chronicity as the significant feature of poor outcome schizophrenia. The St Louis system specifically excludes schizophreniform psychoses which last less than six months; these have an acute onset, more emotional lability, a better prognosis, and may occur in the absence of a family history of schizophrenia. This is in line with the traditional bipolar separation of schizophrenia into process and reactive forms, with the latter corresponding to the acute schizophrenic episode. There is evidence that good prognosis acute episode psychosis may be genetically differentiated from the poor prognosis chronic form, and that the two therefore represent separate and distinct psychopathologies (Roth, 1978; Rosenthal, 1978).

The separation of these two categories cannot be made phenomenologically, i.e., on the basis of symptoms and signs presented at the clinical interview. The ambiguity of these symptoms is emphasized by Carpenter *et al.* (1976), who, again as part of the IPSS, reassessed 680 schizophrenic patients originally diagnosed into the classic subtypes of catatonic, hebephrenic, simple, acute, paranoid, and schizoaffective. Using 27 items from the Present State Examination they showed that symptom profiles for the six subtypes completely overlapped, with all groups scoring highly, for instance, on 'lack of insight'. It appears that only by taking social, environmental, and genetic factors into account along with current symptomatology, can a genuinely useful system for classifying schizophrenics be derived.

Despite the essentially phenomenological nature of classification in schizophrenia, psychiatrists tend to agree on the basic diagnosis. Estimates of inter-observer reliability range from 53–80 per cent, which compares favorably with inter-observer reliability in the diagnosis of some physical illnesses (Falek and Moser, 1975; Helzer et al., 1977). An impressively consistent cross-cultural incidence of around 1 per cent of the population also argues that schizophrenia is a 'real' psychopathology, and not an entirely artificial construction of psychiatry and psychiatrists. A number of individual signs and symptoms are consistently associated with the syndrome, there is a significant genetic loading (Gottesman and Shields, 1976), and two distinct subgroupings exist, one characterized by gradual onset, chronicity, and poor prognosis, and the second by sudden onset, an acute course, and a favorable prognosis.

2. ANIMAL MODELS IN SCHIZOPHRENIA

Schizophrenia is diagnosed mainly on the basis of the diagnostic interview revealing the presence of decisive symptomatology. Few of these symptoms are amenable to direct modeling in animals. Thought disorder, delusional states, and auditory hallucinations are incapable of being recognized in animal subjects, although affective flattening can exist as a general apathy and lack of responsiveness. There is no possibility, therefore, of modeling the syndrome directly, only of drawing analogies. The success of a given analogy is assessed either by its contribution to a novel and effective treatment, or by the impetus it gives to developing a neuropsychological model of the disorder; these two areas are not mutually exclusive, but do follow the traditional differentiation of physical treatments into the surgical and the pharmacological.

2.1. Animal models and brain structure in schizophrenia

The earliest animal model used in schizophrenia was the frontal lobectomized monkey of Fulton and Jacobsen (1935). Impressed by the reports of postoperative docility and calm, Moniz saw the potential of such operations for violent and difficult human psychiatric patients. He returned to Lisbon and supervised the first prefrontal lobotomy. In 1936 he described the results of the first 20 such operations carried out on chronic institutionalized patients, the majority diagnosed as schizophrenic; 15 were rated as improved, ranging from increased docility to complete cure.

Psychosurgery then became a popular therapy for schizophrenia. Moniz himself was not destined to play the leading role, being shot and paralyzed by a lobotomized patient in 1944. Freeman and Watts (Freeman, 1971) were the main exponents, replacing the original destruction of the frontal lobe tissue via injections of alcohol with the prefrontal leucotomy; hooked scalpels were inserted through forehead or temple regions of the skull, and waggled up and down, severing frontal-subcortical fiber pathways. The degree of waggling determined the grade of leucotomy: minimal, standard, or radical (Freeman, 1971). (See Carroll and O'Callaghan, Chapter 16.)

Those using the frontal lobotomy consistently reported favorable outcomes, while critics pointed out the side-effects of gross personality change, with apathy or docility being mistaken for specific amelioration of schizophrenic symptoms. Significantly, after around 50 000 such operations up to 1950, the procedure virtually disappeared with the introduction of phenothiazine drug therapy in the early 1950s.

Over the last decade there has been something of a resurgence of interest in psychosurgery. Improved surgical techniques enable focal lesions a few millimeters across to be made in target structures; the target structures are again identified from animal models of behavior. Since the initial studies of Papez (1937) linking the emotional changes in rabies with the deposition of negri bodies in the hippocampus, the limbic system has been consistently associated with the control of emotional behavior. Most of the evidence for this association comes from stimulation and lesion studies in animals, with septal lesion 'rage' in rats and amygdala lesion 'docility' in monkeys being the classic examples. Many psychopathologies, including schizophrenia, are characterized by variations in emotional behavior. Using a heterogeneous sample of chronic psychiatric patients, Kelly et al. (1973a, b) placed a number of focal cryogenic lesions in fronto-limbic pathways and in limbic structures. The precise sites were chosen on the basis of physiological reactivity—stimulation had to induce signs of peripheral autonomic arousal.

Overall 67 per cent of patients were clinically improved, being less neurotic, less anxious, and less depressed. All had proved resistant to previous psychotherapy and physical therapies. Although given some semblance of a rationale, in that the limbic system is associated with some aspects of emotional control, the procedure is almost entirely empirical. Despite its quite impressive results, it contributes little to an understanding of schizophrenia or of the other psychopathologies represented. Even the reliance upon animal models of limbic function can be criticized (Section 3), and the extrapolation shown to be at best speculative.

2.2. Structural localization of schizophrenic symptomatology

If physical intervention is ever to be completely effective, it has to be aimed at the areas of the brain responsible for schizophrenic symptomatology. Schizophreniform psychoses can be associated with organic disorders of the brain such as epilepsy, various encephalitic diseases, cerebrovascular disorders, and invasive tumours. In an exhaustive review, Davison and Bagley (1969) find an association between left temporal lobe lesions and primary delusions, basal ganglia lesions with catatonic symptoms, diencephalic lesions with auditory hallucinations, and brain-stem lesions with thought disorder and Schneiderian first-rank symptoms. If schizophreniform psychoses are closely related to schizophrenia, then this particular psychopathology could potentially involve almost the whole brain, leaving no scope at all for localized psychosurgical intervention.

Post-mortem studies of the brains of schizophrenics reveal no consistent organic pathology. The results would anyway be confounded by the difficulty of finding a control group of drug-free patients. More interestingly, the recent technique of computerized axial tomography has been used to examine the brains of living schizophrenics, both drugged and drug-free. The most dramatic finding has been the identification of a subgroup with enlarged cerebral ventricles, significant cognitive impairment, and with a poor response to drug treatment (Weinberger et al., 1980; Johnstone et al., 1976). They may represent a biologically distinct group, with substantial loss or shrinkage of brain cells, related perhaps to the chronic poor prognosis subgroup mentioned earlier.

As no evidence for a localized lesion consistently associated with schizophrenia is forthcoming from post-mortem studies, an alternative approach is to define the basic psychological deficit in schizophrenics, and then use animal studies to model the possible brain mechanisms involved. For many years it has been hypothesized that defective attentional or stimulus filtering processes characterize schizophrenia, resulting in information overload. Attempts to cope with the overload produce the clinical symptoms (e.g., Venables, 1972; Hemsley, 1977).

Animal models of attentional processes have emphasized the role of limbic mechanisms in behavioral orienting and habituation, in particular the hippocampus and amygdala (Vinogradova, 1975; Sokolov, 1975; Pribram, 1967). The Pribram model suggests that the amygdala is responsible for the elicitation of an orienting response, while the hippocampus mediates its habituation as stimulus familiarity increases.

In the early 1970s, Gruzelier and Venables (1974) identified two distinct subgroups of schizophrenics on the basis of their skin conductance orienting responses to tones. One group showed orienting responses which did not habituate, while the other group did not orientate at all; they were referred to as responders and non-responders respectively. This paradigm can be easily mapped on to the Pribram model of orientating and habituation; hippocampal lesions should produce orientating which does not habituate, while amygdala damage should result in a failure to orientate at all, i.e., responder and non-responder groups.

To increase the overlap between animal and human paradigms, Bagshaw and Kimble (1972) recorded skin conductance orientating responses to tones in amygdalectomized and hippocampectomized monkeys. The results were as predicted, with non-responder and responder groups emerging to match the human data, supporting the speculation that these skin conductance characteristics of schizophrenics represent pathology of temporal lobe structures such as the hippocampus and amygdala. As the responder group also show significant bilateral asymmetries in their palmar skin conductance responses, Gruzelier concludes (1978) that the pathology is to the left temporal lobe, in accord with the conclusions of Bagley and Davison mentioned earlier.

Although stimulated by animal models of attentional processes, this particular research area has moved on to the specifically human topic of hemispheric asymmetries of function in schizophrenia (see e.g., Gruzelier and Flor-Henry, 1979), in an attempt to characterize the higher cognitive dysfunction in the disorder. The early stages did, however, represent an impressive attempt to match human and animal paradigms, utilizing the advantages of systematic lesion work in animals to illuminate a specifically human disorder.

The problem of localizing schizophrenia to brain structures is that the range of symptomatology—conative, cognitive, affective—could involve so much of the central nervous system that models become over-inclusive and consequently meaningless. Recent limbic hypotheses of schizophrenia (Torrey and Peterson, 1974; Stevens, 1973) demonstrate the point. Although using sophisticated conceptual models of limbic function based on animal experimentation, and ignoring the problem of extrapolating brain function across species, their conclusions are hardly counter-intuitive. The limbic system will obviously be involved in the pathology underlying schizophrenia as will neocortical, extra-pyramidal, diencephalic, and brain-stem systems with which it is massively interconnected. Localization of function can only be a viable approach if the heterogeneous symptomatology of schizophrenia does represent an attempt to cope with a single fundamental malfunction of, for instance, attentional processing (Hemsley, 1977; Hemsley and Richardson, 1980) or arousal level (Kornetsky and Eliasson, 1969). This implies that the description of the psychological breakdown is paramount.

2.3. Animal models and brain chemistry in schizophrenia

The serendipitous discovery of the anti-psychotic (neuroleptic) actions of chlorpromazine in the early 1950s revolutionized the treatment of schizophrenia. In 1954 Olds and Milner discovered electrical self-stimulation of the brain (ESB) in rats, and started a revolution in brain research. However, it was the 1970s before the two events were finally interwoven, and the most intensive use of animal models in schizophrenia research began.

The plotting of ESB sites led to the concept of reward and punishment pathways in the brain, such as the median forebrain bundle and the periventricular system. Investigations, particularly by Stein (e.g., Stein, 1968), into the chemistry of reward and punishment pathways suggested that noradrenaline was the neurotransmitter of the reward system, and acetylcholine of the punishment system (this was later modified to replace acetylcholine with serotonin, Wise *et al.*, 1973). The classic work of Shute and Lewis (1967; Lewis and Shute, 1967) and Ungerstedt (1971) revealed the existence of major long-axon neurotransmitter systems in the brain, of which Stein's reward and punishment pathways were part, and allowed an alternative approach to brain–behavior relationships. Instead of between fifty to a hundred structures of direct interest to the behavioral neuroscientist, there were, alternatively, around eight neurotransmitter pathways, each of which could be investigated using relatively specific agonist and antagonist drugs. Further, assuming that these major fiber systems played correspondingly major roles in behavior, it might be that some categories of behavior were mediated by single neurotransmitter systems. A catalyst to this approach was the early work of Grossman (1960) on the chemical coding of eating and drinking within the hypothalamus, with noradrenergic control of eating behavior and cholinergic control of drinking. On a grander level, Stein's work suggested that 'reward', as a psychological concept used in the analysis of behavior, was coded in the brain by the activity of noradrenergic pathways.

By defining schizophrenia in part as a failure to respond appropriately to rewarding stimuli—anhedonia—Stein (1971) could postulate a fundamental malfunction in the brain's noradrenergic reward system. As the dorsal noradrenergic pathway innervates hippocampal and cortical structures, and the ventral pathway diencephalic and limbic areas, Stein's hypothesis also accounted for the cognitive and affective symptoms of schizophrenia.

He was aware that the disorder has other features beside symptoms—a significant genetic component, gradual onset, a deteriorating course if untreated, and often a positive response to neuroleptic drugs—and elaborated the model to account for them. The basic malfunction would be a genetically controlled enzymatic deficiency in noradrenergic neurons which, given the contingent relationship between dopamine and noradrenaline, would lead to an over-production of dopamine.

Tyrosine ————▶ DOPA ————▶ Dopamine ————▶ Noradrenaline
             tyrosine   dopa   dopamine-β
             hydroxylase   decarboxylase   hydroxylase
                                                  (DBH)

A genetically-based reduction in DBH would prevent the conversion of dopamine to noradrenaline and produce an excess of dopamine in the neuron. This would be broken down by a variety of routes, and one feasible breakdown product would be 6-hydroxydopamine (6-OHDA). 6-OHDA is a neurotoxin, i.e., it destroys neurons, and in this scenario it would eliminate the noradrenergic neuron it was being produced in and around. The gradual build-up of the neurotoxin would explain the slow onset of schizophrenia, the progressive destruction of the noradrenergic system its deteriorating course, the irreversible loss of neurons the ineffectiveness of neuroleptics in chronic schizophrenia, and the blockade by neuroleptics of 6-OHDA uptake into intact terminals their efficacy in the acute onset syndrome.

Stein's model was the first comprehensive and plausible account of schizophrenia in terms of brain chemistry and based on systematic animal experimentation. Whether the rat bar-pressing for ESB is analogous to the human response to natural rewards is debatable (Gallistel, 1973), while the characterization of schizophrenia as a failure to respond appropriately to reinforcement probably does the syndrome less than justice. However, the model generates specific hypotheses which can be tested on human subjects, and it was to these that Stein next turned.

If DBH and noradrenaline are reduced or absent in the brains of schizophrenic patients, then post-mortem studies and analysis of the cerebrospinal fluid (CSF) of living patients for DBH and neurotransmitter metabolites provide possible if imperfect opportunities for corroboration. Stein himself reported the predicted reduction in brain levels of DBH after post-mortem analysis of schizophrenics (Wise et al., 1974), although Wyatt et al. (1975) concluded in their study that patients and controls did not differ; however, a reinterpretation of their data (Wise and Stein, 1975) suggested that paranoid patients showed a trend in the expected direction. CSF studies in schizophrenia have in general been disappointing, with few positive results. Recently Gomes et al. (1980) found increased levels of noradrenaline in the CSF of chronic patients which, together with reports of elevated noradrenaline concentrations in the limbic forebrain of post-mortem samples from chronic paranoid schizophrenics, suggests noradrenergic overactivity as a basic defect in schizophrenia. This is opposite to the prediction from Stein's model, although in all instances, but particularly post-mortem studies, results may be confounded with chronic drug treatment.

The identification of the long-axon neurotransmitter pathways in the brain

(Ungerstedt, 1971) coincided with evidence that dopamine might be involved in rewarding ESB in rats (Crow, 1972; 1973; Liebman and Butcher, 1973; Lippa et al., 1973). This led to a continuing debate on the relative roles of noradrenaline and dopamine in self-stimulation behavior (e.g., Fibiger and Phillips, 1974; Ritter and Stein, 1974; Herberg et al., 1976).

The significance of this debate lay in the behavior under study. Reward or reinforcement is a psychological concept equally applicable to man and rat. Behavioral analogies between the two species are quite common—homeostatic motivation, emotion, perception, etc.—but often at a simple level, such as feeding or aggression. Complex behavior seen in humans often has no counterpart in the rat, but is usually of most interest to psychologists. The concept of reinforcement and theories of how it affects behavior (e.g., Bolles, 1967) straddle different species, and identifying its neural substrate in the rat might tell us something of the human brain. If psychopathologies can be related to defective operation of reinforcement processes, then the significance of the animal investigations increases, particularly if it leads to convincing neuropsychological models and more effective treatment.

In parallel with the rapid growth of the brain chemistry industry in the 1960s and 1970s, the pharmacology of neuroleptic drugs was being investigated. Led by Carlsson's work (see Carlsson, 1978, for a review) it became apparent that of all the actions of these pharmacologically messy drugs, it was their ability to block dopamine receptors that correlated best with their anti-psychotic potency (Seeman et al., 1976; Creese et al., 1976). Chronic treatment with neuroleptics leads to extra-pyramidal motor side-effects, akin to Parkinsonism; it has been known for some decades that Parkinsonism is due to degeneration of the fiber tract leading from the substantia nigra in the midbrain to the corpus striatum in the forebrain. In 1971 Ungerstedt identified the nigro–striatal tract as one of two major dopamine systems in the brain, the other being the midbrain–limbic–cortical (meso–limbic–cortical) pathway. Parkinsonism could then be explained as degeneration of the dopaminergic nigro-striatal pathway, and extra-pyramidal side-effects of neuroleptic medication could be attributed to the drug-induced blockade of this same pathway.

In view of the confluence of these findings, interest in the reinforcement–deficit interpretation of schizophrenic behavior waned rapidly. In fact interest in schizophrenic behavior generally waned, as attention amongst neuroscientists focused upon the pharmacology of neuroleptic drugs and the distribution of dopamine systems in the brain. With few exceptions, there was no attempt to characterize the schizophrenic breakdown and look for behavioral analogies in the rat, but a straightforward acceptance of the argument that, if neuroleptics work via dopamine blockade, schizophrenia represents overactivity in dopamine pathways, and an animal model of the disorder might be produced by stimulating these pathways in rats.

(Before considering these putative models, it should be remembered that it was already common knowledge that neuroleptics were ineffective in a significant number of schizophrenics (Klein and Davis, 1969), and that a dopamine-hypothesis of schizophrenia based upon neuroleptic pharmacology would therefore begin with prescribed limitations.)

Dopamine agonists such as amphetamine and apomorphine produce at low doses hyperactivity and at high doses a syndrome of stereotypy (Randrup and Munkvad, 1970). The syndrome varies slightly from species to species and from strain to strain, but the commonest features are repetitive licking, gnawing, and pawing. At very high doses, 'waxy flexibility' may occur, where the animal remains in any posture in which it is placed (Stein, 1971). The feature of repetitiveness characterizes some aspects of schizophrenic behavior, including repetition of thought patterns and of motor movements, and amphetamine-induced stereotypy has been directly compared with the human disorder. However, stereotyped thoughts are more a feature of obsessional disorders, and stereotyped movement disorders and waxy flexibility are seen in a wide range of psychiatric patients, and may represent non-specific effects of institutionalization (Mayer-Gross et al., 1977). Stereotypy in general does not play a major role in the diagnosis of schizophrenia.

The stereotypy syndrome produced by dopamine stimulants is antagonized by neuroleptic drugs such as chlorpromazine. As we know they have substantial dopamine-blocking activity, it is not surprising that a behavior induced by increasing dopamine activity should be reduced by decreasing it. What is of interest is that some clinically-used drugs, such as thioridazine, do not antagonize amphetamine-induced stereotypy in line with their clinical potency, calling into question the validity of the syndrome either as a behavioral model of schizophrenia or as a pharmacological test-bed for potential neuroleptic agents. The dopamine pathway implicated in the stereotypy syndrome is the nigro–striatal tract (Iversen, 1977).

If low doses of dopamine agonists are injected into rats with the nigro–striatal tract lesioned on one side, increased locomotion occurs, but in circles—the 'rotating rodent'. This circling behavior is, as expected, antagonized by blocking drugs, and is used as a routine test for dopamine receptor blockage. However, as with stereotypy, drugs such as thioridazine do not antagonize amphetamine-induced rotation. Thioridazine has significant activity as a cholinergic receptor antagonist. Studies of the nigro–striatal system show that the ascending dopamine axons synapse on to intra-striatal cholinergic neurons, which they inhibit. Normal striatal function depends upon a balance in the activity of these dopamine and cholinergic neurons, which, if upset by an amphetamine-stimulated increase in dopamine activity, results in abnormal stereotyped behavior. Chlorpromazine blocks the amphetamine-induced increase in dopamine activity, and restores the normal DA/ACh balance, and so eliminates stereotypy. Thioridazine blocks both dopamine and cholinergic receptors; this simultaneous antagonism maintains the dynamic imbalance produced by amphetamine, and sustains stereotyped behavior. A similar argument applies to the failure of thioridazine to block amphetamine-induced rotation in the unilateral nigro-striatally lesioned rat.

Therefore, neither behaviorally nor pharmacologically does increased activity in the nigro–striatal dopamine pathway qualify as an animal model of schizophrenia or of schizophrenic pharmacotherapy. It does have significant value as a test-bed for isolating potential extra-pyramidal side-effects of neuroleptics. These Parkinsonian-like symptoms, a common sequelae of chronic neuroleptic treatment, are based in the nigro–striatal system, and may also reflect a DA/ACh imbalance produced by neuroleptic blockade of dopamine receptors. A drug simultaneously blocking dopamine and cholinergic receptors maintains the DA/ACh equilibrium, and should not produce significant extrapyramidal effects when used in schizophrenia; such is the case with thioridazine (Snyder *et al.*, 1974).

The side-effects of drugs like chlorpromazine may be prevented by simultaneous treatment with an anticholinergic agent, leaving their anti-psychotic potency intact. As, in the absence of motor side-effects, the nigro–striatal system is presumably functioning as normal, the anti-psychotic action must, by exclusion, be located in the other major dopamine tract, the meso–limbic–cortical pathway.

The two dopamine pathways, although distinguishable, are closely related. They arise from allied areas in the midbrain, and only separate appreciably towards their points of termination. It is therefore methodologically difficult to stimulate one independently of the other, and probable that no one behavior reflects solely the activity in one pathway to the exclusion of the other. Thus, even a relatively pure nigro–striatal syndrome such as rotation may have a meso-limbic component (Pycock and Marsden, 1978).

Striatal lesions eliminate amphetamine-induced stereotypy, while lesions in limbic terminal sites of the meso–limbic–cortical tract (the nucleus accumbens septi) do not. However, they do eliminate the hyperactivity produced by low doses of amphetamine, which, in turn, are unaffected by striatal lesions (for a review, see Iversen, 1977). So the increase in locomotion produced by low doses of amphetamine may reflect activity in the meso–limbic–cortical tract; as the dose increases, this effect is swamped by the motor stereotypies of nigro–striatal over-activation.

Neuroleptics, including thioridazine, block low dose amphetamine hyperactivity, which in this sense appears to be a better pharmacological model for selecting clinical drugs than high dose stereotypy. However, the behavior itself is simple, and does not have even the specious similarity to psychosis of nigro-striatal stereotypy. More recently, Borison and Diamond (1978) have suggested that a stereotypy syndrome induced by the amphetamine-like drug phenylethylamine is a better animal model of schizophrenia. Phenylethylamine is a naturally-occurring substance concentrated in the human limbic system, while the stereotypy produced in rats is blocked by all the standard neuroleptic drugs, including thioridazine. It may therefore prove to be a better pharmacological model for schizophrenia than amphetamine-induced stereotypy or turning.

There is as yet no convincing animal model of the behavioral functions of the meso–limbic–cortical dopamine innervation. On the biochemical level, there is evidence that repeated injections of neuroleptics preferentially increase the synthesis and turnover of dopamine (via the feedback effects of receptor blockade) in meso–limbic and meso–cortical regions of the rat brain; initial increases in striatal areas disappear with chronic treatment (Scatton et al., 1976). It is significant that the anti-psychotic action of neuroleptics only develops with chronic treatment (Hamill and Fontana, 1975), a further criticism of the many acute studies with animals. Post-mortem studies on human brains have found elevated levels of dopamine metabolites in the cortex of schizophrenics given long-term neuroleptic treatment (Bacopoulos et al., 1979); the authors suggest that tolerance develops to the drug-induced effects in nigro–striatal and meso–limbic dopamine systems, and that the therapeutic action is concentrated in the cortex.

The dopamine hypothesis of schizophrenia relies heavily upon the un-doubted efficacy of neuroleptic drugs in blocking dopamine receptors, and on the similarity between the toxic amphetamine psychosis and paranoid schizophrenia (Snyder, 1973). Dopamine stimulants such as amphetamine and methylphenidate have also been reported to exacerbate florid symptoms in schizophrenic patients (e.g., Janowsky and Davis, 1976; Janowsky et al., 1977), although negative results have been found (e.g., Van Kammen et al., 1980) which may relate to chronicity of the patient (Kornetsky, 1976). As dopamine-receptor blocking by neuroleptics is of limited effectiveness in schizophrenia (Section 1), there are grounds for suggesting a pragmatic dichotomy between drug-responsive and drug-unresponsive subtypes; the latter automatically then manifest a chronic or process form of the disorder, possibly exhibiting other features such as identifiable organic damage and cognitive impairment (Section 2.2).

Crow (1980) has put forward such an hypothesis, separating Type I and Type II syndromes. Type I exhibit positive Schneiderian first-rank symptoms, show an acute onset and good response to neuroleptic therapy, and represent a fundamental malfunction in dopamine pathways. Type II represent slow onset chronic schizophrenia with a predominance of negative symptoms (flat affect, speech poverty, etc.), a poor response to drug therapy, and possibly reflecting irreversible organic brain damage.

MacKay (1980) points out that Crow's Type II syndrome corresponds to Kraepelin's original description of dementia praecox (Section 1), where florid symptoms, if present, were seen as accessory, and superimposed upon the fundamental defect state. Some post-mortem studies report increased numbers of dopamine receptors in the brains of schizophrenics, which may not be related to neuroleptic drug treatment (MacKay et al., 1980; Owen et al., 1978); post-mortems, by their nature, involve chronic schizophrenics, and MacKay (1980) suggests that the increase in dopamine receptors is secondary to a fundamental reduction in dopamine turnover in the brains of these patients i.e., they have a reduction in dopamine activity rather than the hyperactivity posited by the conventional hypothesis: as florid symptoms may be superimposed upon the chronic syndrome, any clear distinction between Type I and Type II is somewhat artificial, and similarly an unambiguous biochemical separation would seem improbable. Until post-mortem studies or computerized axial tomography scans of the brains of living patients produce reliable and consistent data, the major distinction between Type I and Type II syndromes is still their relative responsiveness and unresponsiveness to neuroleptic drugs. The efficacy of dopamine-blocking agents in the Type I acute psychosis led to the production of pharmacological and quasi-behavioral models of schizophrenia in animals. In contrast, the failure to conceptualize the psychological deficit in chronic schizophrenia and the absence of any effective treatment prevents any attempt to model either its behavioral or biochemical aspects in animals.

3. THE EXTRAPOLATORY PROBLEM

I began this chapter by pointing out the improbability of producing an animal model behaviorally isomorphic with the symptoms of schizophrenia in humans. Other psychopathologies are less constrained. Depression, with its central clinical features of psychomotor retardation and a frequent association with predisposing life events, lends itself to animal behavioral models such as learnt helplessness (Miller and Seligman, 1975) or mother–infant separation in monkeys (see e.g., Lewis et al., 1976). Anxiolytic drugs have specific and characteristic disinhibitory effects upon conflict responding in the rat, in which responses are simultaneously rewarded and punished (Sepinwall and Cook, 1978), a behavior which can be conceptualized as being mediated by 'fear' or 'anxiety', and therefore as a plausible behavioral/pharmacological model of the human state.

Isolated symptoms of schizophrenia have been used to legitimize animal models. Changes in emotional behavior were related to the effects of frontal and limbic lesions upon emotional behavior (almost always aggression) in animals, which in turn were used as a rationale for psychosurgical intervention (Section 2.1). Inappropriate reactions to rewarding stimuli have led to an hypothesized malfunction of the brain's reward pathways, which in turn had been identified through animal experiments (Section 2.3). Perhaps the easiest aspect of schizophrenia to model would be the chronic defect state, as negative symptoms such as flattened affect and lack of volition (psychomotor retardation) could be descriptions of some animal behavior, e.g., in monkeys after injection of the catecholamine-depleting drug reserpine, or in rats after nigro-striatal lesions (Ungerstedt *et al.*, 1977). However, there would be no way of testing the model, apart from it showing the same unresponsiveness to neuroleptics as do chronic schizophrenics.

One of the few solid facts about schizophrenia is that where drugs are effective, the drugs are dopamine receptor blocking agents. Although fresh candidates appear (e.g., Gunne *et al.*, 1977; Gruzelier, 1978) from time to time, it is impressive that still the only consistent neuroleptics have this anti-dopaminergic characteristic. So, although attempts to model schizophrenia as dopamine hyperactivity can be criticized (Section 2.3), the dopamine link is still the best we have.

The tactic, I would suggest, is consciously, though temporarily, to ignore the symptomatology of schizophrenia (rather than inadvertently, as has been the case) and concentrate instead upon a behavioral analysis of the dopamine systems in animals. This has been proceeding anyway as a by-product of the dopamine hypothesis of schizophrenia, but is constrained by the constant and unnecessary appeal to 'clinical relevance'. This is less of a problem with the nigro–striatal pathway, as drug and lesion-induced motor disorders in the rat have a reasonable and predictable resemblance to various human dyskinesias (Klawans *et al.*, 1977). However, if, as hypothesized, the meso-limbic–cortical pathway is the site of delusions, hallucinations and thought disorders in schizophrenics, then we may immediately conclude that this pathway mediates different behaviors in the rat, and begin looking for them.

The anatomical and behavioral homology between rat and human nigro–striatal systems is encouraging, and suggests that a behavioral characterization of the meso–limbic–cortical dopamine innervation in animals might be validly generalized to humans.

Extrapolation from animals to humans is central to physiological psychology, but its validity has often been assumed rather than argued. During evolution brain structures and the behavior they mediate have changed, and the extrapolatory problem consists in deciding whether the changes are fundamental or phenomenological, i.e., whether apparently different behaviors across species can represent activity in homologous brain structures, or whether they represent activity in two structures with the same name but with qualitatively distinct modes of operating. The reverse problem also occurs. Apparently similar behavior across species, e.g., classical conditioning, may not represent the activity of homologous brain structures, but instead represent a shift in structure/function relationships through evolution. (See Oakley, Chapter 13.)

The evidence for and against is sparse. Some of the most impressive human clinical data concern the role of hippocampal damage in anterograde amnesia (e.g., Milner, 1970; Penfield and Mathieson, 1974). Until recently, parallel work in rats emphasized hippocampal mediation of internal inhibition, attention, and orientating (e.g., Douglas, 1975; Vinogradova, 1975; Sokolov, 1975), but now memory models have found supporting data, with evidence that the rat hippocampus is involved in spatial memory (O'Keefe and Nadel, 1978), classical conditioning (Thompson *et al.*, 1980), and perhaps an animal analog of 'working memory' (Olton, *et al.*, 1980). Work with primates (e.g., Mishkin, 1978) also supports an involvement of temporal-limbic circuits in memory processes.

An evolutionary perspective, comparing neocortical, striatal, and hippocampal development across a range of primates, shows that neocortical growth from primitive to advanced primates is matched by striatal growth, suggesting a close functional relationship (Stephan and Andy, 1969). Hippocampal growth has not kept pace with the increase in neocortex, although intralimbic correlations, e.g., between hippocampus and septum, are impressive. There is, therefore, some tenuous evidence for a possible change in hippocampal/neocortical structural relationships, with perhaps a parallel change in their functional relationships.

The variability in neocortex/hippocampus size relationships seen in living primates (Stephan and Andy, 1969) suggests that extrapolating function across species should be done only with caution. More optimistically, the work of Warburton on the behavioral functions of the central cholinergic system does appear to justify across-species comparisons (see Warburton, Chapter 18). Using a signal detection paradigm, he has shown that anticholinergic drugs reduce stimulus sensitivity in the rat, while cholinergic drugs facilitate stimulus discrimination (Warburton and Brown, 1971; 1972). Cholinergic pathways innervate hippocampus and neocortex, providing a convincing substrate for such effects (Warburton, 1977), while recent work has demonstrated a similar cholinergic modulation of stimulus sensitivity in humans (Wesnes and Warburton, 1978), the monkey (Evans, 1975), and in the pigeon (Cleeves and Green, 1982).

Stimulus discrimination is a behavioral function basic to all animals with a nervous system. It can be operationalized, and its chemical or structural bases investigated. The evidence so far suggests that it possesses a similarity across species both phenomenological and chemical. It is also intriguing that the gross impairment of stimulus processing at the cortex produced by high doses of anticholinergic drugs can lead to hallucinatory episodes in human subjects (Warburton, 1979).

If the behavioral functions of the meso–limbic–cortical dopamine pathways could be similarly identified in animals, there would be grounds for extrapolating to the human condition. Once the normal functions were established, speculations on what an abnormality would look like could begin, and perhaps shed some light on the psychological deficit in schizophrenia.

As an anatomically coherent system, it is tempting to hypothesize that the meso–limbic–cortical pathway has a parallel behavioral coherence, similar to the association of cholinergic pathways with the precise psychological function of stimulus discrimination. There are some speculative hypotheses along these lines. Iversen (1977) proposes that the meso–limbic–cortical dopamine system is involved in selecting appropriate responses and, more generally, in motivational arousal; the nigro–striatal system provides the sensory-motor arousal necessary for the response to be emitted. Matthysse (1974) works on a slightly grander level. He draws a parallel between the two dopamine systems and concludes that, as the nigro–striatal pathway controls which of a number of motor action patterns is allowed final expression, the meso–limbic–cortical pathway might perform a similar function for consciousness, i.e., it would act as a filter, deciding which pre-conscious or unconscious material is allowed access to conscious processing.

This latter speculation matches neatly with the proposal by Frith (1979) that the key diagnostic symptoms of schizophrenia—hallucinations and delusions—could be produced by a malfunction of the filter mechanisms that controls the contents of consciousness, i.e., the schizophrenic becomes aware of cognitive, perceptual, and motor processes which normally operate below the level of awareness.

Such ideas are virtually impossible to operationalize in animals, but are attractive in that they also account for a heterogeneous collection of symptoms via a single malfunction in the mechanism. Hemsley (1977), using the persistently popular notion that attentional problems cause an information overload in schizophrenics, details precisely how various coping strategies could produce various psychotic symptoms. Although he later modifies his view of the primary defect, moving from a filtering deficit to problems with response selection (Hemsley and Richardson, 1980), the overall strategy can be retained; individual differences in coping responses can lead to heterogeneous symptomatology.

Consciousness and self-report of hallucinations and delusions are central to schizophrenia and cannot be modelled in animals. If, instead, they could be reconceptualized as attentional dysfunctions leading to impaired stimulus control of behavior (where stimuli are both external and internal), then we move closer to a behavioral analogy between human and animal. Although it has been convincingly demonstrated that the central cholinergic system plays a major part in stimulus discrimination, there is no reason why other neurotransmitter systems could not be involved; indeed, given the comprehensive interplay of chemical pathways in the brain, it is certain that other systems will be involved. In this context, it is tempting to extend the parallel with the nigro–striatal dopamine pathway, and predict that the meso–limbic–cortical pathway will have direct connections with the extensive limbic and cortical cholinergic network.

Previous proposals for animal models in schizophrenia research have emphasized multiple pharmacological criteria (e.g., Matthysse and Haber, 1975). The logical outcome is that any behavior, however bizarre, which responds appropriately to neuroleptic and non-neuroleptic drugs satisfies the criteria. Although this approach is useful for selecting therapeutic agents, a psychological analysis of the functions of central dopamine pathways would in the long run be more fruitful. It may shed light upon the etiology of schizophrenia; it is certain to extend our knowledge of brain and behavior relationships, thereby making extrapolation between species less speculative and more informed. In this sense, the use of animal models in schizophrenia will become, as it always should have been, secondary to the fundamental analysis of brain mechanisms of behavior.

ACKNOWLEDGMENT

I would like to thank Steve Walker for reading an earlier version of this chapter and making several incisive and valuable suggestions.

REFERENCES

Akiskal, H. S., and McKinney, W. T. (1975) Overview of recent research in depression. *Archives of General Psychiatry*, 32, 285–305.

Bacopoulos, N. C., Spokes, E. G., Bird, E. D., and Roth, R. H. (1979) Antipsychotic drug action in schizophrenic patients: effect on cortical dopamine metabolism after long-term treatment. *Science*, 205, 1405–1407.

Bagshaw, M. H., and Kimble, D. P. (1972) Bimodal EDR orienting response characteristics of limbic lesioned monkeys: correlates with schizophrenic patients. Paper read to American Society for Psychophysiological Research.

Bland, R. C., and Orn, H. (1979) Schizophrenia: diagnostic criteria and outcome. *British Journal of Psychiatry*, 134, 34–38.

Bland, R. C., and Orn, H. (1980) Schizophrenia: Schneider's first-rank symptoms and outcome. *British Journal of Psychiatry*, 137, 63–68.

Blashfield, R. K., and Draguns, J. G. (1976) Toward a toxonomy of psychopathology: the purpose of psychiatric classification. *British Journal of Psychiatry*, 129, 574–583.

Bleuler, E. (1950) Dementia praecox or the group of schizophrenias. *Monograph Series on Schizophrenia: No. 1*, New York: International University Press.

Bolles, R. C. (1967) *Theory of Motivation*. New York: Harper & Row.

Borison, R. L., and Diamond, B. I. (1978) A new animal model for schizophrenia. *Biological Psychiatry*, 13, 217–225.

Carlsson, A. (1978) Does dopamine have a role in schizophrenia? *Biological Psychiatry*, 13, 3–21.

Carpenter, W. T., Bartko, J. J., Carpenter, C. L., and Strauss, J. S. (1976) Another view of schizophrenia subtypes. *Archives of General Psychiatry*, 33, 508–516.

Carpenter, W. T., Bartko, J. J., Strauss, J. S., and Hawk, A. B. (1978) Signs and symptoms as predictors of outcome: A report from the International Pilot Study of Schizophrenia. *American Journal of Psychiatry*, 135, 940–945.

Cleeves, L., and Green, S. E. (1982) Effects of scopolamine on visual difference thresholds in the pigeon. In Press, *Physiological Psychology*.

Creese, I., Burt, D. R., and Snyder, S. H. (1976) Dopamine receptor binding predicts clinical potential and pharmacological potencies of anti-schizophrenic drugs. *Science*, **192**, 481–483.

Crow, T. J. (1972) Catecholamine-containing neurones and electrical self-stimulation: 1. A review of some data. *Psychological Medicine*, **2**, 414–421.

Crow, T. J. (1973) Catecholamine-containing neurones and electrical self-stimulation: 2. A theoretical interpretation and some psychiatric implications. *Psychological Medicine*, **3**, 66–73.

Crow, T. J. (1980) Molecular pathology of schizophrenia; more than one disease process? *British Medical Journal*, **280**, 66–68.

Davison, K., and Bagley, C. R. (1969) Schizophrenia-like psychoses associated with organic disorders of the central nervous system: A review of the literature. *British Journal of Psychiatry, Special Publication No. 4*, 113–184.

Douglas, R. J. (1975) The development of hippocampal function: Implications for theory and for therapy. In Isaacson, R. L., and Pribram, K. H. (eds), *The Hippocampus, Vol. 2*. New York: Academic Press.

Evans, H. L. (1975) Scopolamine effects on visual discrimination: Modifications related to stimulus control. *Journal of Pharmacology and Experimental Therapeutics*, **195**, 105–113.

Falek, A., and Moser, H. M. (1975) Classification in schizophrenia. *Archives of General Psychiatry*, **32**, 59–67.

Feighner, J. P., Robins, F., Guze, J. B., Woodruff, R. A., Winokur, G., and Munoz, R. (1972) Diagnostic criteria for use in psychiatric research. *Archives of General Psychiatry*, **26**, 57–63.

Fibiger, H. C., and Phillips, A. G. (1974) Role of dopamine and norepinephrine in the chemistry of reward. *Journal of Psychiatric Research*, **11**, 135–143.

Fox, H. A. (1981) The DSM-III concept of schizophrenia. *British Journal of Psychiatry*, **138**, 60–63.

Freeman, D. (1971) Frontal lobotomy in early schizophrenia: Long-term follow-up. *British Journal of Psychiatry*, **119**, 621–624.

Frith, C. D. (1979) Consciousness, information processing and schizophrenia. *British Journal of Psychiatry*, **134**, 225–235.

Fulton, J. F., and Jacobsen, C. F. (1935) The functions of the frontal lobes, a comparative study in monkeys, chimpanzees and man. *Abstracts from the 2nd International Neurological Congress*, London.

Gallistel, C. R. (1973) Self-stimulation: The neurophysiology of reward and motivation. In Deutsch, J. A. (ed.), *The Physiological Basis of Memory*. New York: Academic Press.

Gomes, U. C. R., Shanley, B. C., Potgeiter, L., and Roux, J. T. (1980) Noradrenergic overactivity in chronic schizophrenia: Evidence based on cerebrospinal fluid noradrenaline and cyclic nucleotide concentrations. *British Journal of Psychiatry*, **137**, 346–351.

Gottesman, I., and Shields, J. (1976) A critical review of recent adoption, twin, and family studies of schizophrenia: Behavioural and genetics perspectives. *Schizophrenia Bulletin*, **2**, 360–389.

Grossman, S. P. (1960) Eating or drinking elicited by direct adrenergic or cholinergic stimulation of hypothalamus. *Science*, **132**, 301–302.

Gruzelier, J. H. (1978) Propranolol and the neuropsychophysiology of schizophrenia: implications for the drug's central mechanisms of action. In Roberts, E., and Amacher, L. (eds), *Propranolol and Schizophrenia*. New York: Raven Press.

Gruzelier, J. H., and Flor-Henry, P. (eds) (1979) *Hemisphere Asymmetries of Function in Psychopathology*. Amsterdam: Elsevier.

Gruzelier, J. H., and Venables, P. H. (1974) Bimodality and lateral asymmetry of skin conductance orienting activity in schizophrenics. *Biological Psychiatry*, **8**, 55–73.

Gunne, L. M., Lindstrom, L., and Terenius, L. (1977) Naloxone-induced reversal of schizophrenic hallucinations. *Journal of Neural Transmission*, **40**, 13–19.

Hamill, W. T., and Fontana, A. F. (1975) The immediate effects of chlorpromazine in newly admitted schizophrenic patients. *American Journal of Psychiatry*, **132**, 1023–1026.

Hawk, A. B., Carpenter, W. T., and Strauss, J. S. (1975) Diagnostic criteria and five-year outcome in schizophrenia. *Archives of General Psychiatry*, **32**, 343–347.

Helzer, J. E., Clayton, P. J. Pambakian, R., Reich, T., Woodruff, R. A., and Reveley, M. A. (1977) Reliability of psychiatric diagnosis II, the test/retest reliability of diagnostic classification. *Archives of General Psychiatry*, **34**, 136–141.

Hemsley, D. R. (1977) What have cognitive deficits to do with schizophrenic symptoms? *British Journal of Psychiatry*, **130**, 167–173.

Hemsley, D. R., and Richardson, P. H. (1980) Shadowing by context in schizophrenia. *Journal of Nervous and Mental Disease*, **168**, 141–145.

Herberg, L. J., Stephens, D. N., and Franklin, K. B. (1976) Catecholamines and self-stimulation: Evidence suggesting reinforcing role for noradrenaline and a motivating role for dopamine. *Pharmacology, Biochemistry and Behaviour*, **4**, 575–582.

Iversen, S. D. (1977) Striatal function and stereotyped behaviour. In Cools, A. R., Lohman, A. H. M., and Van Den Bercken, J. H. L. (eds), *Psychobiology of the Striatum*. Amsterdam: North Holland.

Janowsky, D. A., and Davis, J. M. (1976) Methylphenidate, dextroamphetamine, and levamphetamine: Effects on schizophrenic symptoms. *Archives of General Psychiatry*, **33**, 304–308.

Janowsky, D. S., Huey, L., Storms, L., and Judd, L. L. (1977) Methylphenidate hydrochloride effects on psychological tests in acute schizophrenic and nonpsychotic patients. *Archives of General Psychiatry*, **34**, 189–194.

Johnstone, E. C., Crow, T. J., Frith, C. D., Husband, J., and Kreel, L. (1976) Cerebral ventricular size and cognitive impairment in chronic schizophrenia. *Lancet*, **ii**, 924–926.

Kelly, D. H. W., Richardson, A., and Mitchell-Heggs, N. (1973a) Stereotactic limbic leucotomy: neurophysiological aspects and operative technique. *British journal of psychiatry*, **123**, 133–140.

Kelly, D. H. W., Richardson, A., Mitchell-Heggs, N., Greenup, J., Chen, C., and Hafner, R. J. (1973b) Stereotactic limbic leucotomy: A preliminary report on forty patients. *British Journal of Psychiatry*, **123**, 141–148.

Kendell, R. E. (1976) The classification of depressions: a review of contemporary confusion. *British Journal of Psychiatry*, **129**, 15–28.

Klawans, H. L., Hitri, A., Nausieda, P. A., and Weiner, W. J. (1977) Animal models of dyskinesia. In Hanin, I., and Usdin, E. (eds), *Animal Models in Psychiatry and Neurology*. Oxford: Pergamon Press.

Klein, D. F., and Davis, J. M. (1969) *Diagnosis and Drug Treatment of Psychiatric Disorders*. Baltimore: Williams and Wilkins.

Kornetsky, C., and Eliasson, M. (1969) Reticular stimulation and chlorpromazine: an animal model for schizophrenic over-arousal. *Science*, **165**, 1273–1274.

Kornetsky, E. (1976) Hyporesponsivity of chronic schizophrenic patients to dextroamphetamine. *Archives of General Psychiatry*, 33, 1425–1428.

Kraepelin, E. (1919) *Dementia praecox and paraphrenia*. Translated by Barclay, R. M., and Robertson, G. M., Edinburgh: E. and S. Livingstone.

Langfeldt, G. (1937) *The Prognosis in Schizophrenia and the Factors Influencing the Course of the Disease*. Copenhagen: *Munksgaard*.

Lewis, J. K., McKinney, W. T., Young, L. D., and Kraemer, G. W. (1976) Mother–infant separation in Rhesus monkeys as a model of human depression. *Archives of General Psychiatry*, 33, 699–705.

Lewis, P. R., and Shute, C. C. D. (1967) The cholinergic limbic system: projections to hippocampal formation, medial cortex, nuclei of the ascending cholinergic reticular system, and the subfornical organ and supra-optic crest. *Brain*, 90, 521–539.

Liebman, J. M., and Butcher, L. L. (1973) Effects on self-stimulation behaviour of drugs influencing dopaminergic neurotransmission mechanisms. *Archives of Pharmacology*, 277, 305–318.

Lippa, A. S., Antelman, S. M., Fisher, A. E., and Canfield, D. R. (1973) Neurochemical mediation of reward: a significant role for dopamine? *Pharmacology, Biochemistry and Behaviour*, 1, 23–28.

Mackay, A. V. P. (1980) Positive and negative schizophrenic symptoms and the role of dopamine. *British Journal of Psychiatry*, 137, 379–386.

Mackay, A. V. P., Bird, E. D., Iversen, L. L., Spokes, E. G., Creese, I., and Snyder, S. H. (1980) Dopaminergic abnormalities in post-mortem schizophrenic brain. In Cattabeni, F., Racagni, G., Spano, P., and Costa, E. (eds), *Advances in Biochemical Psychopharmacology*, Vol. 24. New York: Raven Press.

Matthysse, S. (1974) Schizophrenia: relationships to dopamine transmission, motor control and feature extraction. In Schmitt, F. O., and Worden, F. G. (eds), *Neurosciences: Third Study Program*. Cambridge, Mass.: MIT Press.

Matthysse, S., and Haber, S. (1975) Animal models of schizophrenia. In Ingle, D. J., and Shein, H. M. (eds), *Model Systems in Biological Psychiatry*, Cambridge, Mass.: MIT Press.

Mayer-Gross, W., Slater, E., and Roth, M. (1977) *Clinical Psychiatry*. London: Baillière Tindall.

Mellor, C. S. (1970) First-rank symptoms of schizophrenia. *British Journal of Psychiatry*, 117, 15–23.

Miller, W. R., and Seligman, M. E. P. (1975) Depression and learned helplessness in man. *Journal of Abnormal Psychology*, 84, 228–238.

Milner, B. (1970) Memory and the temporal regions of the brain. In Pribram, K. H., and Broadbent, D. E. (eds), *Biology of Memory*. New York: Academic Press.

Mishkin, M. (1978) Memory in monkeys severely impaired by combined but not separate removal of amygdala and hippocampus. *Nature*, 273, 297–298.

Moniz, E. (1936) *Tentatives Operatoires dans le Traitement de Certaines Psychoses*. Paris: Masson.

O'Keefe, J., and Nadel, L. (1978) *The Hippocampus as a Cognitive Map*. Oxford: Clarendon Press.

Olds, J., and Milner, P. (1954) Positive reinforcement produced by electrical stimulation of septal area and other regions of rat brain. *Journal of Comparative and Physiological Psychology*, 47, 419–427.

Olton, D. S., Becker, J. T., and Handelmann, G. E. (1980) Hippocampal function: Working memory or cognitive mapping? *Physiological Psychology*, 8, 239–246.

Owen, F., Cross, A. J., Crow, T. J., Longden, A., Poulter, M., and Riley, G. J.

(1978) Increased dopamine receptor sensitivity in schizophrenia. *Lancet*, **ii**, 223–225.

Papez, J. W. (1937) A proposed mechanism of emotion. *Archives of Neurology and Psychiatry (Chicago)*, **38**, 725–743.

Penfield, W., and Mathieson, G. (1974) Memory: autopsy findings and comments on the role of the hippocampus in experiential recall. *Archives of Neurology*, **31**, 145–154.

Pribram, K. H. (1967) The limbic systems, efferent control of neural inhibition and behaviour. *Progress in Brain Research*, **27**, 318–336.

Pycock, C. J., and Marsden, C. D. (1978) The rotating rodent: a two-component system? *European Journal of Pharmacology*, **47**, 167–175.

Randrup, A., and Munkvad, I. (1970) Biochemical, anatomical and psychological investigations of stereotyped behavior induced by amphetamines. In Costa, E., and Garattini, S. (eds), *Amphetamines and Related Compounds*. New York: Raven Press.

Ritter, S., and Stein, L. (1974) Self-stimulation in the mesencephalic trajectory of the ventral noradrenergic bundle. *Brain Research*, **81**, 145–157.

Rosenthal, D. (1978) The schizophrenia spectrum disorders: implications for psychiatric diagnosis. In Akiskal, H. S., and Webb, W. L. (eds), *Psychiatric Diagnosis: Exploration of Biological Predictors*. New York: Spectrum.

Roth, M. (1978) Psychiatric diagnosis in clinical and scientific settings. In Akiskal, H. S., and Webb, W. L. (eds), *Psychiatric Diagnosis: Exploration of Biological Predictors*. New York: Spectrum.

Scatton, B., Glowinski, J., and Julou, L. (1976) Dopamine metabolism in the meso-limbic and mesocortical dopaminergic systems after single or repeated administrations of neuroleptics. *Brain Research*, **109**, 184–189.

Schneider, K. (1959) *Clinical Psychopathology*. New York: Grune & Stratton.

Seeman, P., Lee, T., Chau-Wong, M., and Wong, K. (1976) Antipsychotic drug doses and neuroleptic/dopamine receptors. *Nature*, **261**, 717–719.

Sepinwall, J., and Cook, L. (1978) Behavioural pharmacology of antianxiety drugs. In Iversen, L. L., Iversen, S. D., and Snyder, S. H. (eds) *Handbook of Psychopharmacology, Vol. 13: Biology of Mood and Antianxiety Drugs*. New York: Plenum.

Shute, C. C. D., and Lewis, P. R. (1967) The ascending cholinergic reticular system: neocortical, olfactory and subcortical projections. *Brain*, **90**, 497–520.

Singh, M. M., and Kay, S. R. (1978) Nosological and prognostic distinctions in schizophrenia. *Neuropsychobiology*, **4**, 288–304.

Snyder, S. H. (1973) Amphetamine psychosis: A model schizophrenia mediated by catecholamines. *American Journal of Psychiatry*, **130**, 61–67.

Snyder, S. H., Greenberg, D., and Yamamura, H. I. (1974) Antischizophrenic drugs and brain cholinergic receptors. *Archives of General Psychiatry*, **31**, 58–65.

Sokolov, E. N. (1975) The orienting reflex. In Sokolov, E. N. and Vinogradova, O. S. (eds), *Neuronal Mechanisms of the Orienting Reflex*. New York: Wiley.

Stein, L. (1968) Chemistry of reward and punishment. In Efron, D. H. (eds.), *Psychopharmacology, A Review of Progress: 1957–1967*. Washington: US Government Printing Office.

Stein, L. (1971) Neurochemistry of reward and punishment: Some implications for the aetiology of schizophrenia. *Journal of Psychiatric Research*, **8**, 345–361.

Stephan, H., and Andy, O. J. (1969) Quantitative comparative neuroanatomy of primates: An attempt at a phylogenetic interpretation. *Annals of the New York Academy of Sciences*, **167**, 370–386.

Stevens, J. R. (1973) An anatomy of schizophrenia? *Archives of General Psychiatry*, **29**, 177–189.

Thompson, R. F., Berger, T. W., Berry, S. D., Hoehler, F. K., Kettner, R. E., and Weisz, D. J. (1980) Hippocampal substrate of classical conditioning. *Physiological Psychology*, **8**, 262–279.

Torrey, E. F., and Peterson, M. R. (1974) Schizophrenia and the limbic system. *Lancet*, **ii**, 942–946.

Ungerstedt, U. (1971) Stereotaxic mapping of the monoamine pathways in the rat brain. *Acta Physiologica Scandanavica, Supplement 367*, 1–48.

Ungerstedt, U., Ljungberg, T., and Ranje, C. (1977) Dopamine neurotransmission and the control of behaviour. In Cools, A. R., Lohman, A. H. M., and Van Den Bercken, J. H. L. (eds), *Psychobiology of the Striatum*. Amsterdam: North Holland.

Van Kammen, D. P., Docherty, J. P., Marder, S. R., Schulz, S. C., and Bunney, W. E. (1980) Lack of behavioural supersensitivity to d-amphetamine after pimozide withdrawal. *Archives of General Psychiatry*, **37**, 287–290.

Venables, P. H. (1972) Input regulation and psychopathology. In Hammer, H., Salzinger, K., and Sutton, S. (eds), *Psychopathology*. New York: Wiley.

Vinogradova, O. S. (1975) The hippocampus and the orienting reflex. In Sokolov, E. N., and Vinogradova, O. S. (eds), *Neuronal Mechanisms of the Orienting Reflex*. New York: Wiley.

Warburton, D. M. (1977) Stimulus selection and behavioural inhibition. In Iversen, L. L., Iversen, S. D., and Snyder, S. H. (eds), *Handbook of Psychopharmacology, Vol. 8: Drugs, Neurotransmitters and Behavior*. New York: Plenum.

Warburton, D. M. (1979) Neurochemical bases of consciousness. In Brown, K., and Cooper, S. J. (eds), *Chemical Influences on Behaviour*. London: Academic Press.

Warburton, D. M., and Brown, K. (1971) Scopolamine-induced attenuation of stimulus sensitivity. *Nature*, **230**, 126–127.

Warburton, D. M., and Brown, K. (1972) The facilitation of discrimination performance by physostigmine sulphate. *Psychopharmacologia*, **27**, 275–284.

Weinberger, D. R., Bigelow, L. B., Kleinman, J. E., Klein, S. T., Rosenblatt, J. E., and Wyatt, R. J. (1980) Cerebral ventricular enlargement in chronic schizophrenia associated with poor response to treatment. *Archives of General Psychiatry*, **37**, 11–13.

Wesnes, K., and Warburton, D. M. (1978) The effect of cigarette smoking and nicotine tablets upon human attention. In Thornton, R. E. (ed.), *Smoking Behaviour: Physiological and Psychological Influences*. London: Churchill-Livingstone.

Wise, C. D., and Stein, L. (1975) Reply to Wyatt *et al*. *Science*, **187**, 370.

Wise, C. D., Baden, M. M., and Stein, L. (1974) Post-mortem measurement of enzymes in human brain: Evidence of a central noradrenergic deficit in schizophrenia. *Journal of Psychiatric Research*, **11**, 185–198.

Wise, C. D., Berger, B. D., and Stein, L. (1973) Evidence of α-noradrenergic reward receptors and serotonergic punishment receptors in the rat brain. *Biological Psychiatry*, **6**, 3–21.

Wyatt, R. J., Schwartz, M. A., Erdelyi, E., and Barchas, J. D. (1975) Dopamine-β-hydroxylase activity in brains of chronic schizophrenic patients. *Science*, **187**, 368–370.

Animal Models of Human Behavior
Edited by G. C. L. Davey
© 1983 John Wiley & Sons Ltd

Chapter 18

Extrapolation in the Neurochemistry of Behavior

David M. WARBURTON

In this chapter I will be arguing that an important aim in psychology is the development of mechanism hypotheses of human behavior and one important group of mechanism hypotheses employs the concepts of biochemistry especially those of brain neurochemistry. The importance of the development of neurochemical theories of human behavior lies in the rational development of drugs for the alleviation of suffering. However, at the present stage of development of the science, the relations between neurochemical events and behavior can only be established in animal studies and consequently hypotheses about the relations between neurochemical events and human behavior are derived by extrapolation. The detailed justification for this extrapolation will be considered in later sections and it will be concluded that it is an empirical question which can be tested like any other hypothesis in terms of the positive and negative evidence.

1. MATURATION OF PSYCHOLOGY AS A SCIENCE

A science can increase both by surface growth, i.e. accumulating, generalizing and systematizing information, or by depth growth, i.e. introducing new concepts, going beyond the available information and explaining it (Bunge, 1968). Until recently, expansion of psychological knowledge has been due to surface growth in which attention has been focused on description, systematization and prediction at the expense of adventurous theorizing because too little information has been available for postulating detailed mechanisms and because the conjecture of mechanisms has been discouraged by certain schools of psychology (e.g. Skinner, 1958). Of course, surface growth is important but it is insufficient in itself to achieve maturity in a science and the maturation of psychology will occur when breadth and depth are sought and achieved.

Depth in science can be achieved by introducing hypotheses that involve unobservables which are interrelated in the form of mechanism hypotheses and can eventually be organized axiomatically (Bunge, 1968). Non-observational hypotheses can merely describe the system from outside (phenomenological hypotheses) or they can be formulated in terms of the inner function of the system (mechanism hypotheses). Phenomenological or 'black box' hypotheses are deeper than information-summarizing statements, but not as deep as mechanism hypotheses. Consequently, there is a transition from information summary to phenomenological hypotheses and then to mechanism hypotheses as that science matures. The introduction of mechanism hypotheses does not mean that the hypotheses are untestable, but, on the contrary, are broader and so commit themselves much more than phenomenological hypotheses. They are more testable, even though the testing may be less direct.

The traditional hypotheses of psychophysics, perception and learning were concerned with relating output variables to a set of input variables as hypotheses of the form of $R = f(S)$ relations (see Spence, 1944). It was the aim of this work to state these interrelations in terms of quantitative laws. Some psychological theorists went further than these simple relations by postulating events mediating between inputs and outputs $S-O-R$. These theoretical constructs were intervening variables which can be thought of as operators that convert the input into an output. Examples of this sort of phenomenological theorizing are to be seen in the work of Tolman, Hull, and Spence (see Koch, 1959). However, some theorists have postulated neural processes that operate on the input and so they have formulated mechanism hypotheses, e.g. Hebb (1949).

2. BIOCHEMISTRY OF BEHAVIOR HYPOTHESES

The biological sciences are concerned with the many phenomena of living organisms, including behavior. A living organism is, by definition, a dynamic system and underlying every biological activity is some chemical change. Pharmacologists have studied the changes in biological activity after the administration of chemical agents, and one of the recent advances in this science has been the expansion of research that has been devoted to the elucidation of the biochemical mechanisms underlying behavioral phenomena. This area of investigation can be characterized as the study of environment–biochemical system–behavior interactions. This characterization conforms to the pattern of psychological experimentation, $S-O-R$, outlined in the preceding section. However, the S variables are stimuli, the O variables are biochemical variables within the organism, and R variables are selected behavioral variables. In psychopharmacology, drugs can be considered as a special class of stimuli.

Theories, which are based on this methodology are designed to explain behavioral phenomena in terms of biochemical states in specific areas of the organism, i.e. to produce biochemically-based theories of behavior. The aim of these theories is not the elimination of psychological theory, but the coordination of its concepts with those of biochemistry. An important special case of these theories are those which coordinate psychological concepts with neurochemistry, i.e. neurochemically-based theories of behavior. This procedure will result in refinements of the theoretical constructs in psychology, so that more accurate predictions of behavior can be made from the theories. In summary, the object of experimentation in this field is the discovery and study of the causal relations between biochemical events and behavior in terms of the variables outlined above, $R = f(O)$.

At first glance it appears that there are only two classes of events to be considered, biochemical events and behavior, but it is often useful to consider other properties of the living organism including structural and electrophysiological, as well as biochemical and behavioral (Russell, 1966). Each of these properties could be an independent variable and one of the other three a dependent variable, but the electrophysiological and structural variable are considered as subsidiary intraorganismic factors which covary with biochemical events in the neurochemistry of behavior. Thus structural and electrophysiological changes are considered as influencing behavior mediated by some neurochemical change and, in the same way, behavior may produce structural and electrophysiological via neurochemical changes.

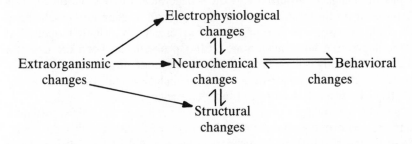

Changes in the intraorganismic variables, when behavior is the dependent variable, are produced by extraorganismic events which interact with organism, including administration of a chemical agent like a drug. In classical psychopharmacology the major hypotheses have been of the drug-behaviour, $R = f(S)$, type which are tested by administering a number of levels of the agent and observing changes in behavior as a function of dose and time to give dose–response and time–response relations (Russell, 1964a). The specificity of hypotheses depends to a great extent on the degree of precision in the statements about the dependent variable. A strong hypothesis is qualitatively very exact in describing the behavior affected and quantitatively very precise in specifying the direction and magnitude of change. From a theoretical point of view the more precise the hypothesis is formulated, the easier it is to test but, most behavior is multicomponent, and so greater ingenuity is required to design behavioral situations to allow unequivocal interpretation of the behavioral mode of action.

The major focus of this research has been on the description and systematization of drug action as a consequence of the Skinnerian atheoretical approach of the early psychopharmacologists. It has resulted in considerable surface growth in psychopharmacology, but has contributed little to a deeper understanding of behavior. Tests of biochemical system–behavior hypotheses are more interesting. These hypotheses are concerned with changes in behavior patterns as a function of changes in particular biochemical systems. From these hypotheses and their tests, mechanism theories can be developed about the biochemical substrates underlying specific types of behavior. The problem with these hypotheses is that they are difficult to test.

Tests of these hypotheses require graded variations in specific biochemical systems, and this is achieved by using chemical agents to produce changes in the biochemical system. Although the administration of drug X is known to produce a change in the biochemical system Y and in the test situation it produces a change in behavior pattern Z, interpretation is equivocal because it cannot be concluded that changes in behavior were related to the biochemical changes measured (Russell, 1964b). Drug X could have changed a second system which was unrelated to biochemical system Y but resulted in the behavior change Z. Alternatively the biochemical and behavioral changes could have been the result of drug X acting on a common biochemical system. In most cases selection of a drug with effects on a single biochemical system is impossible but one solution to this problem has been the use of a set of drugs with only one common biochemical mode of action. If they have the same effects on behavior then specific conclusions can be drawn about the relations between behavior and biochemistry.

As well as narrowing down the biochemical mode of action, research workers are concerned with localizing the effects of the drug within the brain, and formulating hypotheses accordingly. One method of localization is the use of electrical recording. If electrophysiological measures show that electrical activity at one site is greatly affected by the drug, while activity at another is little affected then the experimenter draws up hypotheses about the possible neurochemical pathways that are important for the behavioral effects. A second source of hypotheses are derived from the results of brain lesions and electrical stimulation, and reasoning by analogy enables possible sites of action to be delimited. Other predictions can also be derived from brain assays for the drug; regions with high concentrations can suggest sites of drug action, especially when this technique is combined with histochemical maps of transmitter pathways. These predictions can then be tested by direct injection into possible sites and analyses made of their relative contribution to the observed behavioral changes. In these analyses sites are being compared rather than testing a single site, i.e. the experimenter has multiple working hypotheses. The outcome of the studies is the elimination of many sites and the remaining nuclei are often shown to be organized into a network which is controlling the behavior.

Neural network theory (Warburton, 1975; 1981) proposes that behavior is the outcome of a pattern of activity in networks of neural units rather than the activity at a single center. Instead of a linear chain of neurones, there are multiple interacting pathways combining to produce a behavioral pattern. These networks give the brain considerable resistance to disruption and impairment only results from changes in the pattern of activity in the whole network. This systems approach represents an important change of emphasis in our thinking about the central nervous system and implies that the function of the constituent neurones in the network is constrained by mutual dependence and interdependence. As a result, the whole dynamic complex maintains a unity of action in spite of any unpredictable variability in the function of the units. This means that there can be individual variation in the neural units of the network that do not change the input–output relations of the system. However, the contribution of an individual neurone to the network is considerable and it is the average but particular characteristics of the individual neurones which results in the composite function of a pathway. It is a fallacy to assume that, because a lesion to a pathway has little permanent effect, that pathway does not contribute significantly to the behavior of the intact organism.

Network theory makes the claim that there are a number of basic behavioral systems in the brain that have the same chemical characteristics, i.e. chemically coded (Russell, 1966; Warburton, 1975; Warburton, 1981). A consequence of chemical similarity of the pathways in a behavioral network is that it should be possible to trace these pathways by chemical techniques. Recent research has confirmed that some pathways in the brain with the same behavioral function are chemically coded in the sense that they show similarities in terms of histochemical staining and response to chemical stimulation (Warburton, 1981). These basic systems have their origin in the more primitive portions of the brain so that the cholinergic, catecholamine, and monoaminergic pathways run from the reticular formation through the diencephalon with neocortical and paleocortical projections. In parts of the brain there is a coincidence of the various systems which suggests that the systems may have complementary function in behavior, and this has been supported by direct stimulation of the brain (Warburton, 1981).

It is obvious that research on neurochemical system–behavior hypotheses can only be performed with animals and that systematic studies of neuro-chemistry and behavior cannot be carried out in people. As the depth growth of our understanding of human behavior will only result from the postulation of neurophysiological and neurochemical mechanisms that operate on the various inputs and result in a particular pattern of behavior, the formulation of neurochemical system–human behavior hypotheses must be based on data from neurochemical system–animal behavior hypotheses.

One explicit attempt to use data on animal biochemistry to explain human behavior was analyzed by Schildkraut (1969). He outlined the logical steps involved in the 'pharmacological bridge' strategy to explain human affective disorders, using reserpine's effects as an example.

1. Reserpine produces depression in some people.
2. It is assumed that the depression results from the biochemical changes that are produced by reserpine.
(2a. Naturally occurring endogenous depressions are clinically indistin-guishable from reserpine-induced depressions and so may have the same biochemical substrate.)
3. Reserpine appears to cause the same biochemical changes in various species.
4. Therefore, reserpine's biochemical effects on the animal brain may provide data relevant to the biochemistry of reserpine-induced depressions in man.
(4a. Reserpine's biochemical effects on the animal brain may also provide data relevant to the biochemistry of naturally occurring endogenous depression in man.)

These steps can be reformulated in a more general and more unequivocal form, as follows:

1. A drug produces certain behavioral changes in people.
2. It is assumed that these changes result from biochemical changes induced by that drug.
(2a. The naturally-occurring behavior changes are indistinguishable from these drug-induced changes and so may have the same neurochemical substrate.)
3. This drug produces the same biochemical effects in various species.
4. Therefore, the biochemical changes that are produced by this drug in the brains of animals provide data that are relevant to the drug-induced changes in human behavior.
(4a. The biochemical changes produced by the drug in an animal brain provide data that are relevant to the biochemistry of naturally occur-ring behavioral changes in people.)

In the pharmacological bridge strategy, as outlined by Schildkraut (1969), the *specific* behavioral changes that are induced by the drug are not essential to the logic of the strategy. However, I will argue that a precise analysis of the behavioral changes is essential to the logic of extrapolation in the neurochemistry of behavior.

3. EXTRAPOLATION IN THE NEUROCHEMISTRY OF BEHAVIOR

In science extrapolation is used for both explanation and prediction of phenomena. Both explanation and prediction have the same logical structure and a hypothesis can only predict to the extent that it can describe and explain. However, explanation and prediction are not the same epistemologically (Bunge, 1959) because the phenomenon that it predicted is rarely the same as the observations that were described and explained by the hypothesis. For any hypothesis previous tests will not have explored all possible domains and even exhausted experimentally every possible area of one domain. In any consideration of the possibility that a hypothesis will represent observations other than those on which it is based, a distinction must be made between interpolation and extrapolation.

Scientists have great confidence in predictions which involve interpolation when there are a sufficient number of observations over the interpolation range. It is clear why this should be so because if a sufficient number of facts are established then it will be impossible to formulate multiple hypotheses that give predictions which could ever be differentiated experimentally. In contrast a hypothesis, that is derived by extrapolation, is being extended beyond the limits of the domain. As a consequence it is usually possible to devise many hypotheses which agree within experimental error with the observations inside the domain, but diverge widely outside the domain. There may be no reason at all *a priori* for preferring one extrapolated hypothesis to any of the others, and experimental error would introduce uncertainty into both explanation and prediction. However, it is only by extrapolation that we can extend the limits of the domain of application for our hypothesis and, as I argued earlier, extrapolation is the only way at present of providing neurochemical explanations for human behavior.

Extrapolation of hypotheses in psychobiology depend on the distinction between analogous and homologous behavior patterns. As Russell (1951; 1964a; 1964b) pointed out, homology refers to phenomena which are alike in form and result from the same anatomical structures, while analogy deals with phenomena which are superficially alike but are of different origin. The suggestion that extrapolations can be made from the domain of the neurochemistry of animal behavior to the neurochemistry of human behavior assumes that some behavior patterns are homologous and not merely analogous. Of course, human and animal behavior can never be completely alike in form and origin and so there will be a degree of uncertainty in the explanations and predictions which are derived by extrapolation. As a consequence extrapolation in the neurochemistry of behavior (and in psychobiology in general) can only be evaluated in probabilistic terms.

4. EVALUATION OF EXTRAPOLATED HYPOTHESES

The first step for establishing whether the behavior patterns of two species are homologous is to confirm that the behavior is not merely superficially similar. Similarity is a difficult term to define with clarity and precision because of its many everyday uses. In this context I am using the concept in the sense that it is used in taxonomic classification where similarity is established by the enumeration of the set of biological attributes that are possessed by two species. There are many methodological problems which are involved in the assessment of behavioral similarity (Frey, 1976) but these are not relevant to this discussion. The outcome of this process of enumeration will be a set of behavioral attributes that are common to both species and a set of response patterns which are found in one species but not in the other. The extent of similarity can be given a probability value if an extensive series of behavioral attributes have been recorded. The information could be entered in a 2 × 2 contingency table and a Chi square test performed on the data to establish the degree of association between the behavior patterns. An important assumption of this establishing procedure is that each response attribute is independent, which means that two behavioral measures from the same test cannot be used. A major problem of this method for establishing similarity is that with a large number of observations, significance will be found for a small degree of association and a large degree of association will be needed for significance with a small number of observations. An ideal measure of the degree of association would be independent of sample size.

In the field of numerical classification there are numerous indices of similarity with this property (Goodall, 1978). Some of these indices measure association of characteristics in terms of their presence or absence in the two species, and others are based on quantitative measures of characteristics. Until recently the choice of an index has been a matter of taste, and their merits have not been compared, but Pielou (1979) has presented a way of comparing the different indices objectively and selecting the most appropriate index for use with a given body of data. To my knowledge no-one has attempted to apply these useful indices in psychology.

The second step in establishing homology involves discovering if these forms of behavior in animals and man have the same origins by testing if the behavior is modified in a similar way by the same drugs, i.e. establishing psychopharmacological similarity. A high degree of similarity would constitute evidence for homologous neurochemical processes underlying the behavior. However, there could be other reasons for a low degree of association. Brodie (1962) and Russell (1964b) have cited examples of the marked species differences in the metabolism of drugs which can result in a drug being very active in one species, only slightly active in another, or even have a completely different action due to the production of an active metabolite with different biochemical mode of action. A simple example of these species differences is seen in the effects of hexobarbital on sleep. A dose of 50 mg of hexobarbital per kilogram produces 12 min of sleep in a mouse, but 90 min in a rat. These differences are clearly related to the biologic half-life of the drug in the bloodstream, and the relative activity of the drug metabolizing enzymes in the liver of the two species. Clearly, if such wide differences in metabolism of species in the same genera are found it is not surprising that there can be marked quantitative differences between drug action in rodents and man. However, many responses to drugs are similar for equal plasma levels of the drug (Brodie, 1969), which implies that the neurochemical mechanisms for drug action are similar in man and other mammalian species.

The third step consists of gathering evidence that normal behavioral similarity and the psychopharmacological similarity are homologous resulting from the same neurochemical systems. Evidence from comparative anatomy suggests that the differences in mammalian brains are quantitative rather than qualitative, and that elaborations in structure have been in cortical structures rather than in the subcortical regions. It is these latter regions which are the origins of the neurochemical networks although they project to the paleocortex and neocortex. This sort of evidence gives us some confidence in our original proposition that hypotheses on the neurochemical bases of behavior that were derived from animal studies can be extrapolated to man in order to explain and predict his behavior. The problem is how to test the hypothesis indirectly and discover its limits.

Biochemists have developed a very sophisticated *in vitro* understanding of chemical events occurring in brain structures, but it is clear that simplified test-tube systems may not always accurately represent the dynamic events which occur *in vivo*. However, there is now the possibility of safely acquiring regional *in vivo* biochemical information about the human brain from detection systems which employ positron emission tomography and enable biochemists to monitor the fate of these radioactive drugs *in vivo* in a truly regional and quantitative manner (Raichle, 1979). Emission tomography is a visualization technique in nuclear medicine that yields an image of the distribution of a previously administered radionuclide in any desired transverse section of the body, and this reconstructed image from the radioactive counting data is an accurate and quantitative representation of the spatial distribution of a radionuclide in the chosen section of measurement. The approach may be employed with a variety of radioactive drugs to explore the chemical properties of the brain. One of the most obvious applications of this method is its potential to measure *in vivo* the tissue drug levels in the brain region of humans and animals. In time this technique could permit direct demonstration of the dynamic biochemical events underlying behavior.

One index of activity in a neural system can be obtained from electrophysiological recordings. In normal circumstances records of neural activity in people can only be made with scalp electrodes that measure only gross cortical activity whatever its origin deep within the brain. Nevertheless, similar electrocortical activity in the two species would be consistent with control by the same neurochemical system. Explanations of the neurochemical control of human sleep (Jouvet, 1972) have been based on the identical electrocortical patterns of activity in sleep that were observed in animals and people, although the duration of different types of activity varies across species. In addition to analyzing the normal patterns of activity, it is possible to measure the electrocortical activity after drug administration. Psychopharmacological similarity of activity would give evidence that the drug-induced changes in behavior were a consequence of modifications of the same neurochemical pathways in the brain.

The logical steps that were outlined by Schildkraut (1969) as the 'pharmacological bridge' have been elaborated considerably beyond the simple statement of extrapolation, and use other properties of the organism. The steps in the argument can be stated formally as follows:

(1) If there are similarities in a certain type of behavior between people and animals, allowing for species-specific differences (behavioral similarity);
(2) If drugs produce similar changes in behavior (psychopharmacological similarity);
(3) If these drugs reach and interact with similar neural structures in people and animals (distributional similarity);
(4) If there are similar electrophysiological states correlated with the normal behavior and drug-induced changes in behavior (electrophysiological similarity);
(5) If there are similar anatomical structures in human and the comparison species (anatomical similarity);
(6) Then the neurochemical effects that were determined from animal studies may be extrapolated to explain human behavior.

This form of hypothetical argument is the circumstantial evidence mode of inference which is based upon the recognition of relevant resemblances and relevant differences. It is a form of reasoning in which pieces of evidence cumulatively point to a certain definite conclusion, although no single fact *per se* is sufficient to indicate that conclusion (Stebbing, 1954). The argument for circumstantial evidence is always invalid in the formal logic sense (fallacy of the undistributed middle) because it cannot be maintained that *no other conclusion* is consistent with pieces of evidence. We can only argue that one specific conclusion is more or less probable on the basis of the facts which, in our case, are a set of similarities.

As well as failure of explanation and prediction from extrapolation due to it being an invalid form of inference, there are other reasons why extrapolation may fail. It can be seen that there could be errors in our assessment of the strength of the similarities because either the available information is inaccurate or the information is not complete because the appropriate experiments have not been done. Russell (1964b) has pointed out that there is a lack of reliable and consistent behavioral techniques in psychopharmacology, and consequently large experimental errors are introduced and existing relationships are concealed. Another possible source of error in extrapolation is the inaccuracy or incompleteness of information on the neurochemical substrates. Evidence has accumulated to show that it is erroneous to think of only one controlling pathway for some types of behavior (Warburton, 1975; 1977; 1979b), and it is conceivable that the relative influence of these pathways could be different in people. However, all these uncertainties in extrapolation can be resolved by experimentation and, like any hypothesis, the strength of an extrapolation lies in the weight of evidence to support it. In the next section an example of one of these hypotheses will be given.

5. EXAMPLE: NEUROCHEMICAL BASES OF ATTENTION

As an example of extrapolation in the neurochemical bases of behavior, I will outline some data from our research which is consistent with the conclusion that some human attentional processes are mediated by the cholinergic pathway which ascends from the reticular formation to the cortex. The circumstantial evidence for this hypothesis can be outlined as follows, using the logical steps that were discussed previously.

5.1 Behavioral similarity

The major work on attention in animals has been centered on discrimination learning rather than on the effects of variations in the stimulus properties and information load on stable performance. However, Riley and Leith (1976) have reported a series of animal experiments which have been based on human studies of selective and divided attention. All the evidence suggests that similar stimulus selection processes are operating in a wide range of species, including humans. In our own animal research which was summarized most recently in Warburton (1977), we found evidence for the same stimulus selection behavior in rats and people.

5.2 Psychopharmacological similarity

In one of the animal studies that was mentioned in Warburton (1977), rats were tested with drugs in a 'vigilance' situation in which visual signals occurred on the average once every 15 seconds during the one hour session. Doses of scopolamine produced a decrease in detection of the signal. A comparable study of scopolamine in human subjects with a visual vigilance (signal every 30 seconds on the average) by Dr K. Wesnes gave the same result (Warburton and Wesnes, 1982). In both people and rats, drugs which acted like scopolamine and impair cholinergic function in the brain produced impairments in various forms of attentional performance, whereas drugs which enhanced cholinergic function (like nicotine) improved attentional performance. On these grounds it can be concluded that there was strong psychopharmacological similarity in the action of cholinergic drugs.

5.3 Distributional similarity

No positron emission tomography studies of cholinergic drugs have been done in people, although the technique has been used to look at the distribution of radioactively labeled nicotine in monkeys, and has been recommended for use in people (Mazière *et al.*, 1979).

5.4 Electrophysiological similarity

Patterns of electrocortical activity in a wide variety of animal species including cats and rats are similar to those of people (Thompson, 1967). As well as the changes during sleep, there is the phenomenon of electrocortical arousal or alpha blocking, which is the sudden shift from slower, regular, high voltage waves of alpha activity to the irregular, low voltage fast activity which is correlated with enhanced attention in people (Thompson, 1967). The effects of cholinergic drugs in rats, cats, and humans show the same pattern; drugs which enhance cholinergic function produce electrocortical arousal, while drugs which reduce the function of cholinergic neurones decrease electrocortical arousal (Warburton, 1979a). Thus, there is strong electrophysiological similarity between animal and human electrocortical patterns for both normal states and drug-induced changes.

5.5 Anatomical similarity

Animal studies (Warburton, 1977; 1981) have shown that the neural pathway that controls electrocortical arousal has its origins in the mesencephalic region of the brain-stem and projects to most areas of the cortex. Stimulation of the mesencephalic reticular formation produces electrocortical arousal and cortical acetylcholine release, while lesions abolish electrocortical arousal and decrease acetylcholine release. Histochemical staining techniques have given evidence that the pathway from the mesencephalic reticular region to the cortex is cholinergic. Cholinergic stimulation of this pathway by direct injection into the brain produced changes in 'attentional' behavior in animals. Obviously experiments of this sort cannot be performed with people and evidence for anatomical similarity comes from histological staining and brain damage studies. This evidence indicates the presence of the same neural pathways in people. Damage to the mesencephalic reticular formation and its projections to the cortex decrease electrocortical arousal and impair attentional efficiency (Thompson, 1967).

5.6 Extrapolation

The available evidence indicates that similar attentional behavior occurs in people and animals (behavioral similarity). Cholinergic drugs produce similar attentional shifts in all mammalian species (psychopharmacological similarity). Electrocortical arousal changes are correlated in a similar fashion with natural and drug-induced attention shifts (electrophysiological similarity). Experimental animal and clinical human studies have given evidence for a pathway from the mesencephalic reticular formation to the cortex which controls electrocortical arousal and attention behavior (anatomical similarity) and animal studies have given evidence that acetylcholine is the transmitter for this pathway. This circumstantial evidence on similarities are grounds for the following conclusion. It is highly probable that there is a cholinergic pathway in the human brain which is part of the neurochemical mechanism which can explain some forms of attentional behavior. The evidence does not provide grounds for concluding that it is the only mechanism (see Warburton and Wesnes, 1982) or that this cholinergic pathway controls all aspects of attentional behavior.

6. CONCLUSION

The maturation of psychology depends on development of mechanism hypotheses about behavior. An important class of these hypotheses explain behavior in terms of neurochemical systems. Research on neurochemical system–behavior hypotheses can only be carried out in animals and so the explanation of human behavior can only be achieved by psychology; its validity depends on the weight of confirmatory evidence extrapolation from animal data. Extrapolation depends on the accumulation of evidence which supports this form of inference. The first step is establishing that there is a strong similarity between the animal and human behavior. Then the second step is to gather support for homology, the proposition that the behavior has the same anatomical origins. Relevant evidence comes from psychopharmacological similarities, distributional similarities, and electrophysiological similarities and the validity of the extrapolation will be a function of the strength of these sets of similarities. In this respect extrapolation does not differ from any other form of inference in psychology.

DEDICATION

This chapter is dedicated to Professor Roger W. Russell in his 65th year.

REFERENCES

Brodie, B. B. (1962) Difficulties in extrapolating data on metabolism of drugs from animal to man. *Clin. Pharm. Therap.*, **3**, 374–380.

Bunge, M. (1959) *Causality*. Harvard University Press, Cambridge, Mass.

Bunge, M. (1968) The maturation of science. In *Problems in the Philosophy of Science* (eds I. Lakatos and A. Musgrove), pp. 120–138, North Holland, Amsterdam.

Frey, S. (1976) The assessment of similarity, in *Methods of Inference from Animal to Human Behavior* (ed. M. von Cranach), pp. 7–16, Mouton-Aldine, New York.

Goodall, D. W. (1978) Sample similarity and species correlation. In *Ordination and classification of communities* (ed. R. H. Whittaker), pp. 107–156, W. Junk b.v., The Hague, Netherlands.

Hebb, D. O. (1949) *The Organization of Behavior*, Wiley, New York.

Jouvet, M. (1972) Some monoaminergic mechanisms controlling sleep and waking. In *Brain and Human Behavior* (ed. A. G. Karczmar), pp. 131–161, Springer-Verlag, Berlin.

Koch, S. (1959) *Psychology: A Study of a Science. Vol. 2*. McGraw-Hall, New York.

Mazière, M., Berger, G., Masse, R., Plummer, D., and Comar, D. (1979) The 'in vivo' distribution of carbon-11 labeled nicotine in animals: a method suitable for man. In *Electrophysiological Effects of Nicotine* (eds A. Remond and C. Izard), pp. 31–48, Elsevier, Amsterdam.

Morgane, P. (1964) Limbic-hypothalamic-midbrain interaction in thirst and thirst-motivated behaviour. In *Thirst* (ed. M. J. Wayner), pp. 94–126, Pergamon, London.

Pielou, E. C. (1979) Interpretation of paleocological similarity matrices. *Paleobio.*, **5**, 435–443.

Raichle, M. (1979) Quantitative *in vivo* autoradiography with positron emission tomography. *Brain Res. Rev.*, **1**, 47–58.

Riley, D. A., and Leith, G. R. (1976) Multidimensional psychophysics and selective attention in animals. *Psychol. Bull.*, **83**, 138–160.

Russell, R. W. (1951) *The Comparative Study of Behaviour*, H. K. Lewis, London.

Russell, R. W. (1964a) Psychopharmacology. *Ann. Rev. of Psychol.*, **15**, 87–114.

Russell, R. W. (1964b) Extrapolation from animals to man. In *Animal Behaviour and Drug Action* (ed. H. Steinberg), pp. 410–418, Churchill, London.

Russell, R. W. (1966) Biochemical substrates of behavior. In *Frontiers in Physiological Psychology* (ed. R. W. Russell), pp. 185–245, Academic Press, New York.

Schildkraut, J. J. (1969) Rationale of some approaches used in biochemical studies of affective disorders: the pharmacological bridge. In *Psychochemical Research in Man* (eds A. J. Mandell and M. D. Mandell), pp. 113–126, Academic Press, New York.

Skinner, B. F. (1958) Flight from the laboratory. Reprinted in B. F. Skinner (1959), *Cumulative Record*, pp. 242–257, Appleton-Century-Crofts, New York.

Spence, K. W. (1944) The nature of theory construction in contemporary psychology. *Psychol. Rev.*, **51**, 47–68.

Stebbing, L. S. (1954) *Logic in Practice* (fourth edition, revised), Methuen, London.

Thompson, R. F. (1967) *Foundations of Physiological Psychology*, Harper and Row, New York.

Warburton, D. M. (1975) *Brain, Drugs and Behaviour*, Wiley, London.

Warburton, D. M. (1977) Stimulus selection and behavioral inhibition. In *Handbook of Psychopharmacology Vol. 8* (eds L. L. Iversen, S. D. Iversen, and S. H. Snyder), pp. 385–432, Plenum Press, New York.

Warburton, D. M. (1979a) Neurochemical bases of consciousness. In *Chemical Influences on Behaviour* (eds. K. Brown and S. J. Cooper), pp. 421–462, Academic Press, London.

Warburton, D. M. (1979b) Physiological aspects of anxiety and schizophrenia. In *Human Stress and Cognition* (eds V. Hamilton and D. M. Warburton), pp. 432–465, Wiley, London.

Warburton, D. M. (1981) Neurochemistry of behaviour. *Brit. Med. Bull.*, **37**, 121–125.

Warburton, D. M., and Wesnes, K. (1982) Acetylcholine and attentional disorder. In *Central Cholinergic Mechanisms and Adaptive Dysfunctions* (eds M. M. Singh, D. M. Warburton, and H. Lal), in press, Plenum Press, New York.

Author Index

(Full reference page numbers are in bold type)

355

Subject Index